Find Your Career With Springer Publishing Company

101+ Careers in Public Health

Beth Seltzer, MD, MPH, is a clinical and public health physician, board certified in public health and general preventive medicine. She is currently working on an Indian reservation in western Washington, where her role has included everything from treating the common cold to leading new public health initiatives. Prior to her medical career, Dr. Seltzer was a documentary film producer, earning multiple awards for her work. More recently, she served as a writer and consultant for the Discovery Health and Discovery Channel television networks, developing content for educational television shows and interactive media directed at both physicians and general audiences. She has also written for the *Careers in Public Health* newsletter from the American Public Health Association.

101+ Careers in Public Health

Second Edition

BETH SELTZER, MD, MPH

SPRINGER PUBLISHING COMPANY

NEW YORK

APHA PRESS

AN IMPRINT OF **AMERICAN PUBLIC HEALTH ASSOCIATION**

Springer Publishing Company, LLC
11 West 42nd Street
New York, NY 10036
www.springerpub.com

Acquisitions Editor: Sheri W. Sussman
Composition: Newgen KnowledgeWorks

ISBN: 978-0-8261-9598-2
e-book ISBN: 978-0-8261-9599-9

15 16 17 18 19 / 5 4 3 2 1

The author and the publisher of this Work have made every effort to use sources believed to be reliable to provide information that is accurate and compatible with the standards generally accepted at the time of publication. The author and publisher shall not be liable for any special, consequential, or exemplary damages resulting, in whole or in part, from the readers' use of, or reliance on, the information contained in this book. The publisher has no responsibility for the persistence or accuracy of URLs for external or third-party Internet websites referred to in this publication and does not guarantee that any content on such websites is, or will remain, accurate or appropriate.

Library of Congress Cataloging-in-Publication Data
Seltzer, Beth, author.
  [101 careers in public health]
  101+ careers in public health / Beth Seltzer.—Second edition.
     p. ; cm.
  One hundred and one plus careers in public health
  One hundred one plus careers in public health
  Preceded by 101 careers in public health / Beth Seltzer. ©2011.
  Includes bibliographical references and index.
  ISBN 978-0-8261-9598-2—ISBN 978-0-8261-9599-9 (e-book)
  I. Title. II. Title: One hundred and one plus careers in public health. III. Title: One hundred one plus careers in public health.
  [DNLM: 1. Public Health. 2. Career Choice. 3. Vocational Guidance. WA 21]
  RA440.9
  362.1023—dc23   2015031722

Printed in the United States of America by McNaughton & Gunn.

This book is dedicated to my parents,
Lynn and Robert Seltzer, who have been right there
with me through my own 101 careers.

Contents

Preface

When I was in medical school, I was constantly frustrated by the number of people suffering from preventable diseases. Why was all the effort going into *treating* obesity-related diabetes instead of *preventing* it? We knew that a lot of our pediatric asthma patients would turn up in the emergency room again at some point after we discharged them from the hospital. Why weren't we figuring out why this kept happening, instead of accepting that these kids would be on a merry-go-round of asthma attacks and treatment? Teenagers with serious sexually transmitted diseases (STDs), adults with untreated mental illness—the number of people who could have been helped by population-level efforts was astonishing to me.

I spent about 3½ years railing against all this, until one of my teachers finally introduced me to the world of public health. Here were the people who shared my frustration. Here was a whole world of doctors, nurses, social workers, research scientists, administrators, and activists trying to get those kids off the asthma merry-go-round, trying to shift the way America eats and convince us to ramp up our exercise levels to halt the epidemic of diabetes, and working with teenagers to encourage safer sexual practices and slow the spread of STDs.

I have since completed my medical residency and become board certified in preventive medicine, a specialty with a focus on public health. My fellow "prev med" physicians are an extraordinary group of people, and I think most of us are delighted to have found our way here. As I was interviewing people for this book—health inspectors, civil engineers, pharmacists, and a range of other experts—every single one of them shared his or her excitement about being part of public health.

I had a wonderful time writing the first edition of *101 Careers in Public Health*. I met public health professionals from all across the country and in a wide array of jobs. I got to have fascinating conversations as I learned about the good work they were doing.

For this new edition, I had the privilege to include some new interviewees. The original "career profile" interviews have otherwise been left largely intact. Even though not all of the interviewees are still in the same roles, I've reviewed every one of the profiles and they're just as useful now as when they were first written.

Where I could, I've included "Profile Updates" with interviewees' new roles, titles, and workplaces. I think it's a great way to see how different public health careers can evolve. I've also added an expanded chapter on global health, some insight into public health careers in the military, thoughts on making the decision between a medical or a public health degree, and advice from two expert career counselors. I hope you will find the new information useful!

I am delighted that you have picked up this book, and I hope it will inspire you to pursue a career in public health. It is a great field to be in.

—Beth Seltzer, MD, MPH

Acknowledgments

A heartfelt thank you to the extraordinarily generous people who contributed their time, wisdom, and experience to this book. Much of what you will learn here comes from them. Any errors are entirely mine.

Thank you to all the people who shared their stories for the public health profiles. Many of you agreed to participate with just a brief introduction to the project, because you wanted to help students and career changers learn about your job. Your kindness made working on this book an absolute joy.

Thanks also to everyone who helped me create the list of careers, taught me what people in each job actually do all day, checked my descriptions to make sure they rang true, responded to a request for information, or connected me with another resource. I will try to name everyone here; please forgive me if I have left you out, and know that I very much appreciate your contribution.

Much gratitude to: Pat McConnan, Wanda Manson, Beth Lamanna, Madelaine Fletcher, Candace McCall, Julie Wu, Michael Zwick, Chet Moore, Liz Garman, Aletha Maybank, James Gaudino, Catherine Hayes, Keith Hauret, Mary Anne Bright, Linda Bailey, Chris Anderson, Vickie Wightman, Andrea Circe, Jim Lando, Sheree Williams, Jodee Denneson, Steve Blessing, Leslie Sandler, Kathy Jacobitz, Elizabeth Scharman, Carolyn Barth, Stephen Cina, Stephanie Birch, Robert Burke, Rita Ruel, Julian Kesner, Carol Odnoha, Kate Corona, Susan Johnson, Andrea Gatewood, Douglas Steinke, Rebecca Garner, Kate Migliaccio, Karen Mahoney, Gary Schnabel, Robert Hart, Anne Wright, Vonni Kallemeyn, Ryan Benefield, Jim Kubat, James Tacci, David Hicks, Kelly Classic, Cynthia Jones, Debbie Gilley, Dilcia Granville, Christopher Kelly, Jill Cruickshank, Julie Stallcup, Jennifer McEntire, Martin Lo, Michael Herndon, Wes Long, Stephanie Berger, Irwin Redlener, Patricia Thomas, Nedra Weinreich, John Curtis, Martin Snyder, Paula Kun, Becky Smith, Ephraim Shapiro, Anita Nelson, Steve Smothers, Deb Schnellman, Jeanne Saunders, Theresa Spinner, Reg Hutchinson, Cindy Sweigert,

R. Gerald ("Bobby") Smith, Mark Casanova, Bernadette Burden, Karen White, Sherry Glied, Rachael Wojnowicz, Chuck Young, Eric Wedum, James Schuttinga, Rina Lieberman, Yair Goldstein, Ben Meier, Gene Matthews, Bev Thomas, Jo Ann Saringer, Tyrone Butler, Melissa Lewis, John Porter, Dorothy Lane, Philip Baten, Patti Jo Baber, Laurie Shroyer, Vikas Tandon, Karen Greenwood, Jacqueline Neilsen, Deanna Kramer, John Skendall, Kelly Romero, Christine Clayton, Jody Devoll, Laura Crawford, Ashgar Rastegar, Jennifer Johnsen, Tonia Poteat, Carolyn Hart, Bill Kaizer, and Tanya Cobbs Leslie. Special thanks to George Johns, Tracey Lynn, Kathleen Scanlin, James Horan, Carmit Keddem, Don Griffin, and Julia Goodall.

Thank you to everyone who jumped back in with updates on their profiles and job markets. And thanks to all the new contributors of information and ideas, including Annie Krill, W. David Dotson, Linda Hill, Charmaine Wright, Michael Morrisey, Barb Snyder, Aria Yow, Betty Ruth, Stephen Gloyd, Jennifer Tee, Catherine Johnson, Heather Krasna, Betty Addison, Michael Monopoli, Shelli Stephens-Stidham, Stephanie Callahan, Fran Benton, Aubrey Mellos, Natanya Lott, Barb Boggs, Hugh Cox, Lawrence Gostin, and Ana Ayala.

Thank you to my friends who made connections for me or reviewed parts of the manuscript, including Esther Sitrin, Kevin Hogan, Christy English, Alisa Roost, Katey Coffing, Shannah Whithaus, and Noeleen Walder; to Diana Goodwin, for always being there when I need her; and to everyone else who put up with me while I was working on this project. Sincere appreciation, too, to Professor Steven Jonas at Stony Brook University, for believing that I could do this in the first place.

Thank you to Emily Loeb, who did excellent research work and helped make new connections for the new edition. Gratitude to my father, Robert Seltzer, who tracked down facts and even did one of the new interviews, and to my mother, Lynn Seltzer, who jumped in to help with proofreading. Thanks, again, to the book's original editor, Jennifer Perillo, at Springer Publishing Company, who has not only made my writing better but also demonstrated more patience than anyone has a right to expect.

Finally, so much appreciation to current editor Sheri W. Sussman at Springer Publishing Company, for standing by me as I plugged away at the new edition while juggling my more-than-full-time job. Sheri, my most heartfelt thanks.

PART I

Introduction to Public Health

CHAPTER 1

What Is Public Health?

Public health professionals sometimes joke that nobody understands what they do—until something goes wrong. We tend to take it for granted that the water from our kitchen faucets is safe to drink. We rarely worry about tuberculosis, measles, or diphtheria. We assume that medicine we buy from the local pharmacy will make us better, not make us ill. But when dozens of people are sickened at a restaurant or if there is an outbreak of a deadly illness, *then* everyone asks why the health department has not been doing its job!

Public health is the discipline that aims to keep our population safe from illness. Unlike a doctor who treats individual patients (usually once they are already sick), the public health expert considers health from the perspective of entire communities, neighborhoods, cities, and states. Public health addresses disease prevention and health promotion on a local, national, and global scale.

HISTORY OF PUBLIC HEALTH

Public health measures have been around for centuries (Rosen, 1958). Excavation of a 4,000-year-old city in India revealed covered sewers to carry waste away from people's homes. In Rome about 2,000 years ago, a system of aqueducts brought fresh water to the city. Legend has it that 2,500 years ago, a Greek emperor ended a malaria epidemic by changing the course of two rivers, making a marshy region less hospitable to mosquitoes.

The idea of quarantining people who were contagious became prominent in the Middle Ages. To combat leprosy, church leaders decided to separate people with leprosy from the rest of society, making life very difficult for those patients, but probably saving many healthy citizens from contracting the disease (Porter, 1999). Similar measures were used when the Black Plague hit.

Of course, people have not always understood disease the way we do today. Some misunderstandings actually led to effective public health efforts—the idea that disease was caused by "bad air" eventually led to improvements in sanitation. But confusion about how diseases spread also led to less successful approaches. In Europe in the 1800s, government officials tried to stop the spread of cholera by quarantining people who were ill, destroying their belongings, and burying the dead immediately and away from highly populated areas. But none of these activities actually stopped cholera epidemics.

The roots of modern epidemiology, one of the most important sciences in public health today, are widely thought to lie in work that was done around that time. Epidemiology is the study of how diseases occur within populations and how they can be controlled. Although no one knew exactly what caused cholera, John Snow, a doctor practicing in London, realized that the key to stopping outbreaks lay in figuring out how cholera was being transmitted. Instead of focusing on the disease in individual patients, he looked for patterns in where and when cases of cholera occurred. His investigation led to the discovery that outbreaks were linked to contaminated water and could be halted by providing a clean water supply. Snow was not the only one who attempted to use epidemiologic methods, but his story is among the most well known. It took years for his ideas to be accepted, but approaches similar to his are now widely considered to be at the heart of modern public health.

THE ROLE OF PUBLIC HEALTH TODAY

Today, public health is far more than providing clean water, maintaining sanitation, and controlling the spread of contagious diseases. The field has expanded to include prevention of chronic diseases and cancer, the control of conditions that are linked to disease, like obesity, and attention to mental health. There are public health experts studying disparities in levels of disease among different racial and ethnic groups and trying to bring everyone up to the same degree of health. Public health top-ics also include infant mortality, access to dental care, the prevention of drug and alcohol abuse, and even seat belt and helmet laws. Public health techniques are used to promote workplace safety and reduce on-the-job injuries. Public health can even include clinics and other services to individuals, when those services are offered in the context of trying to raise the health of a community or group.

In fact, the field of public health has become so broad that even the people who practice it sometimes have trouble defining exactly what public health means today. In general, what public health efforts have in common is a focus on promoting health at the population level, instead of focusing on the individual interactions between doctor and patient. The Institute of Medicine offered a definition in their 1988 report *The Future of Public Health* (Institute of Medicine Committee for the Study of the Future of Public Health, 1988). The report specified the mission of public health as "fulfilling society's interest in assuring conditions in which people can be healthy." It also identified three core functions:

- **Assessment.** Public health agencies should collect and analyze information about the health of the communities they serve.
- **Policy Development.** Agencies should promote the use of sound science and act as leaders in the development of comprehensive public health policies.
- **Assurance.** Agencies should assure the provision of services necessary to meet public health goals.

Federal agencies and public health organizations got together a few years later and expanded the definition with the following list of 10 essential public health services (Centers for Disease Control and Prevention, 2014):

1. **Monitor** health status to identify community health problems.
2. **Diagnose and investigate** health problems and health hazards in the community.
3. **Inform, educate, and empower** people about health issues.
4. **Mobilize** community partnerships to identify and solve health problems.
5. **Develop** policies and plans that support individual and commu-nity health efforts.
6. **Enforce** laws and regulations that protect health and ensure safety.
7. **Link** people to needed personal health services and assure the provision of health care when otherwise unavailable.

8. **Assure** a competent public health and personal health care workforce.
9. **Evaluate** effectiveness, accessibility, and quality of personal and population-based health services.
10. **Research** for new insights and innovative solutions to health problems.

Monitoring, Diagnosis, and Investigation

Monitoring is at the root of many public health efforts. If we do not know what patterns of disease are occurring, we cannot create rational programs to address those diseases. In the United States, certain contagious diseases are considered "reportable," which means that doctors or laboratories must alert health officials whenever a case is discovered. If there is an unusually high number of cases, public health experts swing into action to find out why. Public health agencies also monitor diabetes, heart disease, cancer, birth defects, certain types of injuries, and other serious medical problems. A sudden increase in disease, especially if it is in a single location, can signal an immediate problem to be addressed. Even a gradual, widespread change can expose the need for improved health measures on a local or national scale.

Disease Prevention and Health Promotion

Once a problem (such as infectious disease, chronic disease, or injury) has been identified, public health experts use a wide range of methods to try to prevent it from happening. Water treatment plants, free clinics to treat and prevent the spread of sexually transmitted infections, and ad campaigns promoting exercise are all examples of disease prevention efforts. So are programs to reduce pollution and to encourage stores to stock more healthful foods. From low-cost vaccinations for children to national recommendations for exercise, the active prevention of disease and promotion of health are enormous parts of modern public health activities.

Research

The best public health efforts are based on sound research. At schools of public health, government agencies, nonprofit organizations, and even some for-profit businesses, scientists work on finding the best approaches to maintaining and improving health on a population level. Researchers are looking at how our environment affects our health. They are examining why certain populations seem to have consistently better health outcomes than others. They are working on ways to evaluate existing public health programs to see what works and where our tax dollars should be spent. And they are studying public health from many other angles, from the impact of personal choices to the effects of national policy.

Policy

Many public health programs and services are provided by local, state, and federal government agencies. These efforts are created and controlled by laws and regulations. Even nonprofit organizations operate according to overarching policies. A good policy provides for sound, science-based monitoring and prevention and may also support necessary research. But even policies that come from the best intentions can have unintended consequences. There are public health experts who study the outcomes of past policies, examine the impact of current ones, and advise legislators and other policy makers on how to make good choices for the future.

Health Services Research

Health services research is sometimes considered a separate category from public health, but many public health experts consider it a part of the continuum. Health services research looks at how health care is delivered, including the effects of billing and financial structures; the organization of hospitals, insurance companies, and medical practices; the use of health technologies; and the behavior of individuals. Researchers in this area look at patient outcomes, access to care, how people utilize doctors and hospitals, and how health care differs for different populations. The information they collect can be used by doctors, patients, hospitals, insurance companies, policy makers, and others, and the overall goal—at least from the public health perspective—is to improve health care for all.

Direct Service

There are many public health efforts that incorporate direct patient care. There are local and national hotlines to help people quit smoking, provide assistance in cases of accidental poisoning, and direct victims of domestic violence to services. Emergency medical services use a public health perspective, aiming not only to match their services to community needs but also standing ready to serve in case of disaster or attack. Many members of the U.S. Public Health Service Commissioned Corps are assigned to the Indian Health Service, which provides comprehensive health services to American Indians and Alaska Natives.

REFERENCES

Centers for Disease Control and Prevention. National Public Health Performance Standards Program. (2014, May 29). *Ten essential public health services*. Retrieved June 22, 2015, from http://www.cdc.gov/od/ocphp/nphpsp/EssentialPHServices.htm

Institute of Medicine Committee for the Study of the Future of Public Health. (1988). *The future of public health*. Washington, DC: National Academies Press.

Porter, D. (1999). *Health, civilization, and the state: A history of public health from ancient to modern times*. New York, NY: Routledge.

Rosen, G. (1958). *A history of public health*. New York, NY: MD Publications.

CHAPTER 2

Education in Public Health

There are many roads to a career in public health, and it is common to meet people who started out in different careers entirely. Some began as hospital nurses or physicians in clinical practice; others were lawyers, teachers, or even journalists. For many public health jobs, the MPH is considered the most appropriate degree, but there are also jobs for which additional credentials—or entirely different ones—are essential.

BACHELOR'S DEGREES IN PUBLIC HEALTH

Some schools offer a bachelor of arts or a bachelor of science degree in public health. This degree is designed to give students a basic grounding in public health issues and methods, but does not cover the same breadth and depth as an MPH. For some public health jobs, this level of education will be enough, but many jobs do require a more advanced degree. There are also bachelor's degrees available in environmental health, health promotion, community health sciences, and other related majors.

A bachelor's degree in public health is not a prerequisite for an MPH. For students who plan to pursue an MPH, there are many different majors that can serve as a good foundation. Sociology, psychology, or anthropology can be useful majors for those interested in behavioral science or health education; biology or chemistry for those interested in environmental health; and biology or one of the social sciences for those who lean toward maternal and child health issues.

MASTER'S DEGREES IN PUBLIC HEALTH

People who have been in public health for many years often do not have an MPH, but this degree has become much more popular in recent years, and many employers now expect it. MPH programs offer a sound background in core public health topics, including epidemiology, biostatistics, environmental health, health policy and management, and social and behavioral sciences. The educational requirements include coursework, a practical experience or internship in a public health setting, and a final thesis, examination, or other demonstration of comprehensive knowledge and the ability to apply it. Some programs offer a generalist degree, but it is common for schools to require students to choose an area of concentration. In addition to the core topics, various schools offer concentrations such as global health, health promotion and communication, minority health and health disparities, environmental health, and health policy and management.

Different schools of public health can be quite different in their offerings, priorities, and requirements, so it is important to pay attention to which school you choose. Many MPH programs last for 2 years, although some are designed to be completed in a shorter time and some take a bit longer.

The MPH is meant to prepare students for professional jobs in public health practice. There are also Master of Science in Public Health (MSPH) and Master of Health Science (MHS) degrees, which have more of a research focus.

DOCTORATES IN PUBLIC HEALTH

The Doctor of Public Health (DrPH) degree is for people with an interest in public health leadership or a desire for deeper knowledge than an MPH program can provide. It is generally considered a degree for those who intend to be leaders in public health practice or policy making. It requires several years of study, an original research project, and a lengthy written dissertation. A DrPH can serve as preparation for a research career, but a PhD with a narrower focus is often more appropriate for someone interested primarily in conducting research and pursuing an academic career. Some schools offer a Doctor of Science (ScD) degree in areas related to public health. This degree can also be a foundation for a research career.

COMBINED DEGREE PROGRAMS

Many schools offer programs combining the MPH with another degree, such as nursing, medicine, law, or social work. These programs vary in focus, so it is important to explore the coursework and requirements.

OTHER MASTER'S DEGREES

A number of other master's degrees are common among people working in public health. For someone interested in administration—managing a bureau within a state health department, for example—a Master of Public Administration (MPA) degree can be very helpful. A Master of Public Policy (MPP) degree focuses on policy analysis, design, and implementation. A Master of Health Administration (MHA) degree can be good preparation for leadership and policy making specifically related to the provision of health care. Some public health professionals find that a Master of Business Administration (MBA) is useful, either to help them understand how health-related businesses function, or to give them perspective on management issues.

ENGINEERING DEGREES

For those people who handle the nuts and bolts of our water system, design and manage sewer systems, and make sure landfills are properly constructed, a background in engineering is key. These people often do not have degrees in "public health" at all—instead, they have degrees in civil or environmental engineering. There are bachelor's degrees, master's degrees, and PhDs available in these fields. The level of education needed depends on the specific job responsibilities.

CERTIFICATIONS AND OTHER TRAINING

Some public health jobs require other types of training, and some require state licensure. The inspectors who keep an eye on the use of dangerous radioactive materials, for example, receive extensive training on the job. The people who answer the phone at the poison control hotline must pass a test sponsored by a national organization. As you read through this book, you will see examples of training and certifications required for specific jobs.

There is also a general certification for public health professionals. The Certified in Public Health (CPH) credential is voluntary, but it can be a good way to demonstrate both knowledge and commitment. The CPH credential requires an examination for initial certification and then proof of ongoing continuing education. Details on eligibility and maintenance of certification are available from the National Board of Public Health Examiners at www.nbphe.org.

FINDING A SCHOOL OF PUBLIC HEALTH

Schools and programs of public health are located within universities throughout the United States. A list of accredited schools is available through the website of the Council on Education for Public Health (CEPH; ceph.org). The website for the Association of Schools and Programs of Public Health (aspph.org) has more information about requirements for public health degrees and some advice about careers.

As mentioned previously, not all schools and programs of public health are the same. Programs at CEPH-accredited schools all meet the same basic requirements. However, schools have different strengths and offer different combinations of areas of concentration. There is also a wide range of tuition fees. It is worth taking the time to research schools to find out the best match for your interests.

CHAPTER 3

Finding Jobs in Public Health

There are many different ways to join the ranks of people working in public health. It used to be quite common for people to find their way into this field because they had a passion for fighting and preventing illness, but without formal training in public health. In recent years, though, the number of public health degree programs has greatly increased. In 1960, there were only 12 schools of public health. In 2015, there were 160 public health schools and programs accredited by the Council on Education for Public Health (CEPH), including a few in other countries, and 41 more were in the process of applying.

It is becoming more and more common to see employers asking for an MPH, and the training in these programs provides a solid grounding in public health principles that can be used across many different types of careers. At the same time, there are still jobs in public health for people from other backgrounds, including scientists, engineers, and even people with just a high school education.

Here is a basic outline of different ways to begin a career in public health.

TRADITIONAL PATHWAYS

Some people go to school, earn an MPH or other public health degree, and immediately apply for a job that matches the focus of their studies. Many MPH students are hired to work at places where they interned.

Others use the network of people they meet during their studies to find job openings and get recommendations. Some simply answer an ad. Good websites for public health job postings include:

- Publichealthjobs.net, a job board provided by the Association of Schools and Programs of Public Health
- American Public Health Association (APHA)'s Public Health CareerMart, at careers.apha.org
- USAJOBS, the U.S. government's job board for opportunities at federal agencies, at usajobs.gov
- The Careers page at the National Association of County and City Health Officials, careers.naccho.org
- The Job Bank at the Association of State and Territorial Health Officials, astho-jobs.jobtarget.com
- Idealist.org, a job board for nonprofit organizations including groups concerned with public health

It is very common for employers to ask for at least a few years of experience. It can be hard to get that first job, when you are just starting out and you are competing against people who have been in the public health workforce for a while. The good news is that there are many opportunities for people interested in public health to get some experience through internships, fellowships, and training programs. Some even offer a stipend or salary so you can pay the bills while you learn. Not all of these are well known, even among people currently working in public health.

It is worth checking online to find the latest information, because programs may be created when a need arises and end when the purpose is fulfilled—or when funding is cut. Some places to start are the Centers for Disease Control and Prevention (CDC)'s Public Health Training Fellowships page (www.cdc.gov/fellowships); student and fellowship programs at the Food and Drug Administration (www.fda.gov), the Substance Abuse and Mental Health Services Administration (www.samhsa.gov), and other agencies within the U.S. Department of Health and Human Services (HHS); the websites for the various professional associations listed in this book; and the career information web pages from schools of public health.

Here are a few of the programs designed to help public health professionals get started:

- **Public Health Associate Program (PHAP).** This 2-year training program was started in 2007 to help make sure there would be a strong public health workforce. It is open to recent bachelor's and master's graduates and is intended to attract new graduates into public health careers. The program is run by the CDC and participants are assigned to state, local, and Tribal agencies as well as nongovernmental organizations nationwide. It has been a popular program, with many more applicants than spaces available. PHAP does not guarantee a job at the CDC afterward but can be good preparation for public health jobs in many different settings.

- **Epidemic Intelligence Service (EIS).** EIS has been a major training and service program at the CDC for decades, and it is where many of the top people in public health agencies began their careers. EIS is a 2-year postdoctoral program—complete with a livable salary—that combines classroom learning and on-the-job training in applied epidemiology. The program is intended for people with doctoral-level degrees (including MDs, PhDs, dentists, and veterinarians). Those with clinical degrees must be licensed to practice. Participants learn to investigate disease outbreaks and other potential public health problems, analyze patterns of illness and injury, and design a public health surveillance system. About three fourths of EIS officers are stationed at CDC headquarters in Atlanta, and the rest are assigned to CDC offices or health departments all over the United States. EIS officers can also be sent on temporary assignments when there is a need, including sometimes doing international work.
- **Presidential Management Fellows (PMF) Program.** This prestigious program is intended to attract graduate students from various disciplines into federal service, as future leaders in the management of public policies and programs. There are PMFs at the CDC and many other government agencies concerned with public health.
- **Association of Schools and Programs of Public Health (ASPPH) Fellowships.** Most ASPPH fellowships are collaborations with federal agencies. They place recent public health graduates at federal, state, and local agencies, and there are also opportunities in global health. These competitive fellowships are open to recent graduates from ASPPH-accredited schools and programs with advanced degrees (master's or above).

- **Oak Ridge Institute for Science and Education (ORISE).** For students and recent graduates in science and engineering fields, ORISE offers internships, scholarships, and fellowships that can be steps on the way to a public health career. ORISE is affiliated with the U.S. Department of Energy, but it supports a wide range of work at multiple federal agencies. Topics related to public health include occupational hazards, environmental cleanup, emergency preparedness and response, and health communication related to epidemics and emergencies. Programs are geared toward research, often working toward practical goals such as improving air quality or preventing disease. There are opportunities at education levels from undergraduates up to recent PhD graduates.

Many people have found their way to interesting careers through the U.S. Public Health Service (USPHS) Commissioned Corps. Sometimes people new to the field are surprised, when they attend their first public health conference, to see men and women in uniform. In fact, the Commissioned Corps is one of our seven uniformed services—along with the Army, Navy, Air Force, Marines, Coast Guard, and National Oceanic and Atmospheric Administration Commissioned Corps. The doctors, dentists, nurses, pharmacists, engineers, health educators, health information management specialists, and others in the USPHS Commissioned Corps wear uniforms and have military-style rank. They have opportunities to serve in government agencies throughout the United States and even overseas. People in the Commissioned Corps often have interesting stories about where they have been deployed and the work they have gotten to do. Visit the website at www.usphs.gov to find out what positions they are recruiting for and how to apply. There are also some opportunities for students who want to find out what it is like to work for the Commissioned Corps.

There are public health jobs in the U.S. military, as well, both for service members and for civilians. Many of the jobs in this book have counterparts in the armed services.

GETTING IN THE BACK DOOR

Many people, even those with long careers in public health, still express surprise that they "ended up" in this field. Many found their first job through volunteering or through internships. A volunteer experience with a nonprofit or community organization can give you a firsthand look at the needs of communities and provide training in health education, monitoring, and even program design, coordination, and evaluation. It can also introduce you to potential mentors and a network of people who are aware of your abilities and interests. Volunteering or doing an internship can lead to a job with that organization or another one with similar goals. And, because some employers will still accept experience in lieu of a public health degree, a volunteering experience can actually launch a career.

Organizations and associations for public health professionals can also provide networking opportunities. Local meetings and national conferences are good places to meet people who are doing the work you are interested in, and they will usually be happy to talk with you. You might meet someone who knows of just the job for a person with your skills. You might also learn about a fellowship or other paid training program that is a good match for your background and your goals.

COMBINING PUBLIC HEALTH WITH ANOTHER CAREER

Social workers, nurses, dentists, and doctors can sometimes combine public health work with a clinical career, working part time for a health department or community clinic. Some advertising professionals donate a portion of their time to ad campaigns that promote good health instead of selling products. Even executives at for-profit corporations can get involved in "corporate responsibility" programs that promote health on a population scale.

PROFESSIONAL ASSOCIATIONS

Throughout this book, you will read about professional associations and organizations associated with specific jobs and careers. One of the best and most comprehensive resources for people interested in public health work is APHA. APHA's annual meeting attracts thousands of people from a wide range of careers. APHA has low-cost membership options and discounts on annual meeting registration for students and "consumer members" (people not currently working in public health). You can learn more about APHA at www.apha.org.

FEDERAL GOVERNMENT AGENCIES

HHS is the principal federal agency tasked with protecting the public's health and providing certain social services. It incorporates multiple operating divisions, each of which has at least some programs that address public health issues.

- **Administration for Children and Families (ACF).** ACF focuses on the economic and social well-being of families, children, individuals, and communities.
- **Administration for Community Living (ACL).** ACL's mission is to increase access to community support and resources for people with disabilities and for older Americans.
- **Agency for Healthcare Research and Quality (AHRQ).** AHRQ supports research on health care quality, costs, and outcomes, as well as efforts to improve quality, cost-effectiveness, and access to care.
- **Agency for Toxic Substances and Disease Registry (ATSDR).** ATSDR's focus is the prevention of diseases related to toxic substances and exposures to substances that can be harmful.
- **Centers for Disease Control and Prevention.** The CDC's efforts include monitoring, research, programs, services, and policy development related to health promotion, disease prevention, prevention of injury and disability, and preparedness for new health threats.
- **Centers for Medicare & Medicaid Services (CMS).** CMS handles the administration of Medicare and the federal aspects of Medicaid and the Children's Health Insurance Program.
- **Food and Drug Administration (FDA).** FDA is tasked with assuring the safety, effectiveness, and security of prescription medications, over-the-counter drugs, medical devices, radiation-emitting products, vaccines, blood and biologic treatments, as well as cosmetics, tobacco, and some aspects of our food supply.
- **Health Resources and Services Administration (HRSA).** HRSA's mission is to improve access to health care, with a focus on people who are uninsured, geographically isolated, or medically vulnerable.
- **Indian Health Service (IHS).** IHS provides personal and public health services to American Indians and Alaska Natives, with the goal of maximizing these populations' physical, mental, social, and spiritual health.

- **National Institutes of Health (NIH).** NIH is a major funder of medical research and has a major impact on what is being studied. The NIH also employs several thousand researchers at its own research centers.
- **Substance Abuse and Mental Health Services Administration (SAMHSA).** SAMHSA focuses on mental health issues, and its mission is to reduce the impact of substance abuse and mental illness on America's communities.

Several other federal agencies have roles in protecting and enhancing the public's health. Public health-oriented programs and practices can be found at agencies including:

- The U.S. Department of Agriculture (USDA)
- The Environmental Protection Agency (EPA)
- The Consumer Product Safety Commission (CPSC)
- The U.S. Department of Labor's Occupational Safety and Health Administration (OSHA)
- The U.S. Department of Energy (DOE)

STATE AND LOCAL AGENCIES

State, county, city, and Tribal health departments have multiple divisions that add to federal efforts and carry out their own programs to meet local needs. The exact structure of state and local health services varies from place to place, but there is an enormous range of opportunities at these levels for professionals pursuing careers in public health. Visit the websites of your state and city or county health departments to see the roles they play in water quality, environmental health, maternal and child health, nutrition, patient safety, clinical care and preventive services, and more.

PART II

Public Health Careers

CHAPTER 4

Infectious Disease

In spite of advances in clinical medicine, infectious disease remains an important public health concern. Fears about immunization have contributed to outbreaks of diseases such as measles and mumps across the United States. New infectious agents are constantly being discovered. The ease of international travel means that infectious diseases are easily carried from one part of the world to another. The development of resistance to antibiotics and antiviral medications presents new challenges. In some parts of the world, limited access to medicine means that even curable infections can be devastating.

Public health efforts to combat infectious diseases include collecting data about the symptoms patients report and the diagnoses they receive, watching for unusual cases, and investigating outbreaks. When an outbreak or epidemic occurs, public health officials take action to inform the public, educate physicians, and develop policies and systems to contain the infection. There are also policies and programs to keep known infectious agents under control, so that outbreaks are less likely to happen.

This chapter introduces you to some of the careers that involve the control of infectious diseases. To learn about others, also see behavioral scientist, medical epidemiologist, employee health nurse, corporate medical director, food service sanitarian, consumer safety officer, and health educator. The Centers for Disease Control and Prevention (CDC) website (www.cdc.gov) is a great resource for an introduction to infection control and public health.

EPIDEMIOLOGIST

Job Description

Epidemiologists are scientists who study the causes of disease in populations, how diseases spread, and what puts people at risk. They look at issues such as which populations are most affected, what the people who are infected have in common, and whether people who get sick are more likely to have certain risk factors than those who remain healthy. Most epidemiologists' work involves numbers and statistics; they figure out what information should be gathered, how it should be analyzed, and how it can be used. Sometimes they help explain study results to policy makers, the media, and the public. Some epidemiologists also work on ways to prevent disease.

Epidemiologists can study multiple types of diseases, or they can specialize—in infectious diseases, chronic diseases, or other topics such as genetic disorders, workplace injuries, violence or accidents, or how the environment influences people's health. An epidemiologist's job can be very creative and exciting, such as tracking a dangerous new virus. The work can also be more solitary, such as monitoring how many people test positive for tuberculosis (TB) each year. The job is usually office based and involves a lot of computer time. There are also jobs that incorporate fieldwork, such as going out into a community or even traveling overseas to interview people, collect specimens, and search for patterns right where the outbreak is happening.

Education and Certification

Most epidemiologists have at least a master's degree, generally an MPH, with a specific focus on epidemiology. For upper-level positions, a doctorate is usually needed—but a fulfilling career is possible with only master's degree. Some epidemiologists have a background in medicine or nursing, combined with a degree, coursework, or other training in epidemiology. (See "medical epidemiologist" in Chapter 5 to learn more.)

Core Competencies and Skills

- Tendency to think logically and analytically
- Interest in solving challenging research problems
- Ability to work both individually and collaboratively
- Desire to continue learning about new topics and new techniques
- Strong background in math and statistics

- Knowledge of how to use statistics programs and databases
- Ability to explain statistics, study design, and study results to people with different educational backgrounds

Compensation

Nationwide, the median salary for an epidemiologist is about $67,000, with most earning between $43,000 and $112,000, although senior-level epidemiologists can earn more. Epidemiologists with doctoral degrees usually start at higher salaries and have a higher earning potential than those with master's degrees.

Workplaces

Many epidemiologists work for government agencies, such as the CDC; the National Cancer Institute; and city, state, and local health departments. Epidemiologists can also be found at universities, in hospitals, at consulting firms, and in other organizations or companies that do work related to health.

Employment Outlook

The Bureau of Labor Statistics predicts that employment of epidemiologists will grow about 10% from 2012 to 2022, which is about average for all occupations, and that improvements in data collection methods will lead to increased demand. Over the past several years, there has been concern about a shortage of epidemiologists, and the CDC, the Council of State and Territorial Epidemiologists (CSTE), and schools of public health have been working to improve training in this field. According to a CSTE workforce study from 2013, there has been a corresponding increase in formal training among epidemiologists, at least at the state level. It is difficult to predict exactly what the job market will look like, because many public health epidemiologists work for local, state, or federal agencies, and budget constraints can change significantly from year to year. One key to getting started in this career may be to look beyond your primary subject of interest, at least at first; a well-trained epidemiologist who is not tied to any one specialty will have an easier time finding work.

For Further Information

- Council of State and Territorial Epidemiologists (CSTE) *www.cste.org*

- American College of Epidemiology (ACE)
  www.acepidemiology.org
- American Public Health Association (APHA)—Epidemiology section
  www.apha.org/apha-communities/member-sections/epidemiology
- The Society for Healthcare Epidemiology of America (SHEA)
  www.shea-online.org

PUBLIC HEALTH PROFILE: Epidemiologist
Orion McCotter, MPH
Border Infectious Disease Surveillance Epidemiologist
Arizona Department of Health Services, Tucson, AZ

Describe the sort of work you do.

My role at the Arizona Department of Health Services is part of the Border Infectious Disease Surveillance program (BIDS). BIDS was created to survey infectious disease along the U.S.–Mexico border. The participants include local, state, federal, and international public health agencies from each country. My work involves surveillance for infectious diseases near the border between Arizona and Sonora, Mexico. I monitor the occurrence of diseases and watch for new patterns of infection that could signal an outbreak or epidemic.

What is a typical day like at your job?

The daily routine changes constantly depending on what is currently a public health threat. For example, we are in the midst of an influenza pandemic. I have been conducting analyses of emergency room patients that have flu-like symptoms, and trying to determine the proportion of the disease that is confirmed by laboratory tests. When I get results, I notify the hospital, the local health department, and the state epidemiologist. I then write an Arizona BIDS report to share the information with hospitals and public health offices in my region. I am able to perform active surveillance for different infectious diseases in a similar way.

I am often in the field, at clinic, or hospital sites, to train health care staff on surveillance methods. I travel to meet with epidemiologists and public health officials. There are also regular phone conferences with colleagues.

(continued)

(continued)

What education or training do you have? Is it typical for your job?

I have a BS in health education with a community emphasis, focused on disease prevention and health promotion. I have an MPH with a primary concentration in epidemiology and a secondary concentration in health policy. It took a little extra time to do that secondary concentration, but it's been really valuable. It helps me to understand how to translate its findings into policies or interventions that will benefit the public. Many people who do a job like mine would have an MPH with a focus on epidemiology. Some of the people I work with have PhDs, and medical epidemiologists have MDs.

What path did you take to get to the job you are in today?

I discovered public health during my second year at college. I wanted to do something that would help people. Some time after college, I went back to school and I took a class at the public health college. Through that class, I worked with the local health department to do a community assessment of childhood injury. That's when I rediscovered public health and decided to go into the MPH program. I started working for the state as an independent contractor, and eventually I was able to move into my current position.

Where might you go from here, if you wanted to advance your career?

Someone in my job might advance within the health department in several ways. A first step might be to become a program manager. Program managers may be offered promotion to manage an entire section or bureau. Many people continue with higher education in order to advance their careers. I am interested in pursuing a PhD in epidemiology, or potentially a clinical degree.

What is the worst or most challenging part of your job?

Sometimes things don't move at the speed that I would like. Within any agency, there are many layers of approval and review before

(continued)

(continued)

things are able to move forward. Just because I think a project is ready to go, does not mean it is going to start moving yet.

What is the best part?

I enjoy the vast network of people that I get to work with: laboratory directors, emergency room physicians, infection control practitioners, infectious disease physicians, and epidemiologists. I also collaborate with colleagues from the University of Arizona College of Medicine and College of Public Health.

What advice do you have for someone who is interested in your career?

APHA and CSTE are great organizations for networking, and they welcome students. Find out about people's careers and what they typically do. The role of a local epidemiologist is different from a state epidemiologist, and different from a federal job.

Profile Update

Since the time of his interview, Mr. McCotter has moved from the Arizona Department of Health Services to the CDC Mycotic Diseases Branch, where he works as an epidemiologist. His work includes tracking outbreaks, evaluating risk factors and health outcomes, and reporting on fungal diseases. He's enjoying the opportunity to build on his previous work experiences and apply his skills at an even broader level.

MEDICAL OFFICER

Job Description

"Medical officers" are physicians who provide medical expertise for city, state, or federal agencies. Medical officers offer specialized knowledge of disease and treatment that can be essential to making good public health decisions. A medical officer's specific job can include doing direct medical care as part of a government program, but often it involves big-picture work such as developing guidelines and policies, giving advice about the safety of new technologies and products, conducting research on disease prevention and control, making decisions about government grants, or providing guidance for epidemiologic surveillance.

In infectious disease control, there are medical officers who study how infections spread, and then help create recommendations to prevent or control outbreaks. Some help design and carry out disease control programs. Other jobs include helping evaluate antibiotics or other products used to battle infectious disease, participating in infectious disease surveillance and the interpretation of epidemiologic data, and carrying out research. There are medical officers not just in infectious disease control but in many areas of public health, including maternal and child health, chronic disease control, injury prevention, and global health.

Medical officers often enjoy reasonable work hours in comfortable surroundings, although some jobs include emergency response after hours. (For more opportunities for physicians in public health, see medical epidemiologist, medical officer/drug safety, and physician/global health.)

Education and Certification

A medical officer must have an MD or Doctor of Osteopathic Medicine (DO) degree and usually must be licensed to practice medicine. Requirements regarding residency training and other preparation vary according to the needs of each job. For some jobs, earning an MPH or becoming board certified in preventive medicine can make a candidate more competitive. For others, expertise in a relevant clinical specialty is essential.

Core Competencies and Skills

- Good critical thinking skills
- Ability to think flexibly
- Interest in continuing to learn new information and skills
- Willingness to follow government regulations and cope with red tape
- At least a basic grounding in epidemiology and biostatistics

- Understanding of relevant public health regulations and the structure of health-related agencies
- Medical knowledge appropriate to the specific job

Compensation

Medical officers are usually paid well, although not in keeping with the salaries of surgeons or other highly paid specialists. In 2015, typical salaries with the CDC ranged from about $120,000 to $250,000, with the higher salaries for more senior, higher-level jobs. Federal workers also receive generous benefit packages.

Workplaces

The agencies within the U.S. Department of Health and Human Services (HHS) employ a large number of medical officers to do work related to public health. In addition to jobs at federal government agencies, there are similar opportunities with state and local health departments, international agencies, and other organizations, although the job title may be different. (The term "medical officer" is also used in other contexts that do not necessarily have to do with public health.)

Employment Outlook

Most health departments have jobs that are designated specifically for physicians, although those in smaller communities are less likely to do so unless they offer direct clinical care. There are usually several listings for medical officers on the USAJOBS website (usajobs.gov). Finding the job you want can take time, but public health doctors can enjoy broad opportunities for advancement and for lateral moves once they have entered the system. The U.S. Public Health Service Commissioned Corps can also provide steady employment and a long-term career. The skills needed for public health practice are quite different from what's typical in clinical care, so a public health degree can make a doctor quite a bit more competitive for these types of jobs.

For Further Information

- There is no single organization for public health medical officers, but the American College of Preventive Medicine (ACPM; www.acpm.org) is a good resource.

PUBLIC HEALTH PROFILE: Medical Officer
George Pourakis, MD, MPH
Medical Officer
Centers for Disease Control and Prevention, Atlanta, GA

Describe the sort of work you do.

I'm part of a team addressing community measures to prevent the spread of novel H1N1 influenza, the so-called swine flu that was first detected in 2009. Visit the CDC website and go to www.cdc.gov/h1n1flu/guidance. My team creates the guidance documents. We provide recommendations for prevention in various community settings. We're working on guidance for mass gatherings such as business conferences, and next we'll be doing one for homeless shelters. Our recommendations are not binding in terms of law, but people throughout the country look at them to see what they should do.

What is a typical day like at your job?

I'm involved in both gathering information for guidance documents and the actual writing. I spend a fair amount of time reviewing prior guidance documents to identify what aspects are relevant to the new setting I'm writing about. Then, I talk with appropriate subject matter experts. I also search the medical literature to find the best possible evidence about preventing the spread of this strain of influenza and the flu in general. I send our drafts out to various stakeholders, including state and local health officials and professional organizations. They send comments back, and then I review the comments and figure out how to incorporate them. I also respond to questions about the documents.

What education or training do you have? Is it typical for your job?

I have an MD and an MPH. My medical specialty is public health and general preventive medicine. I don't know that an MD is essential for this particular job, but a clinical background is an asset. You have to understand the principles of disease transmission and prevention. Public health training is essential for this work.

(continued)

(continued)

What path did you take to get to the job you are in today?

I did a year of an anesthesiology residency, but I realized I wanted my work to have a broader impact. I switched to preventive medicine, which has a strong focus on public health. During that residency, I did an internship with ACPM in Washington, DC. Through contacts I made, I was able to intern with the Committee on Oversight and Government Reform in the U.S. House of Representatives. I worked on briefings and hearings dealing with H1N1 vaccine manufacturing, distribution, and safety.

After my residency training, I submitted my resume on the usajobs.gov website. I was invited to a CDC job fair in Atlanta. They were recruiting people to work on issues surrounding H1N1, and I had the experience they were looking for.

Where might you go from here, if you wanted to advance your career?

I'm interested in the impact that legislation has on public health. So I'm hoping that the work I am doing now, and my connections at the CDC and elsewhere, will eventually lead to a role focusing more on health policy. For someone who's interested in infectious disease, specifically, the best next step would probably be to do the Epidemic Intelligence Service (EIS) program and become a medical epidemiologist. Having done EIS can help you get your foot in the door in lots of areas.

What is the worst or most challenging part of your job?

When you're at a federal agency, you're in the spotlight. You are subject to the scrutiny of everyone—the public, other experts, and the media. You just can't meet everyone's expectations, and you have to accept that.

What is the best part?

It is great being in an agency where everyone's passionate about the same thing that I'm passionate about. We're making a difference in people's lives on a grand scale, specifically targeting their health.

(continued)

(continued)

Another great thing is having the opportunity to collaborate with people not just here at the CDC, but all over the country.

What advice do you have for someone who is interested in your career?

If you're not happy with what you're doing in medicine, and you're interested in public health, have the courage to make a change. It is not the typical path for an MD, and going against what's typical can be intimidating—but don't be afraid to try it. Keep an open mind, be flexible, be willing to move around and explore your interests.

Profile Update

Dr. Pourakis has changed roles twice since his interview. He has remained a "medical officer," but he has done so in varied capacities with different federal agencies. His next step after working for the CDC came when he was commissioned as an officer in the U.S. Public Health Service Commissioned Corps. His first assignment in the Commissioned Corps was with the Coast Guard, as a Senior Health Services Officer. He did a mix of primary care, occupational medicine, and disability assessments. He says that the military really focuses on keeping the force healthy, so he did a lot of preventive care. Everyone has an annual exam, and people who are exposed to hazardous substances in their work get extra tests and monitoring. For example, he would make sure that someone who was often exposed to diesel fuel during inspections would have their benzene levels tested.

Just recently, he has been assigned to a new role, working for the Health Resources and Services Administration (HRSA) as a senior public health analyst. HRSA provides grants to many different kinds of agencies and organizations, all to support improving access to care for underserved communities. Dr. Pourakis is with the Office of Regional Operations, assigned to Region 2, which includes New York, New Jersey, Puerto Rico, and the Virgin Islands. One of the things he does is meet with representatives of federally recognized Tribes, listen to their concerns, and either make sure they are able to access HRSA resources or connect them with other agencies that

(continued)

(continued)

> might be able to meet their needs. Another example is connecting with rural hospitals, making sure they are aware of funding opportunities at HRSA, and helping them understand how to apply for what they need. In general, his office represents HRSA in the region, and they facilitate interactions between HRSA, state governments, other federal agencies, nonprofit organizations, Tribes, and other entities that carry out work in support of HRSA's goals.

PUBLIC HEALTH NURSE

Job Description

Although most nurses are trained to care for patients one-on-one, public health nurses do everything from providing direct care to leading community assessments and guiding policy change. They can be consultants, administrators, managers, and even leaders of health departments. A public health nurse involved in infectious disease control might run a sexually transmitted infection (STI) clinic, keep track of epidemiologic data on STIs in the community, and lead interventions in response to local trends. There are public health nurses who identify and track TB cases, and others who coordinate immunization clinics. When a disease outbreak occurs, public health nurses help investigate cases, speaking to patients and gathering information.

Public health nurses also work in many areas besides infectious disease prevention and control. Some make home visits and do case management for populations with certain health concerns. Some are involved in designing and carrying out health education programs, advocating for better health policies and laws, planning for emergencies and disasters, and other population-level health efforts.

Education and Certification

A public health nurse needs a current state nursing license. There are nurses doing public health work who have associate's degrees, Bachelor of Science in Nursing (BSN) degrees, Master of Science in Nursing (MSN) degrees, and even PhDs. Leadership roles usually require at least a BSN. An MPH is very useful for a public health nursing career, and some nursing schools offer combined MSN/MPH programs.

California, Minnesota, and New York have specific requirements for the title of "public health nurse," although most states do not. The American Nurses Credentialing Center offers an Advanced Public Health Nursing Certification that can be earned by experienced public health nurses with at least a master's degree and evidence of ongoing professional development.

Core Competencies and Skills

- Passion for social justice
- Interest in community-level health
- Understanding of social issues within target populations
- Desire to work collaboratively across health disciplines
- Interest in health care policy
- Ability to make independent judgments
- Knowledge of both clinical and public health issues
- Knowledge of epidemiologic principles and techniques

Compensation

In 2014, the median salary for all nurses was about $66,000, with most earning between $46,000 and $99,000. Salaries for public health nurses depend on location, tasks, and experience. A 2013 report from the Robert Wood Johnson Foundation showed that public health nurses had high job satisfaction but felt that they received lower salaries than colleagues in other settings. Wages also tended to be lower at local health departments than at the state level.

Workplaces

Many public health nurses work for city, county, and state health departments, in a wide range of roles including infectious disease surveillance and control. There are opportunities at federal agencies, where public health nurses can contribute their knowledge to programs and policies on the national level. Public health nurses in the Indian Health Service provide direct service to patients as well as community assessment and intervention, and there are public health nurses serving as coordinators in the Special Supplemental Nutrition Program for Women, Infants and Children (WIC). There are also jobs at nonprofit organizations, and there are public health nurses who are doctoral-level researchers and professors at universities.

Employment Outlook

Nurses make up a large proportion of the public health workforce, but experts continue to predict a shortage of nurses specifically trained in public health. The actual job description can vary; in some places, "public health nurses" are thought of more as workers in community clinics than as experts on population-level prevention and health promotion, and this can influence the types of jobs available.

For Further Information

- Association of Public Health Nurses (APHN)
  www.phnurse.org
- American Public Health Association (APHA)—Public Health Nursing Section
  www.apha.org/apha-communities/member-sections/public-health-nursing
- Association of Community Health Nursing Educators (ACHNE)
  www.achne.org

PUBLIC HEALTH PROFILE: Public Health Nurse
Donna Westawski, MSN
Tuberculosis Nurse Consultant
Pennsylvania Department of Health, Wilkes-Barre, PA

Describe the sort of work you do.

I'm in charge of TB surveillance and management for a district within a state health department. Each state has communicable disease laws, telling what diseases need to be reported, and TB is one of those diseases. We need to find all of the active cases of TB that exist at any point in time, so that we can prevent transmission and make sure people are getting the right treatment. I'm involved in case finding, case management, surveillance, education and training, consulting, and the enforcement of regulations and communicable disease laws. I also maintain a registry of diagnosed cases, and I coordinate the schedule for directly observed therapy (DOT). DOT involves sending someone out to see certain patients each day, to make sure they take their medicine. If a patient refuses to be treated

(continued)

(continued)

or to stay isolated until he is no longer contagious, we can use legal channels to have that person quarantined.

What is a typical day like at your job?

A large part of my day is working with the state's electronic reporting and surveillance system. Sometimes doctors call to report cases, but surveillance also means hunting and researching and looking for clues that there might be someone out there who has TB. The clue might be an abnormal chest x-ray, or it might be a laboratory report. Automated reports from laboratories come in several times a day.

The same electronic reporting system is also a case management system. The CDC needs certain types of information about patients with TB. I enter data about risk factors, test results, treatment regimens and doses, and interim chest x-rays.

Another thing I do is handle telephone consultations. Some days I get no calls, and some days I get 20. A doctor might call about a patient whose medication is not agreeing with him. I often consult with nursing homes about what to do if a patient is confirmed as having TB. We get a lot of calls from the general public, too. Other tasks include doing trainings for health care providers, testing people for TB, and helping with other health issues that come up in our community.

What education or training do you have? Is it typical for your job?

I have a BSN and a master's in community health nursing. The exact requirements for public health nurses differ from place to place.

What path did you take to get to the job you are in today?

I started with a 3-year diploma nursing program. I worked for a short time in clinical nursing. While I was doing that, I went on and earned my bachelor's degree. That's when I learned about public health nursing, because we had a rotation in community health. It was just a couple of years after finishing the baccalaureate program that I started

(continued)

(continued)

working for the health department. I took several years off to raise a family, and during that time I earned a master's degree in community health nursing. I also did some teaching at 4-year nursing schools and worked part-time at a home health agency. After finishing the MSN, I completed a civil service application and put my name on a list for positions in public health nursing. Some time after that, when the health department was hiring, they called me in to interview.

Where might you go from here, if you wanted to advance your career?

There's not much advancement in my specific job. As a community health nurse, I could become a supervisor or administrator, running a larger program. If I considered anything else, I'd probably consider teaching again.

What is the worst or most challenging part of your job?

There are gray areas in TB diagnosis. Sometimes, my experience tells me that a particular patient does have TB and we need to take care of him, but I can't hand the doctor a piece of paper that tells her what to do.

What is the best part?

I like having enough information and knowledge to be a consultant. I find it gratifying that when people call with questions and concerns, I can give them an answer. Often they'll say, "I wish I'd called you a month ago!"

What advice do you have for someone who is interested in your career?

The APHA public health nursing section is a good resource. I would also say, get some clinical experience before you look for your first public health job. Much of the work you will do in public health is independent. You won't necessarily have a lot of staff or mentors. So if you can work in some different types of nursing, get some experience and build up your knowledge, it can really help.

PUBLIC HEALTH VETERINARIAN

Job Description

Public health veterinarians focus on the interaction between human and animal health. Their jobs can range from inspecting livestock to influencing national policy. Public health veterinarians help protect our food supply, contribute to disaster preparedness efforts, create and enforce regulations for animal shelters, consult with emergency room physicians, and more. Many are involved in infectious disease prevention and control. Some assist with the review and approval of drugs, such as antibiotics, that are used in animals. Others work to monitor and prevent the spread of diseases that can be transmitted from animals to humans (such as rabies, Lyme disease, *Escherichia coli*, Ebola, and many others). At the U.S. Department of Agriculture (USDA), veterinarians' roles include making sure that meat and poultry plants are producing safe food, inspecting animals being brought into the country, investigating disease outbreaks, and seeking new ways to prevent disease in both animals and humans.

Some public health veterinarians work primarily in offices or labs, while others carry out on-site inspections at farms, factories, ports, and border areas. Some work in global health. The job usually involves regular hours; however, a public health veterinarian may need to respond to emergencies on weekends, holidays, or other off-hours.

Education and Certification

A public health veterinarian must have a Doctor of Veterinary Medicine (DVM) degree and, in most cases, must have a current license to practice. Specific public health training or experience is not always required; however, jobs that involve disease surveillance, program design, policy, and other population-level efforts require a strong understanding of epidemiology and other aspects of public health. Some veterinary schools offer combined DVM/MPH programs, and there are opportunities for postgraduate training, including residency programs in veterinary public health. Public health veterinarians can seek certification from the American College of Veterinary Preventive Medicine.

Core Competencies and Skills

- Creative thinking
- Ability to see problems from multiple angles

- Passion for preventing, not just treating, disease
- Interest in working as part of a team
- Good communication skills
- At least a basic understanding of statistics and epidemiology
- Knowledge of veterinary medicine from both individual and population perspectives

Compensation

Salary surveys generally do not separate out public health veterinarians from those who provide direct patient care. The Bureau of Labor Statistics lists the median salary for all veterinarians as $87,500 in 2014, with most earning between $52,500 and $157,000. According to the American Veterinary Medical Association, in 2014 the median salary for veterinarians working for state or local government was $83,000 per year. In federal government, the median salary was $120,000 per year. For comparison, the median for vets in private practice was about $94,000 per year. Specific salaries vary by location, job responsibilities, qualifications, and seniority.

Workplaces

Veterinarians involved in public health activities are employed by local and state health departments and by federal agencies including the USDA, the Food and Drug Administration, the CDC, the Environmental Protection Agency, the Department of Homeland Security, and the Department of Defense. There are also jobs in private industry that use public health skills and techniques.

Employment Outlook

The Bureau of Labor Statistics says that the number of new veterinary school graduates has increased in recent years, which means more competition for jobs. The highest interest seems to be in companion animal care, though; hence, veterinarians interested in public health may have less competition.

For Further Information

- National Association of State Public Health Veterinarians (NASPHV)
  www.nasphv.org

- American College of Veterinary Preventive Medicine (ACVPM)
  www.acvpm.org
- American Association of Public Health Veterinarians (AAPHV)
  www.aaphv.org
- One Health Commission
  www.onehealthcommission.org

PUBLIC HEALTH ADVISOR

Job Description

The title "public health advisor" originally belonged to a team of CDC fieldworkers with basic public health training who went out into local communities to identify and treat patients with STIs. The program later expanded to include TB control and many other issues. Today, public health advisors are closely involved in program design and implementation, providing efficient response to many different kinds of public health needs. They may manage programs or provide technical assistance to state and local agencies, foreign governments, or other organizations. As public health advisors rise through the ranks, they gain more responsibility and may eventually manage large programs. Some public health advisors are stationed at federal agency headquarters; others are assigned to locations around the country or overseas, where they assist with local public health efforts.

Public health advisors are also found at other agencies and in other areas of public health. There are public health advisors working in disaster preparedness, nutrition, mental health, and many other areas of disease prevention and health promotion.

Education and Certification

A CDC public health advisor needs at least a bachelor's degree or equivalent experience in public health, although many of these positions now require a higher-level degree and/or more extensive experience. The CDC's Public Health Associate Program (PHAP), designed for recent bachelor's or master's degree graduates, is technically part of the public health advisor career track. Jobs at the CDC are not guaranteed after the PHAP, but associates are eligible to apply for entry-level public health advisor jobs after completing the 2-year program.

Core Competencies and Skills

- Adaptability
- Initiative
- Good communication skills
- Knack for evaluating situations and determining what is needed
- Ability to apply research findings to practice
- Ability to make decisions independently, but also to collaborate with a team
- Strong understanding of the elements of public health practice, including the use of epidemiologic data, disease surveillance and control, and program design, implementation, and evaluation

Compensation

Public health advisors at the CDC start in the $50,000s to $60,000s, with adjustments for location. Experienced advisors with significant responsibility can reach $100,000, and there are senior-level positions with higher salaries.

Workplaces

Public health advisors have an important role at the CDC. Some work at headquarters in Atlanta. Others are assigned to state or local health departments. It is not uncommon for CDC public health advisors to be assigned where they are most needed, which can mean frequent moves. There are also public health advisors at other federal agencies, including other departments within HHS and U.S. Agency for International Development. Some state and local agencies have similar job titles.

Employment Outlook

Public health advisors are well prepared for a wide range of public health activities. There are many opportunities for advancement, and the skills gained through this job tend to be in demand at state and local agencies and nonprofit organizations, as well.

For Further Information

- Watsonian Society
  www.cdc.gov/watsonian/default.htm

VACCINE RESEARCHER

Job Description

Vaccine researchers look at everything from how the immune system works to how to prevent specific diseases, such as HIV/AIDS and malaria. Other issues include predicting who is likely to respond to a vaccine and figuring out how long the protection from a vaccine will last. There are researchers working to improve on existing vaccines, too—to deliver better protection or make immunity last longer.

Some vaccine researchers examine immune responses on the cellular or molecular level. Some test potential new vaccines in human populations. Some study the safety of vaccines. In general, vaccine researchers must have a strong understanding of the immune system, of the processes involved in infection, and of how vaccines are thought to work. In addition, researchers may write journal articles, present results at conferences, help write medical textbooks, and even give advice to policy makers.

Education and Certification

A researcher who wants to run a laboratory or be primarily responsible for designing and carrying out studies related to vaccines needs a doctoral degree, usually a PhD, followed by additional postdoctoral training. Typical fields for the PhD include molecular biology, immunology, microbiology, or biochemistry, although the name of the degree is less important than the actual topics studied. Some vaccine researchers are MDs who have additional training and experience in research. There are also opportunities in research labs for master's-level graduates and even for those with bachelor's degrees, but the best opportunities for advancement come with a doctoral degree.

Core Competencies and Skills

- Understanding of the scientific method
- Good attention to detail and an appreciation for precision
- Strong sense of ethics, especially when human or animal subjects are involved
- Ability to work as part of a team
- Patience and the ability to accept that studies may not give hoped-for results
- Knowledge specific to infectious diseases and the immune system
- Practical skills for the design and implementation of clinical or laboratory studies

Compensation

According to national statistics, the median salary for a medical scientist, a job category that includes people involved in developing vaccines, is about $80,000, with most earning between $43,000 and $148,000. People in senior positions can reach $200,000 per year or more. Research professors can expect similar compensation levels, although it varies from one university to another. PhDs in postdoctoral positions start at lower salaries, with a jump in pay in their first jobs after this level.

Workplaces

Vaccine research is carried out at multiple places including National Institutes of Health (NIH) and university departments. The U.S. Army Research Institute on Infectious Diseases also develops vaccines, primarily to protect service members from potential biological warfare agents and dangerous endemic diseases.

Employment Outlook

The need for medical scientists with doctoral-level degrees is expected to increase over the next several years, but there is also expected to be strong competition for jobs. In recent years, there has been concern that there are more new science PhD graduates than there are research and faculty jobs available. A job will often require a very specific background, and it may be a challenge to find a position that matches one's training and interests. It is a good idea to talk to people in the field, if you are just starting out, so you will know if your interests match what is likely to be in demand. The availability of federal funding will also influence the number of jobs available in both government and academic settings.

For Further Information

- Vaccine Research Center at the National Institute of Allergy and Infectious Diseases
  www.niaid.nih.gov/about/organization/vrc
- National Foundation for Infectious Diseases (NFID)
  www.nfid.org
- The International Vaccine Institute (IVI)
  www.ivi.int

PUBLIC HEALTH PROFILE: Vaccine Researcher
Mario Roederer, PhD
Senior Investigator
ImmunoTechnology Section
Vaccine Research Center, National Institute of Allergy and Infectious
Diseases, National Institutes of Health, Bethesda, MD

Describe the sort of work you do.

I'm in charge of a research laboratory at the Vaccine Research Center. In my laboratory, we're exploring how immune responses develop. That's important for understanding and treating natural infections, and it is also important for developing vaccines. Every time you test a vaccine, it takes thousands of people, millions of dollars, and several years, so you want to start with a vaccine that is likely to have a good protective response. But at this point, we don't really know which immune system responses are the most likely to be protective. We are trying to determine that, so we can develop vaccines more quickly.

What is a typical day like at your job?

I supervise about a dozen people. My day typically involves providing them with advice on how to design experiments and interpret data, and helping them write up the results for publication. I also participate in outside advisory activities, and sometimes we collaborate with people who are developing similar research programs. There is administrative work, as well. And I go to a number of conferences. At my level, I don't do direct laboratory work. Some people make the choice to stay in the lab. I'd rather focus on providing the best advice and input.

What education or training do you have? Is it typical for your job?

Everyone's a little different. My PhD is in cell biology, and my background is more hard science and technical than most people in my position. I'm an adept computer programmer, I know physics and chemistry, so we do a lot of technology development in my lab, not just application.

(continued)

(continued)

You need a PhD or MD to do my job, and you need additional experience. It takes a lot of years to really learn how to run a laboratory and how to organize it. You also have to think globally—how the different experiments tie together.

What path did you take to get to the job you are in today?

As is often the case in the research world, finding my current job at the NIH was a matter of good timing. The Vaccine Research Center was just being created. I was told by a colleague that they were looking for someone with a background like mine. Usually, for this type of job, there is just one opening and a lot of people apply for it. I applied, not expecting to get the job—and I did get it. It was an outstanding opportunity, a perfect fit for the research I was envisioning.

Where might you go from here, if you wanted to advance your career?

I'm right where I want to be right now, so I would characterize a change not as a step up, but as a step in a different direction. Some people might want to run a department or run an institute. At that point, though, you're not really doing science anymore. It is much more administrative. You could do science policy, you could work for a foundation and do research grants, you could work for a biotech company. There's not one single career ladder.

What is the worst or most challenging part of your job?

My calendar is much more full than it used to be, with conference calls and meetings. I understand the necessity of those, and I even enjoy them—but I don't have the freedom I used to. My job also calls for a lot of traveling. I enjoy the travel, but it gets hard, especially when you have a family. It's hard being away from the lab, too.

What is the best part?

My joy is enabling science, helping research happen. And I love giving presentations. It's my chance to tell people about the cool things that we do!

(continued)

(continued)

What advice do you have for someone who is interested in your career?

You have to experience it. When you're in school, spend some time in the laboratory and discover what it is like to spend 60 or 70 hours a week there. Get into it thinking that you will give it a shot—but it is not for everyone. There are a lot more postdoctoral jobs than there are faculty, and it's partly because people realize this work is not for them. You have to have a love for it!

DISEASE ECOLOGIST

Job Description

Disease ecologists study patterns of diseases in populations, which may include humans, plants, and animals, with an emphasis on understanding the principles that underlie disease patterns. They look at interactions of populations with each other and with the environment, and ask how those interactions influence the emergence of new diseases, the spread of familiar ones, and the appearance of outbreaks and epidemics. Some disease ecologists study the evolution of drug resistance and virulence among infectious agents, and the development of resistance to infection among potential hosts.

Not all disease ecologists do work that is likely to inform public health directly. However, there are some ecologists studying how climate change is likely to impact infectious disease in human populations, how environmental changes may contribute to the emergence of new diseases, and how biodiversity can influence the risk of diseases in humans. Some are directly involved in investigating outbreaks and creating policies to prevent disease. Some work largely with computer models or in laboratories, while others do field research.

Education and Certification

Disease ecologists generally have PhDs or other doctoral degrees. There are some university departments specializing in disease ecology; at others, this work is done within the general ecology department or department of ecology and evolutionary biology. Many established disease ecologists earned their PhDs in fields such as microbiology, ecology, entomology, or zoology, and some are veterinarians. There are a few roles in applied disease ecology for people with BS or MS degrees.

Core Competencies and Skills

- Curiosity
- Persistence
- Ability to collaborate with people who have different types of expertise
- Ability to communicate complex ideas on paper and in person
- Interest not only in clinical manifestations of disease, causes, or risk factors, but also in what causes patterns of disease to occur
- Appreciation of the interactions among epidemiology, ecology, genetics, and medicine
- Good math and statistical skills, and an understanding of how research is designed and carried out
- Willingness to work both in the laboratory and in the field

Compensation

Because "disease ecologist" can refer to people from many different disciplines, there are no national salary statistics. In 2014, the median salary for professors in the biological sciences was about $75,000 and for environmental sciences, $77,000. Low-end salaries were in the $40,000 range and high-end salaries in the low to mid-$100,000s. Variations in salaries make it hard to compare academic and nonacademic jobs, but microbiologists who were not also educators had a median salary of about $68,000, with most earning $39,000 to $125,000; salaries for zoologists and wildlife biologists tended to be a little lower. (These numbers include jobs with various responsibilities and areas of focus, not just disease ecologists.)

Workplaces

Disease ecologists focusing on public health issues work at universities, including schools of public health, at nonprofit organizations that support research, and at government agencies including the U.S. Geological Survey, the CDC, the USDA, and some state health departments. There are also opportunities at organizations that do work in the developing world.

Employment Outlook

Competition for jobs varies. Recent PhD graduates may find it challenging to locate a job that matches their specific research interests. Attending scientific meetings and networking with others in the field is often a good way to find opportunities.

For Further Information

- The Ecological Society of America (ESA)
  www.esa.org
- Society for Vector Ecology (SOVE)
  www.sove.org
- American Society for Tropical Medicine and Hygiene (ASTMH)
  www.astmh.org

INFECTION PREVENTIONIST

Job Description

Infection preventionists are experts on practical methods of preventing and controlling the spread of infectious diseases, typically within a specific population—the patients, staff, and visitors at a hospital or other health care setting. Their work also helps reduce the risk of contagious diseases being carried out into the community. Infection control practices include surveillance, investigation of cases and outbreaks, training of staff members, the development and enforcement of infection control policies, and evaluation of the effectiveness of infection control efforts. If an outbreak occurs, infection preventionists track down the source and control the problem. They must be alert to any unusual illness that could signal an outbreak, a new type of infection, or even the first casualty of a bioterrorism attack. They spend some time collecting and analyzing data, but they also observe staff members' practices, participate in patient rounds, attend meetings, and design and lead interventions to improve infection control.

Some infection preventionists are involved in protecting the health of wider communities. They may provide guidance on controlling epidemics, protecting against emerging diseases, or planning in case of a bioterrorism attack. Many infection preventionists in health care settings have additional responsibilities, such as employee health. (To learn more about jobs in patient safety, see Chapter 19.)

Education and Certification

Requirements depend on the specific job setting. Many infection preventionists are RNs. Some have an MPH or other relevant training. A few schools have begun offering master's degrees emphasizing infection prevention, and some schools offer certificate programs. Although special certification is not necessarily required, job candidates may be viewed more favorably if they have a Certification in Infection Prevention and Control (CIC) credential, which is obtained by passing a test administered by the Certification Board of Infection Control and Epidemiology (CBIC). As of 2015, the Association for Professionals in Infection Control and Epidemiology is working on creating an advanced IP designation, as well. There are also infectious disease physicians and PhDs whose work focuses on infection control.

Core Competencies and Skills

- Curiosity and persistence
- Good problem-solving skills and the ability to think creatively
- Ability to make timely decisions, using good judgment
- Understanding of epidemiology and data-analysis techniques
- Strong enough science background to understand how infections are transmitted and what protective practices are appropriate in a given situation
- Knowledge of infection control guidelines and regulations
- Good understanding of human behavior, to understand how and why people put themselves at risk

Compensation

Salaries vary depending on specific qualifications, responsibilities, and location. Overall, compensation has increased as hospitals and other health care settings have become more aware of the importance of this role. A 2013 survey of infection prevention and control professionals found an average salary of nearly $78,000 per year. Salaries reflected education levels. Most respondents were RNs and about half had a credential from the CBIC. The average salary for someone with an associate's degree was about $66,000, with a bachelor's $74,000, and with a higher degree, $81,000.

Workplaces

Infection preventionists can be found at hospitals and outpatient centers, as well as hospices, home-care organizations, and other settings where health services are provided. Health departments, federal agencies, non-profit organizations, and university centers also employ these experts to enhance infection control practices on a wider scale. Some infection preventionists work with the military, and some are even involved in global health, such as working to prevent outbreaks in developing countries.

Employment Outlook

With a growing emphasis on patient safety, hospitals are paying increasing attention to infection control and job opportunities should be good. In addition, many current infection preventionists are nearing retirement age. Concerns about bioterrorism and emerging diseases also provide opportunities for these specialists.

For Further Information

- Association for Professionals in Infection Control and Epidemiology (APIC)
  www.apic.org

CHAPTER 5

Chronic Disease and Cancer

Chronic disease is an increasingly important concern in the world of public health. The number of Americans with type 2 diabetes has soared in recent decades (American Diabetes Association, 2014). Heart disease is the leading cause of death in the United States; yet many premature deaths from heart disease could be prevented (Centers for Disease Control and Prevention, 2014). Asthma affects about 19 million adults and 7 million children (Centers for Disease Control and Prevention, 2015a). Nearly three out of five teenagers already have dental cavities, and about 15% of teens have untreated tooth decay (Dye, Thornton-Evans, Li, & Iafolla, 2015). Cancer, which many health professionals also classify as a chronic disease, is the second leading cause of death in the United States (Centers for Disease Control and Prevention, 2015b).

There are ways to reduce the risk and lessen the impact of many chronic diseases, but often we do not take advantage of them. Regular exercise and a healthful diet have numerous benefits, but a lot of us do not follow the recommended guidelines. And many people with chronic diseases do not get the care they need.

Public health asks what we can change in our neighborhoods, our communities, and our health care system to get better control of chronic diseases. Some experts focus on measuring disease incidence and prevalence and tracking patterns in different communities. Others look at what can be done about these findings. Many jobs have elements of both. Do people need education about healthy choices? Is there something we can alter in the environment, such as prohibiting smoking in restaurants or posting calorie information on menus? Do we need to train doctors to provide better care? Is there a way to ensure that people who need treatment are getting it?

In this chapter, you will learn about some careers involving chronic disease prevention and intervention. To learn about others, see the descriptions for epidemiologist, medical officer, public health nurse, environmental health nurse, nutrition consultant, corporate medical director, and community activist, and the chapters on maternal and child health (Chapter 7) and on vulnerable and at-risk populations (Chapter 16). The Centers for Disease Control and Prevention (CDC) has a website devoted to chronic disease prevention and health promotion at www.cdc.gov/chronicdisease.

HEALTH EDUCATOR

Job Description

Health educators convey health information to the public in ways that people will understand and, ideally, find interesting and useful, too. They begin by figuring out what people in a given community do and do not know about a particular health topic. In chronic disease prevention, this might be preventing diabetes, controlling asthma, or detecting colon cancer. (Health educators may also teach about many other topics besides chronic disease.) They determine how most people in that community like to learn and what will catch their attention. For example, pamphlets might be good for college students who like to read, but not very useful in an inner-city community where literacy is low. Next, they put together programs—classes, videos, and even cell phone texts—that convey the needed information. When possible, they follow up by evaluating the success of the program, to see what people learned and if their behavior or health changed as a result.

Health educators are involved in all levels of health promotion, from designing local programs to serving as advisors for national health campaigns. In addition to teaching members of the general public, in some places they work on systems-level programs, such as teaching convenience store owners how they can stock healthier foods.

Education and Certification

A bachelor's degree is usually the minimum qualification to work as a health educator. There are bachelor's degrees specifically in health education. At some schools, it is possible to focus on health education as part of another degree. And some employers will accept on-the-job experience or other training. A master's degree, such as an MPH with specialization in public or community health education, broadens the job possibilities and contributes to the chances for advancement. Certification as a Certified Health Education Specialist, which requires an exam administered by the National Commission for Health Education Credentialing (NCHEC), is preferred for many public health jobs and occasionally is required. There is also a Master Certified Health Education Specialist credential, which requires at least 5 years' experience in the field.

Core Competencies and Skills

- Knack for explaining complex information in a straightforward, easily understandable way
- At least basic knowledge of health and medicine, and the ability to understand medical information
- Excellent spoken and written communication skills
- Appreciation of cultural diversity
- Understanding of human psychology and behavior
- Ability to create a curriculum covering necessary information
- Understanding of research processes and survey design
- Ability to write for people with low reading literacy and low health literacy

Compensation

In 2014, the average salary for a health educator was about $50,000. Most earned between $29,500 and $90,000.

Workplaces

Health educators who create and implement public health programs are found in government agencies, nonprofit organizations, college and universities, and sometimes hospitals and medical centers. (In medical settings, they are more likely to provide one-on-one teaching.)

Employment Outlook

Rising interest in the prevention of disease as a way to control health care costs may lead to more opportunities for health educators in public health roles. The Bureau of Labor Statistics describes an increase in insurance companies and employers hiring health educators to teach patients about managing disease, which is more of a direct-care role but can incorporate some community-based efforts. Formal training as a health educator and speaking a foreign language may help in the job search.

For Further Information

- Society for Public Health Education (SOPHE)
  www.sophe.org
- American Public Health Association (APHA)—Public Health Education and Health Promotion section
  www.apha.org/communities/member-sections/ public-health-education-and-health-promotion
- Society of Health and Physical Educators
  www.shapeamerica.org

HEALTH PROMOTION PROGRAM COORDINATOR

Job Description

Health promotion programs can be local, state, or nationwide efforts to get people to adopt healthier behaviors. Examples include a national campaign to remind people to eat their fruits and veggies, cooking classes to help low-income families make healthy food on a budget, and "fit city" exercise campaigns. There are programs that encourage corner grocery stores to carry healthier foods and doctors to talk to their patients about smoking.

Each of these programs has a coordinator or manager (or sometimes more than one) to oversee everything from the planning process, to the daily activities, to the analysis of data that are collected. Responsibilities can include developing educational materials, partnering with other organizations, raising funds, hiring and firing employees, reaching out to the media, and making sure that the program is running smoothly. In small programs, the coordinator may do all these things directly; in larger programs, a director will delegate tasks to employees.

This is primarily an office job, with the usual business hours. Program coordinators may also need to attend evening meetings, be present at weekend events or conferences, and visit community sites. Late hours may sometimes be needed to meet a grant deadline, prepare a report, or respond to media interest.

Education and Certification

A program coordinator usually has at least a bachelor's degree in a health-related field. Some schools offer a major specifically in health promotion, but many people study health promotion as part of another major. An MPH or a master's degree in a related field is often preferred or required; an MPH with a concentration in community health, behavioral and social science, or health promotion and communication would provide useful skills. There is no special certification required for this job, but for larger programs, especially, relevant experience is expected. Some employers look for credentials such as Certified Health Education Specialist (CHES) or Certified in Public Health (CPH).

Core Competencies and Skills

- Good public speaking and presentation skills
- Strong management skills
- Excellent social skills for interacting with program participants and leaders of other programs and organizations
- Strong writing skills
- Understanding of the population that the program serves
- Knowledge of how to apply research results to real-world programs

Compensation

Compensation depends on experience, on the size of the program, and on the budget of the agency or organization. Many jobs, particularly with small organizations or small programs, have salaries in the $40,000 to $60,000 range. Program coordinators can eventually become managers or directors at programs with statewide or national reach, with higher salaries to match the level of responsibility.

Workplaces

Health promotion program coordinators usually work for academic institutions, government agencies, and nonprofit organizations, or for consulting firms that serve these types of organizations.

Employment Outlook

Jobs are most likely to be available in cities and counties with larger and more active health departments, with corporations that have taken an interest in a particular community health issue, or with local nonprofit organizations that have a special interest in promoting public health. Health promotion programs are often grant-funded and may continue for only a limited number of years, but new programs are often being launched, as well.

For Further Information

- American Public Health Association (APHA)—Public Health Education and Health Promotion section
  www.apha.org/membergroups/sections/aphasections/phehp

PUBLIC HEALTH PROFILE: Health Promotion Program Coordinator
John Wedeles, MPH
Program Coordinator
Manhattan Tobacco Cessation Program, New York, NY

Describe the sort of work you do.

I am the program coordinator for the Manhattan Tobacco Cessation Program (MTCP), one of the 19 cessation centers throughout New York State. MTCP is funded by the New York State Department of Health. My job is to give health care providers (doctors, nurses, nurse practitioners, and medical assistants) the knowledge and resources to help their patients successfully quit smoking. MTCP promotes the "5 A's" model, which recommends that providers ask about tobacco use, advise smokers to quit, assess their readiness to quit, assist them in their attempt to quit by referring them to cessation services or pre-scribing pharmacotherapy, and arrange a follow-up visit. We also help clinics develop their paper charts or electronic medical records so that tobacco treatment becomes a standard practice. And we supply them with educational resources for both providers and patients.

What is a typical day like at your job?

During a typical day, I work on collecting or analyzing data from patient charts to determine whether a partner site is adhering to the

(continued)

(continued)

5 A's model. I'll summarize the data and point out achievements, areas where improvements can be made, and so on. I might advise a hospital or clinic about larger policy issues, such as smoke-free grounds. I also might give training to clinic staff on practicing the 5 A's. I represent my group at community health fairs, too, distributing educational materials and answering questions.

What education or training do you have? Is it typical for your job?

I have a master's degree in public health. Most of my colleagues have master's degrees in public health or public administration. Several have clinical backgrounds, including a few who are registered nurses. Also I'm a trained tobacco treatment specialist. Although I don't provide direct patient care, the training gave me an excellent background in tobacco treatment that I use in my staff trainings for partner sites.

What path did you take to get to the job you are in today?

After two jobs in marketing and public affairs, I switched careers and started working as a public affairs assistant for a hospital trade association. I also volunteered at a hospital in order to strengthen my background in health care, with the intention of going to graduate school in public administration or public health. Once I got to graduate school, I volunteered for MTCP. The program coordinator position opened up shortly after I graduated, and at that point they already knew me and liked my work.

Where might you go from here, if you wanted to advance your career?

From here I could continue in program management in more of an administrative role. Because I do a fair amount of data collection and analysis, I could also seek a position at a research organization. A job at a consulting firm might be a good fit as well.

(continued)

(continued)

What is the worst or most challenging part of your job?

Many of the health care providers I work with are often pressed for time. As a result, treating tobacco use is sometimes not a high priority in comparison with other health conditions. In addition, sometimes it is easy to get caught up in the daily tasks without having an eye for long-term strategy and goals. It is essential to always be thinking 6 months down the road and looking at how your daily work will meet your annual deliverables.

What is the best part?

I've been able to impart real change to the partner sites I work with. In certain instances, following staff training, we have observed improvements in the doctors' adherence to the 5 A's. We've also requested changes to the electronic medical record template at the pediatric clinics, which led to improvements in adherence. Another great part about my job is the variety of activities—from research and data collection to training to policy development.

What advice would you give to someone who wanted to do this type of work?

For this particular job, I would tell that person to get trained as a tobacco treatment specialist, so you have those skills to pass on to health care providers. It also helps one to have experience in a clinical setting to understand the flow of patient care. A master's degree in public health or public administration will be very helpful as well. Public health is all about collaboration, so I would be open to partnering with other organizations and administrative departments—anything that will help open doors throughout your work.

Profile Update

Since his original interview, Dr. Wedeles has completed a DrPH program with a concentration in health behavior at the GW Milken Institute School of Public Health. He also worked as a research

(continued)

(continued)

assistant on a tobacco cessation research study while enrolled in that program. Dr. Wedeles now works as a data analyst with the District of Columbia Department of Health Care Finance, which is the District's Medicaid agency. He works on a variety of topics, often with an emphasis on children's health, mental health, home health, and long-term care.

MEDICAL EPIDEMIOLOGIST/CHRONIC DISEASE

Job Description

Medical epidemiologists are public health physicians who bring a strong knowledge of clinical medicine to their epidemiology work. (See the description of epidemiologist to learn more.) Their medical training gives them special understanding of the clinical manifestations of diseases, the underlying pathophysiology, the ways medications work, and the nuances that can make the study of certain diseases especially complex. Medical epidemiologists can do surveillance and monitoring, outbreak investigation, and research, not just in chronic disease (such as asthma, cardiovascular disease, diabetes, and cancer), but in all areas of public health. Some use their skills to help design and evaluate disease prevention programs. Often, medical epidemiologists serve as consultants to nonphysician epidemiologists and other public health experts. They also have the knowledge to talk peer to peer with other physicians about medical information. Some medical epidemiologists are specialists, focusing on one area of health, others are generalists.

Education and Certification

In most cases, a medical epidemiologist must have an MD or DO degree. Many jobs also require completion of a residency program and a license to practice, and some require a specific medical specialty. It is possible for a doctor to learn to do epidemiologic work without a public health degree, but employers usually prefer or require an MPH, completion of the Epidemic Intelligence Service (EIS) fellowship at the CDC, or other relevant education.

Core Competencies and Skills

- Curiosity about patterns of disease
- Logical and analytical thinking
- Creativity
- Ability to explain medical knowledge to nonphysicians
- Strong knowledge of epidemiologic principles
- Knowledge of how to use statistics programs and databases
- Good background in clinical medicine, an interest in learning more, and the ability to search and understand the medical literature

Compensation

Salaries vary by level, experience, and location. Recent job openings have been in the range of $100,000 to $200,000 per year.

Workplaces

Medical epidemiologists work for local and state health departments and for federal agencies including the CDC, the National Institutes of Health, and the Department of Defense. Some are university faculty. There are also opportunities at nonprofit organizations and in consulting firms.

Employment Outlook

There is expanding interest in epidemiologic approaches to chronic disease, maternal and child health, substance abuse, disaster preparedness, and other topics beyond the more traditional focus on infectious disease. At the same time, job listings with the title "medical epidemiologist" have become less common in recent years, and it can take some searching under other job titles (e.g., "epidemiologist," "public health physician," and "medical officer") to find the ones that combine epidemiology skills with a medical background. Some of the strongest candidates are doctors who have been through EIS.

For Further Information

- See the listings under the entries for epidemiologist and medical officer.

PUBLIC HEALTH PROFILE: Medical Epidemiologist
Sarah Schillie, MD, MPH, MBA

Medical Epidemiologist
U.S. Public Health Service Commissioned Corps, Centers for Disease
Control and Prevention, Springfield, IL

Describe the sort of work you do.

I'm a medical doctor with special training in public health and epidemiology. I'm an officer in the U.S. Public Health Service Commissioned Corps and am employed by the CDC. Currently, I'm a chronic disease field epidemiology assignee to the Illinois Department of Public Health, so I am employed by the federal government but work at the state level.

My job is multifaceted, but most of my work revolves around asthma, tobacco, and obesity. I design evaluations for chronic disease programs and interventions, analyze and interpret surveillance data, and collaborate with other agencies to develop public health interventions. Part of my assignment is to help build epidemiologic capacity within the state, which includes teaching others about epidemiologic principles and methods.

What is a typical day like at your job?

A typical day includes working with data, writing, providing technical assistance, and attending meetings. The data analyses range from simple, descriptive statistics to more complex analysis. The writing includes reports, abstracts, and press releases. I provide guidance to coworkers and stakeholders on things such as survey design, data analysis, and data interpretation. My participation in meetings often involves providing subject matter expertise or presentations.

Project managers often ask me to display data using maps. For example, I recently created state maps depicting obesity rates by county over time. Additionally, I spend quite a bit of time creating web-based surveys. I'm currently working on an electronic survey as part of an evaluation for various asthma interventions that are conducted by grantees.

(continued)

(continued)

What education or training do you have? Is it typical for your job?

I have an MD and an MPH, and recently received an MBA. After medical school, I completed residencies in pediatrics and preventive medicine, as well as the 2-year EIS program at the CDC. The medical training provided me with a broad-based background, and also allows for additional flexibility regarding my assignments. For example, in the event of a public health emergency I could respond in several different capacities. The preventive medicine, public health, and epidemiology training provided me with important skill sets necessary to perform my duties. The MBA is somewhat unique for public health work, but that education has impacted the way I think about allocating resources and implementing processes to improve efficiency.

What path did you take to get to the job you are in today?

After my residency training, I worked as the director of performance improvement at a county health department for 4 years. I think that experience has helped to keep me grounded and remember the true meaning of public health. I left that job to enter the EIS program, and this is my first assignment after completing EIS.

Where might you go from here, if you wanted to advance your career?

One of the advantages of being part of the U.S. Public Health Service Commissioned Corps is mobility, including mobility in terms of federal agency, subject area, and geography. As far as advancing one's career, my philosophy has always been that it's important to get as many different experiences as possible, and also a wide variety of experiences.

What is the worst or most challenging part of your job?

There is a lot of paperwork. Although it is not challenging from an intellectual standpoint, it can be frustrating and time-consuming.

(continued)

(continued)

What is the best part?

The work impacts the health of populations, which I believe is a very noble cause. There is also much variety with public health work, and for the most part it is rewarding, intellectually stimulating, and fascinating. Also, the field of public health tends to attract genuinely good people, so having wonderful coworkers has been another advantage.

What advice do you have for someone who is interested in your career?

The importance of a diversity of public-health–related experiences early on cannot be overemphasized, and those experiences could be gained from academia, government, or a nonprofit organization. My advice would be to learn as many skills as possible, including statistical software and survey design. The ability to communicate in another language, such as Spanish, would always be helpful. Finally, become adept at public speaking.

Profile Update

Dr. Schillie is still at the CDC, now at Atlanta headquarters, serving as a medical epidemiologist in the Division of Viral Hepatitis. Her work informs the development of national vaccination policies related to hepatitis B, including those of the Advisory Committee on Immunization Practices. She collaborates with other experts to consider the changing epidemiology of the disease, cost-effectiveness, and implementation issues, and she creates related publications for professional use. Her areas of professional interest include perinatal hepatitis B and infection control in health care settings.

PUBLIC HEALTH DENTIST

Job Description

Public health dentists often combine direct patient care with work focusing on population-level health. Some provide services to patients in underserved areas or those who could not afford dental care otherwise. They are also administrators, advisors, and consultants, helping to create and oversee programs that provide care or promote dental health. There are public health dentists involved in programs such as community water fluoridation, school-based dental screenings, oral cancer screenings, and educational efforts to promote good oral hygiene. Some advise politicians on new programs that should be funded and enacted. Some participate in forensic investigations, using their skills to help identify victims of crimes or disasters.

Education and Certification

Public health dentists need a Doctor of Dental Medicine (DMD) or a Doctor of Dental Surgery (DDS) degree and a license to practice in the state where they work. Extra training may not be needed, but experience or training in the world of public health is often expected. Many public health dentists hold an MPH, and there are also master's programs specifically for dentists interested in public health. Dentists can pursue residency training specifically in dental public health. Public health dentists who meet certain education and training requirements can apply for specialty board certification from the American Board of Dental Public Health.

Core Competencies and Skills

- Strong leadership, management, and communication skills
- Ability to work with a team that may include other health professionals, community leaders, politicians, researchers, and others
- Ability to design, manage, and evaluate community programs
- Interest in research and the knowledge of how to design and carry out studies
- Understanding of epidemiologic principles and at least basic statistics
- Up-to-date knowledge of dental health, oral hygiene practices, and preventive dentistry

Compensation

A typical salary for a public health dentist is similar to what a general dentist would earn. The median salary for dentists in general practice was $149,000 in 2014, with most earning at least $70,000 per year. Public health dentists usually have positions that include benefits such as health insurance and retirement plans, unlike dentists in private practice.

Workplaces

Public health dentists work in many different settings, including community clinics, local, state, and federal agencies, and universities. The U.S. Public Health Service Commissioned Corps has roles for dentists both in clinical care and in policy and development.

Employment Outlook

The number of board-certified public health dentists is small, and only a small percentage of U.S. dentists work in public health. At present, there are jobs available and dentists who take the time to search should be able to find public health work. In recent years, there has been an uptick in interest in public health among dental students, with new and expanding student chapters of the American Association of Public Health Dentistry. It is possible that as more young dentists pursue public health training, there will be more competition in the job market.

For Further Information

- American Association of Public Health Dentistry (AAPHD)
  www.aaphd.org
- Association of State and Territorial Dental Directors (ASTDD)
  www.astdd.org
- American Public Health Association (APHA)—Oral Health section
  www.apha.org/apha-communities/member-sections/oral-health

PUBLIC HEALTH PROFILE: Public Health Dentist
James Lalumandier, DDS, MPH
Professor and Chair of Community Dentistry
Case Western Reserve University School of Dental Medicine, Cleveland, OH

Describe the sort of work you do.

As a public health dentist in an academic position, there are three elements to what I do: research, teaching, and service. What I like to do the most revolves around teaching and service. When I started at my current job, there was a small sealant program serving kids in

(continued)

(continued)

the public schools. (Dental sealant is a material that helps prevent cavities.) Our program sends dental students into schools in low-income neighborhoods to do exams, administer sealant, and teach children about oral hygiene. I've worked to expand the program, and now each year, more than 20,000 schoolchildren are educated, more than 6,000 treated, and approximately 3,000 referred for additional treatment.

What is a typical day like at your job?

When I was setting up the program, on a typical day I would be bringing equipment out to schools, meeting with principals and teachers, instructing dental students and dental hygiene students, and talking to the children. Then I'd oversee the dental students doing the exams and applying the sealant. To get the program into the dental school curriculum, I had to write out exactly what was planned, what the students would do, what they would learn, and why it was important to their education. I also had to obtain funding, which meant looking for opportunities, networking, and writing proposals for grants. Now, I have two full-time health educators to teach the children, two part-time dentists, and eight additional personnel; therefore, my role in the program is primarily administrative.

What education or training do you have?
Is it typical for your job?

I have a DDS and an MPH, and I'm board certified in dental public health. There are a lot of very good public health dentists who don't have an MPH, but I would recommend it. Most schools of public health don't have a dental track, but you can choose a dental school that has a public health track.

What path did you take to get
to the job you are in today?

After dental school, I did a general practice residency through a military program. I went back into the military to get public health training, including an MPH. After I retired from the military, I worked for

(continued)

(continued)

2 years at a health department. I had been thinking that community dentistry was something I would love to do, so when I heard about an opening for chair of community health dentistry at the dental school, I applied for the job. Doing general dentistry would probably not have been enough to qualify for the position, but I already had an MPH with a scholarly record of peer-reviewed publications. I was also board certified in my specialty, and there are only about 150 boarded public health dentists in the United States.

When I first took this job, colleagues said that taking on the sealant program was not a good idea. In academia, publications are very important, and running a program could limit the number of research papers I could publish. But this is what I wanted to do, and it has turned out very well.

Where might you go from here, if you wanted to advance your career?

If I were going to take a "next step," I'd want to be a dean. I'm not much into titles, but as a dean I could focus a dental school on access to care issues. Access to care is a real problem in dentistry. I'd like to devote a larger part of education to showing students how rewarding it is to work in very rural or urban areas, and to help those who need help the most.

What is the worst or most challenging part of your job?

My least favorite part of the job is the administrative stuff. I'd much rather be treating patients and making somebody's life a little better.

What is the best part?

The most fun is interacting with both the children and the students. It is helping the students to be better dentists, and hopefully inspiring some of them to look beyond private practice in suburbia. And it is educating the children to take care of their teeth and to feel comfortable with getting dental care.

(continued)

(continued)

What advice do you have for someone who is interested in your career?

Learn about what public health is. It is not right for everybody. Research it, find out what public health dentists do, and then if you're still interested, give it a shot!

Profile Update

Since his initial interview, Dr. Lalumandier is still in the same job and happy doing what he is doing. He has continued the sealant program and is now in the process of setting up a geriatric program. Eventually, he hopes to have students from the medical school, nursing school, dental school, and social work program all working together, along with students from a nearby pharmacy school. They would bring portable units to nursing homes, geriatric centers, and assisted living homes. He notes that older people in these settings often don't get good oral health care, so they can bring that to them. And with the other disciplines, they can take care of a lot of needs all at once. The program would also help young dentists to be more comfortable with geriatric patients. Dr. Lalumandier says, "We are just getting started, but I think it's going to be terrific!"

TOBACCO QUITLINE COACH

Job Description

At a tobacco "quitline," counselors or "coaches" take calls from members of the public who want to quit smoking. Some also offer online chats or texting services. They help each caller make a plan for quitting and then follow up to see how they are doing. They use special interviewing techniques to increase motivation and guide callers through the quitting process. At some quitlines, the counselors can help callers obtain free nicotine patches or gum. Counselors keep records of calls and often are required to use a computerized charting system, which allows data to be collected for quality assurance and research. Some quitlines offer interactive, web-based services as well. Quitlines tend to be open from early morning to late at night, so counselors usually work either set hours or in shifts. There may be an option to work part time or even from home.

Education and Certification

Quitline services generally look for people with at least a bachelor's degree. Some ask for training in social work, psychology, nursing, or another field that incorporates counseling, and some prefer counselors with master's degrees. There is usually on-the-job training in specific methods and techniques to be used.

Core Competencies and Skills

- Emotional stability
- Strong listening skills
- Patience and empathy to work with callers who may have multiple mental, emotional, or physical challenges
- Ability to help guide people toward finding their own solutions to problems
- Fluency in a language other than English (not required but can be extremely helpful)
- Ability to follow a protocol and to use the counseling style directed by the helpline organization

Compensation

Quitline counselors are not highly paid, but it can be a fulfilling job. A starting salary might be about $18/hr ($37,440 per year), ranging to about $23/hr. It is common to receive a salary premium for working evenings or weekends.

Workplaces

Quitline counselors work for nonprofit organizations, health departments, and universities. There are also for-profit organizations that run quitline services, both for health departments and for corporations.

Employment Outlook

Most states have at least one tobacco quitline, and there seems to be ongoing support for such services, although they do tend to depend on the availability of funding. Working as a quitline counselor can be a good entry-level opportunity for someone interested in health behavior or in direct-service programs. There are also helplines to assist with substance abuse, problem gambling, domestic violence, and other health issues, and working at such places can be a way to learn more about these issues and related needs.

For Further Information

- North American Quitline Consortium (NAQC) *www.naquitline.org*
- Smokefree.gov

PUBLIC HEALTH PROFILE: Tobacco Quitline Coach
Shelley Anderson
Counselor
California Smokers' Helpline, San Diego, CA

Describe the sort of work you do.

The purpose of my job is to give people the tools they need to be able to stop smoking and to provide extra support during the first couple of weeks while they are trying to quit. The California Smokers' Helpline aims to reach as many people as possible, so our protocol is fine-tuned to cover the most important key topics in a call lasting 20 to 30 minutes. We focus on motivation, planning, use of quit aids, and setting a quit date. We discuss any ambivalence the person might feel, help identify smoking triggers, and help callers come up with strategies to avoid or overcome those triggers. We talk about which quit aids might work best for a particular client and in many instances we can help them get their insurance to cover them. We encourage callers to at least *try* to quit.

What is a typical day like at your job?

I usually start taking calls right away. When people call for the first time, they can choose to get materials only, or choose materials and counseling. Our goal is to try and move them right into a counseling call. We ask a series of questions to help determine how to best help

(continued)

(continued)

them. We also collect demographic information, which helps us know whom we are reaching throughout the state. If they want counseling but are not able to do it right on the spot, I set up an appointment and we call them back.

On slower days, I focus more on outgoing calls to clients we have not yet counseled, or clients we want to follow up with. Often, if someone has relapsed, we'll set a new quit date and start the process again. Although I try to cover the main points in our protocol, I can adjust the conversations to each individual caller.

What education or training do you have? Is it typical for your job?

I have a bachelor's in women's studies and sociology. Most of the counselors here have at least a bachelor's degree.

What path did you take to get to the job you are in today?

I started out working in domestic violence centers and rape crisis centers, and later I worked as a drug and alcohol counselor in public schools. Although I loved working with kids, I felt I was ready for something that would be less emotional and stressful. I started at the helpline as a counselor working part time in the evenings, after my day job for the schools. I was promoted to supervisor 6 months later. After working as a supervisor for several years, I left for a while to start my own business in a different industry. But I missed feeling like I was helping people every day, and I'm now enjoying working as a counselor again.

Where might you go from here, if you wanted to advance your career?

One option is to be a supervisor again, either here or in a similar organization. My skills would also transfer to other positions involving counseling or case management, and to many other jobs in the "helping" professions.

(continued)

(continued)

What is the worst or most challenging part of your job?

The repetition can be a challenge. On busy days, the calls start to blur together after a while. Another thing that can be hard is sometimes we work with clients in very sad situations. You have to be careful not to take on the callers' feelings of hopelessness.

What is the best part?

I love the work environment. We're all working toward the same common goal—to help people quit. We get a lot of support from one another in weekly meetings and one-on-one. I enjoy counseling because I'm really interested in people, in their lives.

What advice do you have for someone who is interested in your career?

I got here by following my interests and doing the type of work I felt was right for me. I would say do what's most rewarding to you, and look for work that provides an opportunity for personal growth. That's how I've found satisfaction in my career.

BEHAVIORAL SCIENTIST

Job Description

Behavioral scientists study what makes people do the things they do. In public health, they study why people make good and bad choices about food, smoking, safe sex, wearing seat belts, and many other behaviors. They design and carry out research to find out what helps people make healthy choices or cut down on risky behaviors. Behavioral scientists can be directly involved in community-level studies, or they may concentrate on examining data from local or national surveys to look for patterns. Some are primarily interested in research, while others create public health interventions. They can also be found helping the teams that design campaigns to promote health and prevent disease, and offering guidance on behavioral issues. Hours tend to be reasonable, although projects may sometimes require long hours or weekend work.

Education and Certification

Behavioral scientists usually have doctoral-level degrees in subjects having to do with human behavior, such as psychology, sociology, or anthropology. It is also possible, at some schools of public health, to earn a PhD in social and behavioral sciences. Some behavioral scientists are medical doctors with an interest in human behavior and training in research methods and application. Some are nurses or social workers, often with a PhD in addition to their clinical training.

Core Competencies and Skills

- Initiative and perseverance
- Interest in what makes people tick
- Ability to work as part of a team
- Appreciation of cultural differences
- Tendency to think logically, objectively, and methodically
- Ability to address problems for which solutions have not yet been found
- Understanding of statistics and data analysis (necessary level of expertise varies)

Compensation

The Bureau of Labor Statistics has calculated average salaries for certain social scientists. The median salary for sociologists, for example, was $73,000 in 2014, with most earning between $40,000 and $128,000. This includes people doing many different types of work, not just public health. Psychology professors have a similar range, with most earning $35,000 to $127,000 (the lower end salaries are more likely to be at junior colleges where research is not a major focus). Upper-level behavioral scientists at the CDC can earn in the range of $115,000 to $150,000 per year.

Workplaces

Behavioral scientists are found in government agencies, academic institutions, and nonprofit organizations. Private companies also hire behavioral scientists, either to carry out public health projects funded by the government or nonprofit organizations or to work on for-profit efforts that are intended to earn money while addressing health concerns.

Employment Outlook

Overall, employment opportunities for sociologists and anthropologists are expected to increase, but the total number of jobs will remain relatively small. However, there are no national statistics for behavioral scientists working in public health. Academic and research positions can be quite competitive, in general, but a growing interest in systems-level health promotion may lead to new opportunities.

For Further Information

Behavioral scientists tend to belong to the associations for their specific fields, such as psychology, psychiatry, or anthropology:

- American Psychological Association (APA)
  www.apa.org
- American Sociological Association (ASA)
  www.asanet.org
- Society for Medical Anthropology (SMA)
  www.medanthro.net

STUDY COORDINATOR

Job Description

Public health research studies are usually originated by professors or doctoral-level researchers. But it is the study coordinators who keep these studies going from day to day. They arrange for recruitment of research participants, set up appointments, manage the data, help prepare updates for funders, and supervise staff. If there are samples or other physical materials involved, they make sure they are properly catalogued and stored. They manage communications, serving as a link between the primary researcher and various assistants, technicians, and clinical or laboratory personnel. Sometimes the coordinator also helps carry out the research. Research coordinators may have opportunities to help author scientific papers and other publications. They may also be involved in submitting grant proposals and obtaining approval from their organizations' institutional review boards, which judge studies for ethical acceptability.

Education and Certification

The educational requirements for this job vary widely. A typical requirement is a bachelor's degree in a field related to the research topic, with training in research principles. Some studies require the coordinator to have a master's degree. If there are clinical responsibilities involved, the coordinator may need to be a nurse or physician assistant. The coordinator of a clinical trial—such as a test of a new medication—may need certification as a Certified Clinical Research Coordinator or Certified Clinical Research Professional; however, these studies are less likely to be considered public health research.

Core Competencies and Skills

- Attention to detail
- Good communication skills
- Excellent organizational skills
- Ability to multitask, prioritize, and delegate tasks efficiently
- Ability to follow directions and use good judgment when unexpected situations arise
- Understanding of research practices, study design, and research ethics
- Knowledge of regulations regarding research

Compensation

Compensation is influenced by the size of the study, whether the coordinator oversees more than one study, the level of responsibility, and the specific tasks involved. Job search websites put the average salary around $45,000 per year.

Workplaces

Research coordinators involved in public health research work at universities and government agencies; there are also nonprofit organizations and consulting firms that carry out studies.

Employment Outlook

Research is what drives schools of public health, and there is always more to be learned. National data are not available for this specific job title; however, as long as there is funding for research, these jobs should continue to be available. Study coordinator is often a step on the path to a research career or to other opportunities.

For Further Information

- A good place to learn about public health research projects is at the annual meeting of the American Public Health Association (APHA). Brief research reports from past years' meetings are available at www.apha.org.

REFERENCES

American Diabetes Association. (2014, June 10). *National diabetes statistics report, 2014*. Retrieved April 25, 2015, from http://www.diabetes.org/diabetes-basics/statistics/

Centers for Disease Control and Prevention. (2014, March 13). *Vital signs: Preventable deaths from heart disease and stroke*. Retrieved April 25, 2015, from http://www.cdc.gov/dhdsp/vital_signs.htm

Centers for Disease Control and Prevention. (2015a, May 14). *FastStats: Asthma*. Retrieved June 30, 2015, from http://www.cdc.gov/nchs/fastats/asthma.htm

Centers for Disease Control and Prevention. (2015b, September 30). *FastStats: Leading causes of death*. Retrieved October 10, 2015, from http://www.cdc.gov/nchs/fastats/leading-causes-of-death.htm

Dye, B. A., Thornton-Evans, G., Li, X., & Iafolla, T. J. (2015). *Dental caries and sealant prevalence in children and adolescents in the United States, 2011–2012*. NCHS Data Brief, no. 191. Hyattsville, MD: National Center for Health Statistics.

CHAPTER 6

Public Safety

Public safety intersects with public health in a number of ways. There are nearly 4 million emergency room visits due to motor vehicle injuries each year (Albert & McCaig, 2015). Seat belt and car seat use, drunk driving, drowsy driving, and the safety of teenage drivers are all subjects of public health programs. Public health also addresses playground injuries, drownings and other water-related injuries, sports-related injuries, falls among older adults, and even dog bites. Some public health experts argue that "accident" is not really the right word for these events: Most "accidents" can be prevented with the right engineering, education, and enforcement of safety laws and regulations.

The prevention of violence is another focus of modern public health. Dating violence, child abuse, elder abuse, domestic violence, and suicide all fall under the topic of violence prevention.

In many areas, emergency medical services (EMS) are also considered part of public health. Over the years, emergency response has grown from simply transport to the hospital to a sophisticated system of prehospital care designed to improve survival and minimize disability. EMS systems include dispatchers, ambulance and helicopter services, emergency medical technicians and paramedics, and the emergency rooms and trauma centers where patients are brought for care. The people who oversee these systems use many skills in common with other public health leaders.

More information is available at the Injury Prevention and Control section of the Centers for Disease Control and Prevention (CDC) website (www.cdc.gov). Other careers that can address safety and injury prevention include epidemiologist, medical epidemiologist, public health nurse, medical officer, health educator, behavioral scientist, and community health worker.

INJURY PREVENTION SPECIALIST

Job Description

Injury prevention specialists assess safety problems in communities, determine the leading causes of serious injuries, and then work on outreach, education, and policy changes that will help. They collect data from sources such as hospitals, clinics, trauma registries, and death certificates. They track motor vehicle accidents, assaults, falls, and other events that could cause disability or death. When the best intervention is already known, they tailor those techniques to the local community; otherwise, they devise their own interventions based on the best available evidence. They look for ways to educate the public, to change the environment to reduce the likelihood of injury, and to enforce rules that promote safety.

Modern injury prevention efforts often focus more on systems and environmental changes than on more traditional outreach such as pamphlets and public services announcements. An injury prevention specialist might meet with legislators to educate them on laws and environmental changes that could make streets safer. He or she might meet with city engineers about building sidewalks on a busy street. They might work with school officials to decide the best location for a new school building, so that kids can walk and bike there along safe routes, and then help arrange for secure storage of bikes and helmets. Or they might assist a hospital develop a policy to provide safe sleep information to all parents of newborns.

Education and Certification

There is no single education requirement for this career. Some schools of public health have a certificate program specifically in injury prevention, but most do not offer a special focus on this topic. Some employers look for a degree in environmental health, public health, epidemiology, health education, or another related field, and some specialists are nurses with training in injury prevention. Increasingly, employers are looking for candidates with an MPH or even a PhD in public health.

Core Competencies and Skills

- Good communication, presentation, and teaching skills
- Ability to make decisions independently
- Interest in learning how and why specific types of accidents occur
- Understanding of personal and cultural differences that can influence responses to safety efforts
- Knowledge of epidemiology and methods of data analysis
- Understanding of local laws related to injury prevention
- Skills in evidence-based program design and evaluation

Compensation

Differences in responsibilities, educational requirements, and settings make it difficult to give an average salary. Recent openings for injury prevention jobs have offered salaries ranging from $45,000 to $90,000 per year, and job search websites show an average salary around $55,000. The higher end salaries tend to go to those with extensive experience and high levels of responsibility.

Workplaces

Injury prevention specialists work for local, state, and federal agencies and for nonprofit organizations. Some hospitals have their own injury prevention programs. Nonprofits often have specific interests such as child safety, water-related injuries, or drunk driving. The military employs injury prevention specialists, both to address everyday injuries and to track combat-related injuries so that protective measures can be optimized.

Employment Outlook

The field of injury prevention has been gradually expanding in recent years. At present, jobs often combine injury prevention and other responsibilities, but as the issue gains prominence, more opportunities specific to injury prevention may become available. On the other hand, injury prevention efforts are often grant funded, which introduces uncertainty because funders' interests can change. Overall, the injury prevention workforce is aging and many specialists are nearing retirement, which may open up jobs for new people to enter the field. As injury prevention is not a common focus in public health education, candidates who have either studied injury prevention or done an internship in this field will be at an advantage.

For Further Information

- American Public Health Association (APHA)—Injury Control and Emergency Health Services Section
  www.apha.org/apha-communities/member-sections/ injury-control-and-emergency-health-services
- Safe States Alliance
  www.safestates.org
- National Center for Injury Prevention and Control
  www.cdc.gov/injury/index.html
- Society for Advancement of Violence and Injury Research (SAVIR)
  www.savirweb.org

DIRECTOR OF EMERGENCY MEDICAL SERVICES

Job Description

The EMS system includes government agencies at the local, regional, state, and even national levels. At each level, there are EMS directors or chiefs who are responsible for making sure the system works effectively. On the local level, many cities and small towns have EMS directors who supervise personnel, handle scheduling, and verify that all workers have the proper certifications. At the county level, EMS agencies oversee the work of smaller local departments and set and enforce policies and regulations. State agencies certify EMS personnel and handle statewide coordination and regulation of EMS.

Typical responsibilities for EMS directors include making decisions about spending, reviewing personnel or departments, ensuring that training and safety programs are in place, and coordinating with the leaders of other emergency services including the fire department (if separate from EMS) and nearby EMS systems. The director also must ensure that the department, its various elements, and any contractors all comply with local, state, and national laws and regulations. EMS directors make decisions about purchasing ambulances or hiring ambulance companies; work with hospitals to ensure high-quality emergency care; and plan for emergencies such as natural disasters or attacks. Policy development is another big part of the job, especially at higher levels.

Running an EMS system is essentially an office job. Some directors who are trained as emergency responders also respond to emergency calls, but as the administrative responsibilities become more complex, this may not be an option.

Education and Certification

An EMS director is usually an experienced manager who has risen through the ranks, either locally or elsewhere. Depending on the specific job, it may be necessary to be certified as a paramedic or licensed as a nurse. Some local jobs require additional emergency-response certifications or even firefighting skills. However, many EMS administrators are not paramedics, firefighters, or emergency medical technicians. Especially at higher levels, the director needs a strong understanding of public policy, administration, and how medical systems are run. Degree requirements vary, but large city or county systems may ask for at least a bachelor's degree in public administration or a business-related field, with a master's degree preferred.

Core Competencies and Skills

- Ability to remain calm under pressure
- Ability to handle multiple tasks and responsibilities at once
- Excellent interpersonal skills
- Strong management ability and financial skills
- Good political and negotiating skills
- Patience with politics and red tape
- Ability to understand and interpret data
- Knowledge of EMS systems and of related local, state, and national laws and regulations

Compensation

Compensation varies greatly, but a salary in the range of $50,000 to $80,000 per year for a city or county EMS director is not uncommon. The director of EMS for a large county or metropolitan area can earn over $100,000 per year, although most salaries are not this high.

Workplaces

EMS directors work for cities, counties, states, and the military, and there are also opportunities to shape EMS services at the federal level. EMS may be part of the health department or the public safety department, it may be run by or affiliated with the fire department, or it may be a separate agency. There are also administrator roles at ambulance companies and medical centers that incorporate aspects of policy making and public health planning.

Employment Outlook

There are often jobs available at the local level, although finding an opening in a specific location may be a challenge. Top jobs at the county and state levels are limited and open only to those with strong experience and credentials. However, there are many administrative positions within EMS, particularly in larger systems, which can serve as stepping-stones toward jobs with high levels of responsibility.

For Further Information

- National Association of State EMS Officials (NASEMSO)
  www.nasemso.org
- National EMS Management Association (NEMSMA)
  www.nemsma.org

PUBLIC HEALTH PROFILE: EMS Director
Virginia Hastings, MHA
Executive Director
Inland Counties EMS Agency, San Bernardino, CA

Describe the sort of work you do.

I am in charge of planning, implementation, monitoring, and evaluation for an EMS system that serves three counties in California. That includes overseeing the delivery of paramedic services and the integration of emergency departments and specialty hospitals, such as trauma hospitals or cardiac hospitals. It also includes monitoring and evaluating services to make sure that patients are receiving good

(continued)

(continued)

care. Another of my department's roles is to ensure compliance with regulations and laws.

What is a typical day like at your job?

I check my e-mails first thing. I follow up on quick phone calls. I check what assignments I've given others, and I look through my mail. Then, I'll generally have meetings all day long. I attend all the regular meetings of the key county groups—the fire department association, the hospital association, and the nurses' association. We discuss contracts and criteria, and then I assign staff members to formulate policies on the things we've talked about. On Tuesdays I go to Board of Supervisors meetings, so a good portion of that day is spent with the elected board members, explaining why I want to approve something.

My job involves a lot of talking and consensus-building. I could sit down right now and put out a directive to say, "You shall do this." But if you don't take the time to build relationships, you can write all the policies you want and they won't be followed.

My responsibilities also include reviewing my staff members' work. And I do "ride-alongs" with the ambulances and the fire companies to make sure that I keep a "street" feel, because sometimes what you put on paper sounds good but doesn't apply to the real world.

What education or training do you have? Is it typical for your job?

Because this is a government position with a health emphasis, it is helpful to have an education that covers public administration and health care administration. I have a bachelor's degree in public administration and a master's degree in health care administration. Lately, I have been noticing that newer people coming in tend to have worked as paramedics or emergency room nurses. Those of us who started earlier came up through administrative channels, but the newer people have a field background. I think either type of background could be appropriate for this job.

(continued)

(continued)

What path did you take to get to the job you are in today?

I obtained my very first job while I was still in high school. I started as a medical stenographer. When I came to the EMS agency, I knew nothing about EMS. My title was Staff Assistant II, and my very first assignment was to analyze a consultant's report dealing with what kind of ambulance service there should be. Later, I became the administrator of the paramedic training institute at Harbor-UCLA Medical Center. I continued to move into jobs with more responsibility until I reached the position of Director of the Los Angeles County EMS Agency. After I retired, I was approached personally by a colleague to apply for my current job. I thought I'd give this a try for a year or so—and that was 5 years ago.

Where might you go from here if you wanted to advance your career?

With the experience I have, I could join a think tank organization dealing with EMS or homeland security. I could also become a consultant, which is a financially rewarding opportunity. In my personal goals, I am considering law school because I have become intensely interested in legal issues and legislation related to EMS and health.

What is the worst or most challenging part of your job?

There are sectors that have far more access to local, state, and federal lawmakers than do civil servants like myself. This includes unions that often appear to set policy through powerful legislative contacts. It can be frustrating when policy does not match what I believe would be best for the system.

What is the best part?

I can see the fruits of my labors every time a fire engine, ambulance, or air ambulance is responding, and each time a critically injured person is rushed into surgery at a designated trauma hospital. I know my efforts are worthwhile.

(continued)

(continued)

What advice would you give to someone contemplating a career like yours?

Pursue it. It is exciting and it makes a difference. Pursue education in governmental structure; all our programs come under some federal, state, county, or city statute or regulation. It is also important to understand the different cultures of the various entities involved in an EMS system. You can use the strengths of these cultures as you forge public policy.

SPECIALIST IN POISON INFORMATION

Job Description

Specialists in Poison Information (SPIs) educate consumers and health care providers about potential poisons and about what to do if a poisoning occurs. SPIs have to know about common poisons, and they have to know how to obtain information quickly about more than 1 million different drugs, pesticides, chemicals, and even plants. They use specialized online databases, textbooks, and medical journals, and they consult with toxicologists when necessary. Examples from a typical day might include reassuring someone who accidentally took an extra dose of medicine, helping a father whose child swallowed a household cleaning solution, and advising a doctor who is treating a patient who attempted suicide. SPIs also have to be prepared to deal with chemical spills, snake bites, bee stings, and even calls about possible terrorist attacks.

Some SPIs create informational materials, lead training sessions for other health care professionals, and assist with outreach at schools, businesses, and other community sites. They are also part of broader public health efforts. The data they collect go into a national surveillance system that is used to monitor trends in poisonings, track outcomes, and provide early alerts about problems with prescription drugs. Many poison centers have started to work with local health departments in other ways, such as answering after-hour calls to the health department or helping to disseminate information about an epidemic. Some SPIs are also involved in doing original research. Poison control hotlines are active 24 hours a day, 365 days a year, and SPIs generally work 8-, 10-, or 12-hour shifts.

Education and Certification

SPIs are usually registered nurses or pharmacists with special knowledge of toxicology, which can be obtained through on-the-job training at a poison control center. Some are physicians, nurse practitioners, or physician assistants. In most cases, they must earn the credential of Certified Specialist in Poison Information (CSPI), which is provided by the American Association of Poison Control Centers. For nurses, a current license to practice is essential, and prior clinical experience is helpful and may be expected; some centers prefer nurses who have worked in emergency rooms or intensive care units (ICUs).

Core Competencies and Skills

- Knack for staying calm under pressure and for keeping others calm as well
- Patience and the ability to listen
- Ability to handle multiple tasks at once
- Ability to communicate effectively with people of different backgrounds and educational levels
- Strong research skills, including the ability to use a computer database and to absorb information rapidly
- Good math skills, for calculating doses, estimating blood levels, and interpreting medical information
- Talent for interviewing, to take an accurate, detailed medical history

Compensation

Salaries vary from center to center. Many centers hire primarily nurses, in part because pharmacists can command higher salaries. Typical salaries for nurse SPIs range from about $40,000 to $90,000.

Workplaces

Poison control centers may be independent nonprofits, or they may be associated with medical centers or health departments.

Employment Outlook

According to a 2008 study in the journal *Clinical Toxicology*, many of the workers at poison control centers were in their 40s or older, suggesting that there would be a need for more specialists as current workers move on or retire. The availability of jobs depends in part on centers' funding and also on the economy as a whole. With nurses and pharmacists expected to be in demand in the next several years, and with so many different opportunities available, it seems likely that poison control jobs will remain obtainable for those who are interested. Willingness to begin with a less desirable shift, such as overnight, may be an advantage. Remember, however, that there are only about 60 poison control centers nationwide. Not every city has one, and some cover multiple states.

For Further Information

- American Association of Poison Control Centers (AAPCC)
  www.aapcc.org
- American Academy of Clinical Toxicology (AACT)
  www.clintox.org

PUBLIC HEALTH PROFILE: Specialist in Poison Information
Jean Lubbert, RN, CSPI
Nebraska Regional Poison Center, Omaha, NE

Describe the sort of work you do.

I've worked at the poison center for 23 years. We respond to calls from the public and health care providers about poisonings 24/7. That's our primary role, and it's my main job. The phones always come first. In recent years, we have become more involved with public health issues. Our center also handles calls that come in to the health department about issues like rabies or a potential meningitis outbreak, and we deal with health alerts that come through the CDC.

What is a typical day like at your job?

We have eight incoming phone lines and usually more than one nurse on duty. If I'm doing a morning shift, the night nurse will discuss cases that need further follow-up. There could be one, or there could be eight. This involves home follow-up as well as health care callbacks.

(continued)

(continued)

I'll look through the database to see if there's anything I should be aware of. And then I'll put my headphones on, and off I go. As each call comes in, I obtain a very detailed history, check my references as needed, and enter notes into the computer. I determine how toxic the exposure is and provide detailed recommendations. I need to communicate in a way that each caller can understand. If it is a parent, I'll talk to them differently than I would to a health care provider.

If it turns out to be a nontoxic substance I don't need to follow up with the caller, but if it is gasoline, for example, we do a 1-hour and a 4-hour callback to verify no chemical aspiration has occurred. If I'm not certain about what to do for a particular case, I check with other professionals. There is always a board-certified toxicologist on call for further input depending on the complexity of the case.

If there's downtime on the phones there are many other things to work on. Sometimes health care providers want a copy of our protocols or an article from our files, so we'll fax them. Quality assurance is important, so I may be auditing cases, reading abstracts, or reviewing primary literature to assist with writing protocols. Sometimes I'm scheduled to work on research. We also have pharmacy students and emergency room residents who do rotations here. It adds variety to our job, because we can be mentors and we always work as a team.

What education or training do you have? Is it typical for your job?

Most CSPIs are registered nurses or registered pharmacists. I went to a liberal arts college for 1 year after high school, and then I went to the University of Nebraska Medical Center College of Nursing for an associate's degree nursing program. I have taken classes toward obtaining my bachelor's degree. After working 2 years or taking the equivalent of 2,000 calls, I sat for the national certification examination to become a CSPI.

What path did you take to get to the job you are in today?

I was working as a nurse in a hospital. I worked 3 years in neurosurgery and 2 years in the adult ICU. And then I saw an ad in

(continued)

(continued)

the paper for a poison center specialist, and it really intrigued me. Poison center work was nothing I had learned about in nursing school. The managing director was happy to hear that I had ICU experience. That nursing experience has helped me immensely in my work here.

Where might you go from here, if you wanted to advance your career?

For myself personally, I like the combination of the things we do here. I find the variety of work challenging and rewarding. For someone who wanted to try a different job, the skills would likely translate to certain aspects of public health nursing—like how to collect and interpret data. Critical thinking and communication skills are huge benefits if you were to work in another type of telephone triage service.

What is the worst or most challenging part of your job?

If you're super busy and you've got multiple lines going, you need to prioritize. And sometimes you have difficult callers. They're saying, "Somebody poisoned me," but it could really be a mental health issue. Staying calm, efficient, and precise in recommendations gives the best patient outcome.

What is the best part?

Even though you don't see the patient or the health care provider you're talking to, people are often really grateful that you are helping them. Not only that, but you never stop learning in this job. It is so rewarding.

What advice do you have for someone who is interested in your career?

You have to have good communication skills, you have to be empathetic, and you have to have good listening skills. If you want to help people, it's a great job to have!

FORENSIC PATHOLOGIST

Job Description

A forensic pathologist is a physician who assists with death investigations, often through a city, county, or state medical examiner's office or in affiliation with an elected lay coroner's office. The job varies by state, but the medical examiner is typically involved in investigating cases of sudden, unexpected death; death from accidental injury, violence, or poisoning; deaths outside of a hospital or hospice setting; deaths of infants and children; deaths in correctional institutions and state mental health facilities; deaths of people in police custody; and any other unusual case. When an autopsy is needed, the job goes to a forensic pathologist. These experts use knowledge of medicine, toxicology, criminalistics, and evidence collection and processing to provide information for police investigations, and when necessary they provide courtroom testimony.

In addition, forensic pathologists serve the cause of public health by watching for trends that could indicate a disease outbreak, the emergence of a new infectious disease, or a bioterrorism attack. Their reports contribute to surveillance for child mortality, intimate partner homicide, deaths due to drug abuse, and other types of deaths that public health programs may be able to address. Some also practice clinical forensic pathology, which means examining living patients for evidence of a crime such as rape or child abuse. The job can also include working with local hospitals on quality assurance for trauma and emergency care, collaborating with other agencies to review child fatalities, tracking trends in drug abuse, and participating in programs to promote driver safety.

Education and Certification

A forensic pathologist must have an MD or DO degree, and must have completed residency training in anatomic pathology, or anatomic and clinical pathology, plus a fellowship in forensic pathology. Certification by the American Board of Pathology, which requires an examination and ongoing education, is often expected.

Core Competencies and Skills

- Ability to handle unpleasant sights and smells without becoming ill or upset

- Tendency to ask questions and seek answers that are as complete as possible
- Attention to detail
- Thorough understanding of human anatomy
- Knowledge of toxicology, pathology, ballistics, infectious and chronic disease, and other subjects related to potential causes of death
- Knowledge of laws and procedures for the collection of evidence

Compensation

Salaries vary by location and responsibility. Typical salaries offered for forensic pathologists range from the low $100,000s to well over $200,000. Chief medical examiners and those who consult for coroners can earn quite a bit more.

Workplaces

In some places, the office of the medical examiner is part of the health department. In others, it is a separate part of city, county, or state government. Some areas have only coroners and no medical examiner's office at all; in those jurisdictions, forensic pathologists are hired as consultants on a case-by-case basis. Forensic pathologists also work for hospitals or private medical groups that contract with the local government to provide forensic autopsy services.

Employment Outlook

The need for pathologists in general is expected to be strong over the next few years. With a shortage of board-certified forensic pathologists currently in full-time practice, the job opportunities in this specialty should be good. There has been discussion of converting the existing coroner systems to medical examiner systems within the next decade or two; if this happens, there may be many additional job openings.

For Further Information

- College of American Pathologists (CAP)
  www.cap.org

- National Association of Medical Examiners (NAME)
  thename.org
- American Academy of Forensic Sciences (AAFS)
  www.aafs.org

REFERENCE

Albert, M., & McCaig, L. F. (2015). *Emergency department visits for motor vehicle traffic injuries: United States, 2010–2011.* NCHS Data Brief, no. 185. Hyattsville, MD: National Center for Health Statistics.

CHAPTER 7

Maternal and Child Health

Maternal and child health is a major area of public health. More than half of American women who give birth receive services through programs administered by the Maternal and Child Health Bureau. Millions of women, infants, and children receive nutritional support through a program at the U.S. Department of Agriculture. There are numerous federal, state, and local programs addressing infant mortality, birth defects, and access to prenatal care.

Some maternal and child health efforts apply to everyone, such as newborn screenings to test for certain congenital disorders and hearing ability. Other programs focus on specific populations: teenage mothers, children with developmental delay, and low-income families. There are programs to address perinatal depression, encourage breastfeeding, raise immunization rates, increase the number of children receiving health care services, provide family planning services, reduce the risk of sudden infant death syndrome, and teach parenting skills. Monitoring systems gather data to try to discover why some babies are born healthy and some are not. In addition to programs run by government agencies, there are many nonprofits dedicated to issues in maternal and child health.

Many people working in this area belong to the American Public Health Association (APHA) section on Maternal and Child Health (www.apha.org). The APHA section on Population, Reproductive, and Sexual Health includes family planning issues.

There are many different opportunities in maternal and child health; this chapter outlines just a few. Also see the descriptions for public health social worker, nutritionist, health teacher, injury prevention specialist, and director/officer of minority health.

ADMINISTRATOR, FAMILY HEALTH SERVICES

Job Description

Each state has a department dedicated to public health services for parents, children, and teens. These departments have various names—family health services; maternal and child health services; maternal, child, and adolescent health; and so on. The department typically has a director who handles the upper-level decision making and long-range planning, but also one or more administrators whose role is to oversee the finances, handle personnel issues, and guide the daily work of the department.

These departments house programs such as registries of birth defects, newborn screening systems, programs to track and prevent child abuse, educational programs to reduce teen pregnancies, family planning services, nutrition services, and more. The department or division administrator makes sure that they are meeting goals, staying within their budgets, and identifying and addressing both new and ongoing needs. When there are changes in the budget, they help determine what services must be cut and which should be preserved. They also help program coordinators write grant proposals, participate in personnel decisions, and work with clinical staff to make sure that patients at community clinics receive appropriate care. This is largely a desk job, but there may also be opportunities to go out into the community and observe the department's programs in action.

Education and Certification

This role requires substantial experience with administration, as well as with the programs within the department. An MPH is particularly useful, because it provides a good understanding of maternal and child health issues. A Master in Public Administration (MPA) can also be a good fit, with experience or other training in public health. Some people in this role have clinical training, such as a nursing degree.

Core Competencies and Skills

- Strong management and financial skills
- Excellent written and spoken communication skills
- Good planning skills, including the ability to break large projects down into specific tasks
- Knowledge of health issues that are of particular relevance to parents and children
- Knowledge of state and federal requirements for health and social services programs
- Ability to understand statistical and epidemiologic data
- Experience managing a public health program

Compensation

Salaries depend on the local cost of living, amount of experience, and pay structure within the health department. Recent openings for similar jobs have offered salaries from about $50,000 up to $150,000, depending on the size of the department, location, and qualifications.

Workplaces

This is usually a state government job, but some city and county health departments also have sections dedicated to maternal, child, and family health. County-level programs tend to focus more on public health nursing programs, such as home visits and clinic services.

Employment Outlook

There may be just one job at this level in family health services at a state health department, although larger states may have multiple divisions or be divided into regions. However, there are many administrative opportunities within maternal, child, and family health departments. Individual programs may each have their own managers, there may be directors who oversee multiple areas within the department, and programs may be divided up among different areas of the state. Specific requirements for these jobs, such as an MPH or a clinical degree, vary by department.

For Further Information

- Association of Maternal and Child Health Programs (AMCHP) *www.amchp.org*

PUBLIC HEALTH PROFILE: Deputy Director/Family Health Services
Chris Haag, MPH
Deputy Director
Bureau of Family Health Services
Alabama Department of Public Health, Montgomery, AL

Describe the sort of work you do.

I oversee the finances, administration, and program operations for the Alabama Bureau of Family Health Services. My responsibilities include applying for grants, working on protocols and procedural issues, overseeing the budget, and finding new ways to address specific public health problems. Part of my job is knowing when the time is right to tackle certain issues. When divisions within the bureau propose new projects and programs, I guide them in making strategic decisions. I make sure that the budget includes everything that's essential, I ask if other states have done similar programs and what they cost, and I consider whether it makes more sense to create a new system in-house or to purchase an outside product or service.

What is a typical day like at your job?

I have lots of meetings. Today, there were several meetings on finance. Budgets are being reduced, but people still need public health services, and we have to figure out how to do more with less. I also met this morning with some staff from our child health program. We're launching an online system for our newborn screening program. We walked through what we need to do, what the timeline is, and what it will cost.

When we need approval for a new program or service, I keep track of who is responsible, what has been done, and what needs to be done. I coordinate strategy with my boss, and with the staff who will work with state leaders to get approval and funding. I frequently receive proposed legislation to read, and I provide comments on the potential impact. Personnel management also consumes much of my time.

(continued)

(continued)

What education or training do you have? Is it typical for your job?

I have an MPH and a bachelor's degree in education. The training you get with an MPH is very helpful for this job.

What path did you take to get to the job you are in today?

My first public health job was as a health educator at a county health department. When I moved to Montgomery, I continued working as a health educator, this time with the state health department. Then I spent 4 years as the bureau administrator here, mostly handling the finances. I never really liked that job, but I learned a lot from it. And then the deputy director position opened up, and I decided to interview for it.

Where might you go from here, if you wanted to advance your career?

I'm happy where I am. For me, the next thing may be to earn a doctorate in public administration. In Alabama, currently the Director of the Bureau of Family Services must be a medical doctor, so I couldn't be promoted into that position. Staff assistant to the State Health Officer might be a next step, but being promoted into that position is very difficult and I am not sure I would be interested in that level of work. I enjoy what I do now.

What is the worst or most challenging part of your job?

Having to lay people off is the worst. When funding decreases, we have to identify services or programs we can cut. A close second is firing someone. It can also be challenging to deal with politics. My team and I have to craft solutions that work politically but at the same time meet very real needs.

What is the best part?

I like going out into the community. It is a chance to see how what we do is helping an individual kid or a family. At times, I can even help

(continued)

(continued)

directly. If a family can't afford the special foods for a child with a metabolic disorder, sometimes we can develop a more reasonable fee agreement, which lets families buy the foods at a lower cost.

What advice do you have for someone who is interested in your career?

If you want to work your way up to a leadership position, worry less about what your job description is and more about doing what's needed. I got to where I am because my boss knows that whatever he asks for, I'll give it 100%. I will figure it out and get it done.

Profile Update

Mr. Haag has continued in the same role in the time since his original interview. He says, "If you find your calling—why change? I still wake up in the morning and look forward to work because I know we are making a difference."

HOME VISIT NURSE

Job Description

There are several public health programs that involve home visits by nurses, not to provide traditional nursing care, but to help catch problems and increase the potential for good health. For example, a home visit nurse might spend an hour or two each week teaching a teenage mother life skills (changing and feeding the baby, checking for safety hazards, etc.) that will help her to be a good parent. She makes sure that baby's development is on track, and if there is a problem, she connects the mother with services that can help. She helps mothers access other services, too, from housing to adult education programs to domestic violence hotlines. The home visit nurse might also provide counseling to a teenage parent who is struggling with drugs, alcohol, or mental health problems. Some programs provide continued home visits through the child's early years.

In addition to working with clients, home visit nurses also have to maintain patient charts and keep up with new regulations, requirements, and research. The job may include some evening and weekend visits.

Education and Certification

A home visit nurse must have a current state registered nurse (RN) license. A Bachelor of Science in Nursing (BSN) degree (as opposed to a nursing diploma or associate's degree) may be required. Home visiting experience, training in obstetrics and prenatal care, and experience as a pediatric nurse can all be helpful. Once a nurse is hired for a home visit program, there is usually a period of on-the-job training, as well.

Core Competencies and Skills

- Flexibility and patience to deal with missed appointments, traffic, and challenging patients
- Willingness to travel to low-income, potentially dangerous areas
- Strong initiative and organizational skills
- Knack for teaching and for helping people set and meet goals
- Appreciation of diverse cultures and ways of thinking
- Knowledge of or an interest in learning about pediatric development, parenting skills, and basic mental health care
- Knowledge of local, state, and national programs to assist parents and families
- Fluency in a language other than English (may be needed)

Compensation

In one major city, home visit nurses in a public health program earn from the $50,000s to over $90,000. In a southern state with a lower cost of living, nurses in a similar program start at about $40,000.

Workplaces

Home visit nurses often work for health departments. They also work for nonprofit organizations and for private companies that contract with public health programs. In addition to maternal and child health programs, nurses who make home visits can also be found in outreach programs for the elderly.

Employment Outlook

One of the most prominent maternal–child home visit programs, Nurse–Family Partnership, has been going strong for more than three decades. A track record of good outcomes means that programs like this are likely to continue. Nurse–Family Partnership has expanded significantly in recent years, and its affiliated agencies often have positions available. Competition for jobs varies, but some programs have actually found it a challenge to recruit nurses, because this work is quite different from a typical nursing role.

For Further Information

- Nurse–Family Partnership
  www.nursefamilypartnership.org
- Visiting Nurse Associations of America (VNAA)
  vnaa.org
- Also see the organizations listed with the job description for public health nurse.

COMMUNITY HEALTH WORKER

Job Description

Community health workers (CHWs) go out into neighborhoods, housing projects, barber shops, and other community settings to work directly with populations in need. They are usually members of the communities they serve. CHWs provide health education and can assist with access to care, but they are not licensed health care providers. Instead, their primary role is as a link between underserved communities, where people are often suspicious of government and doctors, and the health service mainstream. Through individual visits, presentations to community groups, and the distribution of written information, CHWs can provide education on many important health issues.

In some maternal and child health programs, CHWs work directly with pregnant women who are at risk of poor birth outcomes. They do outreach to locate these women and interest them in the program, help them find prenatal care services, encourage them to make and keep appointments, provide basic education on health issues, and help them find resources such as adult education programs and safe child care. CHWs are trained to be sensitive to issues such as poverty or violence that might serve as barriers to good health.

In addition to maternal and child health, CHWs are also used with other health issues and populations. This job has many different titles, including "lay health educator," "peer educator," and "promotor" or "promotora" (used in Spanish-speaking communities). In Tribal health settings, there is a long history of laypeople being trained as "community health representatives."

Education and Certification

Educational expectations vary from high school (or an equivalency diploma) to a college degree. CHWs are often trained by their employers for the specific services they will provide. There are also training opportunities at community colleges, local nonprofits, and other health-oriented settings. Some states have specific training and certification requirements.

Core Competencies and Skills

- Patience and a sense of humor
- Outgoing, friendly nature
- Excellent communication skills, including good listening skills
- Ability to help people solve problems, without doing it for them
- Interest in helping build community strength
- Basic understanding of health and health care issues
- Personal understanding of the culture of the community being served
- Ability to be comfortable among different types of people
- Fluency in a language other than English, if needed to communicate with clients

Compensation

In 2014, the Bureau of Labor Statistics (BLS) found that the median salary for a CHW was about $35,000, with most earning between $21,000 and $60,000.

Workplaces

Typical employers for CHWs include local health departments and Tribal organizations, nonprofit organizations, health care facilities, and community health programs based at academic institutions.

Employment Outlook

The idea of using community members to promote health and improve access to care has gained momentum in recent years. According to the

BLS, this field is expected to grow faster than average between 2012 and 2022 because of efforts to improve health outcomes and reduce costs. The best opportunities will be for people who have done some formal training or education to prepare for this role, or who have particularly strong connections or experience with the target community. Speaking a second language can also be helpful.

For Further Information

- American Public Health Association (APHA)—CHW Section
  www.apha.org/apha-communities/member-sections/community-health-workers
- Center for Sustainable Health Outreach (CSHO)
  www.usm.edu/csho
- National Association of Community Health Representatives (NACHR)
  www.nachr.net

WIC NUTRITIONIST

Job Description

The national Special Supplemental Nutrition Program for Women, Infants and Children (WIC) is a long-running federal program that provides supplemental foods, nutrition education, and health care referrals for low-income women who are pregnant or have recently given birth, and for infants and young children at risk of poor nutrition. WIC nutritionists determine whether women and children are eligible for the program and provide vouchers for approved foods. The foods WIC supplies were chosen to help meet specific needs in populations at risk of poor nutrition. But WIC nutritionists do more than hand out vouchers. They ask about health problems that could affect nutrition, like food allergies in a child. They check for anemia and monitor children's growth. They educate women about healthy eating and teach them how to make affordable, nutritious meals. They work to combat child obesity. Some WIC programs encourage exercise, help women obtain car seats, or offer cooking demonstrations.

WIC nutritionists have to strike a careful balance between educating women and allowing them to make their own choices, and they have to be sensitive to social and cultural differences. Some clients are eager to learn, while others may be challenging to work with. The job also requires knowledge of program regulations and requirements, which can be quite complex. Some nutritionists have the opportunity to bring additional creativity to the work, such as designing recipes and menu plans or writing a monthly newsletter. A 40-hour workweek is typical, although some programs offer appointments on evenings and weekends.

Education and Certification

Nutritionists and dietitians generally must have at least a bachelor's degree, with a focus on nutrition or a related subject. Specific requirements for WIC nutritionists vary. Often, they must be registered dietitians (RDs), which requires a bachelor's degree, certain courses specific to nutrition, hands-on training, and an examination. Details on the RD credential are available from the Commission on Dietetic Registration at www.cdrnet.org. A master's degree in nutrition is usually required for supervisory work.

Core Competencies and Skills

- Strong communication skills, including both speaking and listening
- Excellent teaching skills
- Flexible thinking, to adapt recommendations to individual clients' lifestyles and needs
- Understanding of local communities, particularly their cultures and food traditions
- Knowledge of WIC regulations and requirements
- Thorough knowledge of nutritional needs during pregnancy, breastfeeding, and early childhood

Compensation

Dietitians and nutritionists in general earn salaries ranging from about $35,000 per year to about $80,000, with about half earning above $57,000. These numbers are typical for WIC nutritionists, as well.

Workplaces

WIC programs employ a large number of nutritionists nationwide. There are WIC programs run by health departments, nonprofit organizations, and hospitals and health centers.

Employment Outlook

WIC is a very large program—serving more than 9 million women, infants, and children—and there are often jobs available. Some programs find that nutritionists stay in their jobs for many years, which may limit the number of openings, but some also report that job openings can be hard to fill. Overall, jobs for dietitians and nutritionists are expected to increase faster than average between 2012 and 2022 and job prospects are expected to be good, although this may be largely driven by direct-care needs such as counseling diabetes patients or managing diets in nursing homes.

For Further Information

- Academy of Nutrition and Dietetics
  www.eatright.org
- The Public Health/Community Nutrition Practice Group of the ADA
  www.phcnpg.org
- American Public Health Association (APHA)—
  Food and Nutrition Section
  www.apha.org/apha-communities/member-sections/food-and-nutrition
- National WIC Association (NWA)
  www.nwica.org

PUBLIC HEALTH PROFILE: WIC Nutritionist
Rosemary Flynn, MS, RD
Public Health Nutritionist
WIC Program
Nassau County Health Department, Uniondale, NY

Describe the sort of work you do.

I'm a nutritionist with a WIC program run by a county health department. We give women information about nutrition and help them find ways to stretch their food dollars. We see the women for individual appointments, and we also offer classes on topics such as cooking and portion control. We really encourage physical activity, too. In the

(continued)

(continued)

summer, we connect with farmers markets and give our clients coupons to buy fresh produce. One of our goals is to lay down the groundwork when children are young, so they'll make healthier choices later.

What is a typical day like at your job?

I start by preparing for appointments or classes. When I'm teaching classes, I usually have about four sessions, and I don't have patient appointments on those days. On a day with clients, I'll see about 20 women. Visits are scheduled to last 15 minutes each, although sometimes they go over.

At the visits, I measure height and weight and check for anemia, for both mother and child. I ask about physical activity and about television time for the child. We talk about their eating habits, including not just what foods they eat but when and how they have their meals. Once I have that information I can encourage healthy eating habits. I see a lot of overweight children, and many of those moms need guidance on how to make fast food and soda occasional treats instead of everyday things. I ask about substance abuse, conditions at the home, and dental care. At the end of the appointment, I give the woman 3 months of WIC checks.

Appointments don't always go smoothly. Sometimes a woman will come in, and her papers aren't filled out, and the child is crying, and just filling out those papers becomes a big deal. I have to find out what's going on in her life that makes even that first task so difficult. Children present their own challenges. If a child won't eat anything but mashed potatoes, I can't just say, "Have him eat more fruits and vegetables," because he won't! I have to think about getting him better nutrition in ways that he will accept.

What education or training do you have? Is it typical for your job?

I am an RD, licensed by the state as a certified dietitian/nutritionist, and I'm also certified as a lactation consultant. I have both bachelor's and master's degrees in nutrition. Among my colleagues in the WIC program, about half have a master's degree, and supervisors are required to have that level of education.

(continued)

(continued)

What path did you take to get to the job you are in today?

I started as a clinical dietitian, working in hospitals. But then I was given an opportunity to take a part-time job doing public health nutrition. I realized I enjoyed that more than my full-time job! I had to learn a lot to make the transition to public health, because it is very different working in a community than working at the bedside. After I took some time off to raise my family, I went back to school to earn that master's degree. I thought I'd go back to clinical nutrition, because that's where the money was—but then, while I was looking for a new job, an ad popped up for the WIC program. And I thought, that's what I want to do.

Where might you go from here, if you wanted to advance your career?

The next step for someone at my level might be to oversee a WIC program. We have a nutritionist from the city who comes and audits what we do, and there are state supervisors. If I wanted a really high-level career, I'd have to leave the practice of nutrition. I could aim to become a program director, or I could be involved in selling pharmaceuticals.

What is the worst or most challenging part of your job?

There are some clients who are difficult to deal with. There are a few who are so set in their ways, I know that no matter what I say, their behavior is not going to provide the healthiest environment for the child.

What is the best part?

The best part is when I see someone succeed. It is when a really obese child comes back after 6 months, and he hasn't gained any weight, and he's grown 6 inches. It is rewarding to help a mom know what to do when her child is overdue to graduate from a bottle to a cup, and to see the child finally make that change.

(continued)

(continued)

What advice do you have for someone who is interested in your career?

Do an internship first and make sure this is something you really want to do. Then look deep inside yourself, and see if you can be tolerant and empathic and compassionate and nonjudgmental. If a woman is sitting in front of you and tells you she wants to terminate a pregnancy, what are you going to do? Or what if she says she's never going to stop smoking cigarettes? You can't bring your own morals and values to these visits. You have to leave them outside the door.

CHAPTER 8

Aging

The U.S. population is getting older. In 2010, about one in eight Americans was 65 years or older. By 2030, it will be closer to one in five (Vincent & Velkoff, 2010). With age comes a variety of illnesses and conditions that increase the demand on our health care system. We can expect the prevalence of chronic diseases to rise, with more people requiring care for problems such as cardiovascular disease, diabetes, cancer, dementia, and arthritis. More people will need assistance with ordinary activities, such as shopping, cooking, and even bathing and cleaning. We can expect increased hospitalizations and higher needs for rehabilitative and nursing home care, assisted living, long-term care, and hospice. Caring for aging parents and relatives puts physical and emotional strain on family members. And with the increased expense of technology and medications, the cost of health care is expected to keep rising faster than the growth of the economy (Sisko et al., 2014).

The aging of our population is already putting stress on our health care system, and public health efforts are emerging in response. As the percentage of older Americans continues to increase, the need for public health responses is expected to grow.

Although public health includes making sure that the health care system is adequate to meet the need for care, equally important is finding ways to reduce the burden of disease in this population and keep them out of hospitals and nursing homes. The Centers for Disease Control and

Prevention (CDC) recommends that public health agencies, at all levels, increase efforts to maintain the health of older adults, not just focus on diagnosis and treatment for known diseases.

Some public health goals for our aging population are encouraging healthful eating and active living, which can ward off disease; preventing disability through fall prevention and safe driving campaigns; making sure older adults receive preventive care, including immunizations and cancer screening; and providing opportunities for them to be productive and socialize, which can help maintain quality of life.

The CDC also stresses the importance of health care providers' receiving timely information about improvements in practice with the elderly and about the public health resources available for them in the community. For ease of access, services to the aging should be integrated with other networks that serve them, such as community centers where meals are provided. Finally, the CDC asks all public health programs to examine whether they meet the needs of an aging population and to expand their programs if the aged are underserved.

Some public health careers related to aging are well established, such as social workers who help link elders and their families to county or state services. Others are still evolving, as new programs are developed to meet the growing need. Here are some of the jobs we may see more of as time goes on.

"AGE-IN-PLACE" PROGRAM COORDINATOR

Job Description

According to an AARP survey, nearly 80% of American adults aged 65 years and older want to be able to live in their current homes as long as possible. But achieving the goal of staying in one's home can be difficult. Older adults may face deteriorating chronic conditions or memory deficits, which can lead to poor nutrition, loss of mobility, inability to take care of a house, and trouble managing financial matters. Yet "aging in place," living at home instead of at a nursing home or assisted living facility, can be a good choice for an elder's health. Staying home makes it easier to maintain social contact with friends and family and have continuity of medical care, and can improve elders' sense of independence and mental outlook. Some agencies and community organizations are using public health methods to address these issues, to reduce the burden of illness in the population, improve quality of life for elders and their families, and reduce the burden on hospitals and nursing homes. "Age-in-place" programs are one such effort.

Different communities are developing their own approaches to supporting aging in place, and these initiatives are still evolving. In general, the coordinator organizes a network of community resources to keep an aging client at home. They learn what resources are available in the community and how to access them. Some programs focus on coordinating health care services, home health and personal care, and care planning. Others are more creative: They may help arrange for yard work and cleanup around an elder's home, or for a handyman to come in and attach grab bars to a shower wall. For clients who cannot drive, the coordinator may organize a shuttle service to bring them to doctor's appointments or the grocery store. Some programs offer social and educational activities geared specifically toward helping elders stay healthy at home. The coordinator may organize classes on cooking good food on a fixed income or making healthy meals for one. They may arrange exercise classes to reduce the risk of falls. There are programs that help older adults find ways to volunteer and stay useful, or simply offer fun outings to keep elders active and part of the community. The coordinator may also help connect elders with services to help with finances and medical coverage or to assist with chores or daily activities. In some age-in-place programs, the coordinator enlists and trains volunteers, as well.

Education and Certification

Coordinators for these types of programs tend to have at least a bachelor's degree, and may have training in social work, gerontology, or nursing. There can also be roles for community health workers with less education, but with an affinity for working with older adults. Familiarity with gerontology, health conditions of the elderly, community resources for the aged, legal and financial issues affecting the elderly, and ways to stimulate interest in living will all be advantages.

Core Competencies and Skills

- Compassion, good communication skills, and patience
- Creativity in problem solving and attention to detail
- Extensive knowledge of the community resources that help the elderly remain happy, safe, and healthy in their homes
- Knowledge of the physical, mental health, legal, and financial challenges faced by the elderly and how to deal with them

- A large network with many kinds of professionals in the community
- Ability to coordinate and integrate different kinds of care

Compensation

As community-level age-in-place programs are still relatively new, the pay scale is not yet well established. These roles are similar to what the Bureau of Labor Statistics (BLS) defines as social and community service managers, for whom typical salaries usually run from $38,000 to about $104,000; recent job listings seem to place salaries in the lower half of the scale, but it would likely depend on the size of the program and the coordinator's credentials.

Workplaces

Age-in-place programs are typically run by a local government agency or an organization that believes that a long-term care facility is not always the answer. A coordinator can be based in an office, but he or she may also be based in a community center or clinic where the elderly come for other services. If the coordinator trains people to work with the elderly, they will offer supervision and make occasional visits to elders' homes.

Employment Outlook

The BLS reports that jobs with social and community programs for older adults should be expanding between 2012 and 2022. Creative age-in-place programs have made the news, and Medicare supports some programs to help keep older adults in their homes. It seems likely that these types of programs will be increasingly common in the future.

For Further Information

- National Aging in Place Council
  www.ageinplace.org
- Program of All-Inclusive Care for the Elderly (PACE)
  www.npaonline.org
- Beacon Hill Village
  www.beaconhillvillage.org
- American Society on Aging (ASA)
  www.asaging.org

- American Public Health Association (APHA) Section on Aging and Public Health
  www.apha.org/apha-communities/member-sections/aging-and-public-health

DEMENTIA SERVICES COORDINATOR

Job Description

Dementia is a term for a decline in memory, reasoning, and foresight. Alzheimer's dementia is its best known form, but dementia can also be caused by strokes, alcoholism, and other underlying problems. Dementia is a growing problem in the United States and around the world. As the population ages, the number of cases of dementia will increase, and by 2030, it is expected that about 8 million Americans will have the condition. Dementia is a disease that affects all of society: It drains the victim of a meaningful life, requires large amounts of time and energy from caregivers, and costs society billions of dollars in resources every year.

There are public health programs to address dementia, but they have been criticized for being scattered among too many agencies, underused, and of questionable effectiveness. Dementia services coordinator is an emerging concept at the public health level, so its exact description will probably vary as more agencies and organizations consider adopting this role. The underlying idea is to take a comprehensive view of dementia services in a state, region, or city, and develop a system to improve them. A major goal is to identify gaps in services and areas where services are duplicated, and make sure that anyone in need of services can easily find them. Responsibilities may include increasing access to screening for dementia and making it easier to link patients to care if problems are found. The coordinator may disseminate information about caring for patients with dementia to emergency responders and health care providers. They may work on improving connections between caregivers and needed services, so that caregivers can more easily navigate the eldercare system, learn how to safely care for a family member at home, arrange respite care, and obtain help or long-term care when needed. The role may also include surveying the population to identify new or unmet needs, evaluating existing programs, preparing policy recommendations for legislators, and helping to ensure that there are sufficient long-term treatment facilities. Although primarily an office job, the role can be expected to include travel around the region, interaction with the public, and networking with other agencies.

Education and Certification

A dementia services coordinator will generally be an administrative-level job that requires graduate-level education and considerable knowledge of program management as well as of dementia. Typical education for this type of job includes an MPH, a Master of Public Administration (MPA), a degree in gerontology, or a background in social work or nursing. A few schools of public health now offer a certificate or MPH concentration specifically in gerontology or aging. There are also a number of certificate programs designed for caregivers and health care professionals, which could help provide a good background. In smaller communities, a 4-year degree with considerable experience with dementia or public health may be sufficient.

Core Competencies and Skills

- Extensive knowledge of dementia and how it affects individuals, families, and communities
- Ability to translate research findings into practical applications
- Extensive knowledge and experience with state, county, and city resources related to aging and dementia
- Understanding of laws and regulations related to dementia and public health
- Ability to work cooperatively with other agencies, medical professionals, and legislators
- Good communication and interpersonal skills
- Ability to create, implement, and evaluate programs, and suggest new policies
- Creativity and good problem-solving skills

Compensation

A dementia services coordinator would be classified among the administrative occupations. Salary can be expected to vary depending on the size of the population under consideration and the range of responsibilities. According to national statistics, salaries for a "social and community services manager" tend to be in the range of $38,000 to $105,000.

Workplaces

Typically, this type of job is found in public agencies, such as state departments of public health, departments of human services, or departments of aging. Large hospital systems, schools of public health, government health services, and insurance companies may have people with dementia service coordination skills on staff; these are likely to be more traditional social work jobs, connecting individuals to services, but may also have some program and policy work involved.

Employment Outlook

With the growing prevalence of dementia, there is a need for a comprehensive system for treatment and care that meets the needs of the elderly and their families. Over the past few years many states have been developing plans specifically to address Alzheimer's disease and other dementias. It seems likely that more state and local agencies will begin to recognize a need specifically for coordination of dementia services; or, this role may be built into broader services for aging. It is possible that there will be just one or two jobs to coordinate services at the state level, but that there will also be opportunities at county and large city agencies, if funding permits fulfillment of this need.

For Further Information

- National Institute on Aging Alzheimer's Disease Education and Referral Center
  www.nia.nih.gov/alzheimers
- Alzheimer's Association
  www.alz.org
- Alzheimer's Foundation of America
  www.alzfdn.org

RESEARCHER IN AGING AND PUBLIC HEALTH

Job Description

A number of schools of public health have their own centers or institutes focused on aging. There is also research on public health and aging going on at medical schools, nursing schools, and other university departments. The CDC's Healthy Aging Program funds a network of several universities, each with researchers looking at how to promote and support healthy aging; from 2014 to 2019, funding will support a "Healthy Brain Research Network" focusing on cognitive functioning.

A researcher working on issues of aging and public health generally focuses on one or a few specific topics. Some current issues being studied at schools of public health include effects of diet on preventing disease, the impact of stressful experiences on cognition as we age, how doctors can do a better job of talking to patients about end-of-life care, and how communities can support and encourage healthy lifestyles for older adults. Research starts with identifying a problem related to aging and gathering information on the extent of the problem and possible causes. Some researchers focus on biologic patterns, such as why a particular diet might lead to more heart disease, or which type of exercise works best to prevent falls; the idea is to eventually translate the results to public health campaigns. Increasingly, public health researchers are using community-based participatory research, which means collaborating with the target community to help identify underlying causes and come up with realistic solutions. In the area of aging, this might mean working with community members to figure out what they need to support increased exercise for older adults, helping them create programs or make infrastructure changes, and evaluating the results, then working with other communities to see how the same underlying ideas can be expanded to broader populations. Some researchers are more focused on policy issues and do their research by examining what has and has not worked in the past so they can make new recommendations.

Education and Certification

Researchers working on public health and aging are typically PhDs who have chosen aging as a particular focus of their research. Some earned their degrees specifically in gerontology, but there is a wide range of backgrounds in the field of aging research. Some researchers come from a background in nursing or social work, some are sociologists, psychologists, or anthropologists. Some have their degrees in "hard science" areas such as biology. There is room for nutritionists and for experts in physical activity. There are also medical doctors who have chosen this as an area of research.

Core Competencies and Skills

- Extensive knowledge of issues in aging and public health
- Expertise in designing research studies
- Curiosity, analytical thinking, and creativity

- Ability to interact with other researchers and interdisciplinary teams
- Ability to direct others, including students and research assistants
- Good communication skills, and ability to summarize thinking in simple words

Compensation

Salaries will depend in part on the subject area and level of experience. As many researchers are university professors, these salaries can give a general idea. For the 2013 to 2014 academic year, the American Association of University Professors reported an average salary for university professors ranging from $79,000 for lower ranks to $138,000 for full professors.

Workplaces

Researchers in aging and public health are usually based in universities, schools of public health, medical schools, and federal government health agencies. Some work for state and local health departments.

Employment Outlook

The aging of the population calls for more public health research to find programs addressing, for example, how to attain "healthy aging" and how to cope with chronic health problems related to aging in the community. As most research in public health depends on grants from government agencies and nonprofits, openings for researchers will depend on the state of the economy and the budgets of various agencies. Researchers with creative ideas and good communication skills in grant writing will be in the best position to have their research funded.

For Further Information

- CDC Healthy Brain Initiative
  www.cdc.gov/aging/healthybrain/index.htm
- The Gerontological Society of America (GSA)
  www.geron.org
- American Geriatrics Society (AGS)
  www.americangeriatrics.org

DIRECTOR, AREA AGENCY ON AGING

Job Description

Area Agencies on Aging (AAAs) are regional nonprofit organizations or divisions of local or state government designated by state governments to address the needs of older adults. These agencies are concerned with issues such as eliminating physical and emotional abuse of elderly people, making sure that homebound elders have nutritious food to eat, and connecting eligible people to social services. AAAs may support "aging in place" programs. Many sponsor community centers where older adults can socialize, exercise, and take classes, or "day-care" centers for people who need a safe place to go while their caregivers work. AAAs may provide services directly, or contract with local service providers who carry out the day-to-day work of the programs.

The director or chief executive officer of an AAA guides the agency's work. This includes setting short- and long-term priorities, ensuring that programs conform to federal and local regulations, and helping the agency adapt if local needs change. The director is responsible for ensuring that funding is available and that contracts with service providers are appropriate. The director has administrative duties such as overseeing the budget (with the help of a financial officer), hiring and supervising certain personnel, interacting with elected officials to advocate for seniors, and meeting with leaders of other organizations and agencies to collaborate on service and policy efforts and to make sure that goals are aligned.

Education and Certification

These executives generally have at least a bachelor's degree, and most have higher degrees; there are MPAs, social workers, lawyers, and others. Most have prior experience as administrators of services related to aging or as administrators or supervisors in other public programs.

Core Competencies and Skills

- Excellent management skills, for both personnel and finance
- Strong verbal and written communication skills
- Knack for political and community networking and an understanding of public relations
- Awareness of the issues faced by elder adults in general, and of issues specific to the local population

- Understanding of government funding processes and knowledge of how to obtain funding
- Understanding of laws, regulations, and services related to elder affairs
- Understanding of epidemiologic principles and program evaluation techniques

Compensation

Salaries for high-level jobs at AAAs vary considerably, in part because of differences in agency size and geographic location. Some recent examples include a range of $74,000 to $100,000 at an AAA in the Washington, DC, area and $74,000 to $122,000 in a large city in the Northwest, with both jobs requiring a master's degree and several years' experience. Another position, in a rural area in New England, offers $55,000 to $65,000 and will accept someone with a bachelor's degree.

Workplaces

Most states have multiple AAAs, and several have 10 or more. Some AAAs are incorporated into nonprofits that cover other social services, as well; in these cases, the person in charge of the aging component often has the title of director. A few states do not have separate AAAs; instead, programs are administered through a central government office.

Employment Outlook

The prospects for this specific job are limited by the number of AAAs. For those who are interested in administering services to promote the health of older adults, there are many other opportunities within nonprofit organizations and at government offices on aging. Overall, because the U.S. population is aging, the demand for related services is expected to increase.

For Further Information

- National Association of Area Agencies on Aging (n4a) *www.n4a.org*
- American Society on Aging (ASA) *www.asaging.org*

- National Association of States United for Aging and Disabilities (NASUAD)
  www.nasuad.org
- American Public Health Association (APHA)—Aging and Public Health Section
  www.apha.org/apha-communities/member-sections/aging-and-public-health

---

PUBLIC HEALTH PROFILE: Director, Area Agency on Aging
John Skirven, MMS
Chief Executive Officer
Director, Senior Services of Southeastern Virginia
Norfolk, VA

Describe the sort of work you do.

I am the chief executive officer of Senior Services of Southeastern Virginia. We are an AAA. We plan for the needs of the elderly in our region, advocate, and administer aging service funds. One of our main goals is to provide the services that will keep older Americans in their homes as long as possible. Under our roof, we have care coordinators for aging-in-place, wellness coordinators who oversee nutrition and evidence-based preventive and nutrition programs, transit coordinators and drivers who provide our clients with mobility around town, benefits counselors who help people access the benefits to which they are entitled, and other staff who help clients make their wishes known on end-of-life issues. My job is to provide leadership and management to all these different parts of our agency. I oversee administrative issues, marketing, finances, fundraising, public outreach, and program development.

What is a typical day like at your job?

I have a long workday—10 to 12 hours is common if I have some evening meetings. I use the morning to take care of administrative issues that have to do with running the organization, things like hiring a new person. I then meet with different departments—with the

(continued)

(continued)

care coordinators or with my Transit Department, for example. We discuss how our efforts are working and what new needs have arisen. Evidence-based programming is important to us, so we do what research has shown is effective—and we evaluate all we do to know whether those programs are working for us. I represent the agency on other local and statewide boards and committees. Later in the day, I might consult with outside groups who want to start a program to aid seniors. We are in various consortiums to share resources and deal with outside suppliers, so a few times a month we meet to discuss how our arrangements are working. I might say I don't have a typical day, but that's why I like my job.

What education and training do you have? Is it typical for the job?

I earned a bachelor's degree in journalism and wanted to work at a newspaper. The interviewer told me I needed a few years of real life experience, so I became a case aide at a senior center. I enjoyed my work with the elderly and decided to get a master's degree in social work. My master's internships exposed me to management and to the usefulness of data and evidence-based programming in social work. After graduation, I worked in several different settings for the elderly until I assumed my present position. Not too many in the field start out in journalism! Undergraduate degrees in nursing and social work are more common when you look at our care coordinator jobs, but we also see applicants with bachelor's degrees in gerontology, psychology, and the other social sciences.

What path did you take to get to the job you are in today?

After receiving my master's in social work, I ran a geriatric partial hospitalization program. I spent some time in private home health and then became the housing director at an AAA. (I had paid for college with my carpentry skills; who knows when old skills will be useful!) I came to Senior Services of Southeastern Virginia as executive director and then assumed the CEO position.

(continued)

(continued)

Where might you go from here, if you wanted to advance your career?

I see the private sector as a growth area for those who want a leadership position. The federal government has been shifting many of its health care programs to private for-profit companies. We need people with health management skills who desire to help the public in the position to advise corporations and insurance companies so that good work can be done.

What is the most challenging part of your job?

I find that the most challenging part is keeping abreast of trends in health care and public health for the elderly. I want to know what new things are going on in senior health care and how to take advantage of them. These might be new approaches to wellness, or a better way to keep the newly discharged from a hospital readmission, or a new direction in managing chronic conditions. I am always looking for ways to improve our programs, and we have done well with new evidence-based programs, for example.

What is the best part of your job?

The best part of my job relates to the challenging part. The best part is seeing our clients achieve their goals, knowing that we've instituted the best programs and that our efforts have been helpful. Flourishing at home, getting to medical appointments regularly and on time, wishes for end-of-life care that are respected—these are some of the outcomes that tell me we are doing well. I'm also pleased that we're reaching a good portion of the local population that needs our services. Finally, I'm happy we also serve healthy, independent seniors by showing them, for example, which prescription drug plan best suits their needs.

What advice do you have for someone who is interested in your career?

I'd advise them to think of the AAA as a wide-open opportunity. Keeping the elderly and disabled living at home has been a national

(continued)

(continued)

priority since the 1970s, and a lot has been discovered about how to do this well. Yet, changes, such as the arrival of the baby boomers, more for-profit corporate involvement, and programs based on solid evidence of success, can get us thinking in new directions. For example, we are working with several other agencies to renovate a historic school into a services and housing complex in a neighboring town to make it into a "livable community," where it is easy to get around on foot and where what the elderly need day to day is right there. So I would recommend that someone interested in what I do see it as an opportunity to be creative and to engage with diverse groups in a common goal. I would also tell them to stay determined and optimistic—they may be disappointed at times, but if they build on their strengths and stay open-minded, they will succeed.

REFERENCES

Sisko, A. M., Keehan, S. P., Cuckler, G. A., Madison, A. J., Smith, S. D., Wolfe, C. J.,...Poisal, J. A. (2014). National health expenditure projections, 2013–23: Faster growth expected with expanded coverage and improving economy. *Health Affairs, 33*(10), 1841–1850.

Vincent, G. K., & Velkoff, V. A. (2010). *The next four decades, the older population in the United States: 2010 to 2050. Current Population Reports, P25-1138.* Washington, DC: U.S. Census Bureau.

CHAPTER 9

Pharmaceuticals and Drug Safety

How do we know that a prescription medicine will actually do what the manufacturer claims? How can we be sure that a bottle labeled "aspirin" actually contains aspirin? And how can we be confident that a medication is more likely to help than to harm? This is the realm of public health professionals concerned with drug evaluation and safety.

The Food and Drug Administration (FDA) oversees regulation of prescription and over-the-counter medicines. The FDA's many responsibilities include not only determining the safety and efficacy of drugs before they can be sold but also regulating advertising, inspecting manufacturers, ensuring accurate labeling, doing ongoing safety monitoring, protecting against counterfeit medicines, and more. The FDA also regulates blood products, vaccines, and other biological products, as well as tobacco products.

There are many opportunities for public health professionals in drug evaluation and safety. Much of this work goes on at the FDA, but there are also opportunities in other government agencies, industry, academia, and the nonprofit world. Other jobs that touch on drug safety include epidemiologist, veterinarian, medical officer, consumer safety officer, and medical epidemiologist.

PHARMACIST

Job Description

Although "public health pharmacist" is not a widely used term here in the United States, there are plenty of pharmacists helping to promote the health of our population. Some pharmacists combine their pharmacy training with work in policy making, epidemiology, or other areas of public health. They can be involved in analyzing reports about drug side effects and deciding if extra warnings should be added or if the drug should be recalled. They may contribute their specialized knowledge to decisions about new drug regulations or laws. There are public health pharmacists involved in evaluating proposals for new medications, as well.

There are also public health pharmacists performing traditional tasks such as compounding and dispensing drugs. The Indian Health Service (IHS) includes pharmacists in its efforts to protect and improve the health of Native Americans. Some pharmacists are involved in disaster planning. Other roles include managing drugs for rare diseases, studying the safety of dietary supplements, and helping to manage programs that provide medicine for people with HIV/AIDS.

Education and Certification

A pharmacist just finishing training needs a Doctor of Pharmacy (PharmD) degree in order to be licensed. This is a relatively new requirement, so older pharmacists often hold different degrees. Licensure also requires examinations covering drug information and state and federal regulations and laws. Pharmacists who are interested in public health often pursue an MPH, and some pharmacy schools offer combined PharmD/MPH programs. Experience in research and data analysis can be especially helpful. Pharmacy students can apply to do public health oriented rotations at the FDA.

Core Competencies and Skills

- Tendency to be detail oriented
- Aptitude for science and for research
- Ability to break down complex problems into manageable steps
- Ability to see how research and data apply to real-world problems
- Good interpersonal skills, including the ability to communicate with people from other disciplines

- Understanding of statistics and epidemiology (necessary level of knowledge varies)
- Broad knowledge of drugs, how they work, and drug interactions
- Understanding of community dynamics (for pharmacists who will be working in community-level programs)

Compensation

Most pharmacists earn between $89,000 and $150,000 per year. Pharmacists who work for the federal government may earn a little less than those in hospital or retail pharmacies, although government jobs with high levels of responsibility can pay well over $100,000 per year. Pharmacists who work in public health often find that the lifestyle and job satisfaction tend to offset any difference in salary.

Workplaces

In the federal government, the departments within the U.S. Department of Health and Human Services (HHS)—such as the FDA, the Centers for Disease Control and Prevention (CDC), and the Health Resources and Services Administration—employ many pharmacists to work on public health matters. Many public health pharmacists get their start at the IHS. There are many opportunities through the U.S. Public Health Service (USPHS) Commissioned Corps. Pharmacists also fill public health-oriented roles at state and local health departments and in the military.

Employment Outlook

Growth in jobs for pharmacists is expected to be about the same as average job growth overall between 2012 and 2022, with new jobs driven largely by demand for prescription medications as the population ages and as the Affordable Care Act gives more people access to health care. In public health, there will likely be a continued need for pharmacists in drug safety, disaster planning, and public programs. Given the recent interest in quality assurance, medication effectiveness, and cost control, there may be an increasing demand for pharmacists in public health; however, this depends on how the health system evolves and what funding is dedicated to these issues.

For Further Information

- APHA Pharmacy Special Primary Interest Group
  www.apha.org/apha-communities/spigs/pharmacy
- Visit university PharmD/MPH programs and government agencies'
  websites including *fda.gov*
- American Pharmacists' Association
  www.pharmacist.com

PUBLIC HEALTH PROFILE: Pharmacist
Lt. Brian Parker, PharmD
Pharmacist
San Xavier Indian Health Center, Tucson, AZ

Describe the sort of work you do.

I'm a pharmacist with the USPHS Commissioned Corps, assigned to
the IHS. I work at a clinic on an Indian reservation in Tucson, AZ.
Right now, a lot of what I do is similar to what a pharmacist might
do at a drugstore. I answer questions from patients, doctors, and
nurses. I make sure that medications match the conditions they're
prescribed for and that doses are correct. Every 3 or 4 weeks I spend
a few days at our hospital, where I perform similar duties. We're also
working on drug reconciliation and on polypharmacy—trying to help
patients reduce the number of pills they have to take.

What is a typical day like at your job?

On some days I'm primarily doing refills; on others, I'm doing all the
new prescriptions or checking prescriptions our technicians have filled.
If the dose seems too high or too low, it doesn't seem like the right
drug, or it seems like a drug is missing from what's been prescribed, I
call up the doctor or nurse and ask. Usually with new prescriptions, I
tell the patient a little bit about the medicine. A lot of times they have
something they're uncomfortable asking the doctor, so they ask me.

   I'm also helping implement an automated refill line, and I've created a pamphlet and posters to help the patients use it. Hopefully,
I'll be training soon to participate in our pharmacist-run anticoagula-
tion clinic. Our health center is also looking at having pharmacists

(continued)

(continued)

perform medication reconciliation, do patient counseling, and look at other laboratory results, too. Together with the doctor we would make adjustments to the patients' drug therapy.

What education or training do you have? Is it typical for your job?

I have a PharmD degree. I originally went to school to be a physical therapist, so I also have a BS in exercise physiology.

What path did you take to get to the job you are in today?

In the summer during college, I worked at a drugstore, and I'd often hand patients their medications. I found out that I liked talking to people. I only needed one more class to qualify for pharmacy school, and I decided to do it. After pharmacy school, I worked for a while as a traveling pharmacist, and I was sent to different areas on short-term assignments. I had always wanted to work on an Indian reservation, so I asked if I could do that. They sent me here for 8 months, and then a permanent job opened up and I was asked to stay. That's when I joined the Commissioned Corps.

Where might you go from here, if you wanted to advance your career?

I'm thinking about getting my MPH and doing Epidemic Intelligence Service, and I also want to get my Board-Certified Pharmacotherapy Specialist certification. In the public health service I can get out from behind the counter at the pharmacy, become a deputy director or compliance officer, do epidemiology, serve as chair of a public health organization committee, help with disaster response, work in drug approval at the FDA—there are so many options!

What is the worst or most challenging part of your job?

I like Arizona, and my primary site's not too remote, but I'm far from my family. Also, because of how my schedule works, some days it's hard to predict what time my workday will end.

(continued)

(continued)

What is the best part?

The other pharmacists and our technicians and I really get along well, and we help each other out when there is a lot of work to do. I also like talking to the doctors and hearing if they've seen anything fascinating in clinic that day. And I enjoy working with the patients. People will come in with different stories, and I love to talk with them about what's going on in their lives.

What advice do you have for someone who is interested in your career?

Talk to as many people in the job as you can, in as many areas as you can. I can describe my job, and it sounds wonderful—but someone else might not like it at all. It might be different at another IHS site, so it's worth asking three or four people at different sites. You'll get a better understanding of the pros and the cons.

MEDICAL OFFICER/DRUG EVALUATION AND SAFETY

Job Description

The FDA employs doctors as medical officers to help ensure the safety and effectiveness of prescription and over-the-counter medicines. These physicians interpret research and make important decisions about whether drugs should be approved, how they are manufactured, and what precautions should be in place. Some medical officers are involved in reviewing drug studies. Some make sure that drug labels are accurate. Some inspect manufacturing plants to verify that pills, tablets, and other medicines are being made correctly and are not contaminated. Medical officers also evaluate complaints and reports of side effects from drugs, and they have influence over the creation of new warning labels and even the removal of drugs from the market. The FDA hires doctors for other medical officer roles, too, in areas including food safety, vaccine effectiveness, the safety of blood products and medical devices, and radiation control.

Medical officers generally work standard hours, except when important projects or emergencies require extra time. They may also need to take time outside of work to read medical journals and keep up with the latest research.

Education and Certification

An FDA medical officer must have an MD or DO degree and, usually, must have completed residency training and be licensed to practice. Some medical officer jobs require only 1 year of residency, and the licensure requirement may be waived if there is no direct patient care. There are opportunities for many different types of doctors, but training relevant to the focus of the job is important. For example, a medical officer who evaluates drugs that affect the digestive system would be expected to have expertise in gastroenterology.

Core Competencies and Skills

- Ability to work with people from different fields and backgrounds
- Confidence to make decisions that may be controversial
- Patience with paperwork and red tape
- Understanding of research design and data analysis
- Willingness to read complex and sometimes lengthy documents
- Strong medical background, with an understanding of how the body works and of what happens in disease
- Knowledge of basic pharmacology (essentially, how drugs work)

Compensation

Typical salaries for FDA medical officers are in the range of $100,000 to $200,000 per year, with adjustments for location.

Workplaces

The FDA is the primary federal agency concerned with drug safety and effectiveness. There are also opportunities within industry to help monitor drug safety and ensure compliance with regulations.

Employment Outlook

The work of the FDA is ongoing, and medical officers will continue to play an important role. The FDA periodically announces hiring initiatives to meet specific needs, and this can include special outreach to enlist qualified physicians. Finding a specific job in drug safety may take a while, but there are medical officers in many different areas within the FDA.

For Further Information

- Food and Drug Administration (FDA)
  www.fda.gov

PUBLIC HEALTH PROFILE: Medical Officer
Sandra Kweder, MD
Deputy Director
Office of New Drugs
U.S. Food and Drug Administration, Washington, DC

Describe the sort of work you do.

My job is to oversee the scientists and public health experts who make decisions about medicines and determine which ones should be available for use. That includes deciding how drugs should be studied and, once they've been studied, if they're safe and effective and eligible for marketing. This includes prescription medicines as well as over-the-counter products such as headache or allergy medicines. My department also looks at a drug's role in the marketplace and what patients and prescribers need to know. Once drugs are on the market, we monitor them closely for safety. We are really public health agents at the FDA, but we do our job by regulatory oversight of the multibillion dollar pharmaceutical industry.

What is a typical day like at your job?

When I first started, my job was to review individual clinical studies and think about the details of how a specific drug might go from the laboratory to the bedside. Now, my days are about guiding the overall system we have at the FDA for new drug review. I am making decisions that may affect many drugs and how they are studied or marketed. I oversee other medical officers and scientists. My office has more than 900 professionals in it, all of whom are involved with

(continued)

(continued)

overseeing drug development, clinical trials, and marketing applications. I meet with directors of offices under mine to talk about what they are reviewing in their divisions and what the scientific, public health, and management challenges are, including those related to new findings about the safety of drugs already on the market. I often advise them on how to handle problems that come up.

In between meetings, I try to keep up with about 200 e-mails a day. Often, those contain something I need to read and approve, such as a position paper, a review, or a press release. I often interact with very senior executives in the pharmaceutical industry, speak to the press, and represent the FDA at academic conferences, consumer and industry group meetings, and congressional hearings.

What education or training do you have? Is it typical for your job?

You need to be a doctor, an MD or DO. It helps to have been through residency training and have some clinical experience, so you understand how drugs are used. It is also helpful if you've been involved in doing clinical studies.

What path did you take to get to the job you are in today?

I was fresh out of residency when I started at the FDA, as a medical officer in the antivirals division. At that time, there was only one drug available to treat HIV, and we were inundated with new drug proposals. We were constantly hiring new people. Pretty soon I was one of the people with the most experience, and I became a team leader. When the job of Director of the Division of Surveillance and Epidemiology opened up, I was asked to fill that role on a temporary basis—and that turned into 2 years. Next I chose to advance my own knowledge with a fellowship in medical complications of pregnancy. When I came back, I worked as deputy director for an office of drug evaluation and then, with more growth and changes within the FDA, I took on the role of acting director of the Office of New Drugs and then became the full-time deputy director.

(continued)

(continued)

Where might you go from here, if you wanted to advance your career?

If I wanted to advance, it could be to a job with even more responsibility within the FDA or I could seek a leadership role in another agency or organization. Many with the experience I have had find roles in the pharmaceutical industry or even working with large health care organizations.

What is the worst or most challenging part of your job?

It is hard having to be the bad guy. Sometimes I have to deliver bad news to a company, and I have to be tough on them. Sometimes it is a staff member who needs to improve his or her work. Back when I first started as a medical officer, the things I liked least were statistics and chemistry. I was always grateful that I worked with chemists and statisticians who really loved those disciplines and would help me!

What is the best part?

One reason my job is so interesting is that almost no two circumstances are the same. There may be parallels from one drug to another, but there is always something new. There is always a new puzzle, and I am learning all the time.

What advice do you have for someone who is interested in your career?

If you're a physician who likes science, likes puzzles, and is interested in the underpinnings of medicine, you should explore what we do at the FDA. We often have openings, and they're posted on usajobs.gov. We look for people who understand data analysis and research or are interested in learning, and who have a public health outlook.

Profile Update

Since her original interview, Dr. Kweder has continued in her role as deputy director at the Office of New Drugs. She notes that there are still frequent opportunities for qualified physicians to join the FDA, not just in drug safety, but also in premarket assessment work, focusing on clinical trials and drug development.

BIOSTATISTICIAN

Job Description

Biostatisticians use statistical expertise to help researchers investigate issues in all areas of public health. There are biostatisticians at the FDA who develop mathematical models to help find the best ways to do clinical trials. Biostatisticians review data sent in by drug manufacturers to see if their study results match the claims they are making. Some create mathematical models to predict how drugs will be processed by the body or use statistical techniques to help determine if a generic drug is equivalent to the brand-name version. Biostatisticians also analyze data to check the quality of drugs and other medical products.

Typical tasks for a biostatistician might include figuring out how many patients are needed for a clinical trial, determining how many measurements should be taken, and calculating whether a result is likely to represent a real effect or is probably due to chance. If a study is not done correctly the information may be useless, so biostatisticians help look for pitfalls in how data will be gathered and errors in study design. Biostatisticians are involved in many different areas of public health, in addition to drug safety. This is primarily a desk job, with a lot of computer time. Biostatisticians often work with a team of other public health experts, such as epidemiologists, medical officers, research scientists, and policy analysts.

Education and Certification

Biostatisticians have training in mathematics and statistics, as well as knowledge of how medical research is done. For some jobs, a bachelor's degree in mathematics or statistics will suffice, but a master's or doctoral degree allows for far more opportunities. Jobs in research and in academia usually require a PhD. The American Statistical Association (ASA) has offered a voluntary accreditation process since 2010, although it remains to be seen how much this credential will influence hiring decisions.

Core Competencies and Skills

- Knack for numbers
- Strong understanding of statistics
- Basic understanding of epidemiology

- Excellent computer skills, particularly with statistics programs
- Willingness to continue learning (statistical methods are constantly evolving)
- Ability to "translate" statistical information into language that nonstatisticians can understand
- Understanding of how to apply statistical and mathematical concepts to real-world situations

Compensation

For all statisticians, the median salary in 2014 was $80,000, and most earned between $44,000 and $130,000. The ASA surveyed their members in business, industry, and government jobs in 2013 and found that the middle of the salary range was $136,000 although there was quite a wide range, with states paying the least and industry the most. Most respondents had master's degrees or PhDs, and PhDs commanded the highest salaries on average. The salary range in a 2013/2014 ASA survey of biostatisticians at academic institutions showed a range from $95,000 for starting salaries to $150,000 and higher for full professors.

Workplaces

Biostatisticians are employed in virtually every aspect of public health. Within the federal government, those who focus on drug safety work largely at the FDA, but there are many biostatisticians at the CDC, the National Institutes of Health, and other agencies within the HHS. Biostatisticians also work for health departments, nonprofit organizations, medical centers and hospitals, and consulting firms.

Employment Outlook

Biostatisticians are needed for a wide range of research, safety, and health surveillance projects. According to the ASA, in recent years there has been a shortage of biostatisticians with training at the graduate level, so there should be good opportunities for employment.

For Further Information

- American Statistical Association (ASA)
  www.amstat.org

- American Public Health Association (APHA)—Applied Public Health Statistics Section
  www.apha.org/apha-communities/member-sections/applied-public-health-statistics

DIRECTOR, STATE BOARD OF PHARMACY

Job Description

A state board of pharmacy is the regulatory agency for the practice of pharmacy in that state. The board is usually responsible for licensing pharmacies and pharmacists; regulating drug storage, security, and dispensing; and inspecting pharmacies, drug distributors, and manufacturers. The pharmacy board also handles complaints and imposes penalties when people and businesses violate regulations. It informs pharmacists of changes in laws and regulations and provides guidance regarding the scope of what pharmacists can do.

Overseeing all the board's work is the executive director, who advises the members on policy matters and strategic planning, guides the implementation of policies, and supervises certain staff members. The executive director must be aware of pharmacy issues and trends, current laws and policies, pending legislation, and issues in inspection, licensing, and enforcement. Day-to-day tasks can include attending legislative hearings, working on ways to improve processes for licensing or inspection, addressing budget issues, and collaborating with other agencies.

Education and Certification

Some states, but not all, require the executive director to be a licensed pharmacist, and many require a certain amount of experience. Knowledge of pharmacy laws and regulations and of how the board of pharmacy functions is essential. Some executive directors have come to the job after serving as appointed members.

Core Competencies and Skills

- Strong managerial skills
- Excellent negotiating and public speaking skills
- Ability to handle multiple responsibilities at once
- Interest in policy making

- Talent for networking and making connections with legislators, government officials, and local leaders in the pharmacy world
- Thorough understanding of pharmacy laws and regulations
- Ability to communicate complex information to people from many different backgrounds

Compensation

Salaries vary substantially by state. Recent job listings have offered salaries ranging from about $80,000 to $140,000.

Workplaces

State boards of pharmacy may be separate agencies or may be located within health departments, departments of consumer affairs or public safety, departments of regulation and licensing, or other sections of state government. In some states, the director of the board of pharmacy also oversees other agencies, as well.

Employment Outlook

Each state has only one pharmacy board, and these jobs are generally filled by people who have experience with the activities of a state pharmacy board.

For Further Information

- National Association of Boards of Pharmacy (NABP)
  www.nabp.net
- National Association of State Controlled Substances Authorities (NASCSA)
  www.nascsa.org

REGULATORY AFFAIRS SPECIALIST

Job Description

A regulatory affairs specialist is in charge of making sure that a drug company or medical device manufacturer is complying with legal and regulatory requirements. Regulations come into play at all steps of the process from research to marketing, including conducting clinical trials, applying for FDA approval (or approval from agencies in other countries), and manufacturing the drug. A regulatory affairs specialist ensures that an application for a new drug contains all the necessary documents and information. During the research stages, a regulatory affairs specialist examines plans for clinical trials, ensures they conform to requirements, and keeps track of what forms must be submitted and what information must be reported. There are also regulatory affairs specialists involved in drug advertising and promotion. Responsibilities include reviewing advertising copy and label information to be sure they contain essential information and do not make any claims that are not allowed.

Education and Certification

Most regulatory affairs specialists have at least a bachelor's degree, and a major in a scientific or health-related field is helpful. Many have completed at least some graduate work or hold higher degrees. There are now some degree and certificate programs specifically in regulatory affairs, but it is not yet clear how important this type of background will be. Experience in research, laboratory work, clinical medicine, pharmacy, or a related area is often expected, and experience with the FDA is helpful. Experience with project management can also be useful. Some jobs require specialized knowledge, such as an engineering background for work related to medical devices. Companies may also look for employees with certain certifications. Regulatory affairs specialists may be more competitive if they hold Regulatory Affairs Certification (RAC) from the Regulatory Affairs Professionals Society (RAPS).

Core Competencies and Skills

- Patience with paperwork
- Ability to understand complex technical and legal language
- Strong sense of ethics
- Basic understanding of science, medicine, and research principles
- Familiarity with applicable federal requirements
- Good computer skills, including word processing and spreadsheets
- Ability to keep important company information confidential

Compensation

The 2014 salary survey from RAPS shows average salaries starting around $50,000 for the lowest-level jobs and rising to well over $100,000 for managers and directors. Higher salaries roughly correlate with higher education levels. There is also a modest bump for those with an RAC credential. Academia tends to pay less than government or industry.

Workplaces

Regulatory affairs specialists involved in health care work primarily for industry, and sometimes for medical centers, universities, research companies, or other organizations that must meet certain requirements. There are also jobs at the FDA, reviewing compliance and helping to set policy.

Employment Outlook

Because pharmaceutical and medical device companies cannot run without making sure they comply with regulations, these jobs will likely be secure. In recent years, companies have had difficulty finding qualified people to do this work, but they are often looking for seasoned professionals. One way to get started is to begin with a company in a different role and look for opportunities to learn about regulatory affairs.

For Further Information

- Regulatory Affairs Professionals Society (RAPS)
  www.raps.org
- Food and Drug Administration (FDA) Office
  of Regulatory Affairs
  www.fda.gov/ora

CHAPTER 10

Environmental Health and Water Safety

The environment has always had an impact on public health practice, since the earliest development of city water supplies and sewage systems. In modern times, however, public health and environmental health have become somewhat separated. The 1988 report from the Institute of Medicine, *The Future of Public Health*, pointed out that this fragmentation impeded coordination of health efforts and led to inadequate attention to the connection between environmental problems and health (Institute of Medicine Committee for the Study of the Future of Public Health, 1988).

In recent years, public health experts have begun to pay increasing attention to possible links between environmental hazards and disease. In fact, the Centers for Disease Control and Prevention (CDC) now has an environmental public health tracking network that collects data on environmental hazards, exposure levels, and health effects. Researchers are studying the effects of air pollution and chemical exposures through food, water, and personal care products. The impact of the built environment is a current hot topic: Can our neighborhoods make us sicker or healthier? Does a lack of sidewalks contribute to obesity? There is much we don't know about environmental health. Many chemicals used in industry have unknown potential health impacts. Issues such as the health consequences of climate change, environmental radiation exposures, and other pollutants are all subjects of study. As we learn more, there may be increasing opportunities to contribute to public health by focusing on our interaction with the environment.

There is a great deal of information at the CDC's National Center for Environmental Health (www.cdc.gov/nceh). The National Institute for Environmental Health Sciences (www.niehs.nih.gov) is another good resource. The American Public Health Association has a member section specifically dedicated to environmental health.

Job opportunities in environmental health are broad. In addition to this chapter, see also the entries for epidemiologist, medical epidemiologist, public health nurse, biostatistician, injury prevention specialist, specialist in poison information, health educator, health promotion program coordinator, disease ecologist, and study coordinator, and the chapter on occupational health (Chapter 11).

TOXICOLOGIST

Job Description

In public health, toxicologists study the effects of drugs, poisons, environmental contaminants, and other potentially dangerous substances, and then they use that knowledge to help protect the public's health and safety. Some specialize in certain substances or certain aspects of health, such as cancer risk or effects on the nervous system. Others focus on certain locations, such as factories where chemicals are produced or used. Often, it is not simply the presence of a substance that is important, but the amount, the way it is used, and potential interactions with other substances. In addition to environmental health issues, there are toxicologists working in other areas of public health such as helping figure out if a medicine, a food preservative, or an ingredient in lipstick poses any risk. Toxicologists who focus on research might do laboratory work, or they might help figure out if a chemical is causing an outbreak of illness. Toxicologists are also involved in creating and enforcing regulations to ensure that industries produce, use, and dispose of chemicals safely. They often must be able to explain the science behind their recommendations to nonexperts, such as legislators, health department personnel, and company workers.

Education and Certification

About half of all toxicologists have PhDs. Bachelor's and master's degree training are also options, but people with doctoral degrees will likely have the best opportunities. Many toxicologists start with an undergraduate degree in a science such as chemistry or biology, then go on to more specialized graduate study. Physicians, veterinarians, and people with PhDs in other biomedical sciences can pursue postdoctoral training in toxicology. Several certifications are available. The American Board of Toxicology recognizes expertise in general toxicology, and the American Board of Applied Toxicology focuses specifically on the study of poisons as they affect humans and animals. Both organizations require a PhD or a combination of education and experience. The American Board of Emergency Medicine, the American Board of Pediatrics, and the American Board of Preventive Medicine offer a subspecialty credential in medical toxicology for physicians.

Core Competencies and Skills

- Knack for biology, chemistry, math, and statistics
- Ability to learn complex new information rapidly
- Interest in scientific detective work
- Good writing and speaking skills to communicate your findings or explain risks and regulations
- Understanding of research design and implementation
- At least a basic knowledge of epidemiology and biostatistics
- Knowledge of biochemistry, molecular biology, and physiology
- Knowledge of known toxins and their effects on the body
- For work in industry and government, especially, the skills to interact effectively with a team

Compensation

According to a 2012 survey from the Society of Toxicology, average salaries for PhDs in their first few years of receiving their degrees ranged from about $35,000 to over $100,000, and salaries rose substantially with experience. Academic salaries and those at state and local governments tend to be notably lower than those in federal government or industry. Jobs for people with master's and bachelor's degrees tend to have lower salaries than jobs for PhDs.

Workplaces

Based on the same survey, about 15% of toxicologists work for city, state, and federal government institutions. Another 14% are employed by academic institutions, where their jobs can include both doing research and teaching students. About half work for private employers such as manufacturers and pharmaceutical companies. Toxicologists are also found at nonprofit organizations and consulting firms.

Employment Outlook

The job outlook for toxicologists is good. There is a strong need for the kind of work toxicologists do, and the specialized training helps reduce competition from other types of scientists. According to the Society of Toxicology, increasing attention to both health and the environment should make for a wide range of opportunities.

For Further Information

- Society of Toxicology (SOT)
  www.toxicology.org
- American College of Toxicology (ACT)
  www.actox.org
- American Academy of Clinical Toxicology (AACT)
  www.clintox.org

POISONING PREVENTION COORDINATOR

Job Description

The coordinator of a poisoning prevention program manages outreach, education, and cleanup programs to remove dangerous substances from the environment. Many poisoning prevention programs are focused on reducing the risk of lead poisoning in children. Depending on the program, the coordinator's tasks might include maintaining a registry of houses and apartments without lead contamination, directing people to professionals who can help with lead removal, and organizing a program to screen children for elevated lead levels. The coordinator is often responsible for managing employees and takes part in handling the budget, including writing grant proposals and administering grants. Obtaining and analyzing local data are other typical tasks. The coordinator may be directly involved in activities such as conducting community outreach and educational sessions, providing counseling to families when children have elevated lead levels, inspecting homes, and training housing contractors, or they may delegate such tasks to staff members. He or she may also help to develop new programs, based on available funding and local needs. The job can include policy and advocacy work, as well.

Often, it involves meeting with partner organizations to share ideas and encourage cooperation.

Education and Certification

Poisoning prevention coordinators are often nurses or trained health educators. A bachelor's degree and experience overseeing a community service or health-related program will meet some employers' requirements. An MPH can be helpful, and an MPH or a master's degree in a related field is sometimes required. Certification as a lead inspector, which requires a short course and an examination, may be needed if inspection is part of the job.

Core Competencies and Skills

- Excellent organizational and managerial skills
- Ability to multitask
- Flexibility to work with many different types of people, from community members to city leaders
- Strong writing and spoken communication skills
- Knowledge of public health program administration and the ability to interpret regulations
- Working knowledge of epidemiology, data analysis, and program evaluation techniques
- Ability to create educational programs and materials geared to the needs of local communities
- Knowledge of issues specific to the prevention program, such as lead poisoning risks and abatement requirements

Compensation

Salaries vary widely according to location, responsibilities, and the size of the agency or organization. Recent job openings have offered salaries ranging from $35,000 up to nearly $70,000.

Workplaces

Poisoning prevention programs are located in city, county, and state health departments, and there are also programs run by nonprofit organizations and academic institutions. Although jobs will be different from those in local communities, there is also work in lead poisoning prevention at the federal level. The CDC has a lead prevention program, which works with local programs as well as providing information for health care providers and the public. There are lead prevention efforts at the Environmental Protection Agency (EPA) and at the Department of Housing and Urban Development.

Employment Outlook

There are many childhood lead poisoning prevention programs throughout the United States, at state and local health departments. When a city or county health department has its own lead prevention program, it will usually have only one or two coordinator positions. However, there are other opportunities to be involved in these programs and to gain experience. In addition, there are other programs focusing on the prevention of poisoning through environmental exposures, including pesticide poisoning and exposure to lead in the workplace.

For Further Information

- CDC Lead Poisoning Prevention Program
  www.cdc.gov/nceh/lead

ENVIRONMENTAL ENGINEER

Job Description

Environmental engineers (also called sanitary engineers) who work in public health are involved in fields such as air pollution control, waste disposal, and water treatment. They may design systems to keep drinking water supplies safe, to control pollution, to treat wastewater and sewage, and to manage potentially hazardous waste. They may help track down problems at existing facilities and develop regulations to guide future efforts. When a developer is building a new subdivision, it is an environmental engineer who looks over the plans for the proposed water supply. These engineers also ensure that projects comply with laws and regulations. They need not only to understand the principles of design and development but also to have at least basic knowledge of pathogens, disease vectors, toxicology, and other public health issues.

Other typical jobs include working on systems to treat wastewater from manufacturing plants, finding ways to reduce emissions from automobiles or factory smokestacks, planning for the safe disposal of dangerous substances, and finding ways to clean up contaminated sites. In the course of their work, environmental engineers interact with other experts, including health officials, architects, and building contractors. They are often based primarily in offices, but they typically spend about a quarter of their time on-site, inspecting locations or facilities. There are also environmental engineers who primarily do research on environmental control.

Education and Certification

Environmental engineers need at least a bachelor's degree in a related engineering field, and a master's degree in environmental engineering can lead to better employment opportunities; academic programs should be accredited by the Accreditation Board for Engineering and Technology. A PhD is not essential for most environmental engineers but can open up additional possibilities, especially for those interested in research. An engineer who plans to offer his or her services to public or private clients needs to hold a state license and to be certified as a Professional Engineer (PE). Engineers who work for government agencies often need a license and PE certification, and certification is generally necessary for advancement.

Core Competencies and Skills

- Tendency to be detail oriented and analytical
- Strong skills in math and physics
- Curiosity about science and biology
- Understanding of the workings of state or local government, including how government policies can affect engineering projects
- Ability to communicate with scientists and nonscientists in different fields
- High-level computer skills, for the use of technical design and modeling programs and data analysis
- Ability to visualize projects, such as imagining two-dimensional plans in three dimensions

Compensation

In 2014, the median salary for an environmental engineer was $83,000. The top 10% earned over $125,000, and only 10% earned $50,000 or less. More experience and more education will generally lead to higher compensation. The federal government and private industry tend to pay more than state governments, although salaries vary.

Workplaces

Environmental engineers work for city, county, and state governments, usually either with the health department or with a separate division focused on the environment. They also work for corporations that contract to do government work. Some work directly for a corporation in a specific industry.

Employment Outlook

The number of jobs for environmental engineers is expected to grow a little faster than average between 2012 and 2022. The Bureau of Labor Statistics notes that there should be increased demand due to the need to clean up contaminated sites, and also for wastewater treatment related to drilling for shale gas. There is an ongoing need for environmental engineers at utilities and water treatment plants. The need for water conservation and efficiency of use may also create opportunities. Many employers prefer to hire engineers with at least a master's degree, not just a bachelor's.

For Further Information

- American Society of Civil Engineers (ASCE)
  www.asce.org
- American Academy of Environmental Engineers and Scientists (AAEES)
  www.aaees.net
- American Water Works Association (AWWA)
  www.awwa.org

PUBLIC HEALTH PROFILE: Environmental Engineer
Jeff Stone, MBA, PE
Chief Engineer
Engineering Section, Arkansas Department of Health, Little Rock, AR

Describe the sort of work you do.

We protect the public's health with regard to drinking water and wastewater as well as ensure compliance with the federal Safe Drinking Water Act. We approve or disapprove water sources, drinking

(continued)

(continued)

water treatment plant designs, wastewater treatment plant designs, and treated wastewater discharge locations. We monitor everything from the source to the wastewater plant and back to the river.

I manage a staff of engineers and engineering technicians. The technicians carry most of the on-site inspection burden and also review the data from drinking water treatment plants each month. The district engineers carry most of the burden of plan review, both for new sites and for infrastructure improvement, and they do some of the inspections of larger systems and sources.

What is a typical day like at your job?

My door is always open to my staff. People come to confirm judgment calls or to obtain guidance. There are also calls from outside consultants and design engineers. They might call to get my input before they get started on projects. When an issue in the field warrants my firsthand experience, I'll go out. If there's a breakdown of equipment or a treatment interruption that could lead to contamination, we swing into action and try to prevent disease from happening. The health agency has an emergency office manned 24/7. If there's a power failure that makes our water utilities not operational, or if there's a water main break, I get a call.

What education or training do you have?
Is it typical for your job?

I have a bachelor's in chemical engineering and an MBA, and I am licensed as a PE. Some people in this field have a bachelor's degree in civil or chemical engineering and a master's degree in environmental engineering. That master's would give them a bit of an edge. But many environmental engineers don't actually have a degree in "environmental engineering." Their degree is in, say, civil engineering and their work experience and acquired competency is in environmental engineering.

What path did you take to get to the
job you are in today?

I started out working in industry, but the technical skills I was learning were specific to that business. I wanted a skill set that would

(continued)

(continued)

lead me through a 40- or 50-year career, and I decided on environmental engineering. I found an ad in the newspaper for a job at the health department. I had taken some electives in environmental engineering at college, and that may have helped me get the job. After I started here, I became licensed as a PE, and I advanced to jobs with more responsibility. I earned the MBA for my own interest and to learn about finance, personnel law, and other things that a manager needs to understand.

Where might you go from here, if you wanted to advance your career?

I think I have a lot of choices. I've been here with the health agency about 24 years and worked my way up. If I stayed here I might have a chance at higher positions, or I could start a second career after I retire and become a project manager with a consulting engineering company.

What is the worst or most challenging part of your job?

Even though my department is trying to help the public, we still have to deal with people who are upset by things that have happened. Also, my decisions can mean a cost difference to utilities in building their systems, or they can affect someone's property rights. If someone thinks my decision is incorrect or unfair, they can appeal my decision or perhaps litigate. I've never been subpoenaed for a court case, but I've had to answer difficult calls. This is not a job for people who can't deal with conflict in a calm way and strive to find solutions to problems.

What is the best part?

I'm involved in important judgment calls and in responding to emergency situations, and I know that what I do matters. The general public might not be aware of exactly what my department does, or of the problems we prevent, but they rely on us to keep them safe.

(continued)

(continued)

What advice do you have for someone who is interested in your career?

Anyone, in any kind of engineering, should pursue professional licensure. Not only does it enhance your own marketability, it is also the best way I know of to have a career that serves you over your lifetime.

Profile Update

Since his original interview, Mr. Stone has been promoted to Director of the Engineering Section at the Arkansas Department of Health, managing a program with more than 70 employees. In this position, he serves as the Arkansas Program Manager for the federal Safe Drinking Water Act, which is tasked with ensuring that every Arkansan is served by safe drinking water. He also serves on the Board of the Association of State Drinking Water Administrators (ASDWA) and is ASDWA's representative on the Board of the Water Information Sharing and Analysis Center (Water ISAC).

HAZARDOUS WASTE INSPECTOR

Job Description

The job title is not glamorous, but hazardous waste inspectors have very important jobs. They ensure that manufacturers meet local and national guidelines for the disposal of certain types of potentially dangerous waste. They keep our water supply safe and keep dangerous substances out of our soil and air. They visit factories and other industrial settings to help companies understand and comply with waste management regulations. Some serve as site assessors, taking soil samples at vacant properties to determine if hazardous substances are present. They also inspect waste treatment and disposal facilities, and they respond to complaints about improper dumping or disposal. Inspections may require travel throughout the state, including nights away from home. Back at the office, inspectors write reports, research current regulations, interact with other inspectors, and talk with industry managers or clients.

Education and Certification

A typical requirement is a bachelor's degree in environmental science or a related field, or college-level science classes plus related training. Some jobs require specific certification. Courses and certificates are available at some colleges and universities and from professional organizations.

Core Competencies and Skills

- Basic grounding in chemistry, biology, and geology
- Interest in educating workers as well as in uncovering problems
- Strong organizational skills and self-motivation
- Ability to write technical reports
- Understanding of local and national waste disposal and management regulations
- Interest in work that involves travel to multiple sites as well as office work

Compensation

State health department salaries vary according to local budgets as well as cost of living and level of responsibility. Some examples include $40,000 to the low $60,000s in one California county with a requirement of at least 6 months' experience; $46,000 to $60,000 in a Washington county, for someone with a BA and 5 years' experience; and up to $90,000 for an experienced manager in an urban area in the Northwest.

Workplaces

State governments employ hazardous waste inspectors, usually through the state environmental agency, to inspect businesses throughout the state. There are also some opportunities for hazardous materials inspectors in city and county programs. Manufacturers employ people with similar knowledge to oversee waste management within their companies. Industrial waste disposal companies also employ inspectors to make sure they are transporting materials safely and complying with the law.

Employment Outlook

Government jobs are considered relatively stable, even in tough economic times, and in fact some supervisors have reported that it can be challenging to find qualified employees for this type of work.

For Further Information

- Environmental Council of the States (ECOS)
  www.ecos.org
- Environmental Protection Agency (EPA)—Wastes website
  www.epa.gov/wastes

PUBLIC HEALTH PROFILE: Hazardous Waste Inspector
Chad Babcock

Environmental Project Scientist
South Dakota Department of Environment and Natural Resources,
Pierre, SD

Describe the sort of work you do.

I work in the waste management program of South Dakota's Department of Environment and Natural Resources. My primary job involves inspecting commercial businesses and government agencies for compliance with hazardous waste rules and inspecting facilities permitted to accept solid waste for treatment, storage, or disposal. During hazardous waste inspections, I ensure that businesses and agencies properly determine if wastes they generate are ignitable, corrosive, or toxic, and I make sure the wastes are managed accordingly.

What is a typical day like at your job?

Some days I'm out of the office doing inspections, and other days I'm here completing inspection reports and preparing for upcoming inspections. I plan a series of inspections once or twice a month. To prepare for each inspection, I go through all our records on the company, and I put together a preinspection report. I'll look for any compliance issues in the past. Then I call the company to schedule my visit. When I go do the inspection, I like to start by sitting down with a company representative to get an idea of what the company does and the waste that they generate. Then I get out into the actual manufacturing or production area. I walk through, discuss each process, and inspect waste storage areas. If I identify anything new

(continued)

(continued)

or unexpected, I'll request additional information. I usually have a number of questions to follow up with afterward, so after I return to the office I'll contact the company representative again as needed. Finally, I write the official report.

Sometimes I handle complaint calls and do complaint investigations. This usually involves contacting affected parties to gather information about the incident. Many times I will conduct a follow-up inspection. People will also call with questions about the hazardous waste rules that apply to them, or if they have a new manufacturing process they might ask for our assistance.

What education or training do you have? Is it typical for your job?

I have a bachelor's degree in biological chemistry, with a minor in math and physics. A bachelor's degree in life or physical sciences or in an engineering discipline is pretty typical for this job.

What path did you take to get to the job you are in today?

I started out working as a research scientist with an animal vaccines company. I was working mostly in a laboratory. I had more of an interest in environmental health than I did in the animal work, so when I moved to a new city, I began working as an environmental consultant. I think my science background helped me get that position. I did a lot of asbestos and lead paint inspections for renovation and demolition work, also some on-site monitoring. I kept an eye out for openings in the Department of Environment and Natural Resources, and when I saw one advertised, I applied.

Where might you go from here, if you wanted to advance your career?

Experience is valued a lot here, and there are always opportunities to take on new tasks without changing levels. Right now I'm not that interested in supervising. I am more interested in increased responsibilities involved in inspecting, permitting, and compliance assistance. I

(continued)

(continued)

report to a senior scientist who manages the hazardous waste program and an engineering director who manages the solid waste program.

What is the worst or most challenging part of your job?

Tracking the disposal of different wastes involves a lot of paperwork, and that gets tedious at times. Report writing involves evaluation, which I find interesting, but also has some aspects that are repetitive.

What is the best part?

I really enjoy the background research for inspections and reports. There is a lot of learning and often unique application of regulations, so it remains challenging and interesting. And then, I like taking that knowledge and discussing company operations with personnel of various levels. There is constantly something different and I have the opportunity to meet and work with an interesting group of people.

What advice do you have for someone who is interested in your career?

It is helpful to have a background in chemistry, biology, and environmental science. I value my experience as a consultant, working with businesses and seeing how they do things, because it gave me a good perspective on both sides of what I do now. I think it helped me understand my current job a lot more quickly, coming from the background that I had.

Profile Update

Since his original interview, Mr. Babcock was promoted from project scientist in the hazardous waste program to asbestos coordinator in the waste management program. His primary responsibilities now include inspecting commercial and public building renovation and demolition projects to ensure that owners and contractors identify, properly remove, and properly dispose of asbestos-containing materials. He also manages the state asbestos accreditation program, which ensures that asbestos contractors are properly trained and certified to do their work and provides compliance assistance and outreach to building owners, contractors, and local municipal building services departments. He continues to conduct solid waste facility inspections.

HYDROLOGIST

Job Description

Hydrologists study the occurrence, movement, and distribution of water on and within the earth, and the relationship between that water and the surrounding environment. Hydrologists also look at how water can become contaminated or purified by natural processes, and they develop methods to predict changes and monitor effects. Hydrologists who work with public health officials are involved in monitoring water supplies, looking for pollutants, and determining how altering certain aspects of the environment could influence water purity. If a new well is planned, a hydrologist will look at how it could affect water in existing wells. They also help decide where to place new waste disposal facilities, to minimize environmental effects. The job often includes work in the field, such as visiting lakes and streams to gather samples, as well as high-tech work such as statistical modeling and the use of remote sensing technologies. Hydrologists work closely with engineers, geologists, and other experts.

Education and Certification

A master's degree is standard. There are some entry-level jobs for people with bachelor's degrees, and high-level research jobs tend to require PhDs. Degrees specifically in hydrology are available, but many programs have a hydrology concentration within a degree program in geoscience, engineering, or environmental science. There are also nondegree certificates available from some universities, for people who already have a background in a related subject. Several states require hydrologists to be licensed if they will be offering their services to the public. There is also a voluntary certification available from the American Institute of Hydrology.

Core Competencies and Skills

- Good math and statistics skills and an interest in the natural sciences
- Strong computer skills, for statistical and modeling programs
- Ability to collaborate with other scientists
- Ability to communicate information to nonscientists
- Training in how to assess risk and apply theory to actual practice

- Understanding of public health laws and regulations as they relate to environmental issues
- Knowledge of geology, chemistry, physics, and biology with respect to water systems
- Knowledge of how various water contaminants can affect human health

Compensation

In 2014, the median salary for hydrologists was about $78,000. The top 10% earned over $117,000 and the bottom 10%, about $50,000 or less.

Workplaces

There are many different types of jobs, with varying levels of connection with traditional public health issues. About 29% of hydrologists work for the federal government, primarily with the U.S. Geological Survey and the Department of Defense, although not all are directly concerned with public health issues. At state environmental agencies, hydrologists work with engineers and others concerned with the supply and safety of our water and with waste management. There are also many jobs for hydrologists at consulting firms and in industry, and there are opportunities at nonprofit organizations concerned with the environment.

Employment Outlook

Growth in this job market is expected to keep pace with job growth overall, from 2012 through 2022. Concerns about the environment are expected to help drive the need for hydrologists. Population increases, with ongoing development of environmentally sensitive areas, will likely increase the need for these experts, as well.

For Further Information

- American Institute of Hydrology (AIH)
  www.aihydrology.org
- U.S. Geological Survey (USGS)
  www.usgs.gov
- American Water Resources Association (AWRA)
  www.awra.org

ENVIRONMENTAL HEALTH NURSE

Job Description

Environmental health nursing could be considered a subset of public health nursing. These nurses focus on specific dangers in the environment, from lead exposures to air pollution. To help control asthma in a community, a nurse might learn about all the environmental triggers—such as dust mites, pet dander, and other indoor pollutants—and then help develop programs and policies to reduce exposures at home and school. An environmental health nurse may work with other environmental health experts, health care providers, community groups, and even builders and contractors. Often, the job involves going out into the community—including homes, schools, and hospitals—to assess potential dangers and offer interventions. There can also be a lot of deskwork, including data collection, analysis, and writing.

Education and Certification

At present, the best preparation in addition to an initial nursing degree is probably an MPH with a focus on environmental health sciences. Another option would be a master's degree in nursing with an environmental health specialty, but at present these programs focus largely on occupational health and workplace safety, not on wider environmental issues.

Core Competencies and Skills

- Interest in community-level health
- Desire to work collaboratively across health disciplines
- Interest in health care policy
- Ability to understand not only environmental risk factors but the social factors that contribute to those risks
- Knowledge of epidemiologic principles and techniques
- Training in how to design and carry out public health programs
- Knowledge of toxicology and environmental health risks

Compensation

The specific responsibilities of environmental health nurses can vary widely, so it is difficult to give a typical salary. For registered nurses in general, typical salaries in 2014 ranged from about $46,000 to $99,000.

Workplaces

Environmental health nurses work not only for local and state health departments, but also for hospitals, schools, and industry—both at factories and in office settings. There are also opportunities in federal government, including the CDC and the EPA.

Employment Outlook

Environmental health nursing is still an emerging field. In addition to lead abatement programs, public health agencies and organizations are starting to focus on other environmental health hazards, such as identifying and reducing asthma triggers in urban living spaces. There may be roles for nurses in these programs. For now, nurses may have the best luck looking for public health nursing jobs in general, and watching for opportunities to get more involved in environmental health.

For Further Information

- Alliance of Nurses for Healthy Environments (ANHE)
  www.envirn.org
- American Nurses Association (ANA)
  www.nursingworld.org

COMMUNITY ACTIVIST

Job Description

Community activists are involved in many aspects of public health, including environmental health. These committed workers take on issues that are important to the health of a group, a neighborhood, or a city as a whole, and they help community members make their voices heard. Sometimes, a campaign begins with a single individual who rallies others to the cause; sometimes, it is the result of a concern that many people share. Either way, a community activist's work involves bringing people together (through meetings, events, and online forums) to find ways to solve problems. They encourage interest through news stories, local events, and social marketing campaigns. They work with legislators and public officials when possible, but when necessary they use legal challenges, protests, and staged events to make their voices heard. Members of community-focused organizations might be found collecting signatures for a petition to stop the city from building a bus depot near a school. They may meet with local business leaders to get funding to build a park. They might attend a hearing about new regulations to reduce pollution in a local river. Or you may spot them at a playground, taking soil samples to test for lead. Often, community action organizations are small, so just a few people share many responsibilities, including raising funds, writing press releases, planning events, and speaking to the public. When these organizations have more employees, jobs are more clearly delineated; see the section on jobs at nonprofit organizations for more details.

Education and Certification

A community activist can have any educational background, from a high school diploma to a doctoral degree. There is no special certification. People with specific degrees may be able to put them to use in their work. For example, someone with a degree in environmental science might be able to speak with particular authority about pollution, and a nurse might use her knowledge to explain health effects to legislators or the public.

Core Competencies and Skills

- Excellent interpersonal skills
- Dedication
- Ability to see a project through to completion
- Resilience to deal with disappointments and setbacks
- Strong writing skills for creating grant proposals, press releases, and other documents
- Good research skills, to learn about the issues and about the science and medical facts involved
- Knack for seeing all sides of an issue and understanding how different people think
- Belief that it is possible to change the status quo

Compensation

People who work for community activist organizations do their jobs for the opportunity to make a difference. Salaries depend greatly on the specific job description and on the organization's funding but are often less than someone with the same skills and education would earn in the private sector. At a small grassroots organization, an entry-level salary in the mid-$20,000 to mid-$30,000 range would not be unusual for someone with a bachelor's degree; a larger organization, or one in an area with a high cost of living, might start entry-level workers at $35,000 or more. The director can expect to earn more, for example $55,000 at one small organization or $75,000 at a mid-sized one. Larger organizations with larger budgets will typically pay more. Salaries also vary according to the organization's structure, and a group may choose to pay more to recruit and retain the most qualified people.

Workplaces

Community activists work for nonprofit organizations, often small or medium-sized organizations that focus on a specific region or issue. There are also large, national nonprofits with divisions devoted to grassroots work, but the issues being addressed will generally be less specific to the local community. If there is an important local issue that is not being addressed, starting an organization is also an option. It is a risk, and it takes a great deal of commitment, but if it succeeds it can make a real difference to the community.

Employment Outlook

There is always work to be done to help make our communities healthier, but the local organizations that do this work often have limited funding so it may take a while to find a job in a specific area of interest. One way to get started is to volunteer, get to know people involved in the cause, and let it be known that you're interested if a job opens up.

For Further Information

- Idealist
  www.idealist.org

PUBLIC HEALTH PROFILE: Community Activist
Peggy Shepard
Executive Director
WE ACT for Environmental Justice, New York, NY

Describe the sort of work you do.

WE ACT is a nonprofit organization. We work to build community power among people of color in northern Manhattan neighborhoods, in order to improve environmental health, environmental protection, and policy. We do that through research, training of community members, mobilization of the community, and working in public policy.

We got started in the late 1980s, after a new sewage treatment plant began spewing noxious odors and fumes that were making people sick. We convinced the city to spend millions of dollars to fix the plant. Today, we have many different projects and programs. We have been educating people in our local community about climate change, and we are also doing policy work on the city and state level. On the national level, we recently held the first climate justice conference in the country. Some of our other concerns include clean air and water, indoor air quality, sanitation, transportation, and the development and use of our waterfront.

What is a typical day like at your job?

I can give you a better idea by looking at a week. Last week, on Monday I gave a talk about food security and food justice at a large meeting put together by the City Council president. Then I had a paper due for an upcoming conference. On Tuesday, I had a meeting with our board about fundraising, a meeting with one of my staff about performance planning, and a call with a consultant about the theory of change. I had a conference call with the CDC for their National Conversation on Chemicals and Public Health. I lead a workgroup called Serving Communities. That night, I had a board meeting with the Public Health Association of New York City.

On Wednesday, I had a meeting with a major media organization to talk about diversity issues, and I had a meeting at the Environmental Defense Fund, where I cochair the environmental

(continued)

(continued)

justice committee. That was a brainstorming session to talk about new directions. Then, I had a call with the Children's Environmental Health Network to discuss their climate change policy initiative. Later in the week, I had a fundraiser with a Harlem community group, and I had a meeting with the founding dean of a new School of Public Health, to brainstorm about a new initiative to work on health disparities in Harlem.

What education or training do you have? Is it typical for your job?

I have a bachelor's degree in English and background in journalism. Mostly, what you need is commitment. Business skills are helpful, too. WE ACT is a nonprofit, but all the things you have to do with a small business, you have to do with a nonprofit as well.

What path did you take to get to the job you are in today?

I had worked for 10 years as a journalist, a magazine editor, a speechwriter, and a public information director for a state agency. I used my writing skills to work in political campaigns, and I became the public relations director for Jesse Jackson's first campaign for president. After that, I ran for the office of Democratic District Leader for West Harlem. When I was elected, the community asked me to help them organize to address the problems with the sewage plant.

Then, we found out that the Metropolitan Transportation Authority (MTA) was building another bus depot in our community. Diesel exhaust contributes to multiple health problems. We already had multiple bus depots in northern Manhattan, whereas other communities had none. We decided to file a lawsuit against the MTA—and to do that, your group needs a name, and official members. We began developing WE ACT officially, so we were able to file that lawsuit. The city settled our lawsuit for $1.1 million, and it was decided that WE ACT would get $200,000 to staff the organization. That's when I started my job as director.

(continued)

(continued)

Where might you go from here, if you wanted to advance your career?

I could probably have a position at the EPA or at the state Department of Environmental Conservation. A lot of government agencies don't know very much about how to interact with community, so I have a lot to offer. Or, I could move into community-based research. But right now I'm where I want to be.

What is the worst or most challenging part of your job?

Funders will support programs and projects, but they don't usually want to give general operating money. We know what it takes to make a really strong, viable organization, but we don't always have the money to hire the additional staff that would make everyone's job here easier.

What is the best part?

The best part is taking community concerns and developing solutions that are realized. To give you a case in point—we had a dilapidated waterfront. We organized the community to envision a waterfront park, and we got the city to build it! It is also very gratifying to help support the development of a national voice on environmental justice.

What advice do you have for someone who is interested in your career?

You have to be at the right point in your life cycle, and you also have to have the right family situation. Your family has to be extremely supportive. You'll be giving 200% every day for a long time.

HEALTH PHYSICIST

Job Description

Health physics focuses on making it possible for radiation to be used for beneficial purposes. Health physicists are experts in radiation safety, and they work at many different levels and in a variety of settings to protect workers, the public, and the environment. One role is in the licensing and inspection of radioactive materials, which are used in many different industries. Health physicists also observe the workers in these settings, ensure they are taking appropriate precautions, and offer training and guidance when needed. They judge whether safety measures are acceptable.

Health physicists are also involved in planning for radiation safety. Some help design facilities with proper radiation control and create training programs for employees. There are health physicists at nuclear power plants, ensuring compliance with regulations, training workers, and monitoring safety measures. Some health physicists work primarily in emergency preparedness, such as modeling the potential effects of a radioactive dispersal device (a "dirty bomb") and teaching first responders how to deal with a radiation emergency. There are health physicists figuring out how to decontaminate sites where military facilities, research laboratories, or industrial operations used to be. There are also opportunities for these experts in research, in policy and regulations, and in many other areas of health-related work.

Education and Certification

An associate's degree can suffice for certain jobs such as inspecting x-ray equipment, but most jobs in health physics require a minimum of a bachelor's degree in a field such as physics, engineering, or environmental health. It is possible to earn a bachelor's, master's, or PhD degree specifically in health physics, although not all universities offer these degrees. Health physicists also need specific training in radiation safety and preparedness, which is usually obtained on the job and through specialized training courses. Experience is enough to allow career advancement in some settings, and there is a wide range of interesting jobs for which a master's degree is sufficient. Some high-level jobs require a PhD. Voluntary certification as a Certified Health Physicist (CHP) is available through the American Board of Health Physics.

Core Competencies and Skills

- Knack for math and physics and at least basic knowledge of biology and chemistry
- Strong sense of responsibility and ethics
- Good writing and organizational skills

- Ability to interpret situations and make appropriate decisions with limited guidance
- Ability to gather information and apply it to real-world situations
- For inspectors, especially, willingness to travel
- Knowledge of local and federal regulations pertaining to radiation
- Knowledge of radiation hazards, safety measures, and monitoring

Compensation

According to a 2014 survey of health physicists, the median salary is about $101,000 per year, with most in the range of $40,000 to $160,000 depending on education and experience. Health physicists with less than 6 years' experience averaged $81,250 and those with more than 15 years' experience were more typically earning $110,000 to $130,000. Salaries for state-level inspectors tend to be at the lower end of the scale. A health physicist with only a bachelor's degree can also expect to be on the lower end of the pay range, while having the CHP credential correlates with higher salaries.

Workplaces

Health physicists can be found wherever radiation is involved. There are inspectors at state health departments. A few large metropolitan areas have local programs. There are many opportunities in the federal government, including at the Nuclear Regulatory Commission, the CDC, the EPA, and the Department of Homeland Security. There are health physicists working in research laboratories, at decommissioning facilities, and in industry. Some health physicists teach and do research at universities. There are also "medical health physicists" who focus on radiation safety and radiation therapy at medical facilities.

Employment Outlook

There has been concern for several years about a looming shortage of health physicists. Recent years provided a reprieve as there was slower than expected growth in the nuclear power industry, a weak economy that probably kept some workers from retiring, and some growth in academic training programs. However, the workforce is aging and a wave of retirements is expected, and it is not clear that there will be new candidates qualified to take their places. Experts continue to report concerns both about being able to meet regular staffing needs and about our nation's ability to respond to an emergency. Overall, the job prospects for well-trained health physicists appear promising.

For Further Information

- Health Physics Society (HPS)
  www.hps.org
- American Nuclear Society (ANS)
  www.ans.org

REFERENCE

Institute of Medicine Committee for the Study of the Future of Public Health. (1988). *The future of public health*. Washington, DC: National Academies Press.

CHAPTER 11

Occupational Health and Safety

The health of our workers has an enormous impact on the health of our population as a whole. With more than 3 million nonfatal work-related injuries and illnesses and about 4,500 deaths in 2013, there are many opportunities to improve health and safety on the job (Bureau of Labor Statistics, 2014a, 2014b). Occupational health and safety experts approach a given industry's or company's workers not just as individuals but as a population facing certain risks and hazards. They use the techniques of public health to address health and safety concerns and reduce risks in the workplace. In fact, the training for occupational medicine physicians incorporates earning an MPH or a related master's degree.

There are two federal agencies concerned with occupational health. The National Institute for Occupational Safety and Health (NIOSH) is an agency within the Centers for Disease Control and Prevention (CDC; www.cdc.gov/niosh). At the Department of Labor, the Occupational Safety and Health Administration (OSHA) develops, implements, and enforces workplace standards for occupational safety and health (www .osha.gov). There are also state health departments that do their own surveillance and interventions. Many government agencies employ occupational health experts to protect their workers' health, and there are extensive opportunities in the private sector.

In addition to the careers discussed in this chapter, there are many other professionals working in this field, including epidemiologists, toxicologists, environmental health nurses, and health promotion program coordinators.

OCCUPATIONAL MEDICINE PHYSICIAN

Job Description

Occupational medicine is a medical specialty that has a lot of overlap with public health. "Occ med" physicians are trained to look at the health of workers as a population, as well as to know about all the different medical issues that can arise in the workplace. Office workers can suffer injuries from repetitive tasks or even badly made chairs. Warehouse workers can hurt their backs. Factory workers can be exposed to heavy metals, dust, dangerous equipment, and loud noise. The occupational medicine physician watches for these types of injuries and sounds the alarm if a pattern or serious danger exists. For example, if several factory employees develop breathing problems, the physician might investigate the cause. An outbreak of the flu can tear through a company; the occupational medicine physician helps devise and promote ways to prevent such outbreaks.

In their day-to-day work, these physicians may treat injured or ill workers, make official determinations about whether injuries and illnesses are work related, and help workers get back on the job. When workers develop physical or mental illnesses that do not have occupational causes, they help guide them to outside care and make recommendations for any needed work accommodations. Some occupational medicine physicians are primarily administrators, setting policy and investigating patterns; others primarily see patients; and some do a combination of the two. Occupational medicine doctors also work with other experts to help companies put safety measures into place, like muting loud sounds that can damage hearing.

Education and Certification

An occupational medicine doctor needs an MD or DO and a current license to practice. Some doctors transition to occupational medicine careers without specialized training, but the best preparation is to complete a residency program in occupational or occupational and environmental medicine. Board certification, which involves passing a rigorous examination after finishing residency, is not absolutely essential, but it is often expected. It is also possible for physicians in other medical specialties to acquire skills in occupational medicine through continuing education and on-the-job training.

Core Competencies and Skills

- Familiarity with the industry or industries in which the patient population works
- Good interpersonal skills
- Curiosity and a willingness to investigate when the source of an illness is not clear
- Knowledge of medicine, in general, and of hazards present in the workplace
- Knowledge of rehabilitation methods for injured workers
- Knowledge of workplace safety and sanitation issues
- Knowledge of workers' compensation laws and of local, state, and national regulations that apply to worker safety and health

Compensation

The starting salary for an occupational medicine physician is often at or above $100,000 per year. According to the American College of Occupational and Environmental Medicine (ACOEM), in 2012, the median income for someone board certified in occupational medicine was $225,000. Salaries increased with experience: an average of $175,000 for those with less than 5 years, and $240,000 for those with more than 20 years.

Workplaces

Some occupational medicine physicians work directly for large companies. Others work with practices focused on occupational medicine or with groups of doctors from various specialties. These doctors see patients who are employed by many different companies and have work-related complaints. The practice of occupational medicine often includes both direct patient care and visits to worksites. There are also jobs in government, consulting, and academia.

Employment Outlook

The outlook for employment should be good. The current workforce is aging, which should lead to new openings as doctors retire. In addition, the specialty is not well known, even among physicians, which should limit competition for jobs.

For Further Information

- American College of Occupational and Environmental Medicine (ACOEM)
  www.acoem.org
- American College of Preventive Medicine (ACPM)
  www.acpm.org

EMPLOYEE HEALTH NURSE

Job Description

A nurse who works in employee health is responsible for certifying that employees are physically fit and assisting with the care of workers who have been injured; he or she also does work that helps keep a whole population of workers healthy. Like an occupational medicine physician, the employee health nurse must be alert for outbreaks of illness and patterns of injury that could signal a safety problem. He or she encourages employees to have annual flu shots and practice good hand hygiene. If the workplace is a health care center, employees must be tested routinely for tuberculosis and have other immunizations verified, so that they do not expose patients to dangerous diseases. The employee health nurse conducts any required drug tests. When workers are injured, the employee health nurse may be the one to manage and coordinate their care. Responsibilities may also include counseling workers with substance abuse problems or psychosocial concerns. Many employee health nurses are involved in writing health-related newsletters, teaching employees about safety and infection control, designing health promotion programs, and making decisions about safety in the workplace.

Education and Certification

Employee health nurses are usually RNs, and some are nurse practitioners. They must be licensed in the state where they practice, and a bachelor's degree is helpful. Also helpful is certification as a Certified Occupational Health Nurse by the American Board of Occupational Health Nurses. Some jobs also ask for other certifications related to the work, such as Certified Health Education Specialist. Precise job requirements vary according to the setting and workers' needs. Nurses who want to obtain upper-level positions helping to shape occupational health programs or policy, for example at government agencies or in industry, can benefit from earning an MPH with a focus on occupational health, a combined MSN/MPH, or even a PhD.

Core Competencies and Skills

- Familiarity with medical charting and coding
- Excellent communication skills
- Understanding of the company culture
- Background in worksite wellness or general health promotion
- Knowledge of workplace safety and health issues, OSHA regulations, and workers' compensation laws
- Ability to apply research findings and recommendations to real-life needs
- Knowledge of how to interpret data on workers' health
- Skills to design, implement, and evaluate health and safety programs that will have an impact on workers

Compensation

The median salary for an RN in 2014 was about $66,000 per year, with most earning between $46,000 and $99,000. According to a 2013 report from the American Association of Occupational Health Nurses, the median salary for members was $75,000, with higher education and certification associated with higher salaries.

Workplaces

Employee health nurses work for hospitals, factories, railroads, retail businesses, and universities—essentially, any type of company, organization, or agency with enough workers to justify having a department dedicated to their health. Nurses in the broader category of occupational health also work for private medical practices, government agencies, and research universities.

Employment Outlook

The demand for nurses, overall, is expected to continue to be high over the next several years. Opportunities for occupational health nurses will likely be good as well, particularly as many in the current workforce are nearing retirement. A recent NIOSH report has also projected, based on a survey of employers' hiring plans, that there will be a need for more new nurses in occupational health over the next several years.

For Further Information

- American Association of Occupational Health Nurses (AAOHN) *www.aaohn.org*

INDUSTRIAL HYGIENIST

Job Description

The field of industrial hygiene involves the anticipation, recognition, evaluation, and control of occupational health hazards. Industrial hygienists examine workplaces for potential health and safety hazards and make recommendations about what should be done to improve the safety of the workers. This includes not only recognizing current hazards but anticipating future ones. "Workplaces" can be dangerous places such as factories and mines, but they can also be academic settings, hospitals, and corporate offices. Industrial hygienists deal with many different types of hazards—noise that can damage hearing, chemicals that can irritate skin, fumes that can damage lungs, and more. They also work to prevent repetitive stress injuries and physical damage due to other causes. They look for ways to reduce the chance that workers will be exposed to a hazard in the first place. They limit risk further through policies that encourage safe work habits. When necessary, they recommend personal safety measures, such as masks and earplugs; if workers are not following the recommendations, they determine why not and how to increase compliance. Industrial hygienists can also be involved in scientific research. Some participate in determining national regulations and standards. Some do disaster preparedness work, such as helping local emergency medical services professionals understand what chemicals are used at a worksite.

Education and Certification

An industrial hygienist has at least a bachelor's degree in a field such as physics, chemistry, biology, or engineering. Many choose to pursue a master's degree focusing on industrial hygiene, an MPH with an emphasis in industrial hygiene, or a master's in a related field. The exact expectations and requirements vary according to the job. A Certified Industrial Hygienist (CIH) credential is available for industrial hygienists who have met academic requirements, have several years of experience, and pass a certifying examination. Although certification is not required, employers do tend to prefer it.

Core Competencies and Skills

- Good attention to detail
- Knack for the physical sciences
- Appreciation for technical work and measurement
- Good observational skills
- Ability to communicate clearly with employees from entry level to administration
- Good memory for rules and regulations, combined with knowledge of local and federal requirements for the workplace
- Willingness to get dirty during inspections at worksites or on factory floors

Compensation

The median salary for all occupational health and safety specialists, a category that includes industrial hygienists, is about $69,000 per year, with most earning between $40,000 and $101,000. According to the 2013 American Industrial Hygiene Association (AIHA) salary survey, the median salary among respondents was $100,000, with the top 10% earning $150,000 or more. Younger workers, probably early in their careers, reported average salaries around $70,000 compared with $132,000 for those aged 65 years and older. Those with CIH credentials tended to have higher salaries than those without.

Workplaces

Industrial hygienists work in many different industries, wherever workers' safety is a concern. They also work at federal government agencies such as OSHA and NIOSH. Many industrial hygienists travel to worksite locations to do inspections and observe practices, which can require them to face the same (potentially dangerous) conditions that onsite workers do. Others spend much of their time in an office setting.

Employment Outlook

The demand for people who work as occupational health and safety specialists is expected to slow down between 2012 and 2022, expanding more slowly than average. However, job opportunities for people with advanced degrees are expected to be good, and there should be room in the workforce as a large number of current workers retire.

For Further Information

- American Industrial Hygiene Association (AIHA)
  www.aiha.org
- American Conference of Governmental Industrial Hygienists (ACGIH)
  www.acgih.org
- American Public Health Association (APHA) section for Occupational Health and Safety
  www.apha.org/apha-communities/member-sections/ occupational-health-and-safety
- American Society of Safety Engineers (ASSE)
  www.asse.org

PUBLIC HEALTH PROFILE: Industrial Hygienist
Erica Stewart, CIH, HEM
National Environmental, Health and Safety Senior Manager
Kaiser Permanente, Oakland, CA

Describe the sort of work you do.

I work for Kaiser Permanente, the oldest and largest not-for-profit health care organization in the country. In addition to direct patient care settings, we have laboratories, steam plants, distribution warehouses, and optical lens production facilities; we even do construction. My job involves creating standards and policies that will prevent exposures to hazardous substances, or to conditions that could be dangerous. I also collaborate with different departments to come up with solutions to occupational health problems. Kaiser Permanente is very supportive of outside volunteer activity, and so I've been able to become involved in a NIOSH initiative called Prevention by Design.

(continued)

(continued)

We're looking at preventing occupational injuries from occurring by designing the workplace to anticipate and mitigate hazards.

What is a typical day like at your job?

My typical day consists of answering e-mails, meeting with people, and working on projects. One project I'm working on is creating hazardous materials inventories for new hospital construction. That means making lists of what materials will be found in each department and in what quantity, and then creating tables that compare the maximum allowable amount to the amount needed. The lists include all kinds of hazardous substances—even hand sanitizer. I'm also working with our National Facilities Services group, the department that sets our building standards.

I do four or five audits a year, where I go out to see what our employees actually do in practice versus what the policy says they should do, or what they say they are doing. The audits take about 60 hours, with 3 days on the site plus preparing and writing the report. I do department tours, interview employees, assess metrics, and calculate scores.

What education or training do you have? Is it typical for your job?

I have a bachelor's degree in biochemistry, and I'm a Certified Industrial Hygienist. I'm also a Certified Health Care Environmental Manager. It's common for people at my level to have graduate degrees, usually a master's in industrial hygiene or occupational and environmental health and safety.

What path did you take to get to the job you are in today?

My stepfather was an industrial hygienist, and he suggested that I go to work in an industrial hygiene lab. I thought it was really cool. You get to see what people do and then help make the work easier on them. I started doing different kinds of fieldwork, like testing emissions from manufacturing plants, and lab work like spectrophotometry. Later,

(continued)

(continued)

I did asbestos abatement project management, directing the safety aspects of the work. My first job at Kaiser Permanente was as an industrial hygiene technician, doing air sampling in sterile processing, in the lab, and in the operating room. I've been here for 19 years now, with progressive levels of responsibility.

Where might you go from here, if you wanted to advance your career?

The next step might be director or senior director, or even vice president, but I'm satisfied with where my career is now. I enjoy doing work that demands technical expertise, as well as managing people, and a higher-level title might mean that I'd be doing more managing and less technical work. I like to keep that balance of sharp technical skills while still mentoring and coaching junior staff.

What is the worst or most challenging part of your job?

Working with different kinds of people can be challenging. Sometimes it takes all of my skills to make sure I'm working on the problem and not the personality. It's not a matter of whether we like each other, but whether the problem is solved. You have to look at it from their perspective, so you get cooperation rather than resistance.

What is the best part?

My favorite thing is coming up with solutions to problems that have seemed intractable. It's really rewarding when I'm working with a group of people and we come up with something that is quantifiably better than it was before, and everyone benefits.

What advice do you have for someone who is interested in your career?

I don't think there's any one path to getting involved in this career. It can be through education and training, or doing fieldwork, or doing research. You can work in manufacturing, consulting, or services such as health care. I happen to like dealing with engineering

(continued)

(continued)

controls, while other people are more interested in doing training or air sampling. You do bring the experience from each job to your next one, so you can change from one focus to another. For those who are looking for advice I would also say find your local professional organization and get involved. Local chapters of AIHA are very helpful for networking.

CORPORATE MEDICAL DIRECTOR

Job Description

Physicians who serve as corporate medical directors can be in charge of many different aspects of health within a company. The exact responsibilities vary according to the size, type, and values of the corporation. At a large company, the corporate medical director's job can encompass worksites from offices to factories, at locations around the country or around the world. The medical director often oversees employee health services, deciding what will be offered at on-site medical clinics and ensuring that protocols are in place to address illnesses and on-the-job injuries. He may oversee preventive care programs—such as serving healthier food in the cafeteria or rewarding employees for getting fit. He may also advise on workplace hazards, such as identifying toxic substances and safety issues in the workplace. He may be in charge of protecting the health of employees who have to travel overseas, ensuring that they know where to get essential vaccinations and have somewhere to turn if they get sick while away. He guides the preparations for emergencies and disease outbreaks at company worksites. Some medical directors are primarily administrators, while others also provide patient care. Some are involved in health-related research pertaining to company products and in monitoring consumer complaints about injuries or illnesses. This job usually has regular business hours, although there may be after-hours calls for emergencies, and physicians generally use their own time to keep up with medical journals and research news.

Education and Certification

A corporate medical director needs an MD or DO degree and a current license to practice. For those who provide direct patient care in multiple locations, licensure in more than one state may be needed. Typical specialties are internal medicine, family medicine, or occupational medicine; training in occupational medicine or in preventive medicine and public health is particularly useful and can be an advantage when seeking a job.

Core Competencies and Skills

- Strong communication skills, including both writing and public speaking
- Good managerial skills
- Understanding of how the business world works
- Knowledge of epidemiology and the ability to interpret data
- Awareness of issues that arise in medical practice on the population level, in addition to one-on-one patient care
- Good understanding of occupational health issues, particularly regarding the work that the company does or products it manufactures
- Ability to work with business executives who may not understand the principles of occupational medicine and public health, and to educate them as necessary

Compensation

Physicians who share their expertise as corporate medical directors can expect to be well paid. At smaller companies, they may work as part-time contractors, earning from $100 to $300 per hour depending on their experience and skills, as well as on the local market. Typical salaries range from the mid to high $100,000s, for example, at a large manufacturing plant, to well over $200,000 for a high-level director at a major corporation. According to ACOEM, in 2012 the median income for a corporate medical director ranged from $210,000 to about $250,000, depending on the size of the organization.

Workplaces

Corporate medical directors work at all sorts of companies, from manufacturing to office settings.

Employment Outlook

Most large companies offer some type of employee health services, although not all will have their own, extensive health programs. For the past several years, there has been a lot of talk about employee health promotion as a way to keep insurance costs down and productivity up, so there may be expanding opportunities. Typically, a corporate medical director needs some experience in occupational settings and administrative work; one way to obtain this experience is to start by working part time with smaller companies or as an occupational medicine physician in one division or location.

For Further Information

- See the organizations listed with occupational medicine physician.
- American Association for Physician Leadership *www.physicianleaders.org*

PUBLIC HEALTH PROFILE: Corporate Medical Director
Ron Stout, MD, MPH
Medical Director
Procter & Gamble, Cincinnati, OH

Describe the sort of work you do.

I serve as a medical director at a multinational consumer goods company in the Beauty, Health & Grooming Sectors. We develop, manufacture, and market over-the-counter medications, vitamins, minerals, supplements, oral care products, shampoos, cosmetics, perfumes, electric and manual shavers, razor blades, and support our commercial hair salons. Over the past 16 years, I have served in a variety of medical leadership roles, including employee health, safety surveillance, and medical affairs.

Employee health responsibilities include monitoring, maintaining, and improving the health of employees across the world. We assure medical qualification and surveillance (traditional occupational health) and have focused recently on the connection between health and productivity. We are particularly interested in preventing illness and injury. Our safety surveillance organization responds to customer concerns, and reviews aggregate data for signals and

(continued)

(continued)

sentinel events. Medical affairs activities include engaging thought leaders, serving as principal investigator on research studies, and facilitating partnerships. For example, we've partnered with the CDC to develop a product that purifies drinking water in virtually any environment, at a cost appropriate for developing countries.

What is a typical day like at your job?

My days typically start at 6:30 or 7 a.m. with international calls, e-mails, and meetings. Later in the morning are leadership, team, and/or project meetings with global physicians, health leaders, or researchers on a development project. Much of the day involves project-specific work. When launching a new product, we'll review the active ingredients in collaboration with industrial hygienists and toxicologists. We develop surveillance protocols, work practices, and engineering controls to facilitate safe handling of ingredients. We "flow" to the work, assuring we can connect medical leaders around the world during their natural working hours, addressing business critical issues as they arise. The day often ends with an international call or web-based meeting.

When working on a development project, I meet with the project team to understand the objective and help design the research. I stay up to date on best practices in preventive medicine and primary care and provide leadership for our global "Save a Life" function, which is our emergency response system. We ensure that cardiopulmonary resuscitation and automated external defibrillators are available within 4 minutes, for every employee who is at work, around the world.

What education or training do you have?
Is it typical for your job?

I completed a MD and a couple of MPHs (health administration and public health) and am board certified in preventive medicine and general public health, occupational and environmental medicine, and in family medicine. I've studied epidemiology and completed industry-specific certifications. This is a pretty typical background for a corporate physician.

(continued)

(continued)

What path did you take to get to the job you are in today?

I completed a biology undergraduate degree and obtained an Air Force scholarship that paid for medical school. While on active duty in the Air Force, I served initially as the preventive medicine and then as the occupational medical consultant, also teaching in the School of Aerospace Medicine. After active duty, I served as the medical director for preventive medicine and occupational services at a Health Network and in the Air Force Reserves in the Surgeon General's office. I was subsequently offered my current position.

Where might you go from here, if you wanted to advance your career?

I would look for a challenge, perhaps in an organization with significant preventive/occupational opportunities. I'm also interested in further exploring the intersection between health and productivity.

What is the worst or most challenging part of your job?

The "art" of the job is gaining consensus in a global company with many stakeholders.

What is the best part?

My favorite part is the work we do to improve health, both in our own employees and in the developing world. I relish helping to leverage our company's assets to make a measurable difference.

What advice do you have for someone who is interested in your career?

Identify what you are passionate about and then go for it, recognizing that you must be a lifelong learner. Show up, be present, volunteer. Strive for education and experiences that will give you connections to thought leaders, innovators, the people on the cutting edge. Develop mentors, it makes all the difference.

REFERENCES

Bureau of Labor Statistics. (2014a, September 11). *Economic news release: Census of fatal occupational injuries summary, 2013*. Retrieved April 27, 2014, from http://www.bls .gov/news.release/cfoi.nr0.htm

Bureau of Labor Statistics. (2014b, December 4). *Economic news release: Employer-reported workplace injuries and illnesses—2013*. Retrieved April 27, 2014, from http://www.bls.gov/news.release/osh.nr0.htm

CHAPTER 12

Food Safety and Nutrition

When Upton Sinclair wrote *The Jungle* (Sinclair, 1906), he was hoping to raise awareness about abuses suffered by the American working class. But his book—detailing disgusting practices in the Chicago meatpacking industry—had an entirely different effect. An official report on the meatpacking industry confirmed much of what Sinclair had written. In 1906, Congress passed the Federal Meat Inspection Act, mandating certain inspections and sanitary standards (Institute of Medicine [US] Food and Nutrition Board, 1990).

1906 was also the year Congress passed the Food and Drugs Act, which laid out certain requirements for food (Swann, 1998). In the years since then, food safety regulations and requirements have been strengthened and expanded. Today, thousands of researchers, inspectors, educators, administrators, and others keep an eye on the food supply from farm to table and work to ensure that imported food is safe to eat.

Just because our food is very safe, though, does not mean we are always eating right, as the epidemic of obesity demonstrates. Both inadequate nutrition and obesity-related diseases are important problems that concern many public health professionals.

Two good places to begin learning more about food safety and nutrition are the Food and Drug Administration (FDA) and U.S. Department of Agriculture (USDA) websites (fda.gov and usda.gov) and the website nutrition.gov.

The careers described in this chapter are just an introduction to the many jobs concerned with the foods we eat. Others include health teacher, health educator, health promotion coordinator, WIC nutritionist, community health worker, deputy director/family health services, and study coordinator.

NUTRITION CONSULTANT

Job Description

Public health agencies and nonprofit organizations have many different programs to promote good nutrition. There are federal nutrition assistance programs like the Special Supplemental Nutrition Program for Women, Infants and Children (WIC), the School Breakfast Program, the Administration on Aging Nutrition Program, and the Child and Adult Care Food Program. There are also initiatives to encourage healthful eating and to combat obesity. These include improvements in the quality of school lunches, efforts to increase access to healthful foods, and even gardening, cooking, and nutrition classes.

Public health nutrition consultants contribute to these programs in many different ways. A consultant may work on developing the policies and standards that guide local or national efforts. He or she may provide technical assistance at the state or local level, training staff members as they develop their own programs or implement state or national initiatives. The consultant can help when program leaders are not particularly knowledgeable about the nuances of nutrition. He or she may assess statewide or local needs and evaluate programs, gathering and analyzing data to see if they are making a difference in levels of obesity, consumption of healthy foods, or other goals. Some consultants participate in community outreach directly, while some coordinate the work of community health workers, nutritionists, or other staff. The job can include collaborating with other agencies and local organizations. A consultant may also prepare reports and presentations to share with legislators, the media, and the general public.

Education and Certification

The title "nutritionist" can be confusing and somewhat controversial. In many states, this term is not regulated, so a nutritionist could be someone who took a class or two, but could also be someone with a PhD in nutrition. Public health agencies and programs generally seek employees with at least a bachelor's degree with a focus on nutrition, or a bachelor's plus additional nutrition-related coursework. Often, although not always, jobs for nutrition consultants require the registered dietitian (RD) credential from the Commission on Dietetic Registration at the American Dietetic Association. To become an RD, you need a minimum of a bachelor's degree with appropriate coursework, completion of an accredited, supervised practice program, and a passing score on a national exam. A master's degree in nutrition, an MPH, or a master's degree in a related subject can make a job applicant more competitive. A graduate degree also increases opportunities for upper-level positions.

Many states have laws regulating who can be called a dietician, and some do also regulate the title of nutritionist. It is important to seek out accredited training programs and be aware of potential employers' expectations.

Core Competencies and Skills

- Interest in the connection between food and health
- Sensitivity to diverse cultures, with the ability to adjust recommendations to cultural preferences and needs
- Up-to-date knowledge about the connections between nutrition and health
- At least basic knowledge of statistics and epidemiology, with the ability to interpret local and national data and study results
- Ability to develop programs appropriate to a given population's needs
- Knowledge of laws and regulations regarding public health nutrition programs
- Excellent verbal and written communication skills and a knack for teaching

Compensation

In 2014, the median salary for dietitians and nutritionists was about $57,000. Only 10% earned less than $35,000, and 10% earned over $80,000.

Workplaces

Actual job titles vary, but nutritionists doing these types of work are found at public health agencies and programs from the city to the federal level. Examples of employers include "healthy city" initiatives, state health departments, WIC and other USDA-sponsored programs, and the Centers for Disease Control and Prevention. There are opportunities at nonprofit organizations that focus on nutrition and disease prevention, in employee health and wellness programs, in programs at medical centers, and with consulting firms. Jobs with titles such as "nutrition program manager" and "nutrition program coordinator" often incorporate similar responsibilities.

Employment Outlook

A 2014 Association of State Public Health Nutritionists survey showed an increasing emphasis on obesity prevention and nutrition and health education, and the Bureau of Labor Statistics notes growing interest in the role of food for health, wellness, and disease prevention. Some survey respondents noted a need for more well-trained RDs or difficulty recruiting staff. Assuming funding is available to support these jobs, there may be an increasing role for nutritionists in public health. Nutritionists with graduate degrees will likely have the best opportunities.

For Further Information

- Association of State Public Health Nutritionists (ASPHN) *www.asphn.org*
- Also see the organizations listed for WIC nutritionist.

FOOD SERVICE SANITARIAN

Job Description

A sanitarian applies environmental control measures to protect human health and safety. (Sanitarian is an old term; today's sanitarians are often called "environmental health specialists.") Food service sanitarians are experts in the food safety issues that arise in places where food is prepared and served. Many work as city or county health inspectors. They visit restaurants, grocery stores, and other food sales outlets, as well as places such as school cafeterias, day-care centers, and nursing homes, to see whether they are in compliance with city and state food safety codes. They look at how food is stored, cooked, handled, and transported. They ensure that the premises are clean, they check for vermin, and they observe the workers. If they find something wrong, they issue citations and make recommendations about how to correct the problem. Sanitarians also investigate calls from consumers about food poisoning or about practices that look unhygienic. Another role for these inspectors is to review food safety plans submitted by restaurants before they open. If the location of the sinks, for example, looks likely to lead to problems, the sanitarian can offer constructive advice. In some areas, the food service inspector also has other environmental health responsibilities, such as inspecting swimming pools or investigating stream pollution and other community hygiene violations.

Education and Certification

Requirements for food service sanitarians vary. Many health departments require a bachelor's degree including substantial study of the biological and/or physical sciences, but some will accept an associate's degree with appropriate experience in food safety or environmental health. Some states require an examination and special licensing or registration. In addition to state credentials, the National Environmental Health Association offers a Registered Environmental Health Specialist/Registered Sanitarian credential; candidates must have either a bachelor's degree in environmental health or a degree in a different subject plus certain coursework and experience. There are also credentials specific to food safety.

Core Competencies and Skills

- Attention to detail
- Knowledge of food safety
- Willingness to inspect places that may be dirty or unpleasant
- Strong sense of ethics, including the willingness to stand behind the inspection results even if a restaurant owner or worker at an inspected facility objects
- The ability to offer constructive criticism and education
- Familiarity with regulations regarding food service and environmental health

Compensation

Salaries can vary according to location, experience, and level of responsibility, such as whether an inspector also supervises others. Many recent entry-level job listings have offered a range from the mid-$30,000s to the mid-$40,000s; a few other jobs openings, including supervisory roles, have had salaries up to the $70,000s. Most of these employers were looking for someone with at least a bachelor's degree, although some would accept an associate's with additional experience.

Workplaces

Food service sanitarians often work for health departments and other government agencies. They are also employed in the private sector, such as for restaurant chains, where they do quality assurance and risk management work.

Employment Outlook

Budget cuts can affect new hiring; nearly 10% of health departments had to reduce their food safety programs during a recession several years ago. Overall, however, health inspector jobs tend to be fairly stable, because state and local regulations create an ongoing need.

For Further Information

- National Environmental Health Association (NEHA)
  www.neha.org
- National Association of County and City Health
  Officials (NACCHO)—Environmental Health
  www.naccho.org/topics/environmental

PUBLIC HEALTH PROFILE: Food Service Sanitarian
Sara T. Losh, RS
Health Inspector
Health and Food Safety, City of Frisco, Frisco, TX

Describe the sort of work you do.

My department is responsible for inspecting all retail food establishments in Frisco, TX. That includes restaurants, convenience stores, schools, and day-care centers. Each place is inspected from one to

(continued)

(continued)

four times a year depending on its risk category, which is determined by the type of food and population they serve. When a new retail establishment is being built, we review the plans, and then we do a courtesy walk-through to make sure they are on the right track. We do a final health inspection before they can open.

What is a typical day like at your job?

Most days I start in the office, although some days I may start with inspections in the field. When I'm doing an inspection, I enter the establishment and ask for the person in charge. I ask to see their health permit and Certified Food Manager's certificate. Sometimes the owner or manager accompanies me on the inspection, sometimes not. I begin by washing my hands, and I'll check for hot water at the same time. Then I start in the back, looking at the kitchen and storage areas, and work around to the front. I look for insects and rodents, check food temperatures both on the line and in coolers, and check expiration dates. I also make sure the food comes from an approved source; for example, it can't be something that was made at home and brought in. I look for hair restraints on employees and make sure workers are not touching ready-to-eat foods with their bare hands. I look to see that floors, walls, and ceilings are in good repair and that drains are working properly.

Most places pass their inspections. Occasionally, an establishment does have to be closed for an imminent health hazard. I have the manager lock the door and post a sign that they are temporarily closed, and as customers leave the door is locked again behind them. We try to keep closings to a limited time, because we don't want restaurants to lose business, but they have to pass inspection to be able to open again.

What education or training do you have? Is it typical for your job?

I have a bachelor's in nutrition with a minor in business administration, which from my experience isn't typical at all. Registered sanitarians tend to have degrees in environmental health or one of the hard sciences.

(continued)

(continued)

What path did you take to get to the job you are in today?

I learned about this field in college. I was studying nutrition, and I actually overheard someone having a conversation about the type of work I'm doing now. I got a job supervising food service at a hospital and assisting the dietitian, but at the same time I studied on my own for the state RS examination. When I passed that, I answered an ad in the paper for a health inspector job with the city of Dallas. I came to work for the city of Frisco a few years later because it was an easier commute. I heard about the job through the Texas Environmental Association, which usually announces openings at their quarterly meetings.

Where might you go from here, if you wanted to advance your career?

I would accept a promotion if a position became available, but I am happy where I am right now. The next level from here would be a senior health inspector or supervisor position.

What is the worst or most challenging part of your job?

I don't like writing citations and fining people. Depending on how an establishment works, sometimes the manager has to pay the fine even if the problem is not his fault. Sometimes people get fired because of citations. I'm just doing my job, but I don't enjoy that part.

What is the best part?

It is especially satisfying to be able to catch something that might have made someone sick. People can die from foodborne illness, and I can help prevent that. Also, sometimes people in the establishments really don't know the right thing to do, and I can educate them.

What advice do you have for someone who is interested in your career?

When I started as an RS, I had never worked in the food industry before, and I had a lot to learn about that. My suggestion is to get into food service and do that for a while, so you know what it is like

(continued)

(continued)

to be on the other side. I think people with that experience pick up things faster. They know how the dish machine works, and they know how the service industry works. If you are in a food service job, look at the health inspector's report and talk to the inspector when he or she comes in. They will be more than happy to talk with you.

FOOD INSPECTOR/DEPARTMENT OF AGRICULTURE

Job Description

Food inspectors at the USDA or state agricultural departments verify the safety of meat, poultry, dairy products, and eggs, and of products made from these foods. They're involved in every step of food production, from commercial slaughterhouses and dairy farms to the assembling of TV dinners or the making of ice cream. Most inspectors at the USDA's Food Safety and Inspection Service (FSIS) start in privately owned slaughter plants, where they examine animals both before and after slaughter. At processing plants, inspectors help ensure the safe production of foods made with animal products.

Inspectors who want to advance their careers can seek promotion to more complex or less physically strenuous jobs. One career path at the USDA is to the position of consumer safety inspector. Consumer safety inspectors are assigned to one or more plants, where they make sure that sanitation standards are being met and that plans for food safety are properly formulated and carried out. Their responsibilities include working with plant managers, owners, and workers to explain regulations and address any violations; conducting samplings and surveys to assess potential problems; and making sure that products are accurately labeled. Another possibility is to become an import inspector. Import inspectors are stationed at a port or border crossing and are responsible for examining food that is being brought into the country.

Education and Certification

Food inspectors at the USDA need either a bachelor's degree, including a certain number of hours studying the biological, physical, mathematical, or agricultural sciences, or experience that pertains to what an inspector needs to know. Consumer safety inspectors typically need either experience as a USDA food inspector or experience doing similar work.

Core Competencies and Skills

- Attention to detail
- Honesty, with the ability to stand by a decision
- Interest in the science of food safety
- A strong stomach
- Willingness to handle animal carcasses and to be in an environment where animal-based food products are made
- Ability to handle relatively strenuous work
- Knowledge of laws and regulations regarding food safety

Compensation

Food inspector salaries at the USDA's FSIS start at the low $30,000s and go up to the $50,000s, with a few earning up to the low $70,000s. Consumer safety inspectors range from about the $30,000s to the $70,000s, with a few earning more. For agricultural inspectors in general (not just food inspectors), the median salary nationwide in 2014 was about $43,000 per year, with most earning between $25,000 and $63,000.

Workplaces

Many inspectors work for the FSIS. State departments of agriculture also hire inspectors to inspect slaughter plants, dairy farms, and processing plants. Private companies hire inspectors to make sure that they are complying with regulations. There are also inspectors involved in fruit and vegetable production.

Employment Outlook

Overall, the number of jobs in this field is expected to remain about the same over the next decade. However, the FSIS has periodically undertaken recruitment efforts, such as offering bonuses for people willing to work in certain locations, or creating a paid internship to learn the food inspector role. These jobs, including internship opportunities, are listed on usajobs.gov when available.

For Further Information

- U.S. Department of Agriculture Food Safety and Inspection Service (FSIS)
  www.fsis.usda.gov

- National Association of State Departments of Agriculture (NASDA)
  www.nasda.org

CONSUMER SAFETY OFFICER/FDA

Job Description

Consumer safety officers (CSOs) at the FDA fill many different roles related to the public's health and safety; food safety is one of the areas in which they work. Depending on the specific job, a CSO involved in food safety might be assigned to inspect factories where food products are made, warehouses where food is stored, or companies that handle distribution. CSOs make recommendations when violations are found and prepare written reports. When inspections lead to administrative hearings or judicial proceedings, they may be called to testify. They may also investigate complaints about food-related illnesses or about manufacturers' production processes. CSOs can work their way up to higher-level positions. There are CSOs who serve as consultants and advisors, who help shape policy, and who manage projects and programs. They may evaluate state programs to be sure that they adhere to national guidelines, advise industry on the interpretation of regulations, assess new technologies to determine whether regulations should be changed, and train other CSOs. Some CSOs serve as division directors, overseeing multiple staff members and taking on significant administrative and leadership responsibilities.

CSOs are located both at the FDA headquarters in Washington, DC, and throughout the United States, and some jobs involve significant travel. The job can have standard working hours, or—for certain inspectors, for example—it may include regularly scheduled weekend work.

Education and Certification

CSOs can qualify for entry-level jobs either through education or a combination of education and experience. The minimum education requirement is a bachelor's degree with significant study of the biological sciences, physical sciences, nutrition, or other fields related to the work. Alternatively, a CSO can have some college-level work (30 semester hours of relevant study) plus experience or other education that meets the needs of the job. Higher-level positions require further education or additional relevant experience.

Core Competencies and Skills

- Attention to detail
- Ability to make independent judgments
- Interest in food manufacturing and safety
- Understanding of how to assess safety risks
- Ability to understand complex regulations and apply them to real-world settings
- Good communication skills, including writing skills

Compensation

Current federal salaries for FDA CSOs start at the low $30,000s. Those who advance to supervisory positions or to positions requiring work of significant complexity and responsibility can earn substantially more, with top salaries reaching $100,000 and above.

Workplaces

The FDA employs a large number of CSOs. The Office of Regulatory Affairs is the primary department concerned with compliance and enforcement, with investigators who inspect the whole range of FDA-regulated products. There are also CSOs in other FDA centers, including the Center for Drug Evaluation and Research, the Center for Biologics Evaluation and Research, and the Center for Devices and Radiological Health.

Employment Outlook

CSO jobs are periodically listed on usajobs.gov, and at times the FDA has conducted hiring initiatives to meet workforce needs. Future job openings will continue to be influenced by funding, agency goals, and regulatory changes.

For Further Information

- FDA Office of Regulatory Affairs (ORA)
  *www.fda.gov/AboutFDA/CentersOffices/
  OfficeofGlobalRegulatoryOperationsandPolicy/ORA/default
  .htm*

FOOD SCIENTIST

Job Description

A food scientist is just that—a scientist who studies food. It is a broad field, ranging from nutrition to safety. Many food scientists work in industry, helping to develop new products, but they play an important role in public health, too. There are researchers studying food safety, including how much pesticide is found in food or whether genetically modified plants are safe. When a manufacturer proposes a new technology for pasteurizing or preserving food, food scientists test and evaluate the method to be certain that it is effective. Some food scientists study food packaging to evaluate how long a product will stay fresh and how to reduce the risk of contamination. Others look at how well preservatives work or how bacterial contamination spreads. There are jobs related to toxicology, such as exploring the potential effects of specific foods, preservatives, or packaging on people's health. Another focus is nutrition, such as studying the effect of cooking or canning on nutritional content or finding ways to add vitamins without changing the taste. There are food scientists involved in cutting-edge research, as well. All of this is primarily laboratory work.

On the regulatory side, food scientists help develop and implement new regulations and standards for keeping food safe. They gather information from the laboratory scientists and write recommendations, often combining deskwork with visits to factories and laboratories. Some food scientists inspect manufacturing facilities, and some provide education to the public or to manufacturers. Some are involved in protecting the international food supply. Some focus on risk analysis and its application to practice and policy.

Education and Certification

A bachelor's degree in food science will suffice for some jobs, but salaries are lower and the level of responsibility is generally less than with a graduate degree. A master's degree opens up more opportunities and allows for more specialized work. Many people who do food science research at the FDA have PhDs, but there are also opportunities for people with a bachelor's or master's degree. Some food scientists choose to earn MPH degrees, in addition to their other education, to broaden their knowledge of public health issues. The Institute of Food Technologists (IFT) offers a Certified Food Scientist credential, which requires a combination of education and experience plus an exam.

Core Competencies and Skills

- Curiosity and creativity
- Strong critical thinking and reasoning ability
- Good mathematical skills
- Understanding of how and why people make choices about what they eat
- Respect for food as a biological material
- Patience and the ability to see projects through to completion
- Knowledge of food production processes, quality control issues, and other elements of preparing and packaging food for sale
- Understanding of biology and chemistry as it relates to food

Compensation

A survey of members of the IFT found that in 2013, the average salary for a beginning food scientist with a bachelor's degree was about $45,000; with a master's, about $55,000; and with a PhD, $80,000. The median salary for all members was $90,000, and people with extensive experience were earning over $100,000 per year. In 2014, the U.S. Department of Labor estimated that the average salary for all food scientists and technologists was around $61,000, with most earning between $35,000 and $108,000 per year.

Workplaces

In the federal government, food scientists work primarily for the FDA and the USDA. There are jobs at state health departments and departments of agriculture, as well, depending on local needs and budgets. There are opportunities with nonprofit organizations, trade associations, and with individual companies. Some food scientists with doctoral degrees are researchers or professors at universities.

Employment Outlook

The employment outlook for food scientists is expected to remain good. Much of the growth will be in private industry, but increasing interest in food safety and nutrition could also lead to new opportunities in public health. The 2013 IFT survey reports an uptick in job openings, possibly due to economic recovery from a downturn. In general, well-trained food scientists, especially those with experience, should continue to be in demand.

For Further Information

- Institute of Food Technologists (IFT)
  www.ift.org
- International Association for Food Protection (IAFP)
  www.foodprotection.org

REFERENCES

Institute of Medicine (US) Food and Nutrition Board. (1990). *Cattle inspection: Committee on Evaluation of USDA Streamlined Inspection System for Cattle (SIS-C)*. Washington, DC: National Academies Press.

Sinclair, U. (1906). *The jungle*. Project Gutenberg EBook, released March 11, 2006. Retrieved from http://www.gutenberg.org/etext/140

Swann, J. P. (1998). *FDA's origin and functions*. Retrieved from http://www.fda.gov/AboutFDA/WhatWeDo/History/Origin/default.htm

CHAPTER 13

Disaster Preparedness and Response

Disasters—natural or man-made—can have devastating consequences for public health. A breakdown in the water supply can lead to epidemics of waterborne illnesses. Close quarters in shelters can encourage the spread of communicable diseases. People who have lost their homes, possessions, and livelihoods face high levels of emotional stress that challenge their ability to cope.

The events of September 11, 2001, brought home the fact that terrorist attacks could occur on U.S. soil, and many preparedness programs were started as a direct result. In 2005, Hurricane Katrina showed that there were still tremendous gaps in our nation's ability to respond to a public health disaster. Research and planning to ensure a thorough, rapid response to another such emergency continue to this day.

Today, many public health professionals consider disaster preparedness to be part of their jobs. No matter what their primary responsibilities are, health department employees participate in preparedness trainings and drills. Public health responsibilities after a disaster include ensuring availability of essential health care services, monitoring water and sanitation, controlling disease transmission, addressing injury prevention, alerting the public to health concerns, and seeing that vulnerable populations, such as the elderly and the disabled, receive the services they need (Landesman, 2006). Some experts use their skills to help manage the aftermath of disasters around the world.

There are researchers studying the physical elements of disasters—from disease vectors to the potential for bioterrorism—and the human response. There are experts helping to organize hospitals, emergency medical services systems, and individual doctors' offices, and others who are working on the best ways to handle chemical spills or nuclear radiation. Some experts are involved in planning communication networks and data collection systems to allow rapid assessment of public health needs. There are many opportunities in all areas of public health.

This chapter offers a sampling of the jobs in public health preparedness. Many of the people profiled in other chapters also mentioned disaster planning among their responsibilities. The list of specific jobs that could focus on preparedness is too long to include here—but as you look through this book, think about the needs associated with the subject of each chapter. There are disaster preparedness experts working in all of these fields.

EMERGENCY PREPAREDNESS SPECIALIST

Job Description

An emergency preparedness specialist (or "emergency response" or "emergency management" specialist) identifies potential emergencies, draws up plans for government and health care institutions to respond, and ensures that everyone involved is aware of their role if an emergency should occur. Emergency management specialists working in health departments and in other public health settings make sure that needed supplies such as food, water, and medical equipment are in place, and that health, safety, and sanitation service teams are prepared to respond. They write or approve manuals and emergency preparedness plans and make sure that the plans comply with national regulations and take advantage of available assistance. Often, they plan and run practice drills and exercises. They communicate and coordinate with other agencies involved in responding to major emergencies. They may inspect facilities that will be part of disaster response and ensure that communication systems are in place and that workers are properly trained. If an emergency occurs, they alert health care providers, public health professionals, or people involved in other vital services and help coordinate the response.

Education and Certification

A bachelor's degree is usually the minimum qualification, often with education or experience in public administration, public health, social work, or a related field. Because health-related emergency preparedness requires knowledge of the health care fields and the needs of doctors and patients, an MPH or a background in nursing, medicine, or pharmacy can be helpful. Some schools and programs of public health now offer certificates or even MPH concentrations in emergency preparedness. Training in emergency management can also be helpful; there are undergraduate and graduate degrees in this field. Free courses from Federal Emergency Management Agency are available online at training.fema.gov.

Core Competencies and Skills

- Excellent organizational and managerial skills
- Ability to remain calm under pressure and to keep others calm
- Ability to make decisions independently
- Good communication and presentation skills
- Awareness of news events and current risks
- Ability to work with people of different educational backgrounds and responsibility levels
- Knowledge of state and federal programs and regulations for emergency response

Compensation

National salary data is available for emergency management specialists, whose work typically overlaps with preparedness efforts; the median salary is about $64,000 per year, with most earning between $33,000 and $117,000. Some recent job openings specifically in emergency preparedness include a program manager in a major northeastern city with a bachelor's degree and a few years' experience, at $40,000 to $50,000 per year; an emergency preparedness specialist in a southern state, with a bachelor's and 1 to 2 years' experience, $43,000 to $74,000; and a preparedness planner in the Midwest, with similar credentials, $40,000. Salaries can increase with more responsibility and experience.

Workplaces

Emergency preparedness specialists work at all levels of the public health system and in all the areas of public health. They are found at local and state health departments, as well as federal government agencies. Some work with consulting firms or nonprofit organizations. Hospitals often have coordinators for emergency preparedness. Some corporations also employ specialists to plan the company's response to emergencies, focusing on keeping employees safe or protecting the community from events like chemical spills or nuclear power plant meltdowns.

Employment Outlook

Historically, the government has tended to respond to disasters and emergencies with increased funding, but then as time goes on, funding tapers off again. For example, in the years immediately following the events of September 11, 2001, there was a push to greatly increase preparedness efforts, but since then funding has declined to the point that concerns are being raised about our nation's capacity to respond to future emergencies. There does seem to be greater awareness of the need for emergency preparedness than in the past, so these jobs should continue to be available, but the outlook for new openings will depend on local, state, and federal funding priorities. The Bureau of Labor Statistics notes that global climate change could be a driver of new opportunities.

For Further Information

- Centers for Disease Control and Prevention (CDC)
  Office of Public Health Preparedness and Response
  www.cdc.gov/phpr
- Public Health Emergency website from the
  U.S. Department of Health and Human Services (HHS)
  www.phe.gov
- Preparedness Summit
  preparednesssummit.org

PUBLIC HEALTH PROFILE: Emergency Preparedness Specialist
Bindy Crouch, MD, MPH
Primary Care Emergency Preparedness Medical Coordinator
New York City Department of Health and Mental Hygiene, New York, NY

Describe the sort of work you do.

I coordinate emergency preparedness within the primary care community of New York City. For the most part that means outpatient

(continued)

(continued)

facilities, including the federally qualified health centers, some hospital-affiliated outpatient centers, and some private networks. We help the facilities do internal preparation and build capacity so that they can withstand a disaster on their own, and also be part of the New York City plan for public health emergencies. The types of emergencies we prepare for include pandemic influenza, outbreaks due to bioterrorism agents, emergencies due to hazardous materials, and even a nuclear bomb blast.

What is a typical day like at your job?

I spend about 60% of my time in the office and maybe 30% to 40% doing fieldwork. On a typical office day, a lot of my work is related to managing grants. On nonoffice days, I try to get out into the community. I might go to see how a health center is set up and how they are planning to separate infected and noninfected clients during an infectious disease outbreak.

I do a lot of coordinating with other city agencies. I relay information about what capacity the outpatient sites have, where they are, and what roles they could fulfill during an emergency. And I answer questions from the sites and talk with them about how pieces of the plans will be implemented.

My work also includes planning for antiviral distribution from the strategic national stockpile. With the H1N1 flu, I've been managing the process of getting vaccines to sites. Every other month, I also serve as "doctor of the week." For 1 week, I take calls from medical providers about infectious diseases, answer questions, and provide guidance about infection control and outbreak prevention.

What education or training do you have? Is it typical for your job?

Because this is a senior staff position, you have to be a licensed physician and board certified in at least one specialty. I have a medical degree, and I've completed residency training in family medicine and in preventive medicine, which includes an MPH. You could do some of this work without being a doctor, but you'd probably have a doctor overseeing everything you do.

(continued)

(continued)

What path did you take to get to the job you are in today?

I worked part time as a family physician while I was training in preventive medicine. This was my first job after completing my training. I applied for several different positions through the Department of Health website, and I worked with the recruiter at the department. I kept calling them on a regular basis and saying, "I applied for these positions, have you heard anything?"

Where might you go from here, if you wanted to advance your career?

I'm pretty happy with my level right now. At a health department, doctors usually come in as senior staff, and there aren't that many gradations after that. The next level would be medical director of our program—but there are just a handful of positions at that level. Another option would be to stay at this level but move to a different subject, a different area of public health.

What is the worst or most challenging part of your job?

There are some aspects of managing grants I don't like, like bugging people to get things in on time. Also, working within a huge bureaucracy, it can be difficult to get simple things done quickly.

What is the best part?

I am in a really good learning environment. In New York City there are so many other physicians and PhDs that even though it's government work, there is an element of academia. There is research going on, there are opportunities to speak at grand rounds, and there are weekly meetings to review cases.

What advice do you have for someone who is interested in your career?

An important decision to make is what role you want to play. Do you want to be managing people and programs? Do you want to be "boots

(continued)

(continued)

on the ground" and doing the work yourself? I'm in a management job, and that's about the level you come in at here if you're a physician. If you have visions of going out and giving people their tuberculosis medications every day, that's most typically not a physician's role. I think that how much you'll enjoy the job has much less to do with what the subject matter is and more to do with what kind of work you want to do.

Profile Update

Since her original interview, Dr. Crouch has moved on to global health work, first in Papua New Guinea, then in Vietnam, and now in a remote town in western Australia. She is currently a general practitioner at a community-controlled health center working with a federal initiative to "Close the Gap" on health disparities for indigenous people. Her focus is on maternal and child health, working to address the health impact of low education levels, financial and food insecurity, fetal alcohol spectrum disorder, and family violence.

DISASTER PREPAREDNESS RESEARCHER

Job Description

Public health planning for an emergency or disaster requires an understanding of how people are likely to behave and what they will need on both the physical and psychological levels. Providing such knowledge is the job of researchers who focus on disaster preparedness. These scientists study issues such as psychological responses to disasters, ways to help people remain calm, and procedures and programs that are most likely to gain the public's cooperation and prevent chaos. For example, if you recommend that people "shelter in place" (staying home rather than going to a central location), will they listen? Will doctors, firefighters, and ambulance personnel report to work, or will they stay home to try to protect their families? How can technology help keep people informed during a disaster?

Disaster preparedness researchers also share what they have learned with legislators and government officials, and they work to ensure that the knowledge they gather is actually used. The job usually combines deskwork with some degree of fieldwork or clinical research, which can include community visits and even international travel.

Education and Certification

Being in charge of this type of research generally requires a PhD or other doctoral-level degree in a medical, social science, or public health field. A master's degree, such as an MPH, or bachelor's degree will suffice for those who want to assist with the research. In some cases, people with master's degrees can also find work designing and carrying out their own studies.

Core Competencies and Skills

- Interest in problem solving and detective work
- Initiative and ability to see projects through to the end
- Good leadership skills
- Good verbal and written communication skills
- Understanding of human psychology and an appreciation for cultural differences
- Understanding of epidemiology and statistics, and the principles of designing and conducting research studies
- Awareness of current knowledge in emergency planning and the public's reactions

Compensation

Many people who do disaster preparedness research are university faculty. According to the 2013 to 2014 salary survey by the American Association of University Professors, the average salary for professors of any rank at institutions granting a significant number of doctoral degrees was $98,902; full professors earned an average of $138,472. Salaries were lower at schools focusing on master's or baccalaureate degrees. Faculty at private universities tend to earn more than those at public ones, and salaries are often higher in urban areas.

Workplaces

Researchers in the public health aspect of emergency preparedness are often based at universities, including schools of public health.

Employment Outlook

This is a specialized field, and there is a limited number of job openings. At the same time, however, there are a limited number of people who are interested in or qualified to do this type of work. Competition for jobs will depend on trends in government funding and in the decisions that today's degree candidates make about the direction of their work. Also, many current job openings are for accomplished scientists; a new graduate who does not find an immediate opening may be able to begin with a job in a related field, then look for appropriate grants and work toward making this a focus of his or her studies.

For Further Information

There is no single association for disaster preparedness researchers. However, these may be helpful:

- Columbia University's National Center for Disaster Preparedness (NCDP)
  ncdp.columbia.edu
- Natural Hazards Center at the University of Colorado, Boulder
  www.colorado.edu/hazards
- Disaster Research Center (DRC), University of Delaware
  drc.udel.edu
- Johns Hopkins Center for Public Health Preparedness
  www.jhsph.edu/research/centers-and-institutes/
  johns-hopkins-center-for-public-health-preparedness

PUBLIC HEALTH PROFILE: Disaster Preparedness Researcher
David Abramson, PhD
Director of Research
National Center for Disaster Preparedness
Columbia University, Mailman School of Public Health, New York, NY

Describe the sort of work you do.

The NCDP is a multidisciplinary academic center within the Mailman School of Public Health. We do public health research related to disaster preparedness, response, and recovery. We look at the health consequences of an event and ask, "What are the problems that can occur? How can they be prevented?" We think about the effects of policy, system readiness and interorganizational relationships, and

(continued)

(continued)

the impact of disasters on vulnerable populations. We consider solutions that can occur at the individual, community, or organizational level, all the way up to federal policy.

What is a typical day like at your job?

On any given day, I spend at least some of my time managing my research projects. That could mean running focus groups, speaking with assistants who are out in the field collecting data, or looking at the best way to make a research operation run. If I want to send 20 people to the Gulf Coast, I have to plan how to do that.

My days also include thinking about research questions and designing studies to answer those questions. For example, we know that people are generally not physically or emotionally prepared for disasters. My team and I have a hypothesis that people who have taken cardiopulmonary resuscitation (CPR) classes are more likely to be prepared—not just to do CPR, but to evaluate their environment, to make good decisions, and to help others in an emergency. If that's the case, it could be because the types of people who take a CPR class are themselves more likely to be prepared or because the class itself has had some effect. We need to figure out how to design a study to explore this.

Often, I spend part of the day writing up study results or writing grant applications. And part of the day is administrative. There are about 15 people working here, and many report to me. There are a lot of meetings, too—with staff here and with external parties such as government officials, funders, and subject matter experts.

What education or training do you have? Is it typical for your job?

I have a PhD and an MPH. The PhD is in sociomedical sciences, which in my case involved doctoral work in both public health and political science. I also have a BA in English, and I'm a former paramedic. To serve as primary investigator on the types of studies we do at NCDP, you generally need a doctoral-level degree.

What path did you take to get to the job you are in today?

When I was in my 20s, I was a journalist writing for national magazines, including *Rolling Stone* and *Esquire*. I lived in a rural area,

(continued)

(continued)

and I joined a volunteer ambulance corps just as something to do for the community. To work on the ambulances, I became certified as an emergency medical technician (EMT). Then, I wrote an article on trauma care in the United States, which allowed me to travel around the country and hang out with paramedics. And I thought, this is even better than being an EMT. I trained as a paramedic and thought about going to medical school, but I decided an MPH would be a better fit. I wanted to do my own research, and so after the MPH, I started working on my PhD. Shortly after I finished my PhD, I pitched an idea for a disaster-related research project to the director of NCDP. He liked it, and eventually he invited me to join the Center.

Where might you go from here, if you wanted to advance your career?

As faculty, I could work toward becoming a full professor and eventually a center director. Personally, I think my career may loop back to writing. I see the progression being toward writing books, a blend of popular and scientific writing. I could see doing a half writing and half research and teaching role.

What is the worst or most challenging part of your job?

I'm not fond of administrative minutiae and bureaucracy. Often, guidelines for submitting a grant proposal to the National Institutes of Health (NIH) or the CDC are filled with what seem like silly, stupid, or arcane rules. More often than not, it seems like a barrier to the work you want to do.

What is the best part?

My favorite part is thinking about a question and coming up with a study design to answer it. It's that whole formative process of getting the thoughts together, getting the people together, and building the teams. There are a million things to think about and it's very intellectually stimulating. The teamwork aspect is fun too. After years of being a solitary writer, going for days without talking to anyone—the camaraderie is terrific.

(continued)

(continued)

What advice do you have for someone who is interested in your career?

If you are not a very curious person, this is not the career for you. If you're never satisfied with what you read as being "the answer," then it's a career to consider. You also have to feel there is something fundamentally important about research. You have to be committed to the concept that research is a reasonable and laudable thing to be doing, and that it adds to the good of society.

Profile Update

Since his original interview, Dr. Abramson has transitioned from Columbia University to a faculty position at New York University's College of Global Public Health, where he created and leads a program on Population Impact, Recovery, and Resiliency (PiR2). The program's mission is to use social science and public health theory and methods to improve the well-being of populations affected by disasters and other major stressors. He manages several federally funded, state-funded, or foundation-funded "disaster science" projects, with a particular focus on the impacts of disasters on children and their recovery and resiliency. He is also a founder of SHOREline, a peer-to-peer program to help kids and teens affected by disasters.

BIODEFENSE RESEARCHER

Job Description

Biodefense researchers are involved in preparing for the possibility—hopefully remote, but still very real—of a major infectious disease outbreak or an act of bioterrorism. This type of preparedness requires understanding what pathogens or toxins could be used against a population, how tools to diagnose a new disease can be developed *fast*, whether vaccines can be developed, what can be done to ward off biologically based toxins or minimize their effects, and so on. Some of the research is highly practical, whereas some is designed to improve the base of knowledge for future work. Much of this research involves cellular- or molecular-level work using sophisticated equipment. Some researchers do animal studies. As researchers advance through their careers, they may move from doing hands-on work to leading laboratory teams. In most cases, applying for funding to support the research is also part of the job.

Education and Certification

This type of research almost always requires a PhD. Typical areas of expertise include microbiology, virology, bacteriology, immunology, biochemistry, and molecular genetics. Some researchers also have MDs, DVMs, or other clinical degrees. Some have pursued public health training, such as an MPH, in addition to the doctoral degree.

Core Competencies and Skills

- Interest in "hard science" and laboratory research
- Willingness to work nontraditional hours if the research requires
- Ability to think creatively and devise innovative solutions to problems
- Interest in collaborating with other experts to share knowledge and ideas
- Experience with designing studies, carrying them out, and interpreting the results
- Knowledge of cellular and molecular mechanisms of infectious diseases and biologic toxins, as well as their effects on the body as a whole

Compensation

Salaries for researchers focusing on biodefense depend on experience, location, and specialty. A typical range for faculty in the biological sciences, according to the Bureau of Labor Statistics, is $40,000 to $150,000, with about 10% earning less and 10% earning more. As with other types of laboratory research, new PhDs doing postdoctoral work start at lower salaries, whereas directors of research centers are at the top of the scale.

Workplaces

Until 2014, the NIH supported several Regional Centers of Excellence (RCEs) for Biodefense and Emerging Infectious Diseases Research, which brought together researchers from universities and research centers around the region. More recently, a newer program, Centers of Excellence for Translational Research, was established to build on the work of the RCEs. Scientists who do biodefense research are often employed at universities but can also be found at medical centers, non-profit research institutes, government-run laboratories, and other places where basic research is carried out. There are also opportunities in the federal government, including the military.

Employment Outlook

Future opportunities will depend largely on the availability of government funding, as well as on the number of new PhDs interested in this type of work. The level of funding for preparedness work, as well as the specific research grants available, is often influenced by which events and risks have received prominent attention in recent years.

For Further Information

- National Institute of Allergy and Infectious Diseases (NIAID)—Biodefense
  www.niaid.nih.gov/topics/BiodefenseRelated/Biodefense/default.htm
- CDC—Emergency Preparedness and Response/Bioterrorism
  www.bt.cdc.gov/bioterrorism
- U.S. Army Medical Research Institute of Infectious Diseases
  www.usamrid.army.mil

REFERENCE

Landesman, L. Y. (2006). *Public health management of disasters: The pocket guide.* Washington, DC: American Public Health Association.

CHAPTER 14

Health Communication

Communication is an essential part of public health work. Health departments and government agencies need to be able to share information with the public and with doctors and other clinicians. Within the public health system, different offices and agencies need to be aware of changes in regulations and policies. Research findings must be disseminated to have an impact.

Sometimes, public health communication is urgent. Citizens need to know when a water purification plant has problems and if they must boil water before drinking it. Doctors need to know if a batch of vaccines is contaminated. And when there are public health scares—a rumor about a contagious disease, for example—people need to know the facts before fears get out of hand.

Other types of communication are planned in advance to address public health issues. There are public campaigns to promote exercise, healthful eating, condom use, HIV testing, and other choices that prevent disease and promote good health. And there are day-to-day outreach efforts to keep important issues in the public's consciousness or remind them of an organization's role. These campaigns may be carried out by local or federal agencies, or by outside organizations concerned with the public's health.

Then there are the research reports, policy papers, regulations, and myriad other documents that circulate among public health professionals, the people who collaborate with them, and the legislators and other stakeholders whose cooperation is essential. Many of these documents are written by researchers or policy makers, but others are created by experts in public health communication. They gather the information and present it in a format and style that match the intended audience.

This chapter has some typical jobs in public health communication. Several other careers in this book may include heavy communications responsibilities; these include medical officer, veterinarian, health promotion program coordinator, medical epidemiologist, injury prevention specialist, community activist, nutrition consultant, consumer safety officer, emergency preparedness specialist, advocacy director, policy analyst, grant writer, and the several different researchers.

JOURNALIST

Job Description

Is journalism really a part of public health? It can be. The media is a major source of health information. Newspapers and magazines run regular stories about health issues, and television news often includes a daily health segment. Health journalists are specifically trained to report on these kinds of stories. They give people information that they need to stay healthy. A health journalist with an interest in promoting public health can seek out opportunities to investigate food contamination hazards, expose dangerous practices at a factory, explain how to avoid infectious or chronic diseases, and correct myths and misunderstandings. He can also focus on policy, such as helping the public to understand discussions of health system reform.

Journalists divide their time among gathering information by phone and online, conducting telephone interviews with experts, participating in press briefings, attending hearings and events, and writing their articles or reports. Television reporters may do on-site reporting at medical centers and laboratories. Investigations may take reporters all over the country or even the world, and health reporters are often called to the scene after hurricanes, earthquakes, and other disasters that require a public health response. In today's media world, reporters may also need to be able to write stories geared toward the Internet, take their own photos, and even shoot and edit videos.

Education and Certification

A bachelor's degree in journalism or mass communications, with classes in science or health reporting, is the most straightforward path to a medical journalism career. A degree in another subject can also be acceptable, if it is combined with experience such as writing for a high-quality college newspaper or interning at a newspaper or television news program. A master's degree provides additional training, makes a candidate more appealing to employers, and can offer entree into the field for those who have an undergraduate degree in a different subject. Any journalist can find himself writing health-related stories, but some master's degree programs allow a focus on health reporting. Some schools offer a master's degree specifically in health journalism. Multimedia skills can also be useful. A few organizations offer fellowships for journalists to get more in-depth experience on policy or health issues, or courses and workshops to help journalists learn more about specific topics.

Core Competencies and Skills

- Superb written and spoken communication skills
- Basic understanding of biology, medicine, and public health issues
- High level of comfort with "cold-calling" experts, patients, company executives, and other people who are strangers to you
- Curiosity
- Good interpersonal skills
- High level of integrity
- Ability to work under pressure and to meet tight deadlines
- Ability to tell a story in different ways for different audiences
- Understanding of what facts are important and of what will be interesting to readers
- Knowledge of how to create and use video and social media

Compensation

It is difficult to find salary information specifically for health journalists, but in 2014 the median salary for reporters in general was $36,000 per year. Most earned between $21,000 and $82,000. Top journalists can earn $100,000 and more.

Workplaces

Journalists work for newspapers, magazines, television stations and networks, websites, and other media outlets. Typically, staff reporters cover multiple beats, not just medicine and public health. There are also many freelancers who come up with story ideas, pitch them to editors, complete the assignments they receive, and send out their own invoices for payment.

Employment Outlook

Journalism jobs are constantly in demand, because people tend to think of them as glamorous and exciting. However, good journalism jobs are getting harder and harder to find due to declining revenue and a shift to online media with less in-depth reporting, as well as a proliferation of bloggers and other unpaid writers whose work is increasingly accepted by the public. A combination of training, talent, persistence, and patience remains the best route to landing a health journalism job. Agreeing to intern at a newspaper or television station has traditionally been a good way "in," but it is increasingly important to consider the future of the organization and if it is realistic to expect a paid job to follow. Today's journalists often cobble together multiple types of work—from news reporting to writing for foundations or niche publications—to create a career.

For Further Information

- Society of Professional Journalists (SPJ)
  www.spj.org
- Association of Health Care Journalists (AHCJ)
  www.healthjournalism.org
- National Association of Science Writers (NASW)
  www.nasw.org

COMMUNICATIONS DIRECTOR

Job Description

A communications director (also sometimes called a public relations director or director of public affairs) manages the interface between a corporation, government agency, or nonprofit organization and the outside world. It is this person's job to ensure that communication with the public or news media is accurate, timely, and clear. Communications directors also aim to put the organization in the best possible light and to further its goals. There are many opportunities for communications professionals in public health. Government agencies and nonprofit organizations have communications teams to field questions from reporters, connect journalists to the most appropriate experts, and prepare fact sheets, press releases, and information updates that reporters can use. In small organizations, the director may also carry out most of the work; in large ones, he or she oversees a staff. At a health department, the communications director helps control what information is released in case of an outbreak, epidemic, or other public health crisis. He or she is also in charge of managing any public concerns or criticisms about the organization and its work.

This is generally an office job with standard hours, but when events are scheduled, emergencies happen, or important campaigns are launched, weekend work and late evenings can become the norm. Outside meetings and travel may also be important elements of the job.

Education and Certification

A communications director needs at least a bachelor's degree, and a master's degree may be preferred. Typical subjects are communications, journalism, public relations, and marketing. Often, a degree in a field that matches the agency's or organization's interests is also acceptable. Some employers now look for candidates with an MPH in addition to other training. Communications professionals generally start in lower-level jobs and work their way up to higher-level positions; a communications director usually needs at least several years of experience. No special certifications are required, but voluntary certifications are available, such as the Accredited in Public Relations designation through the Public Relations Society of America.

Core Competencies and Skills

- Excellent written and spoken communication skills
- Good time management and organizational skills, to help reporters meet deadlines
- Knowledge of public health issues important to the agency or organization
- Understanding of the needs of reporters, bloggers, and others who share information with the public
- Understanding of marketing principles, including how to plan a campaign and evaluate its success
- Knowledge of how to use the Internet and social media to get a message out
- Ability to write a press release and prepare other materials for reporters to use

- Good sense for business strategy and for planning toward long-range goals
- Ability to handle topics that are sensitive or controversial
- Good interpersonal skills and initiative to develop connections with reporters, other media professionals, and experts

Compensation

For public relations specialists in general, the median salary in 2014 was $56,000, with most earnings between $31,000 and $106,000. The median salary for public relations and fundraising managers was about $101,000, with the top 25% earning $143,000 or more. Salaries at nonprofits are often lower than in industry, and some communications directors choose to accept these smaller salaries to work for causes and organizations they believe in.

Workplaces

Just about every large company, nonprofit, and government agency has a communications director. Communications specialists who are interested in public health can be found at local and state health departments, federal agencies involved in health or safety, and nonprofits devoted to specific health issues or focusing on the quality and availability of health care.

Employment Outlook

There is likely to be growth in the public relations job market, especially with the rise of new media and increasing channels for communication. However, like jobs in journalism and advertising, these tend to be competitive positions because people think of them as exciting, creative, and even fun. It can be hard to find a job in a specific agency or subject area, so it is often a good idea to accept a job in a related area, get some experience, and then watch for other openings. Starting with an unpaid internship can be a good way to get experience and make connections, too.

For Further Information

- Public Relations Society of America (PRSA)
  www.prsa.org
- National Black Public Relations Society (NBPRS)
  www.nbprs.org
- The Association for Women in Communications (AWC)
  www.womcom.org

PUBLIC HEALTH PROFILE: Communications Director
Katherine Hull
Vice President of Communications
Rape, Abuse and Incest National Network, Washington, DC

Describe the sort of work you do.

I handle communications for the Rape, Abuse and Incest National Network (RAINN), a national nonprofit dedicated to preventing sexual violence and helping victims of rape and abuse. This is an enormously important issue: 1 in 6 women and 1 in 33 men in the United States will be sexually assaulted in their lifetimes, and victims are at increased risk of depression, substance abuse, and even suicide. RAINN addresses these issues on a population level by operating a national telephone and online hotline, educating the public, and working toward improving policy. At the communications department, we promote the work of RAINN to the public through a variety of different means. That includes public relations, marketing, social networking, and even working with members of the entertainment industry.

What is a typical day like at your job?

A main aspect of my job is working with the media, which is a balance between proactive and reactive interactions. Proactively, I'll contact specific reporters when we have a story that I think they will be interested in—and reactively, I'll help reporters who call for information on stories they are working on. I also look for ways that RAINN can contribute to a breaking story. For instance, when a celebrity recently disclosed her experience with being sexually abused as a child, we were able to work with key reporters to talk about the impact on Americans, as demonstrated by the large number of calls to our hotlines. We transformed the media coverage from a story about just one celebrity to a story about how a celebrity inspired thousands of people to reach out for help.

As the organization's spokesperson, I sometimes participate in radio or television talk shows. We also work with the entertainment industry on their depictions of sexual violence. In one of my favorite

(continued)

(continued)

experiences, I helped the writers of a soap opera craft a scene accurately depicting the aftermath of a sexual assault, to teach viewers how to preserve forensic evidence and report to police. Another aspect of my job is working with our celebrity supporters. I'll coordinate with publicists and brief celebrities before events or media interviews.

Some of my other responsibilities are managing the organization's website and social networking presence, overseeing our newsletter, and writing press releases.

What education or training do you have? Is it typical for your job?

You don't necessarily need a degree in communications to do this type of work. My bachelor's degree is in political science and history. Many people at my level have a bachelor's or a master's degree.

What path did you take to get to the job you are in today?

I moved to Washington, DC, because I wanted to get involved in politics. My first position was an internship on Capitol Hill for a senator. It was a fabulous experience, but it left me with a desire to explore other areas of work. I took a job with a public affairs firm where I gained experience in crisis management while working for the firm's client base of large for-profit companies. I learned more about communications and the media, and the importance not just of doing good work, but of telling people about it. I realized that I wanted to help a good nonprofit organization tell its story. A friend sent me the job posting from RAINN.

Where might you go from here, if you wanted to advance your career?

I'm constantly setting new goals, finding new partnerships and new ways to reach out to our target audience, so every day is different and exciting. In my current position, I head up the department, so I suppose if I wanted to make a change, the next step would be working for a larger organization. Knowing how to tell the story behind an organization or company is a valuable skill set that could translate to any issue.

(continued)

(continued)

What is the worst or most challenging part of your job?

It's frustrating when a reporter omits information I've pushed for in a piece. For example, there have been times when I've invested a lot of time with a reporter on a specific story, only to find that a mention of our organization didn't make the final cut. Sometimes, it is not even the reporter's fault—the editor makes the cut. At the end of the day, you can't let it bother you too much. It is just part of the job.

What is the best part?

I really enjoy working with the entertainment industry and working with television show writers on plotlines related to our issues. I also love having the flexibility to pursue goals that further the organization's mission and on a personal level, feel challenged on a daily basis. It can be difficult to hear stories of people who have suffered, but what gets me through the day is knowing that the work we are doing is helping people turn their lives around.

What advice do you have for someone who is interested in your career?

Determine what you're passionate about. When you read the news and look at advertisements, notice what topics you're drawn to, and from there look for jobs in a related field. For nonprofit positions, look for job postings in places where companies can place ads for free, because a lot of nonprofits don't have the resources to pay for ads. As you're applying for jobs, remember that details matter! Spell-check your resume, don't leave in the track changes notes, and ensure that the cover letter is geared toward the organization you are applying to.

SOCIAL MARKETER

Job Description

Social marketing practices have been used by international health organizations for many years. Social marketing firms and departments use the same techniques and concepts that advertisers use to sell televisions, fast food, and new cars—but they use them to sell healthy behaviors, instead. (Make sure not to confuse social marketing with social media marketing, which uses online communities, blogs, and social networks like Twitter to sell products.)

A social marketing team usually begins with an established need, such as convincing young adult men to be tested for HIV. They do marketing research to figure out what appeals to the population in question. Do these men watch television? Are they likely to pay attention to cell phone text messages? Why aren't they being tested for HIV, and what would make them more likely to do so? Next, the team comes up with slogans, scripts or ad copy, sample text messages, and so on. They test them with members of the population; then they create final versions and launch the campaign. Afterward, they track the response through surveys, data on web page views, and other measurement techniques. Often, a social marketing expert must figure out how to help an organization accomplish a big goal on a very modest budget.

Social marketing agencies work for many different clients and on many different topics. Some organizations have in-house social marketing departments focusing just on their own causes. The job itself is largely office based but can include conducting focus groups, collaborating with community organizations, attending video shoots, and other outside meetings and events. There may also be travel to meet with clients.

Education and Certification

There is no single set of qualifications for social marketing. Increasingly, employers are looking for master's degrees and/or strong experience in the field. An MPH, a degree in communications, marketing, or journalism, a background in social psychology or another social science, or a background in advertising can all be appropriate. Training or experience in marketing and advertising is helpful. A few schools do now offer graduate-level training specifically focused on social marketing or behavior change communication, such as an MPH with a social marketing focus or a certificate in public health communication and marketing.

Core Competencies and Skills

- Excellent written and spoken communication skills
- Creativity
- Awareness of current social trends and fads, or the ability to find out
- Appreciation of diversity, including the fact that different community groups have different priorities

- Strong understanding of marketing and media, including how to place ads, gain reporters' attention, and appeal to the general public
- Ability to meet deadlines
- Understanding of how to present information for people with low health literacy
- Knowledge of survey and evaluation techniques

Compensation

Salaries for people involved in social marketing will vary depending on the type of organization, the amount of funding available, and the scope of the work. A starting salary in the $40,000 to $50,000 range would not be unusual, with higher salaries for people with more experience and responsibility.

Workplaces

Many people involved in social marketing work for independent firms that offer their services to health-oriented nonprofits and government agencies. Some of these are established advertising or consulting agencies, while others are small start-ups with just a few clients. Other people involved in this field work directly for government agencies, for university departments, or for nonprofit organizations that focus on specific health issues. A great deal of this type of work is focused overseas.

Employment Outlook

Awareness of social marketing seems to be increasing, but many people in American public health are still either unaware of this discipline or uncertain about what the term means. On the other hand, this means that a creative, ambitious person has the opportunity to blaze new trails, such as helping to start a company or create a new department. Overall, opportunities will depend on interest from government and nonprofits and on the funding available. One way to get a toehold in this field is to begin with an internship at a social marketing firm; another is to begin with a job in communications or community outreach that incorporates some social marketing efforts.

For Further Information

- You can learn about social marketing campaigns by visiting companies' websites and looking at their work. Also look for university departments focusing on Social and Behavior Change Communication.

- Centers for Disease Control and Prevention (CDC's) Gateway to Health Communication and Social Marketing Practice *www.cdc.gov/healthcommunication*
- Johns Hopkins Center for Communication Programs *ccp.jhu.edu*
- International Social Marketing Association *www.i-socialmarketing.org*

PUBLIC HEALTH PROFILE: Social Marketer
Les Pappas
President and Creative Director
Better World Advertising, San Francisco, CA/New York, NY

Describe the sort of work you do.

I own an agency that does social marketing with a focus on health and social issues. We work closely with clients to make the most effective use of their resources. We do needs assessments, help clients understand how to get a message out, develop campaigns and interventions, and evaluate the effects of our campaigns. We work in all communication vehicles, including television, radio, print, and billboards, and we're doing more and more on the Internet. We do most of the creative work in-house and also hire photographers and illustrators and other help as needed.

We've done campaigns on many topics, and each one requires its own approach. Doing suicide prevention with teens is very different than trying to get adults to stop smoking. Right now I'm doing an AIDS prevention project in Indonesia. The setting, culture, values—everything has to be taken into account.

What is a typical day like at your job?

As the president and creative director, I have a hand in just about everything. A typical day could involve working with our designers on developing concepts for ads, writing copy for brochures, facilitating focus groups, and doing media buys and strategies. Yesterday, I was

(continued)

(continued)

talking to a cable company about adjusting the time slots for some commercials, and then I was writing proposals to potential clients for some web and brochure work. I write and edit reports on focus groups, I write recommendations for clients on what we advise for campaigns, and I create annual reports for clients—lots of writing, editing, and reviewing documents.

I also have a lot of meetings with clients, other stakeholders, and advisors. We have lots of brainstorming sessions, too. The heart and soul of what we do is coming up with ideas and developing concepts for campaigns. And then of course we find the best ways to carry them out.

What education or training do you have? Is it typical for your job?

I have a bachelor's degree in government and history and an MPA degree. We have people on our staff who have MPHs, people who have experience in advertising, people who have degrees in communications, graphic designers, and artists. This kind of work is generally very collaborative, so it is nice to have people with different backgrounds and different experience.

What path did you take to get to the job you are in today?

I started out working on political campaigns. I worked for Ted Kennedy and for Paul Tsongas in Massachusetts. Then I moved to San Francisco in the early 1980s, at the same time that HIV/AIDS was coming onto the scene. As a gay man, I was very drawn to that issue, and I started working for the San Francisco AIDS Foundation. That's how I got into public health and social marketing. I learned about market research, focus groups, all that sort of thing, in order to do the work we needed to do. Eventually, I decided I wanted to expand to other issues, and I wanted to share what I had learned. I started Better World Advertising in 1996.

Where might you go from here, if you wanted to advance your career?

I own the company, so for me the "next step" would have to be pretty impressive. The independence would be very hard to give up.

(continued)

(continued)

For the people working within the company, there are lots of different career avenues. There are many issue-oriented organizations that have in-house people to work on social marketing, so that would be one option.

What is the worst or most challenging part of your job?

One challenge lies in educating the clients. We're known for creating campaigns that are kind of edgy, that push the envelope. Sometimes being controversial or confrontational helps to get people's attention. But clients often work within bureaucratic systems that don't reward taking risks. That means most of the social marketing you see is kind of boring and safe, and we don't do that. We have to educate our clients about the fact that they have to take some risks to get results.

What is the best part?

Before I started doing social marketing, I didn't even know I was a creative person. But I found that I am. It is in the ability to communicate, to come up with ideas, to write copy. I also enjoy having the opportunity to put my ideas out there—that I can be walking down the street and see a bus go by, and my company's ad is on that bus.

What advice do you have for someone who is interested in your career?

You need to be passionate about the issue you are working on, but you also need to have some objectivity and distance to create a good social marketing campaign. The people who do suicide prevention or adoption work or HIV vaccine research are completely immersed in that issue all day every day. I do that for part of my day. You have to have a balance between passion and objectivity.

Profile Update

A few years after his original interview, Mr. Pappas is still with Better World Advertising and loving his job. He's enjoying the fact that, as he continues to gain experience and seniority in this field, he has more and more interesting opportunities. During the past few years

(continued)

(continued)

he's been working on new public health issues, targeting different audiences with new clients. He is working on two American Indian social marketing campaigns, one with the FDA and one with a consortium of Tribes in Michigan. He says he especially loves meeting new people and learning about other cultures, particularly through a public health lens. He is also working on emerging topics like e-cigarettes, the heroin overdose epidemic, and PrEP for HIV prevention. He says that every day there's a new challenge and a new way to use both his time and his skills to help make life better for people.

MEDICAL WRITER

Job Description

Medical writers create informational articles, reports, and educational materials for consumers, health professionals, and public health experts. (There is an overlap between this role and that of "science writer," which encompasses a much broader range of writing about issues in science and health.) Their work may appear in magazines, on websites, on television, and in other media outlets. Or, they may write documents, newsletters, and articles targeted to very specific audiences. Unlike journalists, medical writers generally do not seek out news stories or investigate health claims or questionable practices. Instead, they organize and summarize health information. For example, a medical writer might be behind a series of website articles, sponsored by a government agency, offering information for parents about children's health problems. There are medical writers who compose educational materials to keep health professionals up to date about new developments in patient care and public health. Medical writers are also involved in helping researchers craft grant proposals, and some write regulatory documents for government agencies. Medical writers must be able to understand complicated research studies, policy issues, textbooks, and experts' opinions and present the information in a readable, straightforward, and useful way.

Education and Certification

Some medical writers come from journalism backgrounds. Others have bachelor's or higher degrees in biology, chemistry, or physics. Some are trained as doctors or nurses. People with advanced degrees are common in medical writing—among the writers responding to an American Medical Writers Association (AMWA) survey in 2011, more than a third had degrees above a master's. Although there is no specific educational pathway to this job, a medical writer must have the knowledge to interpret health information accurately. Medical writers can pursue training through self-study modules or in-person workshops, such as those provided by AMWA. Writers can also apply for a Medical Writer Certified credential, a certification program from the AMWA and the Medical Writing Certification Commission.

Core Competencies and Skills

- Excellent writing skills
- Curiosity about medical and public health issues
- Knack for "translating" information from medical research and complex reports into less difficult language, and for matching the reading level to the audience
- Ability to write in multiple styles
- Understanding of what sort of information doctors, nurses, other professionals, and the general public need to know
- Ability to meet deadlines, which can sometimes be tight

Compensation

According to a 2011 survey of members of AMWA, the median entry-level salary for a medical writer was about $60,000. For early-career writers, with less than 5 years' experience, median salary was about $72,000. Salaries for people with strong skills and experience or advanced degrees can range to $100,000 or higher. Writers for government agencies and medical education companies do tend to be at the lower end of the pay scale, compared to those in for-profit industries. Full-time freelancers can often earn over $100,000 per year in gross income, although they do not receive employee perks such as paid vacation or health insurance.

Workplaces

In public health, medical writers work for government agencies like the CDC or the U.S. Department of Agriculture (USDA), state and local health departments, research organizations, consulting firms, and nonprofits. There are also jobs at websites focusing on medical information for the public. Many medical writers are freelancers, taking on specific assignments for various clients. Medical writers can also find work with pharmaceutical companies and other for-profit industries, but these jobs are usually related more to selling products than to promoting health.

Employment Outlook

Medical writers are consistently in demand, and in fact the field has expanded in recent years, although some of this may have been due to new drug approvals and jobs at pharmaceutical companies, which are not usually public health roles. Breaking into the field can be challenging, however. Writing for smaller organizations and publications, even for free, can be a way to collect some "clips" (sample articles) to show potential employers.

For Further Information

- American Medical Writers Association (AMWA)
  www.amwa.org
- National Association of Science Writers (NASW)
  www.nasw.org

CHAPTER 15

Education

This chapter is about the people who ensure that our children learn basic information about health, our public health professionals are prepared for practice, and our doctors, nurses, and dentists are up to date. All of these types of education contribute to our nation's capacity for health and safety.

For the general public, lack of basic health knowledge can have serious consequences. Misunderstandings about disease transmission can lead to personal illness—or a citywide epidemic. Myths about sex can lead to HIV infection and other serious infections, as well as unintended pregnancies.

There are educational needs for health professionals, too. The training that they receive when they earn their degrees is just the beginning. Health information can change *fast*, thanks to new discoveries—and if our providers' knowledge is out of date, it becomes a problem for everyone. "Continuing education" classes and activities help health professionals keep their knowledge sharp.

Training for public health professionals is vital, as well. Schools of public health help ensure that the public health professionals are equipped to meet local, national, and global needs. They also support the research that leads to new innovations. Federal agencies, health departments, nonprofits, and other organizations offer courses and webinars to share the latest public health tools and information.

HEALTH TEACHER

Job Description

Health teachers educate children and teens about their bodies and about healthy choices in areas such as nutrition, personal hygiene, disease prevention, and safe sex. In public schools, they are generally required to follow a set curriculum; some private schools allow teachers to design their own courses. Health teachers sometimes have to avoid certain topics, too—for example, some school districts forbid teaching about contraception. Most states have adopted some form of health education standards, often following the National Health Education Standards, which emphasize skills for healthy living (U.S. Department of Health and Human Services, Centers for Disease Control and Prevention, 2013).

Health teachers usually teach several classes per day. Depending on the school, they may teach just one age group, or multiple levels. They adapt their lessons to meet the needs of each group of students. In some settings, health teachers work with other teachers in the school to dovetail lessons or to promote schoolwide health campaigns. Many health teachers serve as physical education (PE) teachers, as well. In addition to classroom time, health teachers spend time preparing their lessons, decorating their classrooms, and grading assignments. They enjoy summers off, although many use that time to earn extra money or take classes to further their own education.

Education and Certification

Public school teachers must be licensed, which requires completing a teacher training program and usually an examination, plus taking continuing education classes to maintain the license. The most straightforward path to becoming a health teacher is to earn a bachelor's or master's degree in health education, in a program specifically designed to lead to teacher certification. Many schools look for health teachers who can also lead PE classes; this requires extra preparation, such as a double major with PE. For people who are already certified, each state has its own requirements regarding additional training for health teachers. There are alternative paths to licensure to fill certain teacher shortages; these also vary by state and subject. Private schools can generally hire teachers who are not licensed, although they may choose to make it a requirement.

Core Competencies and Skills

- Adaptability
- Good organizational skills
- Good time management skills
- Sense of humor
- Ability to keep kids focused and well-behaved
- Ability to explain complicated information in a way kids can understand
- Knowledge of how to find reliable information in the library and on the Internet

Compensation

The median salary for a teacher in 2014 was about $57,000 per year at the elementary school level; $58,000 at the middle school level; and $59,000 at high schools. Most teachers at elementary through high schools earned between $36,000 and $88,000. Salaries can vary substantially from one school district to another.

Workplaces

Health teachers work at public and private schools. Middle and elementary schools are most likely to require health education. High schools are most likely to require that health education be carried out by teachers specifically trained in this field, followed by middle schools and then elementary schools.

Employment Outlook

The need for health teachers will vary by location, because it depends on student enrollment and local requirements. Enrollments are expected to increase in the South and the West over the next several years, decline in the Northeast, and remain steady in the Midwest. Job prospects for teachers will likely be better in urban and rural areas, compared to suburban districts. Health teachers will find the best prospects in areas with high enrollment and in districts that require health education to be delivered by certified health teachers.

For Further Information

- Society of Health and Physical Educators (SHAPE America) *www.shapeamerica.org*

- American Public Health Association (APHA)—School Health Education and Services Section
  www.apha.org/apha-communities/member-sections/school-health-education-and-services
- American School Health Association (ASHA)
  www.ashaweb.org

PUBLIC HEALTH PROFILE: Health Teacher
Steve Haines, MA
Health and PE Teacher
Newtown Friends School, Newtown, PA

Describe the sort of work you do.

I teach at a private school for children in prekindergarten through eighth grade. I cover sixth- to eighth-grade PE and health, I'm the athletic director, and I coach three sports teams. I also teach a section of eighth-grade history. There was no PE or health curriculum when I started here, so I created it, and I add to it constantly. Sixth-grade health class covers human development, including puberty, male and female anatomy, pregnancy, and some sex education. In seventh grade, the focus is on nutrition. Eighth grade involves independent student or group research and a lot of class debate. We investigate difficult issues such as abortion, right to die, capital punishment, alcohol and drugs, and even intimate partner violence.

What is a typical day like at your job?

My day starts with homeroom. Then some days I teach two classes, and some days I teach four out of the six periods. I supervise students during lunch, recess, and study hall. I coach after school, too, usually 3 or 4 days a week. I use my free periods to grade tests and papers.

I'm constantly updating my lesson plans with new information and activities. Each health class starts with something to pique my students' interest. I'll look for a short video clip, for example, that pertains to what we'll be learning. And then I give them some information, and then we transition into an activity that they can do. We close with something that provides a practical application, like a change they might consider making in their own lives.

(continued)

(continued)

In PE, I try to teach a lot of personal fitness. I'm trying to get the kids to take responsibility for their strength and their core muscle development. When we do team sports, I try to choose ones that kids can do socially, not just at school. I try to set games up so that no one's sitting out for very long, and I'm a constant cheerleader for the kids at all levels of fitness.

What education or training do you have? Is it typical for your job?

I attended a private Christian school, and then I went to Philadelphia College of Bible as a double major in Bible and PE and health, with a minor in history. My teaching certification is only for private school; if I wanted to teach at a public school, I would need a different certification. I earned a master's degree in history after I started teaching, for my own interest and because I wanted to have options—I couldn't imagine still chasing third graders around at age 50!

What path did you take to get to the job you are in today?

My goal was always to teach PE and health in a private school, and this was my first job after graduating. I had driven by this school for 4 years going to college and never knew what a "Friends School" was. But then when I was looking for a job, I decided to call them. They didn't have anything at the time, but they said to go ahead and send a resume, and I did. And shortly thereafter, a job did open up.

Where might you go from here, if you wanted to advance your career?

A lot of people end up in administration, as division head or as principal. I could see myself doing that, but I don't know that I really want to. Many people find the type of teaching they enjoy and just keep doing that, and that may be what I'll do.

What is the worst or most challenging part of your job?

The kids have all this tech stuff, and educators are thinking that the only way that kids can learn in the 21st century is if we wow them with technology. But I think we're losing content in the process, and

(continued)

(continued)

I'm disappointed by that. I also think it leads to a failure to hold kids accountable. If you forgot your homework, it's going to be online on the class website. You're not expected to write it down anymore.

What is the best part?

What I enjoy most about teaching is the relationships I'm able to form with students. I have the opportunity to see these kids grow for 3 years, because I teach them in sixth grade through eighth grade. I see them develop their skills. To me, teaching is about more than the subject itself. I'm helping these kids learn the skills they need to live a successful life.

What advice do you have for someone who is interested in your career?

Decide what age groups you want to work with. If you can, take opportunities during your training to visit schools or classes with age groups you might be interested in. If you think you only want to teach kindergarten through third grade, try to get into that age group when you are student teaching, so you can see for sure if you like it.

CONTINUING EDUCATION COORDINATOR

Job Description

Continuing education is required in many different professions. There are continuing education courses specifically addressing public health topics, such as updates about controlling a measles outbreak, guidelines for new vaccines, methods for widespread cancer screening and prevention, and disaster preparedness. Courses providing clinical updates help encourage doctors, nurses, and pharmacists to provide high-quality care. A continuing education coordinator is part of a team that helps get information to the professionals who need it. These organizers take on the day-to-day tasks of connecting with topic experts, working with venues or scheduling space within a medical center, and making sure that online programs are working properly. They keep an eye on deadlines and verify that programs meet national requirements. They handle registration for events, scoring of any tests, and approval of credit for participants. They also help to promote the activities to the appropriate doctors, nurses, or other professionals. Coordinators may be involved in writing grant applications to fund programs, too.

Education and Certification

Some coordinator jobs focus on administrative duties. These generally require a bachelor's degree plus good office skills. Some jobs require a bachelor's or master's degree in a related field, such as public health, nursing, or biomedical sciences. There is a new, optional credential available from the Commission for Certification of Healthcare CPD Professionals, part of an effort to standardize skills across the profession. (CPD stands for Continuing Professional Development.)

Core Competencies and Skills

- Ability to multitask
- Excellent organizational skills and the ability to track elements of a project until it is completed
- Ability to work as a member of a team
- General understanding of educational principles
- Strong sense of ethics, to avoid bias in educational programs
- Knowledge of the requirements for continuing education programs

Compensation

The 2010 to 2011 Medical Meetings Salary Survey found a wide range of salaries for continuing medical education professionals, from under $50,000 to over $150,000. Many were in the range of $50,000 to $100,000, but a substantial number earned less than $50,000, particularly at medical schools. Most people answering the survey had been in this career at least 5 years.

Workplaces

Continuing education coordinators are found at health professions schools and at hospitals and medical centers that provide continuing education programs. There are also many private companies that provide continuing education; these tend to be for-profit companies, and people interested in public health will need to assess the balance of profit versus educational motives.

Employment Outlook

There are no national statistics on job outlook for this particular job title. However, with so many doctors, nurses, and other health professionals needing to meet continuing education requirements, there is an ongoing need for programs. One aspect to watch, however, is how much continuing education transitions from in-person meetings to online education; a shift toward online programs could mean lower staffing needs.

For Further Information

- Alliance for Continuing Education in the Health Professions (ACEHP)
  www.acehp.org
- Society for Academic Continuing Medical Education (SACME)
  www.sacme.org

PROFESSOR, SCHOOL OF PUBLIC HEALTH

Job Description

Schools of public health have professors teaching classes in just about every public health-related topic imaginable. There are courses on health economics, cancer epidemiology, the influence of gender on health, the medical issues that arise in refugee camps, and many other issues. The professors who teach these classes usually have personal experience with the subject matter, either as researchers or through experience in previous careers. They share their expertise with undergraduates, graduate students, or both, depending on the school. They decide what information will be included in a class, assign readings, projects, and papers, and grade their students' work. In large lecture classes they often have help from teaching assistants. Sometimes, professors bring in outside experts to share their experiences, too. Professors often teach two or three classes each semester, with each one taking up a few hours of weekly classroom time plus many more hours in preparation and grading. They may also serve as advisors to individual students working on independent projects. With the rest of their time, they do research, write papers or textbooks, and prepare applications for grants to fund their work. Some offer consulting services to government agencies or businesses, or collaborate with nonprofits and community groups. Professors' research interests may bring them into medical laboratories or clinics, out into the community, and even to exotic locations overseas.

Education and Certification

Becoming a professor at a university usually requires a high-level academic degree, such as a PhD, MD, or DrPH. Some public health professors hold MBAs or JDs. Often, those who were originally trained in a field other than public health have earned an MPH, as well.

Core Competencies and Skills

- Patience
- Creativity
- Initiative (to conceive of research projects, find support, and see them through)
- Strong written and spoken communication skills
- Ability to motivate students
- Ability to break information down into manageable segments that people new to a topic can understand
- Deep understanding of one or more aspects of public health, with an interest in learning more

Compensation

Professors usually start at an entry-level job with a title such as "assistant professor." With a strong track record of research and publications, they eventually reach the rank of "full professor." The average salary for faculty of any rank at universities with a significant focus on doctoral-level education was $98,902, based on the 2013 to 2014 salary survey by the American Association of University Professors. Assistant professors earned $78,797 on average and full professors, $138,472.

Workplaces

In addition to schools of public health, professors specializing in public health can be found at medical schools, schools of veterinary medicine, dentistry, and nursing, and university departments focused on related topics such as ecology, sociology, and psychology.

Employment Outlook

The number of schools of public health has been increasing steadily, and this is expected to continue as interest in the field grows. Between 1998 and 2008, the number of applicants to schools of public health went up from about 20,000 to 35,000 per year. The number of undergraduate public health degree programs has also substantially increased, from 45 in 1992 to 176 in 2012.

Overall, the need for postsecondary teachers—professors and others who teach students who have already completed high school—is expected to expand, and it appears this will be true in the field of public health as well. At the same time, however, academic jobs, particularly tenure-track jobs, are quite competitive. (Tenure is a designation, based on accomplishment, which guarantees a certain level of job security.) Many colleges and universities have been rethinking how tenure works and are offering fewer-tenure-track positions and more part-time and non–tenure-track positions as a cost-saving measure.

For Further Information

- Association of Schools and Programs of Public Health (ASPPH) *www.aspph.org*

DEAN, SCHOOL OF PUBLIC HEALTH

Job Description

The dean at a school of public health is both an academic and administrative leader. Working with faculty and with other leaders at the university, the dean is instrumental in shaping the school's educational programs, research, and service, and in raising the funds that keep the school running. He or she also represents the school in the public and professional community. Day-to-day work can include meetings with professors and administrators about educational strategy, discussions about the budget and how the school is funded, conversations with other public health leaders, and events to keep funders aware of the school's plans and accomplishments. The dean provides guidance on what is best for the school and its students, as well as on how the school can maximize its contributions to the science and practice of public health. To do so, he or she must have extensive knowledge of public health practice and must keep up to date on developments in the field. Another important part of the job is knowing how to delegate tasks effectively. A school of public health will generally have assistant or associate deans who oversee specific areas of responsibility, such as financial matters or human resources. This job requires a significant time commitment beyond standard working hours, including evening events and travel to meetings and conferences.

Education and Certification

A dean must be an experienced and accomplished scholar in a public health field. The job requires a terminal academic degree, such as a PhD or DrPH, and significant achievements in research and practice. Institutions look for people who have demonstrated abilities in leadership and strategic planning. The traditional way to become a dean is to begin as a faculty member and rise through the academic ranks. However, people with other types of public health leadership experience can be considered for the job, if they meet the qualifications.

Core Competencies and Skills

- Strong management skills
- Excellent communication skills
- Ability to manage multiple responsibilities and delegate tasks effectively
- Ability not only to get along with diverse faculty members, but to help them get along with each other
- Extensive knowledge of and experience in a public health field
- Understanding of potential funders' interests and of how to connect their interests with those of the school
- Sense of dedication to maintaining high standards, developing effective new programs, and integrating the school with the community and the larger world of public health

Compensation

According to the 2014 to 2015 salary survey by the College and University Professional Association for Human Resources, the median salary for a public health dean was about $292,000. Salaries do vary according to the institution's funding and the individual's qualifications and experience.

Workplaces

This job is found only at universities with schools of public health.

Employment Outlook

The role of dean is open only to particularly accomplished scholars and leaders. There are about 50 accredited schools of public health in the United States, so the number of openings is extremely limited. Faculty members who are interested in becoming dean of a school of public health should look for opportunities to demonstrate leadership in addition to conducting research, publishing scholarly papers, and maintaining an excellent reputation at the school and in the wider public health world.

For Further Information

- See the information in the description for professor, school of public health.

PUBLIC HEALTH PROFILE: Dean, School of Public Health
Linda P. Fried, MD, MPH
Dean
Mailman School of Public Health, Columbia University, New York, NY

Describe the sort of work you do.

The Mailman School of Public Health has about 300 full-time faculty and more than 1,000 students. We are dedicated to the development of knowledge that will improve our society, and we have the privilege of creating knowledge that will have an impact not only today but in 20 to 30 years. We translate information and research results into innovative and impactful ways to prevent disability and illness, both for the community and for the use of individual clinicians, and we bring that knowledge to bear in educating future leaders. As a dean, my job is to guide the school as we strive to accomplish our mission. It's about finding what will have the most impact and make the most difference.

What is a typical day like at your job?

I come in around 8 or 8:30 a.m., and I'm done in the office around 6:30 or 7 p.m. Then, there is often a meeting in the evening or a dinner with someone to talk about raising funds for the school or other important issues.

(continued)

(continued)

There are many things I might do on a typical day. An important part of my day right now is meeting with members of my core team for strategic planning. We've set the goals of the school for the next 5 or 10 years, and we are working hard on implementing a strategy that will allow us to meet those goals. I direct and oversee the shaping of this entire effort. I appoint leaders, but I stay engaged and attend the meetings. I'm the guide, the cheerleader, and the coach.

Another big part of my job is finding the resources to accomplish our school's goals. I'm responsible for seeing that the school is in good financial shape. I plan the budget, together with the vice dean who is in charge of that. I work with my development office to identify grants we should apply for. I meet with individual philanthropists who might be interested in funding our efforts. I have also been involved in improving our research infrastructure, and I work with faculty on changes to our curriculum. I serve as the school's representative to the outside world, too, so I talk to reporters, I write articles and op-eds, and I even get involved in public policy. And I meet with students to find out how their educational experiences are going.

What education or training do you have? Is it typical for your job?

I have an MD and an MPH, and I have a great deal of experience in the worlds of public health, geriatrics, science, medicine, and leadership. A dean is usually someone who has had an influential career as a scientist or educator and has already led programs of significance.

What path did you take to get to the job you are in today?

I majored in history and had several jobs before working as a welfare caseworker, which is what sparked my interest in health care. My medical training focused on general internal medicine, geriatrics, and cardiovascular epidemiology. I spent many years as a professor at the Johns Hopkins University, where I served as director of multiple research centers and led many studies on aging and health. I'm also a cofounder of Experience Corps, a program that engages older adults to tutor and mentor elementary school students and is also a health promotion program for the older adults. I was elected to the National Institute of Medicine in 2001, and I have participated in

(continued)

(continued)

many national and international conversations related to issues in gerontology, how we transform well to an aging society, and how to keep all of us healthy. The job of a dean is usually offered by invitation, and I was invited to take on the leadership at Mailman.

Where might you go from here, if you wanted to advance your career?

A dean could go on to be a university president, to lead a foundation, to take a high-level position in a government agency. As for me, I love my job! I could be happy doing this for a long time.

What is the worst or most challenging part of your job?

My workdays can be long, so I would say one of the hardest parts has been learning how to balance a demanding professional life with a fulfilling personal life.

What is the best part?

I care greatly about the issues that I am working on. I also get to be deeply intellectual, and I get to be a scientist at a level that I love. I like thinking about the big picture, how to make a change, and how to lead so that the school achieves the best possible outcomes.

What advice do you have for someone who is interested in your career?

You're smart to think about it, because it's fabulous! I would say to invest in understanding the stages of a career, go in directions that you care about, and try to make a difference. Learn the skills of leadership and management, even if it's not part of your job description. Learn time management, how to handle conflict constructively, and how to set a clear long-term goal. At each stage of your career, look for ways to add to those skills, and think about the next step so you are prepared to move into it.

REFERENCE

U.S. Department of Health and Human Services, Centers for Disease Control and Prevention. (2013). *Results from the School Health Policies and Practices Study 2012.* Retrieved from http://www.cdc.gov/healthyyouth/data/shpps/pdf/shpps-results_2012.pdf

CHAPTER 16

Health Disparities, Vulnerable Groups, and At-Risk Populations

Certain groups are at particularly high risk of health problems compared to the population as a whole. Health disparities between certain ethnic and racial minority groups and White populations are one major concern. There are significant disparities in many types of cancer, diabetes, infant mortality, and the prevalence and incidence of HIV, for example (U.S. Department of Health and Human Services Office of Minority Health, 2014, 2015a, 2015b).

The reasons for many of these disparities are not completely clear. Causes probably differ from one health problem to another, and from one population to another. Does it have to do with where people live? Their culture or lifestyle? It is an effect of racism? Differences in income or access to care? Public health professionals throughout the country are working to find the answers and to bring our entire population to the same standard of health.

Other types of populations are at elevated risk of certain health problems, too. The elderly, people with physical and/or mental disabilities, people living in poverty, recent immigrants, and refugees are all vulnerable to certain health concerns. Prison inmates are a special population with elevated health risks and a limited ability to control their own care.

In addition to the careers in this chapter, many other public health jobs focus on improving the health of vulnerable groups or can incorporate this goal as part of a larger scope of work. They include medical officer, public health nurse, study coordinator, health educator, health promotion coordinator, public health dentist, behavioral scientist, injury prevention specialist, environmental health nurse, community activist, emergency preparedness specialist, social marketer, health teacher, behavioral health program manager, public health social worker, public health advisor, outcomes researcher, and program officer, as well as several of the jobs in the chapters on health care administration and leadership and maternal and child health.

DIRECTOR, OFFICE OF MINORITY HEALTH

Job Description

Many state health agencies have offices dedicated to alleviating health disparities. The exact names vary, but "Office of Minority Health" is a common variation; other names include "Office of Health Disparities" and "Office of Health Equity." Some city and county health departments have their own such offices, focusing on local needs. These departments use a combination of activities to accomplish their goals, and they have directors who are closely involved in the day-to-day work. Typically, the work of a county Office of Minority Health will be based on information about the health of different population groups, including things like premature births, vaccination coverage, and diabetes prevalence. The director, often working with a small staff, attempts to identify where the disparities are and to begin figuring out why they exist. Then, the office sponsors programs or works with community groups to address the problem. Some of the programs are traditional, but some can be quite creative—like training barbershop staff to talk to their clients about cancer screening or sponsoring health-related contests at high schools. The director oversees these efforts, helping to plan programs and events, drawing up and managing the department budget, applying for funding, making long-range plans, and collaborating with the leaders of other departments and outside organizations. Bringing community groups together, guiding and assisting with their efforts, and providing information and resources they need can be a significant part of this job.

This is an office job, but one with a lot of interaction with community organizations and outside agencies. The director may be expected to represent the department at events that occur in the evenings and on weekends.

Education and Certification

At some local minority health offices, the director is a physician. At others, the director has an MPH, a master's degree in another related field, or a bachelor's degree with experience in local community health programs.

Core Competencies and Skills

- Ability to interact with and gain the trust of people from many different backgrounds
- Ability to handle multiple projects at once
- Understanding of epidemiologic principles
- Awareness of health equity issues and of existing programs to address health disparities
- Experience planning different types of outreach programs and knowledge of how to evaluate their success
- Experience with local minority groups and with the community organizations that are working to address their needs

Compensation

Salaries for local minority health directors reflect their qualifications as well as local budgets. Recent job listings, generally seeking candidates with master's degrees in public health or public administration, have offered salaries ranging from about $45,000 to $90,000.

Workplaces

Minority health offices are found in health departments at every level of government. At the federal level, there is an Office of Minority Health and Health Equity at the Centers for Disease Control and Prevention and a separate Office of Minority Health at the U.S. Department of Health and Human Services.

Employment Outlook

Each state has a division or department focusing on health equity, often as part of the health department. Some cities and counties have their own minority health departments, or a community partnership focusing on this issue. Attention to health disparities is now a standard part of grant proposals and of public health planning, so this should continue to be an active area of interest. People interested in minority health can also find positions elsewhere in local health departments, at universities, or with nonprofit organizations; eliminating health disparities is a common theme in many public health programs.

For Further Information

- Office of Minority Health, U.S. Department of Health and Human Services (OMH)
  minorityhealth.hhs.gov
- National Association of State Offices of Minority Health (NASOMH)
  www.nasomh.org
- Office of Minority Health and Health Equity (OMHHE), Centers for Disease Control and Prevention (CDC)
  www.cdc.gov/minorityhealth/index.html

PUBLIC HEALTH PROFILE: Director, Office of Minority Health
Duane Herron, MPH
Minority Health Program Coordinator
Toledo-Lucas County Health Department, Toledo, OH

Describe the sort of work you do.

I work for the combined city and county health department, and I'm primarily assigned to a coalition of community groups that address health disparities through a number of different activities. I'm sort of a mediator, coordinating the activities within the coalition, supporting the work of the different groups, and helping them work together. The four major goals of my office are to report and monitor the health status of minority populations; to inform, educate, and empower our communities; to mobilize community partnerships; and to support policies and programs that focus on minority health initiatives.

What is a typical day like at your job?

Here's one recent day. I started in the office, spending a couple of hours writing and editing a strategic plan for the Office of Minority Health. Then I attended a conference on obesity. That meeting brought together local nonprofits, health care organizations, local government agencies, schools, and individuals from the community.

(continued)

(continued)

Next, I had a lunch meeting with my program evaluator. We're working on a grant proposal for a youth development program, and we'll be replicating a program that another organization uses. Afterward I met with some of that organization's key staff members. I spent the rest of the day compiling what I learned and getting it back to the program evaluator.

Other tasks include looking at research data to learn where the most serious disparities are or to find other information we can use. I plan monthly coalition meetings with various community groups. Sometimes an organization wants me to contribute an article or a column to their website, and I'm also responsible for our own website. I serve as a resource for various grant-funded programs in our area, too. Someone may be writing a grant proposal and want my advice.

What education or training do you have? Is it typical for your job?

My undergraduate degree is in community health, and my MPH focuses on health promotion and education. Not all the minority health program coordinators in Ohio have MPHs, but I think it's pretty common for a job like this.

What path did you take to get to the job you are in today?

I was working as a waiter when I decided to volunteer for an HIV prevention program. A year later, I was hired as that organization's HIV risk reduction specialist. My boss encouraged me to get a degree, and so I went to school to study community health. By the time I finished, I realized that I wanted to have an important influence, and the best way to start down that path seemed to be an MPH. My internship for the MPH was at the health department here, and I was assigned primarily to the local commission on minority health. I had a job as a health coach after graduation, but my supervisor at the health department knew I was interested in the coordinator job. When they needed to fill the position, they asked me to join their team.

(continued)

(continued)

Where might you go from here, if you wanted to advance your career?

Eventually, I'd like to go back to school for a PhD in public health epidemiology. I'm not sure whether I'll end up working in minority health or health disparities, specifically, but I'd like to have an upper-level job influencing health policy at the state or national level.

What is the worst or most challenging part of your job?

There are so many programs, and so many organizations trying to help, but the rate of disease is still rising. Because this is a relatively new field, we don't always know yet what works best. I'm trying to help the community think critically about that, so we can work toward having effective programs that are driven by outcomes and will really make a difference.

What is the best part?

I like not knowing what's going to come next. Minority health is an emerging field, there is a lot of money available right now, and the field is growing. We have lots of opportunities for funding to continue addressing health disparities, and many states are looking to us for direction. I also enjoy the fact that I'm working on behalf of the community—and the people that I serve really do appreciate it.

What advice do you have for someone who is interested in your career?

Never underestimate the value of volunteer experiences. I understand community issues better because I was a volunteer in a community organization. After I got my degree, that experience also made it easier for me to find a job. Have a blend of academic experience, too, but also be able to apply it. When I was studying, I worried less about my grade point average than about learning what I needed to do a good job.

Profile Update

Mr. Herron currently administers and manages two federal grants for 14 hemophilia treatment centers in five states, for the Great Lakes

(continued)

(continued)

Hemophilia Foundation. From 2010 to 2014, he served the State of Wisconsin AIDS/HIV Program as their Linkage to Care Coordinator. He assisted the department in locating persons living with HIV who were not taking medications. He then served as a liaison between the client and health care system to reengage or engage persons into care. He was also assigned to special projects relating to health for gay and bisexual African American men in the Milwaukee area, and he helped launch a successful HIV mentoring retreat for 24 local youth.

PATIENT NAVIGATOR

Job Description

Some public health programs use "patient navigators" or "health navigators" to help patients find their way through the health care system. Although this is closely linked to individual patient care services, it meets a public health need by connecting people to services they might not be able to access otherwise. Many patient navigator programs focus on making cancer screening programs more useful, such as by connecting members of underserved populations with timely medical care when a screening turns up a positive result. The role of a navigator stems from the fact that our health care system can be pretty confusing and intimidating. Big hospitals can seem like mazes. Dealing with bills and insurance can be frustrating and frightening. It can be especially hard for people who do not have good insurance, who are not fluent in English, who do not fully understand how the health system works, or who come from communities that tend to think about health in ways doctors do not seem to "get." Navigators help patients set up the right appointments, find transportation, communicate with physicians (in English or otherwise), learn about their illnesses, and get answers to questions about insurance and costs. Some navigators even guide patients from the medical center entrance to the doctor's office. Navigators are also employed in public health research to guide patients through studies. There are navigators working with patients who require cancer care, refugees, people with HIV, and low-income patients.

Education and Certification

The required education depends on the program's design and on what services the navigator will provide. Some navigators do not need any special education at all. Some programs look for a bachelor's degree in a field related to health or experience as a community health worker. Some look for social workers or nurses. A few universities and colleges have begun to offer certificates or associate's degrees focusing on patient navigation. There are also online and in-person training programs available. There is a national credential available for navigators who focus on breast cancer, and one is planned for nurse navigators who help with general cancer care and prevention.

Core Competencies and Skills

- Compassion
- Patience
- Good teaching skills
- Understanding of the different ways people react to stress and illness
- Ability to remain calm under stress
- Ability to judge the seriousness of situations and to prioritize needs
- Knowledge of how the health care system works, with at least a basic understanding of medical terms

Compensation

Patient navigator salaries are related to the skills and knowledge required. They tend to be comparable to salaries for community health workers, nurses, or social workers, depending on the specific requirements.

Workplaces

Patient navigators work at universities, health departments, medical centers, and nonprofits.

Employment Outlook

The use of navigators is a developing field, and their role is still being studied. These jobs sometimes overlap with those of community health workers, social workers, or public health nurses. Overall, it appears that opportunities may be expanding with implementation of the Affordable Care Act and increasing focus on cost control, quality, and patient-centered care.

For Further Information

Patient navigators don't have a national organization as of this writing. For more information about patient navigation, visit:

- Patient Navigator Training Collaborative
  patientnavigatortraining.org
- Harold P. Freeman Patient Navigation Institute
  www.hpfreemanpni.org
- Academy of Oncology Nurses and Patient Navigators (AAON+)
  www.aonnonline.org

CORRECTIONAL MEDICINE PHYSICIAN

Job Description

A correctional medicine physician works within the city, county, state, or federal correctional system. These doctors provide clinical care for prisoners, and many also take part in designing and overseeing programs to protect the prisoners' health. Correctional medicine physicians may help to screen patients when they come into a facility, both to check for chronic illnesses like diabetes and to identify contagious diseases. Their work may include quality improvement efforts, such as working on changes that will help prevent medical problems, increase efficiency, and raise the standard of care. They may oversee disease control efforts, plan educational programs for inmates, help to write system-wide policies for the isolation and treatment of patients with certain infections, participate in disaster preparedness planning, or work in other ways to prevent illness and the spread of disease. They must adjust to changing population profiles, such as an increase in older patients with dementia. Rather than simply deal with problems as they occur in individual patients, a good prison health program incorporates surveillance, investigation of health problems, policy development, and evaluation—all elements of public health practice. These jobs tend to have predictable hours, with a limited number of nights and weekends on call. Physicians may be assigned to just one facility or may see patients at multiple locations.

Education and Certification

Correctional medicine physicians are usually trained in family practice or internal medicine. They must be able to handle a wide range of medical problems. Special certification is generally not required, but a Certified Correctional Health Professional credential is available from the National Commission on Correctional Health Care.

Core Competencies and Skills

- Interest in handling complex cases
- Willingness to work with difficult people
- Broad knowledge of general medicine
- Understanding of the mental health issues common in correctional settings
- Tough skin and the ability to recognize and avoid attempts at manipulation
- Comfort with the atmosphere of a correctional facility, including locked doors and the presence of guards

Compensation

Salaries vary according to location, demand, local budgets, and responsibilities, and may or may not be comparable to typical physician salaries. In general, most internal medicine physicians earn at least $60,000, and the median salary is above $187,000. The median salary for family practice doctors and general practitioners is $180,000.

Workplaces

Correctional medicine physicians work at local jails and at state and federal prisons. Some states and local jurisdictions hire their own physicians. Others contract with private companies that hire physicians and assign them to sites.

Employment Outlook

Advertisements for correctional medicine physicians appear regularly. Increasingly, correctional systems are turning to outside corporations for medical staff, and many of these jobs are with such companies. However, these may be more typical direct-care jobs, with less of a public health and population-based focus. Although government-run correctional health care can have its own problems, critics worry that privatizing these jobs has put the focus more on profits than on patient or system needs. For physicians interested in the public health aspects, it will be important to understand the job description and the company's culture.

For Further Information

- National Commission on Correctional Health Care (NCCHC)
  www.ncchc.org
- Society of Correctional Physicians (SCP)
  www.corrdocs.org

PUBLIC HEALTH PROFILE: Correctional Medicine Physician
Elizabeth Sazie, MD, MPH, CCHP
Chief Medical Officer
Coffee Creek Correctional Facility, Oregon Department of Corrections, Wilsonville, OR

Describe the sort of work you do.

Coffee Creek Correctional Facility is the Oregon Department of Correction's intake center for all male and female inmates sentenced to more than 1 year, and it is also the women's prison. (Men move to a male facility after the intake process.) Inmates can receive off-site medical care when needed, but we provide most of the care here on site.

As chief medical officer, my top responsibility is to ensure that we offer high-quality care. In addition to my own clinical work, I provide leadership and staff development, do evaluation and supervision of the clinical staff, and help develop protocols and guidelines. I participate in continuous quality improvement, which includes making sure we are following protocols and examining statistics on deaths, adverse events, and hospitalizations. Another of my roles is overseeing the tuberculosis (TB) program for the state correctional system.

What is a typical day like at your job?

I usually come in and check my e-mail, and then I go to the infirmary and make my rounds. The patients there are people who don't need to be in the hospital but do need extra care. They might be on oxygen

(continued)

(continued)

or IVs, be recovering from surgery, or have something contagious so they can't be among the general population.

At noon, I call in to a statewide conference call for an update about patients who are in the hospital. In the afternoon I handle certain special cases and consultations. I'm interested in HIV, so I do most of our HIV care. If I have patients going off-site for subspecialty care, I may need to call the consultants to coordinate care.

I fit my other work in around these responsibilities, including answering questions for the TB program and doing quality improvement. The past few days I've been going through charts to see who is receiving opiates, how often and why, and who is prescribing them. The nurses noticed that an increased number of patients were receiving these medications. I'm looking to see if there's a problem in our system and if so, what we need to do to address it.

What education or training do you have? Is it typical for your job?

I'm a licensed physician, which is essential for this job. Ideally, someone in this role should have a background in general medicine, either family practice or internal medicine.

What path did you take to get to the job you are in today?

After my internal medicine residency, my first job was at a university student health center. While I was there, we had an outbreak of *Campylobacter*. I worked with the health department and the CDC, and it was through that experience that I got connected to public health in the county. I took a part-time job as county health officer, investigating foodborne outbreaks and communicable disease cases and serving as medical director of the jail. I earned my MPH during that time. When the health department downsized, there weren't a lot of other opportunities in our area for public health doctors, so I practiced with an internal medicine group. But at a local forum on criminality, I happened to meet an administrator of the Department of Corrections Health Services. She asked me, "Why don't you come work with us?" I said, "But you guys don't do public health." And she said, "Yes we do!"

(continued)

(continued)

Where might you go from here, if you wanted to advance your career?

The only way to advance in this department would be if my director left—and I really like him, so I want him to stay. I suppose if I wanted to I could work for a private corporation that provides health care in prisons. Or I could do clinical medicine somewhere else.

What is the worst or most challenging part of your job?

The way things work in government can be really inefficient. At one point we had a temporary assistant we really wanted to hire permanently, but there wasn't a job category that she officially fit into. And so we couldn't hire her.

What is the best part?

Back at the health department, I was the only MD doing that kind of work, and even within the state there weren't a lot of us. I felt isolated. Here, my staff and I bounce cases off each other, and we help each other out. It makes it fun. Also, I take care of patients with very complex problems—both physical and mental—and it is just fascinating. I like figuring out how to help them.

What advice do you have for someone who is interested in your career?

We like to hire people who are experienced and who are nonjudgmental. We have a lot of patients who are very practiced at manipulating people, and you have to be able to differentiate between the real problem and the secondary gain. If we had a real newbie in here, I think he or she would be at risk of being taken advantage of.

DISEASE PREVENTION ACTIVIST

Job Description

This isn't necessarily a job title you'll find in the help wanted ads, although it does sometimes turn up. It describes a range of opportunities to work for improvements in disease prevention and health promotion, sometimes with established organizations and sometimes as part of something new. Many of these activists are working to reduce health disparities and raise the overall health of certain minority groups. These people are the heart of upstart community health organizations and small foundations that focus on preventing breast cancer or heart disease or birth defects or AIDS. They give presentations at town council meetings, put together community events, devise creative ways to encourage behavior change, raise money for programs, and inform the media about overlooked populations or hidden dangers. These activists help keep health issues in the public eye, pick up the slack where health agencies are not meeting needs, and encourage public policy that will support a healthier society.

Their day-to-day work varies, but it can include gathering signatures, writing grant proposals, sending out press releases, and organizing public events. Activists may also work directly with groups and individual patients to provide health or nutrition education, encourage safe behaviors, hand out supplies such as condoms or clean needles, or do screening tests. As an organization grows or an activist's career advances, these same people may find themselves running organizations, advising health officials, and overseeing large health promotion campaigns.

Education and Certification

Just about anyone, at any level of education, can take a stand to promote public health. Commitment to the cause is the most important qualification. Jobs with activist organizations may require specific skills or knowledge: a public relations person to raise the organization's profile in the press, a community organizer to pull together broad support for a ban on smoking in restaurants, or even a gardening expert to get neighborhood kids interested in eating their veggies.

Core Competencies and Skills

- Creative thinking
- Belief that change is possible
- Stubbornness about accomplishing goals, plus flexibility about how to reach them
- Knack for persuasion
- Excellent communication skills
- Initiative and the ability to see projects through to the end, in spite of obstacles
- Knowledge of the medical, social, and cultural issues surrounding disease prevention

Compensation

People who do this type of work often feel that personal satisfaction is the most important reward. Then again, this work can lead to increasing responsibility and respect, and it can be a stepping-stone to other opportunities. Compensation varies greatly according to funding, responsibility, and the size of the organization.

Workplaces

Activists generally work for nonprofit organizations, although there are also some business models that aim to make a profit by doing good. These can be small, local organizations—or groups that started out small and have since grown to have a national reach.

Employment Outlook

Finding paid work as a disease prevention activist can be somewhat challenging, because organizations often have limited funding and there are many young people who are interested in starting out in this type of work. Employee turnover and the ongoing need for improvements in public health make it likely that jobs will continue to be available, but it may take patience and persistence to find one.

For Further Information

- There is no single organization for activists involved in disease prevention. Instead, explore the websites of local and national advocacy organizations that focus on a particular health topic and/or population. Also see the websites of local minority health coalitions.

REFERENCES

U.S. Department of Health and Human Services Office of Minority Health. (2014, June 13). *Profile: Black/African Americans*. Retrieved June 30, 2015, from http://www.minorityhealth.hhs.gov/omh/browse.aspx?lvl=3&lvlid=61

U.S. Department of Health and Human Services Office of Minority Health. (2015a, February 19). *Profile: American Indian/Alaska Native*. Retrieved June 30, 2015, from http://www.minorityhealth.hhs.gov/omh/browse.aspx?lvl=3&lvlid=62

U.S. Department of Health and Human Services Office of Minority Health. (2015b, August 6). *Profile: Hispanic/Latinos*. Retrieved October 11, 2015, from http://www.minorityhealth.hhs.gov/omh/browse.aspx?lvl=3&lvlid=64

CHAPTER 17

Mental Health

The World Health Organization (2014) defines health as "a state of complete physical, mental, and social well-being and not merely the absence of disease or infirmity." People who are mentally healthy are best able to cope with life's stresses, do productive work, realize their own potential, and contribute to their communities.

Mental illness is not rare. The National Institute of Mental Health (NIMH) estimates that in 2012, 43.7 million adults in the United States experienced some form of mental, behavioral, or emotional problem, and 9.6 million experienced mental illness that substantially interfered with their daily lives (Substance Abuse and Mental Health Services Administration [SAMHSA], 2013). The financial cost of serious mental illness in the United States, including health care costs, lost wages, and disability benefits, has been estimated at over $300 billion each year (Insel, 2008). And yet, many people who suffer with mental health problems are not receiving treatment. There are also important differences in mental health outcomes among various socioeconomic, racial, and ethnic groups.

Public health professionals are addressing mental health in several ways. They are exploring patterns of illness and looking for risk factors that could lead to targeted interventions or new methods for prevention. They are working to increase awareness of mental health problems and reduce the stigma associated with them. They are seeking ways to improve the efficiency and effectiveness of our mental health system. And they are creating many different types of programs that address mental health needs at the community, state, and national levels.

This chapter is relatively short, for two reasons. First, other types of public health efforts sometimes incorporate mental health issues, and related jobs appear elsewhere in this book. And second, mental health and public health have, historically, been treated as separate fields. In recent years, there has been emerging interest in integrating mental health and public health, and in how public health models might be applied to preventing and mitigating mental illness (Giles & Collins, 2010; Satcher & Druss, 2010; Williams, Chapman, & Lando, 2005). In addition, public health professionals are looking at how to integrate mental health with primary medical care to reduce stigma and improve outcomes, and how attention to mental health can impact the prevention and treatment of chronic diseases, such as cardiovascular disease, asthma, and cancer.

With the Affordable Care Act making mental health services more accessible, specific needs related to mental health promotion at the community level may also become more apparent. The future may bring new efforts and new career opportunities as this connection continues to evolve.

Other jobs that may involve work related to mental health include medical officer, public health nurse, health educator, health promotion coordinator, helpline advisor, behavioral scientist, injury prevention specialist, corporate medical director, disease prevention activist, program officer, medical director, and the careers in the chapter on maternal and child health.

MENTAL HEALTH RESEARCHER

Job Description

Researchers in mental health study the causes and effects of mental illness and hunt for new ways to treat and manage psychiatric disorders. In the public health realm, this includes population-level issues such as how neighborhood characteristics influence mental health, how a disaster might trigger psychiatric problems, why people in certain groups might be more likely to develop mental illnesses, or how the health care system can do a better job of helping people who are mentally ill. Mental health researchers often work in partnership with other researchers and clinical staff. They raise funds for their projects by applying for grants from the government, nonprofit organizations, or industry.

Projects might include examining national data to look for trends in the use of mental health care, gathering information from community members to find out what people with similar mental health problems have in common, or trying to find the best way to provide mental health services. Researchers share what they have learned through conference presentations and journal articles. Some mental health researchers are involved in designing and implementing public health programs based on the results of their studies. A mental health researcher might also speak to the media or offer advice to policy makers. This can be primarily a desk job, or it can involve going out into the community, conducting focus groups, and interviewing patients. Experienced researchers often have assistants carry out the day-to-day research tasks while they focus on designing studies, raising funds, and analyzing and presenting results.

Education and Certification

Most public health scientists who specialize in mental health have advanced degrees, usually PhDs, in fields such as clinical psychology, sociology, social work, or other related subjects. Some have alternative degrees at the doctoral level, such as Doctor of Science (DSc) or DrPH, and some are doctors or nurses. It is possible to become a researcher in mental health with just an MPH, but as a general rule, a doctoral-level degree will allow access to more prestigious jobs. Many researchers are also university professors, and this title almost always requires a doctoral-level degree.

Core Competencies and Skills

- Curiosity
- Initiative
- Persistence
- Appreciation for cultural and socioeconomic diversity
- Strong writing skills
- Training in study design, epidemiology, and statistics
- Ability to work independently and also to work with a team
- Knowledge of or experience in the clinical side of mental health treatment

Compensation

Salaries depend on type of employer, background, and responsibilities. As an example, according to the American Psychological Association, in the 2012 to 2013 academic year, average salaries for psychology professors in doctoral departments ranged from about $67,000 per year for assistant professors, to $119,000 for full professors. Past surveys have shown that salaries for psychology research positions tended to be higher at other types of organizations, including government and nonprofits.

Workplaces

Researchers in the field of mental health often work at universities, where they may also teach classes, and at government agencies and non-profit organizations. There are also opportunities at private consulting firms, where researchers do work requested by government agencies or other organizations.

Employment Outlook

The outlook depends on the availability of funding, as much of this type of research depends on government grants. Keeping an eye on federal grant topics at grants.gov and watching for research priorities at the SAMHSA, the Centers for Disease Control and Prevention, and the NIMH can be helpful for understanding trends. Overall, the job market in research and academia can be very competitive, and it may take time to find a job that matches a particular interest. Being creative about proposed research—looking for ways to connect ideas with government interests—can be helpful when looking for a job or applying for grants.

For Further Information

- American Public Health Association (APHA)—
  Mental Health Section
  *www.apha.org/apha-communities/member-sections/
  mental-health*
- Substance Abuse and Mental Health Services Administration (SAMHSA)
  www.samhsa.gov
- National Institute of Mental Health (NIMH)
  www.nimh.nih.gov

PUBLIC HEALTH PROFILE: Mental Health Researcher
Leigh Ann Simmons, PhD, MFT
Assistant Professor of Medicine
Duke University School of Medicine, Durham, NC

Describe the sort of work you do.

I'm based at Duke University's Center for Research on Prospective Health Care. There are two aspects to my work. One is trying to understand the contributors to mental health. I study biological factors, psychological factors, social factors, and even environmental factors—everything from how your brain works to where you live. Then I take that information and develop interventions. One example is a program called Blue to You. My colleague and I conducted a survey about depression and then used the results to create tailored educational modules for youth group meetings, senior centers, churches, and other community settings. Another project I'm working on is developing a parenting education and mindfulness intervention for mothers with depression. The goal is to improve mom's mental health and reduce the risk of problems for the child.

What is a typical day like at your job?

I don't have a typical day, and that's what makes it fun. There are several elements in a typical week. One is sitting with my team members, hashing out research ideas and brainstorming about papers or grant proposals to write. Another is reading. To inform my work, I look up other people's research papers and read their findings. I spend about 50% of my time writing, creating grant applications, research papers, and institutional review board (IRB) proposals. The IRB is the ethics committee at the university, and all research projects require their approval.

I'm personally involved in the design and implementation of all my research projects. Once a study is up and running, my research assistants often handle the day-to-day work, and I check in with them to see how things are going. I train them to recruit patients, explain the study, and collect information, and I'll sit with them the first few times to ensure they understand what to do.

(continued)

(continued)

My research assistants are usually undergraduate and graduate students, and I serve as a mentor to them. I also have conference calls and e-mail correspondence about multicenter studies I'm involved in.

What education or training do you have? Is it typical for your job?

My job requires a doctoral-level degree. In addition to my PhD in Child and Family Development, I have a Master of Family Therapy (MFT) degree. At the University of Kentucky, where I had my first academic job, I learned more about women's health and clinical research through a faculty training program.

What path did you take to get to the job you are in today?

I had originally thought I would go to medical school, so after college I worked at an adolescent medicine practice. I really liked talking with the patients about their lives, but I wasn't as interested in clinical practice. I worked in medical publishing for a while, and then decided to go back to school and earn the MFT. During my master's program, I got a job as a research coordinator, and I just loved it. That's what led me to earn a PhD. My dissertation focused on the relationship between poverty and health in rural, low-income mothers. While doing this study, I noticed that a huge number of these women were suffering from depression, far more than the national average. I found that really interesting, and I wanted to learn more about why that was and what I could do about it.

Where might you go from here, if you wanted to advance your career?

At an academic center, rising through the ranks to full professor is one possible goal. Many universities have centers that focus on mental health research and policy, so directing a center, at some point in my career, is also a possibility. I could even start my own research center someday, if I get really ambitious.

(continued)

(continued)

What is the worst or most challenging part of your job?

There can be an ivory tower phenomenon. People are working on their own research in isolation. I try to keep that from happening in my own work, but you can end up working with the same group of people most of the time and not knowing what is going on in another department.

What is the best part?

I love collaborating with people. I love the synergy of getting into a room of people with different perspectives, and working together to come up with a really great research idea. If I could just come up with ideas all the time, I would be thrilled!

What advice do you have for someone who is interested in your career?

I believe I'm doing something for the larger good, and I think that belief has helped me be successful. Sitting around reading research articles won't be any fun if it's not something you are really interested in. It is being interested, and caring, and wanting to make a difference that gets me through the harder days. Whenever you consider participating in research, think: "Is this aligned with who I really want to be?"

Profile Update

Since her original interview, Dr. Simmons has transitioned to the Duke University School of Nursing, where she is an associate professor. She has continued her work on how to address depression in rural areas. She also has been working on a pilot project, with both human and animal subjects, looking at the relationship of diet and weight gain during pregnancy to postpartum depression. The study identified a potential diet-related marker for postpartum depression, and the next step will be to conduct further studies to learn more about this connection. She also has been working with the Veterans Health Administration to teach their providers about health behavior management and how to integrate health coaching into their practices. She says, "One of the cool things about my job is you never know what kind of collaboration you'll get to do next!"

PUBLIC HEALTH SOCIAL WORKER

Job Description

Social workers help people use the resources available to them to cope with physical and mental illness, as well as other challenges they face in their lives. They connect people with available services, provide counseling and guidance, and look for ways to maximize functioning and minimize disability. Public health social workers are trained to use epidemiologic methods and research evidence to identify psychosocial challenges and find solutions at the population level. They can use this training in many different ways; mental health is just one option. They can be involved in creating and running city, county, or state social work programs, shaping public policy, tracking social and mental health problems, and finding new or better ways to address these issues, often with the goal of preventing the problems from occurring in the future. A public health social worker might provide guidance for domestic violence prevention programs, helping the planners understand the personal issues that community members face. He or she might identify an emerging trend of substance abuse in a neighborhood and devise a way to intervene. Or, he or she might help evaluate social work efforts to see if they are making a difference. Public health social workers can help to integrate different services and bridge gaps between other areas of health care.

Some public health social workers provide direct service to individual clients at community clinics or through health department programs, as part of systematic efforts to address problems in specific populations. Typical roles include helping adults and their families find services and develop coping skills to reduce the risk of elder abuse, assisting teenage mothers as they learn to become good parents, helping refugees overcome past trauma and new challenges, and helping HIV/AIDS patients deal with the illness so they can continue working, avoid complications, and reduce the risk of transmitting the infection to others.

Education and Certification

A bachelor's degree in social work is enough for some entry-level jobs. However, it would be difficult to get a broad enough education at this level to be truly qualified for a public health social work job. Social workers with Master of Social Work (MSW) degrees will find more opportunities in public health, particularly if they have pursued an MPH or other training in public health. Some schools of social work offer combined MSW/MPH degrees. Social work students interested in public health may want to look for a program that specifically takes a big-picture view. All states require licensing for social workers; exact requirements vary.

Core Competencies and Skills

- Empathy
- Patience and willingness to appreciate slow or incremental change
- Good listening and communication skills
- Strong problem-solving skills and the ability to think on your feet
- Ability to assess needs on a community level, and to use epidemiologic principles and research evidence to design and evaluate interventions
- Ability to work with people from different backgrounds, and to encourage consensus among people with different interests and needs
- Knowledge of local, state, and federal programs that provide assistance to people in need

Compensation

The National Association of Social Workers published salary guidelines in 2012, suggesting entry-level salaries for MSWs of $43,000 to $58,000, ranging up to about $80,000 for those with 20 years of experience. A 2009 salary survey found that the median salary for social workers in public health was $59,500. Bureau of Labor Statistics data give a wide range of salaries, from about $26,000 to $85,000 or more, without separating out public health social workers specifically. Overall, public health social workers tend to have opportunities for higher salaries than their colleagues who do more individualized health care or counseling work.

Workplaces

Public health social workers are found at state, city, and county health departments, and at federal agencies dedicated to serving the country's physical and mental health needs. They also work at nonprofit organizations, on both the local and national levels.

Employment Outlook

The number of job openings for social workers is expected to increase over the next several years. Not all employers recognize the special combination of skills that public health social workers offer, so finding work that makes full use of public health skills can require a bit of creativity and patience. However, keeping an eye out for opportunities, making use of networking resources, and pursuing a big-picture outlook can lead to a very interesting career.

For Further Information

- American Public Health Association (APHA)—
  Social Work Section
  www.apha.org/apha-communities/member-sections/
  public-health-social-work
- National Association of Social Workers (NASW)
  www.socialworkers.org

PUBLIC HEALTH PROFILE: Public Health Social Worker
Mamie Elmore, LMSW

Social Work Director
Region 4, South Carolina Department of Health and Environmental Control (DHEC), Florence, SC

Describe the sort of work you do.

My title is director of social work for a 10-county region in rural South Carolina. I monitor and facilitate professional social work practice for the region, provide direct services, assist with personnel issues and staffing assignments, provide guidance to staff as they do their work, and ensure they receive up-to-date training. The counties here have limited resources. Our social workers address the psychosocial issues and/or barriers that prohibit individuals from reaching their optimal status, and assist citizens to effectively utilize available resources.

We provide social work services to patients in the following program areas: home health, HIV/AIDS, BabyNet, breast and cervical cancer, maternal and child health, family planning, and tuberculosis. Presently, I am working with a collaborative network of diverse stakeholders to

(continued)

(continued)

recruit and educate leaders on how to manage arthritis and to develop a network of leaders to promote the message in the local community.

What is a typical day like at your job?

A typical day is fragmented, with numerous interruptions. The primary focus of my work is the Arthritis Foundation Initiative. I schedule events and assure that the leaders are qualified to teach assigned classes. In the midst of a scheduled assignment, such as ordering supplies for a class, I might receive a telephone call concerning a referral or an ethical issue that requires immediate attention. I may get a call that an HIV client has presented for "walk-in" services and there is no social worker available, so I have to stop and assess the client's needs. On return to my office my supervisor may call for an administrative report that is needed to meet an unscheduled deadline. The Arthritis Foundation DHEC State Director may call and need immediate information. I may receive a call from a client who has been newly diagnosed with breast cancer and does not know how she can pay her hospital bill. A social worker from another county may call, needing consultation in working through a difficult situation with a client. The day is gone and the initial project I started on is still pending.

What education or training do you have? Is it typical for your job?

My educational background is standard for a public health social worker. I have a bachelor's degree in sociology and a Master of Social Work degree.

What path did you take to get to the job you are in today?

Between the bachelor's and the master's I was a tuberculosis disease investigator with the New York City Department of Health. After graduate school, I worked for a nonprofit organization, monitoring home day-care centers to assure they were compliant with standards of operation. I observed that the day-care providers were overwhelmed with the issues that children and their families were facing—child abuse, drug addiction, and domestic violence. The organization obtained funding for preventive services, and I was

(continued)

(continued)

instrumental in setting up that program. On relocating to South Carolina, I was employed as a home health social worker with DHEC. I have since worked in all program areas (children with developmental delays, HIV, family planning, maternal and child health, environmental quality control, tuberculosis, arthritis, and chronic disease, etc.). Then I was selected as director of social work.

Where might you go from here, if you wanted to advance your career?

For someone who desires to move up the career ladder, the next step would be a state program director or consultant position. The Office of Public Health Social Work career ladder consists of direct practice social workers, region social work directors, state program consultants, and a State Office of Public Health Social Work director. Research and epidemiology are areas social workers need to explore, as we have so much insight and pertinent information that can affect societal change.

What is the worst or most challenging part of your job?

Our region ranks close to the top in the state for health disparities, unemployment, and illiteracy. With the high health disparity, limited resources, and nine master social workers to cover 10 counties, we are stretched and pulled in numerous directions. Issues, concerns, and needs are identified but we have limited staff to address or promote policy change or policy development. Given these challenges, the staff is not able to be a true change agent.

What is the best part?

The best parts are working with people who care about their community and want to make a change; promoting communication strategies that are responsive to community issues, priorities, and solutions; and engaging a broad range of stakeholders in prevention and intervention strategies to promote optimal health.

I love being able to tell someone, "You can get through this. You have power hidden within you that you have not used." This is the mission for which I awake every day of my life.

(continued)

(continued)

What advice do you have for someone who is interested in your career?

I would first ask, is the field of social work a true interest? One should not become a social worker just because of a desire to help people, as you can do that in many other ways. To me, this is a calling. It is very rewarding, yet emotionally challenging. One should search their heart for their true calling. Make sure you are ready to work in communities with limited to no resources and to help people who do not yet know their innate abilities or are afraid to take a risk. As a public health social worker you will be on the front lines every day, fighting and advocating for those disenfranchised citizens who need your expertise and skill.

COORDINATOR, BEHAVIORAL HEALTH PROGRAM

Job Description

There are behavioral health programs that address certain mental and behavioral health issues on a population or community level. For example, there are community-based efforts to reduce methamphetamine abuse. Colleges often have campaigns to convince students that binge drinking is dangerous. There are programs to destigmatize depression and other forms of mental illness, so that sufferers will seek help. The people who run these programs assess community needs, examine past efforts, and determine, based on the best evidence, what is most likely to help. They may have hands-on roles, such as leading classes or visiting community members, or they may be primarily office based—coordinating the health educators, nurses, substance abuse counselors, and other experts who go out into the field. Applying for funding and managing the budget is part of the job, as well.

Education and Certification

Requirements depend on the needs of the specific program. Some managers or coordinators of these programs are social workers, some are trained as substance abuse counselors or as health educators, some have master's degrees in public health or public administration. There is an optional Certified Prevention Professional certification for people doing drug and alcohol abuse prevention work, requiring a certain amount of education and experience and an examination.

Core Competencies and Skills

- Creativity
- Good management skills
- Ability to handle multiple responsibilities at once
- Knowledge of how to assess community needs
- Understanding of issues in mental and behavioral health
- Ability to locate and understand research evidence for behavioral health programs
- Understanding of the population being targeted
- Knowledge of how to implement and evaluate programs

Compensation

There are no national statistics for this type of job, but salaries tend to be relatively modest. One recent example is $32,500 as a starting salary for a coordinator in a violence prevention program in southern California, requiring a bachelor's degree and a year of experience. A substance abuse prevention program in Texas, focused on teens, offers $34,000 to $37,000 for a candidate with a bachelor's degree and at least 2 years doing similar work. A substance abuse prevention program in New York City pays their coordinator $50,000 to $65,000, and asks for at least 2 years' experience and, preferably, a master's degree.

Workplaces

There are behavioral health programs based at local health departments, human services offices, public school districts, community mental health facilities, and colleges and universities. Some are run by nonprofit organizations or for-profit companies. There are also programs at Tribal organizations and in the military.

Employment Outlook

These types of programs often depend on state and federal funding and grants, so availability of jobs will depend on funding priorities. There can be significant employee turnover, due in part to relatively low salaries, and also because some people will see these positions as opportunities to gain skills and knowledge for other public health jobs.

For Further Information

See the links in the mental health researcher description. Also of interest are:

■ National Association of State Alcohol/Drug Abuse Directors (NASADAD)
www.nasadad.org

REFERENCES

Giles, W. H., & Collins, J. L. (2010). A shared worldview: Mental health and public health at the crossroads. *Preventing Chronic Disease, 7*(1). Retrieved from http://www.cdc.gov/pcd/issues/2010/jan/09_0181.htm

Insel, T. R. (2008). Assessing the economic cost of serious mental illness. *American Journal of Psychiatry, 165*(6), 663-665.

Satcher, D., & Druss, B. G. (2010). Bridging mental health and public health. *Preventing Chronic Disease, 7*(1), A03. Retrieved from http://www.cdc.gov/pcd/issues/2010/jan/09_0133.htm

Substance Abuse and Mental Health Services Administration. (2013). *Results from the 2012 National Survey on Drug Use and Health: Mental health findings.* NSDUH Series H-47, HHS Publication No. (SMA) 13-4805. Rockville, MD: Author.

Williams, S. M., Chapman, D., & Lando, J. (2005). The role of public health in mental health promotion. *Morbidity and Mortality Weekly Report, 54*(34), 841–842.

World Health Organization. (2014). *Fact sheet 220. Mental health: Strengthening our response.* Retrieved from http://www.who.int/mediacentre/factsheets/fs220/en

CHAPTER 18

Public Health Law, Regulations, and Policies

There is a difference among public health laws, regulations, and policies (Wing & Gilbert, 2007). Laws are enacted by legislators—by votes in Congress, state legislatures, or city councils. Regulations are the rules put in place by government agencies to carry out the laws. Policy is a more general term used variously to describe laws, regulations, and agencies' overall plans and strategies.

Another important clarification is the difference between "health law" and "public health law." A prominent public health lawyer, Lawrence Gostin (2001), has defined public health law as referring to the government's powers and duties to "assure the conditions for people to be healthy." His definition also includes the limitations on these powers, which prevent the state from unduly restricting citizens' rights. For example, it is generally accepted that the government can enforce a quarantine for someone who might have the deadly Ebola virus, if he or she could be putting other people at risk. But it is unlikely that the courts would uphold a law that made it a crime to drink sugary soda, no matter what it does to our teeth or our waistlines.

Health law is a much broader category. Practitioners of health law include medical malpractice attorneys and lawyers who represent hospitals and insurance companies.

Although nearly every public health professional's work interacts with laws and regulations in some way, the jobs in this chapter focus largely on the laws and regulations themselves.

ADVOCACY DIRECTOR

Job Description

The advocacy director is the connection between a public health organization and the political world. "Advocacy" is about encouraging government officials to support policy that favors the organization's goals. That means getting laws passed and getting line items in federal, state, and city budgets. It also means working to get services provided in a way the organization thinks will be most effective. To make these things happen, the advocacy director keeps up to date on the latest news and policy issues, gets to know politicians and their staff members, and encourages the public to call their representatives and show their support. The advocacy director plans events to raise awareness about public health issues and prepares reports summarizing current policy issues and needs. The advocacy director also maintains relationships with related foundations, companies, and agencies, so they can present a united front. Some advocacy jobs are primarily at the "grassroots" level, focused on enlisting the local community or the general population to help put pressure on policy makers. The job often involves a combination of deskwork and meetings outside the office. It may also require travel. (This job can also be called "policy director," "director of government relations," or another variation.)

Education and Certification

An advocacy director's background usually includes at least a bachelor's degree plus training and experience in politics and health care issues. A master's degree in a related field (such as public policy, nonprofit management, or the organization's health focus) makes a candidate more competitive and is required for some jobs.

Core Competencies and Skills

- Understanding of relevant health care issues
- Tact and a knack for persuasion
- Excellent written and verbal communication skills
- Personal interest in the organization's goals
- Knowledge of the legislative process
- Experience with advocacy or grassroots organizing

Compensation

Salary depends on the size of the organization and the scope of the job. The *NonProfit Times* published a salary survey in 2014 with some average salaries for advocacy and government affairs jobs. The average for a government relations director or manager was about $90,000 and for a grassroots advocacy/campaign manager, $52,500. Salaries can be much lower at small organizations, while a high-level job at a large nonprofit could pay well above the average.

Workplaces

Advocacy directors usually work at nonprofit organizations. The job title also exists at for-profit businesses, but the work is generally geared toward increasing the company's opportunities for profit.

Employment Outlook

In 2015, the National Council of Nonprofits identified an increasing focus on advocacy as "a trend to watch" in the nonprofit world. It is possible that this will lead to more jobs in this field. Landing a job working on a very specific cause or for a particular organization can be challenging; a good bet is to look for opportunities to gain experience in organizing or advocacy, and then work toward eventually obtaining a job in the desired area.

For Further Information

- National Council of Nonprofits (NCN)
  www.councilofnonprofits.org
- Center for Lobbying in the Public Interest (CLPI)
  www.clpi.org

POLICY ANALYST

Job Description

A policy analyst keeps track of laws, regulations, and funding related to an organization's or government agency's interests. This includes current policy, changes that are being discussed, and changes that might occur in the future. The policy analyst also tracks the impact of existing laws and policies, looks at current public health programs, and explores the potential effects of policy changes. To do this, he or she consults with outside experts, conducts research, and keeps up with news reports, government documents, and outside organizations' and agencies' efforts. Then, he or she prepares reports incorporating all this information. The reports may be used to argue for a certain policy change, or they may be intended to help with decision making. Policy analysts also share their knowledge with legislators, agency officials, and community stakeholders. A policy analyst job can incorporate elements of program evaluation, data analysis, and policy development, as well. Some policy analysts also create fact sheets, write editorials, speak to the media, or even appear on television. Policy analysts spend much of their time on the computer, researching the issues and writing reports; they also attend meetings on- and off-site and sometimes travel to program locations and conferences.

Education and Certification

A policy analyst generally needs at least a master's degree in public health, public policy, or another field related to public health policy issues. A bachelor's degree with strong experience in policy, such as a job as a legislative aide, will suffice for some positions. For some positions, a PhD, MD, or JD is most appropriate, and some policy analysts were originally trained as social workers or nurses. It is helpful to have at least some work experience that relates to the policy topic when applying for a first job as a policy analyst.

Core Competencies and Skills

- Excellent writing and presentation skills
- Knack for analytical and strategic thinking
- Ability to understand complex information and to summarize it in a logical way
- Ability to create working relationships with experts from outside agencies, organizations, and academic centers
- Knowledge of government and legislative processes and of how to find information related to laws and policies
- Additional knowledge relevant to the organization's or agency's interests
- For some jobs, good negotiation skills to bring scientists, public health experts, and legislators together on policy plans

Compensation

There is no national summary of policy analysts' salaries. According to a 2014 survey from the *NonProfit Times*, the average salary for a policy analyst at a nonprofit is about $58,000. In federal government agencies, policy analysts who are very experienced can earn $100,000 per year or more. Certain well-funded nonprofits also offer generous pay to well-qualified analysts.

Workplaces

Policy analysts interested in public health usually work for nonprofits or government agencies. Some work for consulting firms or "think tanks" that specialize in interpreting policy issues.

Employment Outlook

It is difficult to assess the employment outlook, because policy analyst jobs can have various titles. Some have responsibilities that overlap with other jobs, such as program officer. However, since this job is essential to major organizations that seek to influence policy, it is likely that job openings will continue to be available. The Bureau of Labor Statistics (BLS) estimates that the demand for political scientists, who may work as policy analysts, is expected to grow faster than average between 2012 and 2022, but the field itself is small so there is likely to be strong competition for jobs. Looking for a lower-level job related to policy, where you can start to gain the required experience, is one way to get your foot in the door.

For Further Information

Policy analysts often belong to organizations that match their specific interests, including the American Public Health Association. Here are some other related links:

- Association for Public Policy Analysis and Management (APPAM)
  www.appam.org
- Health Affairs
  www.healthaffairs.org
- AcademyHealth
  www.academyhealth.org

PUBLIC HEALTH PROFILE: Policy Analyst
Jennifer Greaser, RN, MSN
Public Health Analyst
Centers for Disease Control and Prevention, Washington, DC

Describe the sort of work you do.

I work for the CDC's Washington office. The office has two main functions. The first is analysis, analyzing legislation and other policies and their impact on public health. The second is communicating with policy makers in Congress, at other federal agencies, and at the state and local levels, to provide the information they need when they are creating legislation that may affect public health. A good example is the work we did for the Child Nutrition Reauthorization. We worked with colleagues to provide the latest scientific evidence about nutrition, so that legislators could make the best decisions as they updated child nutrition programs.

What is a typical day like at your job?

The work can be very fast paced. Policy makers are under their own deadlines, and sometimes their staff will call and want an answer within an hour. At other times, I have days or weeks to do an analysis.

An analysis starts with reading the original legislation or policy and any related materials. I talk with CDC scientists and other researchers to learn about the science behind a policy and how a new decision could impact research. I speak with public health planners about potential effects on public health programs. Then I have to find out what happens in the day-to-day world. Say I'm looking at a policy that aims to increase children's fruit and vegetable consumption by changing what's in school lunches. I'll talk to experts about issues such as what children are likely to eat, whether schools have enough refrigerators, and if their kitchens are equipped to steam vegetables.

At times, I go out to see the programs that would be affected or arrange for congressmen or staff members to do a site visit. Once I have the background information, I arrange conference calls or meetings with legislators and their staff members, and sometimes also with CDC scientists, and we'll talk through the issues. I help "translate" the science and summarize what I have learned. Sometimes

(continued)

(continued)

I'm also asked to write policy papers for my director or to provide a written review of legislation.

What education or training do you have? Is it typical for your job?

I have a BSN and a master's in nursing health policy, but people in this job tend to have MPHs, JDs, or MPAs. There are also some MDs and other RNs. With experience in a legislative office, a bachelor's degree can be enough.

What path did you take to get to the job you are in today?

I started out as a nurse doing clinical care. I got my master's degree while I was still working in the hospital, and then I was accepted into a U.S. Department of Health and Human Services (HHS) career development program called the Emerging Leaders Program. This was a program where you would start at a low- to mid-range job and do rotations to different agencies. You could be promoted after each year, and at the end of 2 years you could be hired on full time. That's how I got started in my current job.

Where might you go from here, if you wanted to advance your career?

To round out my experience more, I might want to spend some time at another federal agency whose policies impact public health—such as the Department of Education or the Department of Transportation. When you're trying to influence policy through the public health lens, it is helpful to understand the lenses that other agencies are looking through. More generally, the next step for someone in my role might be to become director of legislative affairs for a nonprofit organization.

What is the worst or most challenging part of your job?

With policy, you can be working on something for years before you see the results. Policy making involves a lot of steps, a lot of influences, and a lot of players. You really have to have patience to see it through. I also find that sitting at a desk all day long can be tough. Sometimes I just have to get up and take a walk.

(continued)

(continued)

What is the best part?

For me, the eye-opening moment was when I realized that there are so many things that impact public health, and so many things that policy makers haven't necessarily thought of. I like knowing that we provide really good quality science to legislators and that we are helping them make the best decisions. Working at the federal level is really exciting, too. I'm close to the action, working directly with the people who are making important decisions.

What advice do you have for someone who is interested in your career?

If you're interested in this job and want to have a competitive edge, get experience in some kind of a policy office. That will also help you decide if this is the kind of work you want to do. If you can't get an internship in Congress, look for state or local opportunities or do a summer internship in the legislative affairs office at a nonprofit. If you're already out of school, look for fellowships and other government programs designed for people with your background.

HEALTH LEGISLATIVE ASSISTANT

Job Description

State legislators and members of Congress have a lot to keep track of—bills, constituents with concerns, lobbyists raising new issues. Legislative assistants help make it possible for legislators to do their work by serving as the in-office experts on vital issues. The health legislative assistant focuses specifically on health care matters including public health, does the background research on important issues, and helps the legislator to shape his or her stance on current topics. When a new issue comes up, the health legislative assistant pulls together information to make sure the legislator is informed. He or she meets with stakeholders, such as health advocacy organizations, gives formal presentations, and may draft new bills related to health issues. The job can include preparing speeches for the legislator and helping him or her prepare for media interviews. Legislative assistants also respond to questions from individual constituents and talk with members of the press. Often, a legislative assistant who handles health issues also covers other topic areas, dividing his or her time among multiple subjects. This job can be very fast paced and stressful, and can require long hours.

Education and Certification

The requirements for this job differ according to the legislator's expectations and needs. There are jobs for people just starting out after college who have had policy-related internships or some experience on Capitol Hill. And there are jobs that require significant expertise, with previous congressional experience or a strong policy background. Some come to this job from a policy analyst role; some come from industry; some come from a clinical background with training in public health or health policy. Many have an MPH, an MPP, or a master's in health management and policy.

Core Competencies and Skills

- Ability to work under pressure and willingness to work long hours
- Ability to multitask
- Good attention to detail
- Ability to analyze information, determine what is most relevant, and present the information in a concise and logical way
- Ability to work under pressure and to meet tight deadlines
- Good political judgment and an understanding of how the legislative process works
- Understanding of health policy issues, including Medicare, Medicaid, and insurance reform

Compensation

A review of legislative assistant salaries for the U.S. Congress in 2015 showed many in the $40,000 to $50,000 range, some in the $30,000s, and a limited number at $70,000 or above. Salaries for congressional staffers in Washington, DC, have typically been lower than in the private sector; people tend to take these jobs because of commitment to the issues, not the rate of pay.

Workplaces

There are legislative assistants at both state and federal levels. Legislators at the state level usually have fewer staff members than senators and representatives in Washington, DC, and are less likely to have designated assistants focusing on health.

Employment Outlook

There is a lot of turnover in these jobs, both because people often use them as stepping-stones to other opportunities, and because of changes following elections. It means that jobs are available fairly regularly. However, there is also a lot of competition for each position. Doing an internship at a legislative office and taking advantage of networking opportunities can be a good way to get in the door.

For Further Information

- National Conference of State Legislatures (NCSL)
  www.ncsl.org
- The Committee on House Administration (keeps a running list of congressional staff organizations)
  cha.house.gov

HEALTH ECONOMIST

Job Description

A health economist working in public health uses specialized knowledge of economics and finance to promote sound health policy. A health economist might focus specifically on the economic effects of policies such as a national health care plan. He or she might help an organization or agency decide which public health programs are most financially sound or cost-effective. Some economists help evaluate health technology. Some assess the cost-effectiveness of different treatment options. Economists also help evaluate existing programs to see if money is being wasted. Overall, the role often includes tracking down data on economic indicators, analyzing trends over time, and developing models to predict the future balance between costs and health benefits. This is usually a desk job with a lot of computer time, but it can also involve creative problem solving and the opportunity to have a direct impact on policy.

Education and Certification

A bachelor's degree in economics is the absolute minimum educational requirement. Opportunities beyond entry-level jobs often require a master's degree, and a PhD is the standard for a health economist who leads a team or a project.

Core Competencies and Skills

- Interest in health policy and a thorough understanding of economics as applied to health care
- Ability to sort through information and decide what elements are most relevant
- Strong written and verbal communication skills, including the ability to explain the work to noneconomists
- Persistence and patience for projects that take significant time to complete
- Knowledge of economic issues in relevant fields such as health insurance, medical technology, pharmaceuticals, or hospital finance
- Strong statistical knowledge and analytical skills and a high level of comfort with math and numbers

Compensation

The median salary for all economists was about $96,000 per year in 2014. Most earned between $50,000 and $171,000. According to a 2012 survey of members of the American Society of Health Economists, the average salary was about $145,000, and it was similar for academics and nonacademics. Salaries tended to be higher in the for-profit sector and lower at government agencies. Overall, the range was from around $60,000 to $400,000. Members with PhDs in economics earned higher salaries than those with PhDs in other fields.

Workplaces

Health economists serve the cause of public health in city, county, and state governments, at federal agencies (including the CDC, the Centers for Medicare & Medicaid, the Food and Drug Administration, and the Government Accountability Office), and at nonprofits, think tanks, and consulting firms. There are also health economists doing cost-effectiveness research at pharmaceutical companies and insurance companies.

Employment Outlook

Compared to the national average for all occupations, employment of economists is expected to grow about as fast as average from 2012 to 2022. With cost-effectiveness becoming an increasingly important concern, opportunities related to health care may expand over the next several years. At the same time, employment for economists in the federal government is expected to decrease overall.

For Further Information

See the description for policy analyst. Also:

- American Society of Health Economists (ASHEcon) *ashecon.org*
- International Health Economics Association (iHEA) *www.healtheconomics.org*

PUBLIC HEALTH LAWYER

Job Description

A public health lawyer uses legal expertise to assist with efforts to safeguard and promote the public's health. At a health department or federal agency such as the CDC, a public health lawyer gives advice to policy makers and reviews plans and policies to identify potential legal pitfalls. Can the government require every doctor to get a flu shot? If city officials want restaurants to post calorie information, how should the policy be worded, and what legal challenges might come up? A significant part of the work at state and local agencies has to do with regulatory matters, for example, looking at the legal aspects of creating ordinances to limit indoor air pollution. Another typical role is helping defend patient confidentiality. Public health lawyers handle lawsuits against public health agencies, as well, and help fight challenges to laws that protect people's health and safety. Some public health lawyers help nonprofits and community organizations take full advantage of existing laws and regulations. For example, they can figure out how to use economic development resources to get public land set aside for a community garden.

Education and Certification

A public health lawyer needs a law degree, a license to practice, and knowledge of public health law, which can be obtained through education or practice. Many public health lawyers have an MPH in addition to the JD. There are also opportunities for lawyers in public health that do not require passing the bar; these are typically positions in academia or management, and some in policy or advocacy.

Core Competencies and Skills

- Commitment to serving the public and a passion for public health
- Persuasiveness
- Ability to explain legal principles to nonlawyers
- Understanding of the legal framework for public health, including government agencies' roles and the scope of states' powers
- Awareness of issues in public health ethics
- Knowledge regarding the areas of public health that the work will address

Compensation

In the profession as a whole, most lawyers earn between $55,000 and $172,000. The median salary is about $115,000. According to a recent survey of lawyers who also had public health degrees, most were earning between $50,000 and $100,000.

Workplaces

Public health lawyers work for the government and for nonprofit and political organizations. At the state and local levels, they are usually at the health department or the attorney general's office; there are also public health lawyers at federal agencies. Some lawyers with public health knowledge work in industry, advising corporate leaders about what government agencies might do and how best to work with them. Some public health lawyers work in academia; public health law research is an emerging field.

Employment Outlook

There is significant competition for job openings for lawyers, including those that are directed toward public service. The BLS predicts that, overall, there will continue to be more lawyers than available jobs, and also that budget constraints may affect hiring at federal government agencies. The Network for Public Health Law notes that in recent years, public health law has been increasingly utilized in efforts to achieve public health goals. At the same time, the number of joint JD/MPH programs has increased from just a small number to more than 25 in the past few decades; so there is an increasing number of lawyers who will be qualified for these jobs.

For Further Information

- Centers for Disease Control and Prevention (CDC)— Public Health Law Program (PHLP) *www.cdc.gov/phlp*
- The Network for Public Health Law *www.networkforphl.org*

ADMINISTRATIVE LAW JUDGE

Job Description

Administrative law judges conduct hearings and make rulings in cases having to do with so-called administrative issues, such as the enforcement of health and safety regulations. When a doctor is accused of professional misconduct, the administrative law judge hears the case and makes recommendations for disciplinary action. An administrative law judge might hear an appeal by a woman who has been denied WIC coverage, or make a judgment about a violation of the sanitary code. A case of a store selling cigarettes to children would go to the administrative law judge, as well. These judges' tasks include holding conferences before official hearings, issuing subpoenas, conducting hearings, listening to oral testimony or reading written documents, and issuing written findings and decisions. State administrative law judges may have significant amounts of travel, as they go to hear cases in different regions. They usually have 8-hour workdays and weekends off.

Education and Certification

Becoming an administrative law judge at the federal level requires a law degree and a specific examination set by the U.S. Office of Personnel Management. At the state level, a law degree may or may not be required. Some departments require a certain level of experience practicing law.

Core Competencies and Skills

- Fairness
- Logical thinking
- Patience and good listening skills
- Excellent problem-solving ability
- Good time management skills
- Strong understanding of public health law and health department regulations
- Knowledge of court procedures and related rules and regulations
- Ability to understand multiple points of view

Compensation

The median salary for administrative law judges and hearing officers was about $88,000 in 2014. Most earned between $41,000 and $157,000.

Workplaces

Administrative law judges who hear health-related cases are employed at the state and federal levels and by some cities and counties. An administrative law judge may work directly for a health department or for a separate agency that focuses on administrative law hearings. Administrative law judges at state environmental agencies sometimes hear health-related cases, too. In federal government, administrative law judges work for many agencies including the HHS.

Employment Outlook

Administrative law judge is a civil service job, which provides some job security. National statistics for employment outlook cover all types of judges, not just administrative law judges; in general, employee turnover tends to be low and there is competition for available jobs. However, pay for lawyers is higher in the private sector, and this may lessen competition. The total number of jobs for judges is expected to remain steady from 2012 to 2022.

For Further Information

- National Association of Administrative Law Judiciary (NAALJ) *www.naalj.org*

- National Association of Hearing Officials (NAHO)
  www.naho.org
- National Conference of the Administrative Law Judiciary (NCALJ)
  *www.americanbar.org/groups/judicial/conferences/
  administrative_law_judiciary.html*

CONSUMER ADVOCATE

Job Description

"Consumer advocate," like "activist," is a title that can represent many different jobs. But essentially, a consumer advocate is someone who helps people obtain safe products and fair services. Consumer advocates do not necessarily focus on health, but those who do help protect the public from products that could cause injury and from inadequate medical care. There are consumer advocates working to improve the laws and regulations that govern the safety of consumer products, pharmaceuticals, or medical devices. Some focus on health insurance restrictions or on the quality of care at hospitals and doctors' offices. They track down data on product- or service-related injuries, read current laws and policies, and write reports and recommendations based on this information. They speak with industry executives, give testimony at legislative hearings, talk to reporters, and meet with people from the community and from other advocacy organizations. Some consumer advocates make regular appearances on television and radio. Consumer advocates may also lead grassroots efforts to encourage consumers to take a stand themselves, or they may use legal skills to go after manufacturers who make harmful products.

Education and Certification

Educational needs differ according to the job. A consumer advocate may be a lawyer, a policy or public health expert, a community organizer, or simply an ordinary citizen with the zeal, persistence, and networking skills to get things done.

Core Competencies and Skills

- Passion for public safety and consumers' rights
- Excellent communication skills, including public speaking skills
- Persuasiveness

- Ability to select information that will gain the attention of reporters, policy makers, and the public
- Understanding of laws and policies related to consumer safety
- Understanding of the political process

Compensation

Salaries depend greatly on the type of organization and type of work. A small grassroots organization might pay as little as $25,000 to $30,000, while someone with significant experience at a large organization could earn $100,000 or more.

Workplaces

Many consumer advocates work for nonprofit advocacy organizations. Some states have a "consumer advocate" office that deals with insurance issues, including health insurance; these offices handle complaints against insurance companies and may also offer consumer education. There are jobs for people interested in consumer protection at federal agencies including the Federal Trade Commission and the Consumer Product Safety Commission (CPSC); there are opportunities for inspectors, program analysts, attorneys, and others.

Employment Outlook

There is no national tracking for jobs at consumer advocacy organizations. However, many of these groups are nonprofits, and at least as of 2014 the nonprofit sector was continuing to expand, The budget at CPSC is relatively modest, and there has been some political controversy in recent years about how its regulations affect private businesses. The number of future opportunities at this agency will depend on congressional decisions about funding each year.

For Further Information

- Consumer Product Safety Commission (CPSC)
  www.cpsc.gov
- Center for Science in the Public Interest (CSPI)
  www.cspinet.org
- Consumers Union (CU)
  consumersunion.org

- Public Citizen
  www.citizen.org
- National Consumers League (NCL)
  www.nclnet.org

PUBLIC HEALTH LOBBYIST

Job Description

A lobbyist's job is to influence legislators to make decisions that support his or her client's interests. Traditionally, lobbying is thought of as interacting directly with legislators and their staff members, to persuade them to pass a favorable law, or prevent passage of a damaging one. Lobbyists contribute to political debate by sharing information and perspectives from the groups they represent. There is also grassroots lobbying, which involves enlisting the help of the public, such as organizing rallies or demonstrations, or asking people to call their congressperson.

A lobbyist for an organization concerned with public health will have face-to-face meetings with legislators, legislative assistants, and influential government officials. The lobbyist observes relevant legislative hearings and sometimes offers official testimony. He or she might arrange for organization members to visit Washington, DC, or a state capitol and meet with legislators. The job requires keeping up with the news and new developments, as well as finding out about legislators' political interests, tracking how they plan to vote, and looking for approaches they will find persuasive. The lobbyist may also be tasked with persuading state and federal agencies to create regulations that support his or her organization's cause. This job may require long hours and travel. A lobbyist's job description can overlap with that of an organization's advocacy director.

Education and Certification

A lobbyist will usually have at least a bachelor's degree and some experience in the political world. Many have master's degrees or law degrees.

Core Competencies and Skills

- Excellent interpersonal and networking skills
- Persuasiveness and strong negotiation skills
- Excellent organizational skills

- Ability to work independently, to meet deadlines, and to handle stress
- Good understanding of politics
- Familiarity with medical and public health issues
- Knowledge of how laws are passed and regulations are created
- Understanding of public relations and media

Compensation

According to the Sunlight Foundation, a nonprofit that advocates for open government, an experienced lobbyist could earn in the range of $110,000 per year, and former legislators or legislative staff could earn a great deal more. Health advocacy organizations tend to have smaller budgets than industry, however, and nonprofits can spend only a limited amount on lobbying. Lobbyists working for nonprofit organizations earn salaries averaging about $70,000.

Workplaces

Most lobbyists work in large cities, particularly Washington, DC. They may be employed directly by organizations and associations concerned with health issues, or they may work for lobbying firms or other private companies that contract with such organizations. A public health lobbyist may work for multiple organizations, each with a limited budget, or do this work as part of another job.

Employment Outlook

The BLS does not offer outlook data for lobbying jobs. Experience, even an internship, in a congressional office can be one way to get in the door. Another option is to begin doing public relations and advocacy work for an organization and then look for opportunities to focus on lobbying. Lobbying skills can also translate to other policy-related careers. Many lobbyists do other government relations or advocacy work, as well.

For Further Information

- Association of Government Relations Professionals (AGRP) *grprofessionals.org*
- Also see the websites in the description for advocacy director.

REFERENCES

Gostin, L. O. (2001). *Public health law: Power, duty, and restraint.* Los Angeles, CA: University of California Press.

Wing, K. R., & Gilbert, B. (2007). *The law and the public's health* (7th ed.). Chicago, IL: Health Administration Press.

CHAPTER 19

Evaluation, Safety, and Quality

The careers in this chapter focus on making sure that both public health and individual health care services are accomplishing what we want and expect them to do.

Historically, funding for the evaluation of many public health programs was limited or nonexistent. Now, funders expect programs to include evaluation, and government agencies require that programs be based on scientific evidence whenever possible. Slowly, public health is building up a base of evidence that can be used to design future programs for maximum impact.

There is also an increasing focus on health care quality and patient safety, as we recognize that there are significant problems in these areas. Modern patient safety practices encourage health care providers to report errors, analyze the causes, and look for ways to improve systems so that errors are unlikely to recur (Kohn, Corrigan, & Donaldson, 2000).

Health care quality includes the effectiveness of the care that doctors, nurses, dentists, and other health professionals provide. The Institute of Medicine has defined quality care as being "safe, effective, patient-centered, timely, efficient, and equitable." The movement to pay health care providers based on patient outcomes instead of by the number of appointments and procedures is one example of a public health approach to improving quality.

Those interested in the connection between medical care and public health can get involved with the American Public Health Association section on Medical Care, at www.apha.org.

Many public health jobs include elements of evaluation or quality improvement. Infection control specialists are concerned with one element of patient safety. Other related jobs include medical epidemiologist, hospital administrator, and pharmacist.

PROGRAM EVALUATOR

Job Description

A program evaluator is responsible for determining whether a public health program is accomplishing what it was designed to do. This includes how the program is being run, whether it is properly designed, how services are being delivered, and—most important—whether the program is making a difference. Sometimes program evaluators are involved in planning public health projects, as well. If you want to know whether a bike safety campaign got more people to wear helmets, you need to know what percentage of people were using helmets in the first place. Then, you need to be able to measure how many people changed their behavior and whether they did so because of the campaign or for some other reason. Program evaluators can give advice about how to collect this information in the most accurate and efficient way.

Specific tasks might include researching medical information, determining exactly what data will be most informative, creating surveys, and setting criteria that will show whether the program is meeting its goal. Once a program is underway, an evaluator might monitor staff performance, look at preliminary results, keep an eye on how well the effort is working, and make suggestions for improvement. If the program has a set end date, the evaluator collects and analyzes information about the final result. Throughout the process, the evaluator reports back to the people who run the program, to the funders, or to others. This job can include a lot of computer time, doing data analysis and writing reports, but it can also involve visits to program sites and interacting with staffs and participants.

Education and Certification

This job requires training in program evaluation or related knowledge and experience. MPH, Master of Public Administration (MPA), or Master of Public Policy (MPP) coursework can provide the necessary skills.

Some senior-level and leadership positions require a PhD. Research or program planning experience can sometimes take the place of specific evaluation training, but an understanding of statistics and data analysis, including how to use statistics programs on a computer is essential. Some schools offer a nondegree certificate in program evaluation. It is also possible to earn a master's degree in program evaluation, although this is usually associated with another course of study such as psychology or education.

Core Competencies and Skills

- Good organizational skills
- Analytical thinking
- Ability to work within time constraints
- Familiarity with quality improvement techniques
- Ability to summarize findings for different types of audiences
- Knowledge of statistical techniques used in program evaluation
- Familiarity with public health programs in general and with the type of program being evaluated
- Cultural competency and sensitivity to the needs and values of the community where the program is being carried out
- Ability to use computer programs to run statistical analyses and to create charts and graphs

Compensation

Compensation varies with duties, education level, and experience. The last salary survey from the American Evaluation Association was in 2006, at which time the majority of evaluators earned between $30,000 and $100,000. More recent job listings suggested that a salary in the range of $60,000 to $70,000 is not unusual for someone with a master's degree and a few years of experience.

Workplaces

Public health program evaluators do their work at government agencies, nonprofits, universities, and consulting firms.

Employment Outlook

The public health world has been paying increasing attention to program evaluation, and funders often require evaluation plans in grant proposals.

It seems likely that public health program evaluators will continue to be in demand.

For Further Information

- American Evaluation Association (AEA)
  www.eval.org

PUBLIC HEALTH PROFILE: Program Evaluator
Allison Meserve, MPH
Research Associate
Public Health Solutions, New York, NY

Describe the sort of work you do.

I work for a nonprofit organization. We have more than 600 employees, whose responsibilities include running WIC centers, early intervention programs, and reproductive health clinics; offering consulting services and technical assistance for nonprofits; and distributing grant money for programs that provide care for people with HIV.

I work in the research and evaluation unit. We evaluate programs to determine whether they are meeting goals during the process and then to determine the impact of the project. My main focus is reproductive health issues, such as contraceptive choice.

What is a typical day like at your job?

Most of my time is spent with program data or research data, getting it ready for analysis, analyzing it, and writing reports about it. A smaller part of what I do is pre- and post-program development—figuring out what indicators we should track, then what worked well and what didn't, and what recommendations we should make for the future. Occasionally, I go to our clinics to supervise the research being done. My major project right now is an evaluation of a computer module that suggests birth control methods to fit individual women's needs. Later today, I'll be looking at some data from an online survey that we did with men who have sex with men. I'll also be doing a literature review for a grant proposal we are going to write for another research project.

(continued)

(continued)

What education or training do you have? Is it typical for your job?

I have an MPH. My undergraduate major was women's studies. Some people doing monitoring and evaluation have another type of master's degree, but for public health work, it is better to have an MPH because you'll understand the issues and the literature. You also need to have experience with data analysis and statistics programs, which you can get as part of your MPH training. For higher-level jobs in project evaluation, you'll need a doctoral degree.

What path did you take to get to the job you are in today?

When I was in college, I thought I was going to go to medical school but after taking a few classes on women's issues in developing countries, I decided I wanted to go into international development. I spent 4 years in Mali.

My personal life led me back to the United States. I decided to get my MPH, and I learned about my current job when I was working for a professor in my MPH program. She heard about this position, and she e-mailed my current boss and said, "I know a great candidate!" This job involves a really interesting patient population, mostly immigrants, so it is a way for me to still be involved with people from different backgrounds.

Where might you go from here, if you wanted to advance your career?

When I think about next steps, I'm thinking several years from now. I could probably stay in program evaluation, possibly moving to an organization that wants an in-house evaluator, which would give me more responsibility. I've also considered running a nonprofit organization. I have the program and finance background from my previous work, and the monitoring and evaluation experience is a nice addition.

What is the worst or most challenging part of your job?

The most frustrating part is trying to translate for people who don't have experience with evaluation. I have to explain why certain things

(continued)

(continued)

are important. Often people want to use anecdotal evidence, and it can be hard to explain why that is not enough.

What is the best part?

On the contraceptive choice project I've been working on, it is nice to see that a module we designed is actually making a difference in women's contraceptive choices and their reproductive lives. One of the things we see is that the methods they're interested in are not the most effective. We hope that this module will help them to choose more effective ones.

What advice do you have for someone who is interested in your career?

Take classes in quantitative and qualitative analysis, but also make sure you are getting actual work experience that uses those skills. A lot of people graduating with an MPH are going to have taken the same classes, so you'll have an advantage if you can show that you have been responsible for data analysis. Also, try to learn about how programs really function. The fact that I've worked in public health programs makes it easier for me to interact with program staff. I know how hard it can be for them to get things done with time and budget constraints.

QUALITY IMPROVEMENT SPECIALIST

Job Description

A quality improvement specialist works either as a consultant or within an organization to make the organization function better. That can include making the organization more efficient, improving the way services are delivered, or improving the services themselves. The goal could be providing safer care throughout a hospital, increasing the number of adults who receive the flu vaccine, or streamlining health inspections so that more restaurants can be checked each month. Quality improvement experts begin by figuring out where improvements are needed. Next, they study organizational culture and the systems that are currently in place. They do their best to gain the cooperation of employees and to work with them to decide what steps to take. Then, they help to implement changes, monitor results, and continue to work with staff members to adjust plans as needed. If an organization has to follow certain government regulations or medical guidelines, quality improvement also means making sure the rules are being followed.

Education and Certification

These jobs usually require a bachelor's or master's degree, with relevant training or experience. The coursework for an MPH or MPA typically includes training in quality improvement, and an MPH is the preferred training for some jobs. There are also quality improvement jobs that require a doctoral degree, such as a PhD or MD, because specialized knowledge is needed to understand the training offered, services provided, or outcomes. Some jobs require a nursing degree or other clinical training. Employers usually look for knowledge of quality improvement requirements and processes that are typical for health care or public health settings. The National Association for Healthcare Quality has a certification for professionals in clinical care quality management. The American Society for Quality (ASQ) offers several certifications in quality management, but these tend to be geared toward corporate and industrial settings.

Core Competencies and Skills

- Good presentation skills
- Good understanding of human nature and how to enlist cooperation
- Good understanding of how workplace and health care systems work and where they are likely to break down
- Knowledge of quality improvement theory and techniques
- Understanding of program evaluation principles
- At least basic skills in statistics
- Ability to use computer programs to create charts and graphs

Compensation

It is difficult to give a typical salary for a quality improvement specialist, because salaries depend on the size and type of the organization and the level of expertise needed. The 2014 salary survey by the ASQ magazine *Quality Progress* found an average of about $88,000 per year for quality professionals (Hansen, 2014). The survey covered all industries, however, not just health care and public health. Recent job openings in health care and public health have offered a range from about $40,000 for a position at a community-based organization to the low $100,000s for a director of quality improvement at a large medical center.

Workplaces

Quality improvement specialists work for all sorts of health-related organizations and government agencies. There are jobs at health departments, at consulting firms, and at Quality Improvement Organizations (QIOs). (QIOs are organizations, usually nonprofits, that contract with the Centers for Medicare & Medicaid Services [CMS] to work on improving the quality of Medicare.) Many hospitals and health care systems hire specialists who use public health techniques to improve direct care.

Employment Outlook

There are often job openings in direct-care settings, such as hospitals and medical centers. In more traditional public health settings, quality improvement can be a separate full-time job, but it is frequently part of a broader job description. There is increasing interest in measuring health care quality that may translate into an expanding job market. For example, the CMS has been expanding its star ratings for quality, which are based on patient feedback, to include physician groups, hospitals, and other types of health care providers. Medicare and regulatory agencies require health care facilities and practices to report progress on meeting quality goals, and Medicare can impose financial penalties for failing to meet certain quality measures. Since 2011, there has been an optional accreditation for public health departments from the Public Health Accreditation Board, and this process includes extensive evaluation and quality improvement efforts.

For Further Information

- American Health Quality Association (AHQA)
  www.ahqa.org
- American Society for Quality (ASQ)
  www.asq.org
- Agency for Healthcare Research and Quality (AHRQ)
  www.ahrq.gov
- National Association for Healthcare Quality (NAHQ)
  www.nahq.org

OUTCOMES RESEARCHER

Job Description

An outcomes researcher studies the results of health care practices and interventions. This means measuring not just, say, how many people got the right medicines after a heart attack, but how long those people lived afterwards and whether they had good quality of life. It means looking at treatment for pneumonia in the hospital compared to treatment at home, to see if the less expensive home option can save Medicare money without compromising patients' health or safety. Outcomes research can also identify practices that are not helpful—and sometimes, it even catches treatments that are causing harm. Collecting outcomes information can be challenging. How do you follow up on patients after they have left the hospital? Outcomes researchers work with clinicians to decide what information is important and how to gather it. They organize the data, decide the best way to analyze it, and carry out the analysis. Then, they present the results to stakeholders. Outcomes researchers may also be involved in writing grant proposals, writing scientific papers, and presenting at conferences. There is a lot of number crunching and computer time in this job, plus communications and meetings with stakeholders.

Education and Certification

Because of the level of knowledge required, including experience with original research, many of these jobs require a doctoral-level degree or at least a master's in public health, epidemiology, or a related field. Most important is having training or experience in this type of research, and experience with managed care institutions or the pharmaceutical industry is often helpful.

Core Competencies and Skills

- Strong study design and statistical analysis skills
- Good organizational skills
- Proficiency with computer programs for statistical analysis
- Understanding of how patient data are collected and reported
- Strong creative problem-solving skills
- Ability to work with both clinical personnel and administrators
- Ability to translate research results into a language and format that nonexperts can understand

Compensation

People who do outcomes research are often classed as biostatisticians, epidemiologists, health scientists, or medical officers. There are no national salary statistics for this job title, but recent job listings and salary reports show a range from about $60,000 to over $100,000.

Workplaces

Outcomes researchers work at government agencies, at hospitals and health systems including the Veterans Administration, in academia, and for private consulting or research firms. Pharmaceutical manufacturers are also a major employer of outcomes researchers; there are public health aspects to these jobs, but the ultimate intention tends more toward improving marketing and sales.

Employment Outlook

Again, national statistics are lacking, but there is significant interest in outcomes and in the related field of cost-effectiveness research within the agencies of the U.S. Department of Health and Human Services (HHS).

For Further Information

- Agency for Healthcare Research and Quality (AHRQ)
  www.ahrq.gov
- Society for Medical Decision Making (SMDM)
  www.smdm.org
- International Society for Pharmacoeconomics and Outcomes Research (ISPOR)
  www.ispor.org

INFORMATICS SPECIALIST

Job Description

Informatics is about the collection, organization, storage, classification, and retrieval of information. "Public health informatics," specifically, uses computer science and technology to facilitate public health research, practice, and education. Informatics specialists might look at how to integrate disease surveillance data from different systems, how to help public health officials share information in an emergency, or how to have public health alerts appear automatically in electronic medical records systems. There is also a significant role for informatics in health services research, making use of patient data to reveal spending patterns, flag infection risks, or track patient safety. Informatics specialists handle complex organizational and computing challenges on a regular basis. For example, a single surveillance system can bring together hundreds of thousands of data points from laboratories, hospitals, other health care facilities, and individual doctors. This job typically involves a lot of computer time and has standard business hours, although tricky problems or tight deadlines can sometimes require staying late.

Education and Certification

Training requirements vary, particularly because this is a relatively new field. There are jobs for people with bachelor's degrees, but these are usually at an assistant level. More interesting and challenging jobs require at least a master's degree, such as an MPH with an informatics focus. An MPH can also be good training for someone who is already working in computer programming or informatics and would like to transition to public health work. Some jobs involving electronic medical records require a nursing or medical degree. Advancement can be through education, experience, or both. In addition to degree programs, as of 2015 there are training opportunities in public health informatics at the Centers for Disease Control and Prevention (CDC) and in medical informatics through the National Institutes of Health.

Core Competencies and Skills

- Excellent computer skills, including programming knowledge and knowledge of available hardware and software
- Strong organizational skills, not just for job tasks but also for information
- Interest in solving complicated problems
- Understanding of how people use databases and information systems, and of how to create systems that are intuitive to use
- Ability to communicate with people who are experts in other fields, and who may not be computer-savvy
- Understanding of relevant public health or medical issues

Compensation

The Bureau of Labor Statistics does not track informatics as a separate job title. An experienced leader of an informatics team at a large agency or consulting firm, with a master's degree or a PhD, could earn $150,000 to $200,000. A 2013 survey of nurse informaticists by the Healthcare Information and Management Systems Society found a median salary of $95,000 for health care information technology jobs, which can include informatics. Starting salaries for entry-level jobs would typically be lower.

Workplaces

There are informatics specialists working at the CDC and other agencies within HHS, at health departments, at universities, at nonprofits concerned with public health or global health, and at private consulting firms. Hospitals, medical centers, and consulting firms often employ informatics specialists to work on improving electronic medical records systems and quality surveillance.

Employment Outlook

This is a fast-growing field. There should be very good opportunities in informatics as more and more health care systems move to electronic medical records, and as the CDC and other health agencies continue to build and improve public health information systems.

For Further Information

- American Medical Informatics Association (AMIA)
  www.amia.org
- Healthcare Information and Management Systems Society (HIMSS)
  www.himss.org
- American Public Health Association (APHA)—
  Health Informatics Information Technology section
  *www.apha.org/apha-communities/member-groups/
  health-informatics-information-technology*
- Centers for Disease Control and Prevention (CDC) Public
  Health Information Network (PHIN)
  www.cdc.gov/phin
- Public Health Informatics Institute (PHII)
  www.phii.org

PATIENT SAFETY SPECIALIST

Job Description

Patient safety specialists track reports about safety hazards at hospitals, medical centers, doctors' offices, or pharmacies. Instead of focusing on individual errors, they look for places within the system where mistakes or problems are likely to occur. This could include opportunities for nurses to give the wrong medication by accident, for patients to slip and fall, or for doctors to overlook abnormal lab results. They investigate incidents, and they work with clinical teams to figure out whether systematic changes—such as flagging lab results in a more obvious way, or adding extra safeguards on medication dispensing—could prevent future problems. They recommend specific changes to "error-proof" a procedure when necessary. Then, they teach the new procedures to staff and follow up to see if plans have been implemented and safety has improved. Patient safety specialists also assess systems to look for places where problems could occur, even if nothing has gone wrong yet.

Some health departments have their own patient safety specialists who work with local health care providers to track incidents and encourage good safety practices. The job combines deskwork with presentations and visits to various clinical departments to observe current practices.

Education and Certification

Patient safety specialists in hospitals are usually, but not always, registered nurses. A master's degree (such as a Master of Science in Nursing [MSN] or MPH), with training in patient safety and quality management, is often preferred. Health departments sometimes look for people with a PhD or MPH to oversee local patient safety efforts. However, there is no single, specific educational pathway. Since 2012, a Certified Professional in Patient Safety credential has been available from the Certification Board for Professionals in Patient Safety, and employers have begun to seek candidates with this credential. There is also a Certified Patient Safety Officer credential available from the International Board for Certification of Safety Managers. Both require a combination of education and experience, as well as an exam.

Core Competencies and Skills

- Computer skills, including databases and presentation software
- Confidence in public speaking and presenting information

- Knowledge of quality improvement techniques
- Understanding of at least basic epidemiology and statistics
- Knowledge of safety regulations
- Knowledge of national patient safety organizations and initiatives
- Familiarity with health information, including clinical knowledge and awareness of how the health care system works

Compensation

Patient safety specialists earn about $43,000 to $77,000 per year, according to national data from salary.com, with higher salaries for managers and department heads.

Workplaces

Patient safety specialists are usually found in hospitals and large health care systems. There are also people working on patient safety at local and state health departments, medical and nursing schools, and nonprofit organizations.

Employment Outlook

There should be good opportunities for nurses in this field. People without clinical degrees will have a harder time finding hands-on patient safety work, but there are opportunities for people with public health training to get involved in patient safety in other ways, such as an analyst role.

For Further Information

- Agency for Healthcare Research and Quality (AHRQ)
  www.ahrq.gov
- National Patient Safety Foundation (NPSF)
  www.npsf.org
- National Academy for State Health Policy (NASHP)
  www.nashp.org
- Institute for Healthcare Improvement (IHI)
  www.ihi.org

PUBLIC HEALTH PROFILE: Patient Safety Specialist
Iona Thraen, ACSW, PhD
Director
Patient Safety Initiative, Utah Department of Health, Salt Lake City, UT

Describe the sort of work you do.

My job is to develop Utah's patient safety program and to liaise with health care industry representatives, including pharmacists, hospital administrators, risk managers, quality managers, and infection control practitioners. I collect information, analyze data, and work with industry representatives to devise interventions, tools, and other resources that will improve the safety of care. We have developed a web-based error reporting system and I'm working on ways to integrate the patient safety initiative with other parts of the health department.

What is a typical day like at your job?

Yesterday started with a rule revision committee meeting. We have a set of rules for reporting intravenous line infections in ICUs, and now we're looking at creating a set of rules for reporting another type of hospital-associated infection. We were talking about creating an umbrella approach, with a single rule for reporting multiple types of infections instead of separate rules for each one. Later, I met with executives from the health department to report on patient safety activities. On other days, I might meet with our infectious disease epidemiologists to talk about infections that occur in hospitals, or work with the neonatal screening program on assuring blood specimens from hospitals are submitted in a timely fashion. I also spend time writing reports on patient safety issues and preparing presentations.

Recently, I presented data to our Patient Safety Users group, which includes hospital representatives, the Utah Hospital Association, the Department of Health, and our region's QIO. At those group meetings, we also discuss upcoming projects, in terms of where to focus our efforts and resources.

What education or training do you have?
Is it typical for your job?

A lot of people doing patient safety work are nurses. I have a bachelor's in psychology, a master's in social work, and some graduate

(continued)

(continued)

work in health care economics. I'm now working on a PhD in medical informatics and social work. To me, this job is less about specific clinical expertise than about consensus building and process: getting people to agree to report errors, finding the best way for them to do that, and using the data from the reports to create change and improve the safety of care.

What path did you take to get to the job you are in today?

Since moving to Utah, I spent a year with a QIO as a project manager, and then I was the administrator for a small nonprofit that had gotten a Robert Wood Johnson Foundation grant to work with rural hospitals on quality improvement. I was recruited to the health department as a division director, and later patient safety was added to my responsibilities. When there was a change in political leadership, I used the opportunity to propose a half-time position dedicated exclusively to patient safety. At first, they said no, and I was prepared to leave and take another job—but then they changed their minds. The job has since expanded to 35 hours per week.

Where might you go from here, if you wanted to advance your career?

For me, completing a PhD in medical informatics is a means to an end. The way in which we collect data today is a manual, voluntary reporting system, and only a small fraction of medical errors are reported each year. It is not that they're being hidden, necessarily, but they often don't show up on the radar screen. The future for health care quality and patient safety is in electronic medical records and automated reporting. I would like to be the liaison between the information technology staff and the clinical staff, making sure that we capture and use data in such a way that we can prevent errors and create better safeguards.

What is the worst or most challenging part of your job?

Before we had the web-based reporting system, I had to enter data by hand. Developing administrative regulations and rules can also be

(continued)

(continued)

tedious, because it takes a lot of going back and forth with attorneys and a lot of legalese.

What is the best part?

The best part is that patient safety is a fairly new domain, and so I'm constantly learning. We are all still learning about how to improve patient safety and figuring out how to create new systems.

What advice do you have for someone who is interested in your career?

Patient safety is a rapidly changing field. What is going on today may not be happening a few years from now. There was no patient safety position at the health department when I started—I created this job! So keep in mind that the field of public health evolves and changes, and you have to keep current and change with it. People worry about age discrimination—but I'll be 60 years old when I graduate with my PhD, and I'll be one of the most currently trained people in the marketplace.

Profile Update

Since her original interview, Dr. Thraen has completed her PhD and now serves as Director of Patient Safety in the Family Health and Preparedness section at the Utah Department of Health. She is the lead primary investigator for a State Innovation Model Design award from the CMS, with the goal of transforming Utah's health care sector from a volume based system to a value based care delivery system. She also continues as chair of the department's institutional review board, and she is an associate instructor with the College of Social Work at the University of Utah. She notes that, with the deployment of electronic medical records throughout the health care sector, "patient safety" is evolving from a process to identify rare events to a surveillance and improvement process. Using clinical records to better identify patterns of potential harms, near misses, and adverse events requires developing new approaches for efficient and accurate data capture and analysis. She suggests that students interested in patient safety build their skills in computer technology, data analysis, and information analysis.

HEALTH FACILITY SURVEYOR

Job Description

A health facility surveyor visits nursing homes, other long-term or residential care facilities, dialysis centers, and other health care settings to verify that they are following state and federal regulations, and sometimes to investigate complaints. The surveyor travels to the facility, where he or she observes the staff and speaks with patients. The surveyor reviews medical records, examines administrative policies and procedures, and looks at other documents and records as needed to make sure that the facility is complying with regulations and providing appropriate care. Surveyors who are clinically trained also examine patients for signs of maltreatment or improper care. In some positions, the surveyor's role extends to inspecting the fire safety systems, as well. The surveyor shares his or her findings, including any violations, with the facility management, and writes an official report. When legal cases arise, the surveyor's report may be subpoenaed, and he or she will occasionally need to testify at a hearing. Some health facility surveyors also help with provider training, assist facilities in doing what is needed to meet requirements, and take part in planning when changes to state regulations are needed. The job can involve overnight travel to facilities throughout a region or state.

Education and Certification

Health facility surveyors are often nurses, who must be licensed to practice. Many employers prefer applicants with experience providing patient care in a facility like the ones being inspected. Depending on the specific job, a surveyor may, instead, have a bachelor's or higher degree in a relevant field such as public health or hospital administration, plus experience with health care administration or inspection. Some surveyor jobs require training and certification in more specific fields such as nutrition or environmental health. Surveyors who inspect long-term care facilities that receive money from Medicare and Medicaid must also pass the federal Surveyor Minimum Qualifications Test either before or within a set time after beginning work. The CMS offers an online training site for surveyors at surveyortraining.cms.hhs.gov.

Core Competencies and Skills

- Understanding of proper medical record-keeping and appropriate care

- Willingness to travel
- Good "people skills," including the ability to give criticism honestly but tactfully
- Excellent observational skills
- Physical ability to be on your feet and moving all day
- Ability to work both independently and as part of a team
- Writing skills that are adequate to convey findings, plus the ability to translate between medical jargon and plain English
- Ability to use state computer programs for making reports or entering data

Compensation

Health care surveyors earn about $35,000 to $80,000 per year, depending on experience and location. The higher-paid jobs, for surveyors with more experience, often involve supervisory and management tasks.

Workplaces

Surveyors work for state health departments or regulatory agencies. There are also regional CMS offices that oversee and provide guidance to state certification agencies. Some private companies employ surveyors to do "practice" inspections and help health care facilities ensure they are meeting regulations.

Employment Outlook

Employment of surveyors will likely be stable, as there is an ongoing need for this type of work. The demand may increase as the population ages and more people enter hospitals, rehabilitation facilities, and nursing homes.

For Further Information

- Centers for Medicare & Medicaid Services (CMS)
  www.cms.gov

REFERENCES

Hansen, M. C. (2014). Satisfaction not guaranteed. *Quality Progress, 47*(12).
Kohn, L. T., Corrigan, J. M., & Donaldson, M. S. (2000). *To err is human: Building a safer health system.* Washington, DC: National Academies Press.

CHAPTER 20

Nonprofit Organizations

Nonprofit organizations serve an important purpose in public health. There are nonprofits providing policy analysis and synthesizing information about vital public health issues. Some nonprofits advocate for policy change related to cancer prevention, the prevention of violence, workplace safety, or other public health needs. There are foundations that provide large amounts of funding for research projects and public programs, shaping the picture of public health both locally and nationwide.

The jobs in this section are not unique to public health; they are found in nonprofits of all types. They are included here both as a reminder of the role of nonprofits in promoting health and preventing disease and as an introduction to some of the careers in these helpful organizations.

GRANT WRITER

Job Description

A lot of public health work is funded by grants from nonprofit organizations or from state or federal government agencies. Grant writers create the applications, often called "grant proposals," that tell funders about a project and invite them to support it. A grant writer begins the work on each proposal by learning about the organization or program that is seeking funds. The writer seeks out information about the potential funder and looks for ways that the organization's and the funder's goals might coincide, so that he or she can present the program in the best possible light. The writer checks the funder's requirements for the proposal and follows the specified structure. Most grant proposals include details about the project, its goals, the evidence behind it, the people involved, the time line, and the budget. There will usually be some back and forth between the writer and the program planners or other leaders at the organization or agency seeking funds, to ensure that the proposal matches what is really planned. In some cases, the grant writer also helps locate potential funding sources and stays in touch with them after the grant proposal has been submitted, in case additional information is needed.

Education and Certification

Excellent writing skills and a sense of what will appeal to funders are the most important qualifications. Most grant writers have a bachelor's degree and many have advanced degrees. A major that is heavy on writing, such as journalism or English, can be a good background, so can a major in one of the social sciences. Advanced knowledge of science, medicine, or public health can be helpful if the grant has to do with a complex health issue. There are online courses to help grant writers get started or build their skills (the Foundation Center is one well-known resource), and some universities offer certificate programs in grant writing. There are also optional professional certifications from the American Association of Grant Professionals and the American Grant Writers' Association.

Core Competencies and Skills

- Ability to learn new and complex information quickly and present it in a clear, organized manner
- Ability to meet deadlines
- Strong writing skills, with a high level of efficiency
- Excellent skills for researching and tracking down information
- Understanding of what is of interest to funders
- Ability to construct an accurate budget plan
- Willingness to accept criticism and make changes

Compensation

According to a salary survey by the Grant Professionals Association, the median salary for grant professionals in 2014 was $56,500. Salaries increased with experience and also tended to be a bit higher for jobs that incorporated managing grants or doing other types of fundraising. Many grant writers work as independent contractors and are paid by the hour or by the project; hourly rates may be as low as $20 or as high as $100 or more, depending on the writer's experience and credentials. Experienced grant writers who worked as consultants reported charging about $60 to $75 dollars per hour, on average.

Workplaces

Grant writers with a public health focus work for nonprofits, academic research institutions, state or local agencies, and some private companies. Some write grant proposals for these types of organizations but do so as freelancers, which means they have their own offices or work from home and set their own hours.

Employment Outlook

Grants are what keep many public health programs running and allow innovative new programs to start, so there will always be a need for people with the skills to write grant applications. Getting started can be tricky without experience; volunteering in the fundraising department at a reputable organization can help.

For Further Information

- The Foundation Center
  foundationcenter.org
- Grant Professionals Association (GPA)
  grantprofessionals.org
- American Grant Writers' Association (AGWA)
  www.agwa.us

DEVELOPMENT DIRECTOR

Job Description

Not-for-profit groups dedicated to public health can require a lot of work to keep running, and that means finding money to support their day-to-day operations and services. The development director is the one who keeps the money coming in. He or she makes short-term and long-range plans for fundraising, coordinates efforts to carry out these plans, maintains relationships with funders, and looks for new ways to find support. Funders can include government agencies, other nonprofits, local or national corporations, and wealthy individuals. Depending on the size of the organization, development directors either do specific fundraising tasks themselves or oversee the people who do. This includes tracking down the right people, arranging meetings, explaining why a particular funder might want to support the organization, and writing grant proposals. When funding is received, they keep in touch with the funders and let them know how their money is being used. They also plan fundraising events and keep people aware of the organization, such as through writing newsletters or press releases. Development directors are usually outgoing, social people who enjoy interacting with funders and are not afraid to ask for what an organization needs. These jobs are based in comfortable, professional office settings but also include many outside meetings and often a number of evening or weekend fundraising events.

Education and Certification

There is no specific educational requirement for development directors, but a bachelor's degree is usually the minimum and a higher degree is common; for example, an employer may seek someone with an MPH, a master's degree in business, or a degree in public relations. A master's in philanthropic studies or fundraising can give an extra edge when there is competition for jobs. Experience with grant writing or other fundraising, in a lower-level job or one with related responsibilities, is extremely helpful. Increasingly, employers are looking for fundraising and development professionals who understand social media as well. Organizations also look for people with connections in the area of public health they serve or with the proven ability to make such connections. For those who want to pursue specialized training, certificate programs are available at a number of universities. Many employers look for candidates with the Certified Fund Raising Executive (CFRE) credential from CFRE International, although it is not generally considered essential.

Core Competencies and Skills

- Outgoing personality, good social skills, ability to network
- Creative thinking
- Excellent communication skills

- Knack for seeing how funders' interests might coincide with those of the organization
- Good long-term planning skills
- Ability to meet deadlines
- Understanding of budgeting and of how fundraising works
- Passion for the work the organization does

Compensation

The Association of Fundraising Professionals (AFP) reports that among their members, the average salary in 2013 was about $75,000. Survey respondents with the CFRE credential tended to earn more than those without. A survey by the *NonProfit Times* found an average salary of about $70,000 for this role at nonprofit organizations. A "chief development officer," at the executive level in a large organization, can earn well over $100,000.

Workplaces

Development directors are typically found at nonprofit organizations and at other organizations, such as academic institutions, that rely on grants from outside funders.

Employment Outlook

Fundraising will always be an important part of the nonprofit world, and at any given moment, there are multiple openings for development directors around the United States. However, people who want to get started in fundraising and development may need some flexibility. At smaller nonprofits, people tend to wear many hats, and if there is a dedicated development department, it may have just one full-time employee. The Bureau of Labor Statistics does predict that prospects for fundraisers will be good over the decade from 2012 to 2022; they cite ongoing needs at nonprofits, colleges and universities, and political campaigns.

For Further Information

- Association of Fundraising Professionals (AFP)
  www.afpnet.org

PROGRAM OFFICER

Job Description

A program officer oversees grantmaking by a nonprofit foundation or a government agency, for a specific area of research or services. He or she is involved in deciding who should receive grants and how funding should be distributed. This includes planning a long-term strategy to meet the foundation's goals, keeping track of what has already been funded, and identifying areas where new work would be especially valuable. The program officer writes requests for proposals, outlining the type of projects the foundation or agency would like to support, and may also contact researchers directly to suggest projects. As grant proposals come in, the program officer evaluates them to decide which projects should receive funding. Once a grant has been given to an organization or researcher, the program officer keeps an eye on the recipient's work. He or she looks at periodic reports and may pay a visit to the laboratory or community site. The program officer reviews the progress of the project, checks to see if goals are being met, ensures that grant money is being spent appropriately, and recommends specific changes if needed. Program officers also connect with other organizations and speak to the public to promote the foundation's or agency's goals, and they attend research meetings and conferences to keep up with current trends.

In addition to program officers who focus on funding for research, there are also many people with this job title who handle funding for health promotion programs and other public health efforts.

Education and Certification

A bachelor's degree is the minimum requirement for a program officer job. A master's degree is often preferred and may be required. In some situations, the program officer must have an MPH, a PhD, or another master's or doctoral degree in the organization's area of focus, because he or she needs a high level of expertise to understand the proposed projects and make judgments about them; this is typical in the federal government. Relevant experience is usually required, and people with experience doing the type of work a foundation or agency funds will often have a competitive edge.

Core Competencies and Skills

- Tendency toward critical thinking and the ability to see how a project fits into larger goals

- Excellent verbal and written communication skills, including the ability to give constructive criticism
- Confidence in public speaking and making presentations
- Ability to handle multiple projects at once
- At least a basic understanding of statistics and epidemiology
- Strong understanding of the field of work being funded, including current knowledge, needs, past successes and failures, and ongoing research and services
- Awareness of needs assessment methods, such as determining the true need for a proposed research study, or for community services in a specific location
- Knowledge of regulations and requirements regarding grantmaking and nonprofit organizations

Compensation

Program officer salaries vary widely, depending on the complexity of the work, the funding available, and the experience and education required. According to the *NonProfit Times*, in 2013, the average salary for a program officer at a nonprofit was about $68,000; senior program officers and those at executive levels can earn $100,000 per year or more.

Workplaces

Program officers work at nonprofit organizations and also at government agencies. Many large companies also sponsor foundations to manage their philanthropic goals.

Employment Outlook

There tends to be competition for program officer jobs, because many people find the idea of grantmaking appealing. Employers tend to prefer people with real-world experience, such as someone who has directed public health programs similar to the ones the organization wants to fund.

For Further Information

- Council on Foundations
  www.cof.org
- Grantmakers in Health (GIH)
  www.gih.org

PUBLIC HEALTH PROFILE: Program Officer
Brenda Henry-Sanchez, PhD, MPH
Research and Evaluation Program Officer
Robert Wood Johnson Foundation, Princeton, NJ

Describe the sort of work you do.

The Robert Wood Johnson Foundation (RWJF) gives grants to organizations that help us achieve our mission, which is about improving health and health care for all Americans. We fund programs that improve health directly, programs that inform citizens and policy makers, and original research. The area I work in involves grants to support new research that helps fill in knowledge gaps, as well as grants to support program evaluation. My specific grant areas are public health and vulnerable populations.

What is a typical day like at your job?

My assistant keeps track of my calendar, so I start by looking to see what's scheduled. Then, I spend my day on a number of different tasks. There are calls with grantees to get status updates, find out what's going on with their programs, and talk about any issues. I read grant proposals, and I write new requests for proposals on topics our foundation is interested in. I do a lot of presentations at conferences, so on many days I work on creating slides and writing talks.

Our funding team meets regularly to decide which proposals to approve. I write and present summaries of the proposals I think should be funded. The other team members ask questions, and then they vote.

My job involves a fair amount of traveling. I often attend academic meetings to hear grantees present their findings. For the evaluation grants, I'll sometimes go to see the program that is being evaluated. I also go to conferences to get ideas and to see if there is something we might want to be involved in supporting.

What education or training do you have? Is it typical for your job?

I have a bachelor's in health science, an MPH, and a PhD in public health. Our program officers come from many disciplines and have

(continued)

(continued)

different levels of education. You need to have the right education and experience to understand the grant proposals. A few of my colleagues are RNs or have other relevant degrees.

What path did you take to get to the job you are in today?

I worked for about 4 years with an academic research group, as a research assistant and then as program coordinator. But I wanted a job that would let me take the research results and actually translate them into programs that would benefit the populations we were studying. So I went back to school for the MPH, and then on to earn the PhD. I worked at a small nonprofit for a couple years, helping organizations that ran programs for teens to improve their services. I wasn't looking to leave that job, but I met someone who was working at RWJF—and she suggested that with my interests, I might like to work there, too. I thought, "I won't lose anything by interviewing!" And it turned out that this job would give me a chance to have an even larger impact.

Where might you go from here, if you wanted to advance your career?

A lot of people make their whole careers being program officers, and it never gets boring because the work you're focusing on changes all the time. I do want to go back into academia eventually, but I'm not sure exactly when. If I decide I'd like to stay, the next step would be senior program officer, with more of a role in shaping initiatives. From there, one might move to deputy director, handling more of the administrative functioning, and then gain increasing responsibility from there.

What is the worst or most challenging part of your job?

I have to make hard decisions about what we are and aren't going to fund. We're a large foundation, but we have a finite amount of resources. The worst part is coming to terms with the fact that there might be something that I'm passionate about, but because it isn't in line with our strategic direction, we just can't support it.

(continued)

(continued)

What is the best part?

Everything that I do has the goal of making a positive impact on the health of Americans. I love every single aspect of my job! I also like the fact that I've been here for 2 years now and my job still challenges me in 101 different ways every day.

What advice do you have for someone who is interested in your career?

Hands-on work experience is essential. I wouldn't be good at this if I hadn't done what my grantees are doing, at some point. When I sit down and review a proposal, I have a sense of whether it is realistic, whether it can be done in the time frame suggested, and if the budget makes sense. There are questions I can ask that I wouldn't have known to ask if I hadn't done similar work.

Profile Update

For the past 2 years, Dr. Henry-Sanchez has served as director of research for special projects at the Foundation Center, a national nonprofit organization that harnesses knowledge about organized philanthropy to strengthen the social sector. She has developed and directed international, national, and regional research projects on a wide range of issues across the field of philanthropy, such as diversity, violence, and democracy. Next, she will be transitioning to become chief operating officer in New York City's Administration for Children's Services Division of Early Care and Education, which oversees Head Start and child care programs that serve over 100,000 low-income children in the city. In this new role, she will be overseeing the division's data systems, quality improvement, and research and evaluation work, in addition to general operations.

VOLUNTEER COORDINATOR

Job Description

Nonprofit organizations that deal with public health issues tend to rely a lot on volunteers. But someone has to round up those volunteers, keep them organized, give them useful work to do, and ensure they follow any required regulations. That is what a volunteer coordinator does. Sometimes this person is a volunteer, too! But many organizations have someone on staff to do this job. An important part of the volunteer coordinator's work is attracting new volunteers with the skills that the organization needs. The coordinator keeps in touch with volunteers by phone or e-mail, schedules projects for them to do, and oversees their efforts.

The volunteer coordinator works with various departments at the organization to learn where volunteers are most needed and to find the most appropriate tasks for them to do. If volunteers must be trained or need to take certain classes, he or she arranges for this to happen. If something goes wrong—a volunteer makes a mistake, or someone gets upset—the coordinator steps in to handle the situation. Another part of the job is letting the volunteers know they are appreciated, with frequent thank-yous, small treats, and occasional special events. The volunteer coordinator might also write a newsletter, set up training workshops for volunteers, and pursue quality improvement efforts. This job combines deskwork with attendance at events where volunteers are needed and visits to locations, such as clinics or outreach centers, where volunteers are used.

Education and Certification

No special education or certification is required to become a volunteer coordinator, although most organizations will want someone with a bachelor's degree and/or supervisory experience. Volunteer administrators with a few years of experience can choose to earn a Certified in Volunteer Administration credential from the Council for Certification in Volunteer Administration.

Core Competencies and Skills

- Patience
- Empathy
- Flexible thinking
- Good management skills
- High degree of comfort with meeting new people
- Ability to motivate people
- Dedication to and understanding of the organization's work
- Appreciation for the special role of volunteers, including an understanding of how expectations differ for volunteers and employees

Compensation

Salaries for volunteer coordinators tend to be modest. The 2014 *NonProfit Times* salary report suggests that the average is about $36,000 for a "volunteer coordinator" and $55,000 for a "volunteer director." The website salary.com, which offers information based on human resources data, gives a median salary of $48,500 in 2015, with most earning $36,000 to $64,000.

Workplaces

Volunteer coordinators whose work addresses public health issues often work for nonprofit organizations. Some health departments and other government agencies have volunteer coordinators, too. They may have duties similar to those at a nonprofit, enlisting volunteers to help with public health campaigns and community programs. Some manage a reserve corps of health care professionals and other skilled workers who have agreed to help in case of a public health emergency; this job involves more administrative and program management tasks.

Employment Outlook

Finding a paid volunteer coordinator job requires patience and a bit of luck. The website idealist.org can be a good place to start. Sometimes this position is combined with another one, so that the office manager or program director might also manage the volunteers. Sometimes, especially at smaller organizations, it is a part-time job. Larger nonprofits that rely on an extensive volunteer network sometimes have a volunteer manager and one or more assistants. Job stability depends on available funding.

For Further Information

- Corporation for National and Community Service (CNCS)
  www.volunteeringinamerica.gov
- Association of Leaders in Volunteer Engagement (AL!VE)
  www.volunteeralive.org

DIRECTOR OF A PROFESSIONAL ASSOCIATION

Job Description

Professional associations are not-for-profit organizations with members comprising physicians, nurses, or other health care or public health professionals. A coalition of community organizations might also form a professional association. Professional associations focus on one aspect of medicine or public health and serve to educate the public, set professional and ethical guidelines for the membership, give members opportunities for networking and education, and advocate for public health issues. These organizations have boards of directors consisting of members who have been elected to help guide the organization. But they also employ executives to lead and manage the organization on the administrative side. These top managers have various titles, such as chief executive officer, executive director, or president; they are different from the elected chair or president, who serves for a year or two at a time.

The executive director is, essentially, the business manager. He or she focuses on the nuts and bolts of improving membership, arranging partnerships with other organizations, finding funds, communicating with local chapters, making sure that the association keeps to its annual budget, and ensuring that the association remains influential and viable over the long term. Depending on the size of the association, he or she may oversee a small number of employees or a large staff. The job includes making and maintaining connections with political leaders and other influential people and serving as a spokesperson for the association. The executive director also offers recommendations to the elected board members and works with them to further the association's objectives.

Education and Certification

There is no set pathway to becoming the chief executive at a professional association. Some organizations prefer people with degrees related to the association's work, such as an MD, DO, PhD, or MPH. Others look for people with administrative experience and a degree in business, such as an MBA. Experience managing an organization or department is key. Some administrators choose to pursue the Certified Association Executive (CAE) credential, which requires several years of experience in association management, relevant continuing education, and an examination.

Core Competencies and Skills

- Superb organizational skills
- Excellent leadership and strategic planning skills
- Ability to manage a large number of projects at once
- Ability to remain calm under pressure

- Confidence in the face of differing opinions
- Strong skills in business, such as financial management and negotiation
- Deep understanding of the association's focus and of important issues in that field, including health, economic, and legislative issues

Compensation

Salaries for the directors of professional societies have an extremely wide range. They tend to be associated with the size of the association and also of its budget. For example, one local association with an annual income of $850,000 pays its director $63,000 per year. The director at a much larger, national association with an income over $2.5 million earns $160,000. At the higher end are the top administrators at some of the best known and most influential public health associations, who make over $300,000 per year.

Workplaces

This job is found at nonprofit professional societies and similar associations, such as coalitions of community organizations.

Employment Outlook

The relatively small number of professional associations puts a cap on the growth of these jobs. According to the American Society of Association Executives, the number of associations is growing every year; however, there are no statistics specifically for associations with links to public health. Top positions at major national organizations require extensive experience, but smaller associations will sometimes be open to hiring someone with the right credentials but a limited track record. It is also possible for someone with good management skills to start out at an entry-level position, gain experience and education along the way, and eventually work up to a director role.

For Further Information

- American Society of Association Executives (ASAE)
  www.asaecenter.org

PUBLIC HEALTH PROFILE: Director of a Professional Association
Mike Barry
Executive Director
American College of Preventive Medicine (ACPM), Washington, DC

Describe the sort of work you do.

ACPM is a professional medical society for physicians in preventive medicine. Our members occupy a unique niche at the intersection between clinical medicine and public health. ACPM's mission is two-fold: to serve as the leader of the specialty of preventive medicine and to work toward the broader goal of improving population health. As executive director, I'm responsible for carrying out the strategic plan set by our board of directors. I oversee operations, finance, business development, and the whole array of activities that are carried out by the college. That includes managing internal functions such as our annual conference and membership support, and also forging partnerships with aligned external corporations, nonprofits, and government agencies to develop new ways to promote better health. Those partnerships increase our visibility, expand our capacity, and provide revenue to keep the organization running.

What is a typical day like at your job?

On any given day, I usually have several meetings and teleconferences: for example, meeting with a government agency, industry, or professional association partner about potential synergies or collaboration; talking with my associate executive director and business innovation officer about pricing models for our new certification program or with my office manager about prospects for subleasing office space; or holding a teleconference with our board to help advance the organization's strategic goals. I also spend significant time reading and responding to e-mail, reviewing documents, writing proposals, working on legal agreements, and attending to finances and other administrative matters.

One important part of my job is deciding what projects and partnerships we should pursue. Preventive medicine writ large is a broad field that not only touches many aspects of health care and public health but also is rapidly growing in importance and recognition

(continued)

(continued)

within the health system. Opportunities abound, and we have to be judicious in determining where to devote our resources, especially our staff time. To help with this, our board recently adopted guidelines and a checklist for vetting potential business opportunities to assure alignment with our mission, strategic direction, capabilities, and our ethical codes. Once we decide to pursue a business opportunity or a partnership, I'm also very involved in negotiating the agreements. For example, currently we are finalizing a joint teaming agreement with a partner organization around sales and distribution of an educational curriculum we have developed, while also exploring a broader affiliation agreement with that organization.

What education or training do you have? Is it typical for your job?

I have a bachelor's degree in mathematics and a CAE credential. Different organizations have different requirements. Some boards want their executive director to have the same credentials that members have. In its most recent search, ACPM decided that my experience with professional associations and background in public health matched their needs.

What path did you take to get to the job you are in today?

When I started my career, I had no aspirations to work in public health or associations. I wanted a job that dealt with statistics and data analysis. I responded to an ad for a statistical assistant at an organization called the Public Health Foundation and discovered that I really liked the nonprofit world and doing research, policy, and other kinds of work around public health. I stayed with that organization for 14 years, learned to do project management, and eventually rose to the level of senior director. And then the executive director of ACPM, who earlier had been the deputy director at the Public Health Foundation, recruited me. I was deputy director here for 5 years, and when the executive director stepped down, I threw my hat in the ring.

(continued)

(continued)

Where might you go from here, if you wanted to advance your career?

I haven't thought much about life after ACPM. I like what I'm doing. I think with the path I've taken, I could move on to any other association in the same role. Or, if I decided I didn't want to be the chief executive anymore, I could take on a lower-level senior position in a larger organization, one with more divisions and staff and a higher budget.

What is the worst or most challenging part of your job?

The decisions I make every day affect the success of the organization. That can bring a lot of stress! One of the most difficult things about my job is that we are a small organization with limited financial resources, and the world of preventive medicine is so broad. So we have to say no to some opportunities, and sometimes we can't do what the board or president wants to do. I have to find other ways to approach those goals.

What is the best part?

No two days are alike. I'm never bored. The job fits my personality well, because it is a generalist job. I deal with the entire gamut of the organization, but do not get mired in the technical aspects.

What advice do you have for someone who is interested in your career?

I don't know of anyone in this field (running nonprofit associations) who planned it as a career. Most people start at a nonprofit because they are interested in the cause. Once you realize you are good at it and you enjoy it, you naturally work your way up the ladder. If you aspire to be a senior director or chief staff executive, learn everything you can about all aspects of the organization. Talk to colleagues, learn what they do, pay attention at staff meetings. The more you understand the big picture, the more ready you'll be to assume a leadership position.

CHAPTER 21

Public Health Administration and Leadership

There are several careers in earlier chapters that could fall into the category of "administration and leadership," and many of the others can be steps on the way to a leadership position. This chapter offers a special focus on the jobs that help to shape public health efforts at local, state, and national levels.

All of these roles require significant leadership skills. Some are more administrative, some are more in the public eye. They all share a need for excellent strategic planning skills, with the ability to see the "big picture" both for the immediate moment and for years down the road.

In most cases, these are not jobs you will apply for straight out of school. They are jobs you grow into. There are a number of programs designed to help shape future public health leaders. There are training opportunities at the Centers for Disease Control and Prevention (CDC), and an Internet search for "public health leadership institutes" will bring up many organizations that provide leadership training. There is also an American Public Health Association section for Health Administration (www.apha.org).

To learn more about jobs where leadership is a primary focus, revisit director/emergency medical services (EMS), deputy director/family health services, director/state board of pharmacy, and dean/school of public health, and see the Public Health Profile for medical officer/drug safety. Strong leadership and administration skills are also particularly important for corporate medical director, director/Office of Minority Health, president, chief executive officer/Area Agency on Aging, director of a professional organization, and nongovernmental organization founder/director.

HEALTH COMMISSIONER

Job Description

"Commissioner" is a title used for the head of a health department, with "deputy commissioners" overseeing specific areas within the department. (Not all health departments use these titles; the top person may be called "director" or "secretary of health.") The commissioner has the final word on many decisions about future directions, major programs, and how the budget is managed. He or she decides where and how resources should be used and what health issues should be addressed. When an important choice must be made, such as whether to close the schools to combat a flu outbreak, the commissioner takes responsibility. He or she advocates for the department with city, county, or state government and makes sure that the department has the budget, personnel, legal and policy framework, and overall capability to respond to the city's, county's, or state's public health needs, now and in the future. The commissioner also represents the department in conversations with media, legislators, leaders of other health agencies, health care providers, and other stakeholders.

Health departments often have deputy commissioners to manage sections of the department. Under the direction of the commissioner, they develop short- and long-term goals for specific areas of public health, set priorities, and play key roles in policy development. They manage decisions about spending within their areas of responsibility. Other tasks include leading quality improvement efforts, supervising staff, and collaborating with other agencies and community groups.

Education and Certification

Some jurisdictions require the health commissioner to be a licensed physician; there are also commissioners who are nurses, who have an MPH, or who have other credentials. Many physician commissioners also have an MPH or a Master of Public Administration (MPA), and some have MBAs or JDs. Similarly, deputy commissioners may be MDs or DOs or may have other training, depending on local requirements. It is typical to have prior experience within the health department or as an administrator in another health-oriented agency or organization.

Core Competencies and Skills

- Excellent management skills
- Ability to juggle multiple projects at once
- Good political skills and understanding of local politics
- Patience with bureaucracy and red tape
- Ability to remain calm under pressure
- Excellent public speaking skills
- Understanding of epidemiology and of the principles of public health
- Knowledge of the public health infrastructure at both local and national levels
- Knowledge of local, state, and national health issues, programs, laws, and regulations

Compensation

Health commissioners earn comfortable salaries, but the actual amount depends on the location, size of the department, and the education level required. As an example, a small midwestern city was recently seeking someone with a bachelor's or master's in public health and at least 5 years' experience, with a pay range from the mid-$50,000s to the high $80,000s. A much larger county employs a commissioner with an MPH and extensive experience, with a salary of $175,000. Deputy commissioners are generally paid less than the top executive.

Workplaces

Health commissioners and deputy commissioners (or executives with similar jobs but different titles) lead health departments at the city, county, and state levels.

Employment Outlook

The top jobs go to people who have substantial administrative and leadership experience and are well respected in the local community or in the field of public health. In some cities and counties, there are opportunities for physicians and others with appropriate training, but without extensive administrative experience, to obtain assistant or deputy commissioner jobs. Most top state and territorial health officials and many local commissioners or directors are political appointees, so elections can affect job stability.

For Further Information

- National Association of City and County Health Officials (NACCHO)
  www.naccho.org
- Association of State and Territorial Health Officials (ASTHO)
  www.astho.org

PUBLIC HEALTH PROFILE: Deputy Health Commissioner
Teré Dickson, MD, MPH
Deputy Commissioner of Health, Director of the Center for Social Health and Advocacy
Nassau County Department of Health, Uniondale, NY

Describe the sort of work you do.

As a deputy commissioner, my official role is to assist the county health commissioner in advancing the mission of the health department, which is to "protect, promote, and prevent." I have several specific responsibilities. I oversee the bureaus of HIV, sexually transmitted disease, and tuberculosis (TB). I am in charge of HIV prevention and outreach, and I manage our health disparities grants. I advocate for the health needs of minority communities in ways that will address health disparities. And I act as community liaison to minority groups, as well as to the county legislature.

What is a typical day like at your job?

I usually start my day with tasks related to payroll. Then I'll answer e-mails from people like the commissioner, community representatives, my staff, and staff from other agencies. I often have a couple

(continued)

(continued)

of meetings in the morning. There may be a staff meeting, or an update about a disease outbreak. I might meet with community-based organizations, and sometimes we invite individual community residents to share their thoughts with us. We also meet with hospitals to discuss potential collaborations.

In the afternoon, I'll have a couple hours to handle any writing I have to do, such as a grant proposal, a monthly report to the Board of Health, or talking points for the head of our county government. Sometimes I work on presentations for the commissioner to use. I prepare my own presentations to give at schools, community groups, and government programs. Sometimes I'll have grant reports to review and approve. I also use my afternoons to return phone calls and respond to requests for information. Some evenings I'll have an additional meeting.

What education or training do you have? Is it typical for your job?

I have an MD and an MPH. You have to have a professional degree to hold a job at this level. Some counties will have a director who is a nurse, but county commissioners and deputy commissioners tend to have medical degrees. For my position, the county wanted someone with both a medical degree and an MPH, but it is common for our commissioners not to have an MPH. Sometimes one will have an MPA.

What path did you take to get to the job you are in today?

I volunteered at a hospital during college, and just being in that environment was very energizing. But then I got to medical school and my pediatrics residency, and I found that my patients were struggling with problems that, as a clinical physician, I had no control over. The turning point was a teenage girl, 15 years old, who came to me for a checkup. She had multiple sexual partners in the past year—and when I mentioned birth control, she didn't know what that was. She was from an ethnic minority group, and it made me wonder—this information is out there in abundance, how come it hadn't

(continued)

(continued)

reached this girl? I started thinking about health communication and how it could be used to address these kinds of problems in minority populations.

I went on to do a second residency, this time in preventive medicine. During that time, I worked at a county office of minority health, and that helped me to see how to get things done. I also spent some time at a news organization and working on health media and marketing projects, so I learned more about communicating health information. Around the time I graduated, Nassau County was looking for a deputy commissioner with an interest in health disparities, and they liked the set of skills that I had.

Where might you go from here, if you wanted to advance your career?

In a health department, one potential career ladder is to go from medical supervisor to division director, then to deputy commissioner, and then, if the job is available, to commissioner. For myself, though, one possibility I'm considering is to create a consulting service for health disparities programming and communications. I also like the idea of working as a media doctor or medical correspondent, using television, radio, print, and the Internet to educate people and help them to make better choices about their health.

What is the worst or most challenging part of your job?

Personnel management can be tough. There is a lot of office politics, too. As someone relatively new to the department, I've had to find my way through that.

What is the best part?

I like doing community presentations. It is the only communications piece that I get to do right now, and it gives me a chance to be creative. I like interacting with people, learning their mind-set, and getting a sense of the knowledge level in the communities. I especially like talking to kids—they have fun questions.

(continued)

(continued)

What advice do you have for someone who is interested in your career?

Get as much experience as you can before you become the boss. Look at people who are successful, and observe and try to understand the communication and time management skills they use. Test the waters while it's not crucial—try to spend some time at the health department during residency, for example. Make sure to learn about the work before you're in a position to be held accountable for it.

Profile Update

Dr. Dickson is now working for the New York City Department of Health and Mental Hygiene. She is a city medical specialist in the Office of School Health. She serves as a school health physician, with a panel of about 20 schools. Her work is part of the city's vulnerable populations program, which targets schools in areas of poverty, with large new immigrant populations, or with a high prevalence of difficult-to-manage chronic conditions. These include conditions affected by the social environment, such as asthma and diabetes. Her duties include school admission exams and case management for students with chronic conditions that interfere with their ability to stay in school and do their best. She also develops programs that will pull in more resources to help those students. For example, she is involved with a Community Schools Initiative that brings opportunities for parents, such as language classes or classes to prepare for the test for a high school equivalency diploma, into the schools. She is also working on a program to link schools with medical specialists and other health care resources.

PUBLIC HEALTH LABORATORY DIRECTOR

Job Description

Public health laboratories are different from hospital laboratories. They are charged with helping to protect everyone's health and safety. They diagnose and monitor infectious diseases and other health threats, screen for genetic problems in newborns, and do certain types of environmental testing. They are part of our defense against emerging diseases and bioterrorism agents, too. Certain complex or unusual tests, such as rabies and smallpox, are done only at public health labs. (The actual scope and quantity of testing differs from place to place according to local needs.) A public health laboratory director leads diagnostics and monitoring within his or her jurisdiction and serves as the point person for coordination of laboratory response when there is a public health crisis. Together with other public health and health care leaders, the director develops plans to meet current and future needs, so that the laboratory can provide essential services as completely and efficiently as possible. He or she advocates for funding and resources to maintain a state-of-the-art facility with the capacity to do all necessary testing. The director keeps an eye on the quality of work at the laboratory, making sure quality improvement systems are in place, and also oversees employee schedules, equipment maintenance, disease reporting, and compliance with federal regulations.

Education and Certification

In the 2011 survey by the Association of Public Health Laboratories (APHL), 63% of the top lab jobs required a doctoral degree, and 10% required an MD. Typical fields for the PhD include chemical, physical, biological, or clinical laboratory science. Doctors typically need pathology board certification or related experience. PhDs must also be certified by one of several boards approved by the U.S. Department of Health and Human Services. Individual states have their own specific requirements, such as a state license or certification. APHL provides some opportunities for fellowships and training (see their website, aphl.org). The CDC has a fellowship program called the Laboratory Leadership Service, designed to prepare early-career laboratory professionals for future leadership at public health labs.

Core Competencies and Skills

- Strong administrative and management skills, for oversight of budgeting, personnel, and equipment
- Good public relations and public speaking skills
- Knowledge of grant writing and business development
- Experience with quality monitoring and improvement
- Knowledge of public health principles and of the public health infrastructure
- Expertise in microbiology, bacteriology, biochemistry, or a related discipline

- Up-to-date knowledge of testing methods used in health care and environmental monitoring
- Understanding of federal regulations and requirements for laboratory work

Compensation

The salary for a public health laboratory director depends on the size of the laboratory, the population it serves, and the department budget. The 2011 salary survey from APHL found most salaries for laboratory directors were in the range of $78,000 to $146,000, with a median of $104,708.

Workplaces

Public health laboratory directors serve at all levels of government, usually working within health agencies.

Employment Outlook

Public health laboratory scientists are in great demand, and there should be increasing opportunities as current public health laboratory workers retire. There is also a strong need for other laboratory scientists, from entry-level technicians to laboratory managers and senior scientists with master's and doctoral degrees.

For Further Information

- Association of Public Health Laboratories (APHL) *www.aphl.org*

MEDICAL DIRECTOR

Job Description

"Medical director" is a title that can refer to a lot of different jobs. Throughout public health settings, medical directors are physicians who contribute their specialized knowledge to the development and implementation of services and programs. A medical director at a health department provides medical expertise regarding the many health care and health policy issues that arise. He or she serves as the liaison with outside clinical professionals and professional associations. He or she may also oversee the department's clinical services and even provide direct patient care. Public health agencies may also have medical directors in more specific roles. For example, a city health department's bureau of emergency management might have a medical director to guide planning for the medical response to a disaster. In an EMS system, a physician keeps an eye on the training of emergency medical technicians and paramedics and makes decisions about care protocols, so that the services provided are consistent with the latest medical knowledge. Departments of corrections have medical directors to ensure that inmates receive quality care that not only protects their health, but also helps to protect the health of the community after they are released.

Education and Certification

A medical director must be a licensed physician with training and experience appropriate to the role. A job may require experience in medical practice, supervisory experience, public health experience, or some combination of these. EMS systems often look for emergency medicine specialists. An MPH or board certification in public health and general preventive medicine can be an advantage.

Core Competencies and Skills

- Strong management skills
- Excellent written and verbal communication skills
- High degree of comfort with public speaking
- Ability to work with both medical and nonclinical personnel and to explain medical concepts in plain English
- Good understanding of epidemiology, statistics, and how to read surveillance reports and research studies
- Strong knowledge of clinical medicine, particularly of issues that are commonly addressed by public health efforts
- Thorough understanding of public health techniques and principles
- At least a basic understanding of the public health system and of public health law

Compensation

Medical directors' salaries are fairly typical for physicians, although generally closer to a primary care doctors' salary than to that of a highly paid specialist. A range of $100,000 to $200,000 is common, although jobs may pay less or more depending on budget, experience, and level of responsibility. Recent examples include about $117,000 for a medical director in an emergency preparedness program in a major midwestern city and up to $160,000 for the medical director at an early intervention program in a city in the Northeast.

Workplaces

There are medical directors overseeing various services at local and state health departments. When public health services are divided among other local or state agencies, these agencies may also employ medical directors. Nonprofit organizations that provide services often have medical directors, as well.

Employment Outlook

Many medical directors are public health physicians, and there has been concern about a shortage of doctors trained in public health. The number of new doctors trained in preventive medicine, a public health specialty, declined 29% between 2008 and 2013, in part due to funding constraints. The total number of doctors in this specialty declined about 5% in the same period. The number of jobs within each agency is limited, but a doctor with a strong background in both clinical medicine and public health should be able to find interesting opportunities.

For Further Information

- American College of Preventive Medicine (ACPM)
  www.acpm.org
- Also see the organizations listed with health commissioner.

FEDERAL AGENCY DIRECTOR

Job Description

The CDC has a top director to guide the agency's work, and each of its many divisions also has a director who shapes that division's agenda. Other federal agencies dealing with the public's health, such as the Food and Drug Administration (FDA), have similar structures, although the titles may be different. Directors can have enormous influence, serving as nationally and internationally recognized experts. They provide leadership on public health issues and encourage research on disease prevention and health promotion. They develop and maintain relationships with other federal agencies, state and local health departments, academic institutions, and national organizations. They are involved in creating health policy, carrying out new policies, and maximizing the efficiency and effectiveness of the department. Although they delegate much of the day-to-day administrative work, they bear responsibility for all major activities within the agency, from financial matters to decisions about drug approvals or health initiatives. They also have the privilege of providing direction and vision to the agency on a wide range of public health issues.

Education and Certification

Becoming the director of a federal public health agency, or of a division within such an agency, requires a doctoral degree in a related field and a strong track record in public health work. Many people start out in lower-level jobs at local health departments or at federal agencies, and then work up through the ranks. For example, the current CDC director, at the time this book was published, started as a "disease detective" in the Epidemic Intelligence Service, led a TB control program in New York City, and spent 5 years helping with TB control in India before becoming the head of New York City's health department and, finally, the head of the CDC.

Core Competencies and Skills

- High degree of expertise in public health, with specific expertise related to the agency's work
- High degree of prominence in the world of public health
- Experience in public health leadership, program development, and program implementation
- Experience with government, academia, and health-related organizations, to allow effective communication and collaboration
- Experience interacting with reporters and the public

Compensation

Leaders in the federal government are well compensated, although often not as well as people with similar levels of responsibility in the private business world. For example, in 2014, the director of the CDC earned a base salary of $179,700, according to a federal salary database, and the FDA commissioner earned $155,500.

Employment Outlook

As with other leadership jobs, there are only a few top positions, and they are open only to people with proven leadership skills and a high level of accomplishment. There are many lower-level leadership opportunities, however, which can lead eventually to positions of greater influence.

For Further Information

- To learn more about how federal agencies such as the CDC are run, visit their websites and look for links labeled "about" or "organization."

SURGEON GENERAL OF THE UNITED STATES

Job Description

Known as America's doctor, the Surgeon General is responsible for helping Americans understand how to improve their health and reduce their risk of illness and injury. The Surgeon General's duties include educating the public, advocating for effective public health programs, and serving as a symbol of the nation's commitment to protecting and improving our citizens' health. Through the Office of the Surgeon General, he or she oversees the U.S. Public Health Service Commissioned Corps. The Surgeon General advises the president, the secretary of Health and Human Services, and other government officials on a wide range of health issues, based on the best scientific evidence and policy analysis. He or she works with other agencies to promote specific initiatives, such as preventing HIV infection or reducing obesity. Responsibilities also include raising the standards for and quality of public health practice, promoting essential research, and contributing to emergency preparedness planning. The Surgeon General oversees the publication of major reports on health issues, convenes workshops with key leaders in public health, encourages community programs, and speaks out in the media about priority issues. In many ways, each Surgeon General is able to decide how to shape the job and how best to use the public influence it offers.

Education and Certification

The Surgeon General must be a physician and is typically an accomplished public health leader.

Core Competencies and Skills

- Passion for public health
- Understanding of public health issues on both the local and national scales
- Excellent management and interpersonal skills
- Ability to juggle multiple projects while keeping up with a busy schedule
- High level of comfort with public speaking, including media appearances
- Ability to select issues that can and should be addressed on a national scale
- Understanding of the use of evidence-based practice
- Ability to mobilize public health leaders and the public to take effective action

Compensation

The Surgeon General's salary is about $180,000.

Employment Outlook

There is only one U.S. Surgeon General. It is not the sort of job you can apply for. The president selects someone to hold this post, and only the most accomplished physicians are considered. The doctor President Obama chose in 2009, Regina Benjamin, was "just" a family physician who ran a clinic in a rural area of Alabama—but she also had a long list of achievements and awards. She had been chair of the Federation of State Medical Boards of the United States, president of the American Medical Association Education and Research Foundation, and associate dean at a medical school. She had served on many influential boards and committees and been recognized, multiple times, for her accomplishments. Dr. Vivek Murthy, who became Surgeon General in 2014, had a long list of accomplishments even though he was only 37 at the time. He had cofounded an HIV/AIDS education program that reached tens of thousands of young people, as well as an organization in India training women to provide health care and education. A company he helped to create supports collaboration among researchers around the world. And he is a cofounder and served as president of Doctors for America, a group dedicated to improving the health care system.

For Further Information

- Office of the Surgeon General
  www.surgeongeneral.gov

CHAPTER 22

Global Health

Defining "global public health" is a bit of a challenge. Some experts differentiate "global health" as a separate discipline from public health, suggesting that "public health" focuses on specific countries or communities (Koplan et al., 2009). Some also believe that global health should be considered distinct from international health. They define international health as wealthier countries helping poorer ones, with each effort limited to specific countries or locations, while global health emphasizes sharing knowledge, with all participants around the globe having something to contribute.

Meanwhile, other experts share this book's perspective that global health is public health. The modern definition of public health includes the same emphasis on population-level policies, overcoming health disparities, international and interdisciplinary collaboration, and health as a broad concept encompassing physical, mental, and social well-being (Fried et al., 2010). Furthermore, attention to health around the world is important for controlling infectious disease transmission, preventing or ameliorating chronic diseases, and creating the most efficient and effective systems for the delivery of health care.

At present, while the exact definition of global health continues to evolve, all three terms—public health, global health, and international health—continue to be used when talking about public health efforts beyond U.S. borders. Global health serves as something of an umbrella term, encompassing direct care, public health, economics, policy, and other influences on the health of individuals and communities. The work may take place in localized areas, or it may try to span the globe, addressing everything from classic public health issues like the risks of epidemics or pandemics, to environmental pollution, climate change, and how to overcome economic challenges to equitable care.

A look at courses and departments at American schools of public health reveals a wide range of "global health" work attached to public health research, education, and practice. There are programs focused on HIV prevention, infant nutrition, water and sanitation, the control of malaria, family planning, and many more areas of health. There are programs to build or strengthen the public health infrastructure. There are projects examining health disparities, studying ways to prevent violence, addressing health impacts of globalization, and more.

Many of the jobs and careers in the other chapters of this book either have equivalents in global health organizations or can incorporate global health issues. Most of the careers in the infectious disease chapter (Chapter 4) and several in the chronic disease chapter (Chapter 5) include at least indirect connections with global health. There are jobs with global health elements for pharmacists, biostatisticians, environmental engineers, nutrition consultants, emergency preparedness specialists, social marketers, professors, program evaluators, and many others.

However, breaking into international work can be a challenge. Job titles and expectations can be different from U.S.-based careers. Employers usually expect candidates to have experience in international work already and to understand the terminology associated with this work. In recent years, there has been increasing interest in global health careers, with new MPH programs and global health degrees. At the same time, many global health employers are focusing on hiring in-country national staff rather than expatriates. There may be more competition than ever. So how do you get that first job?

This chapter will share some of the more common roles in global health organizations, some information on how to get started, and where to look to find out more. It will also touch on humanitarian assistance roles, which focus on intervening to help populations during emergencies and political conflicts; some of these roles overlap significantly with the broader arena of public health.

ONLINE OVERVIEW: GLOBAL HEALTH WEBSITES

There are many nonprofits, government agencies, intergovernmental organizations, and business firms concerned with global health. Exploring their websites can be a good way to start to understand what's going on in public health around the world. Here are a few places to start:

- The Global Fund (theglobalfund.org)
- World Health Organization (WHO; www.who.int)
- United Nations Programme on HIV and AIDS (UNAIDS; www.unaids.org)
- United Nations Children's Fund (UNICEF; www.unicef.org)
- Centers for Disease Control and Prevention (CDC) Global Health (www.cdc.gov/globalhealth)
- U.S. Agency for International Development (USAID; www.usaid.gov)
- The Gates Foundation (www.gatesfoundation.org)
- Global Health Council (globalhealth.org)

The American Public Health Association (APHA) section on international health (www.apha.org/apha-communities/member-sections/international-health) is another good resource. APHA members can join this group to connect with people working in public health all over the world.

IS THIS REALLY THE CAREER FOR ME?

Going into global health is a pretty popular career goal. There are many, many people in schools of public health who imagine themselves working overseas, especially in the developing world, learning a new culture, practicing a new language, and helping to overcome some of the enormous inequities in health, sanitation, access to care, and quality of care.

But one of the biggest challenges of going into global health is just that: If you're going to do a job that involves traveling to other countries, especially in less developed regions, you actually have to learn new cultures, practice new languages, and do without conveniences you take for granted in the United States. You may find that your new colleagues or the population you are working with have different expectations, different values, even different ideas about time and deadlines than you are used to.

Some people thrive on the challenges. They jump into learning new ways of thinking and finding creative ways to overcome obstacles and create collaboration. Others last a week or a few months and come home frustrated, disappointed, and even angry.

Even if your job is based entirely in the United States, global health means being open to different ways of thinking and different ways of approaching the world. Making assumptions based on how we do things in the United States has led to the failure of countless global health efforts.

A commitment to global health also means understanding that you might not get to travel a lot or live in another country, at least not at first. Increasingly, global health work that is based in other countries emphasizes training and employing local community members to carry out the work. Some global health work is research that can be carried out right here in the United States. For example, there is biological research to investigate infectious diseases and computer modeling to try to predict disease migrations or outbreaks related to climate change. Many nongovernmental organizations (NGOs) and USAID contractors also have a U.S. headquarters office with a variety of relevant positions.

WHY PURSUE SPECIFIC TRAINING IN GLOBAL HEALTH?

People outside public health often think that doing global health work is straightforward: You go to a less developed country and provide medical care, vaccines, and mosquito nets. However, the global health world is filled with stories of "simple" efforts that failed or even backfired. A classic example is the large number of donated mosquito nets that are being used to catch fish instead of to protect against malaria, because fishing nets are expensive and food is essential. Using the nets for fishing creates a round of new problems, too: They catch far more fish than traditional methods, and so can put stress on fish populations. Moreover, the nets are coated with pesticide, which can leach into the water.

Another is the distressing situation with arsenic contamination of wells in Bangladesh. UNICEF and the World Bank funded the installation of tube wells throughout Bangladesh in the 1960s and 1970s to provide clean water for drinking, because the surface water was contaminated with dangerous bacteria. Unfortunately, the planners did not test for arsenic, which naturally occurs in groundwater in that region. The effects of low-level arsenic poisoning take years to develop, but they are serious: cancer, neurological problems, and chronic sores on hands and feet. By 2009, an estimated 43 million adults were dying each year from arsenic poisoning.

Of course, not all unintended consequences can be avoided. Even the best efforts can fail, and complications cannot always be predicted. However, a well-trained global health professional will have learned from the past and will understand how to assess a situation, look for potential problems, enlist the necessary help (from local community members to outside scientific experts), and avoid repeating mistakes.

Today's global health professionals also understand that combating inequity is not simply a matter of stepping in and fixing a problem with money or technology. Instead, there is a focus on cultural competency, collaboration, and building on strengths so that people around the world can achieve and sustain the same high level of health and safety. There is also a trend toward looking at health needs as broad and interconnected, instead of focusing in on just one country or community.

EDUCATION AND AREAS OF STUDY

As with many public health jobs, there is no single route to getting to work in global health. One of the more straightforward paths is an MPH, but there are other degrees and other backgrounds that can also lead to global health careers.

MPH Programs in Global Health

An MPH can be good preparation for global health work, particularly at a school with a strong international or global health program. Some schools and programs of public health offer a specific MPH concentration in global health. Some offer a global health certificate program that lets students combine global health with any other area of study. Because global health encompasses so many different public health disciplines, it can make sense to specialize in, say, maternal and child health or infectious disease, but with extra training related to international issues.

A typical global health concentration will require specific courses along with the core MPH curriculum. The course offerings can be quite different from one school to another. Subjects run the gamut from hard science—such as microbial risk assessment—to the social sciences, such as how religious beliefs impact health.

Someone interested in the sociological side of health might look for courses on health as social justice, social entrepreneurship, and communication for behavior change.

Someone interested in economics and policy could choose to study international health policy and how health care systems are structured in other countries.

If engineering or biology is a strong interest, it is possible to focus in on water, sanitation, and control of water- and foodborne illness.

In some programs, you can even find classes on emergency management or humanitarian assistance in resource-limited areas, including logistics, disease control, food distribution, management of complex emergencies, and the needs of refugees.

In every MPH program, students complete a practicum experience, in which they start putting their skills to use in a workplace setting. Students also complete a major project during their practicum, which could be research, program design, program evaluation, or something else the organization needs. Schools of public health with established global health programs often have extensive lists of organizations that will accept their students for the practicum and that offer experiences around the world. For a global health student, this is your chance to start making connections and showing that you can do this type of work.

Global Health Competencies

In 2011, the Association of Schools and Programs of Public Health published a list of competencies for global health education. They noted that existing programs were so varied, it was not clear that graduates from different programs would even have the same knowledge or qualifications. The competency model is an effort to standardize the training and education, so that an MPH in "global health" would at least guarantee the same core knowledge across the board. It is also intended to make sure students are well prepared with a good base of knowledge for their future careers.

Schools of public health do not necessarily have to follow these competencies, but they provide a good framework for thinking about what a global health professional needs to know.

The competencies incorporate seven major domains:

- *Capacity strengthening*: Be able to design workforce development strategies, assure sustainability, and help communities strengthen their ability to respond to health challenges.
- *Collaborating and partnering*: Know how to recruit and collaborate with stakeholders from many different backgrounds.
- *Ethical reasoning and professional practice*: Be able to recognize and respond to difficult ethical issues, and promote

accountability for the impact of policies and public health efforts.

- *Health equity and social justice*: Understand how to address health disparities across different types of populations.
- *Program management*: Know how to design, implement, and evaluate health programs that will be effective and sustainable.
- *Sociocultural and political awareness*: Be able to work effectively in many different cultural settings and across political landscapes from local to international.
- *Strategic analysis*: Learn to analyze complex factors, think about the systems they are part of and how they interact, and use this knowledge to create effective programs.

This list of skills is not meant to stand alone, but to build on the core competencies for all MPH programs, which include the following discipline-specific domains:

- Biostatistics
- Environmental health sciences
- Epidemiology
- Health policy and management
- Social and behavioral sciences

The general core competencies also include seven interdisciplinary domains: Communications and Informatics, Diversity and Culture, Leadership, Public Health Biology, Professionalism, Program Planning, and Systems Thinking.

Even if a program follows these competencies, different schools do still have their own specialties within the field, and the emphasis may differ from one school to another. Different schools also have strengths in different areas and connections in different parts of the world. It is worth doing some research to figure out what a school offers before deciding where you would like to attend.

Global Health Master's Degrees

Some universities offer global health master's degrees, which are distinct from the MPH. The content of these programs overlaps with that of an MPH, and they may even include a practicum experience. At present, the master's degree in global health seems to be still evolving; one program will be more research-based, while another aims to give a broad understanding of global health to people who will be doing practical work in the field. Some programs are only 1 year and some longer. Some are geared toward established professionals from other disciplines who want to augment their knowledge of global health.

It seems likely that at this point, the MPH will give a more practical and well-rounded education for someone who is just starting out and wants to go into public health. The master's in global health may be a more appropriate choice for someone who already has a career or an advanced degree in another area, but wants to either increase their knowledge or bring their experience to international work. Some programs emphasize their interdisciplinary nature, combining classes from different subject areas around the university. It is worth checking on these programs as time goes by, to see how they evolve and what they offer as this area of study continues to develop.

Bachelor's Degrees

As the public health bachelor's degree becomes more common, undergraduate programs are also offering public health majors with international concentrations, as well as undergraduate degrees in global health. These programs provide an introduction to global health and usually include either an opportunity or a requirement to spend time studying abroad. Some graduates of these programs go on to entry-level jobs in public health. Others use this training as a foundation for an MPH, a medical degree, a nursing degree, law school, a Master of Public Administration (MPA) or Master of Public Policy (MPP), or other graduate education.

Doctoral Degrees

For those interested in policy-making and leadership positions in global health, a Doctorate of Public Health (DrPH) with an international concentration or a PhD in a related field can be helpful. Different degree programs have different emphases; the DrPH tends to be directed more toward the practice of public health, while a PhD is focused more on research.

One option is a PhD in global health, but many jobs look for a specific field of knowledge such as business, health policy, or economics. Many people have found that working in the field for a while helped them identify what to study, so that they could choose a PhD program and advance their careers in a specific direction. It is important to remember that in most cases, even with a doctoral degree, it is real-world experience that makes a candidate stand out for a leadership position in global health.

Other Backgrounds and Degrees

An MPH (or other public health degree) is definitely not the only way to a global health career. As with public health in general, there are jobs in global health for engineers, economists, environmental experts, doctors and nurses, lawyers, logistics specialists, and people from many other backgrounds. In some cases, an MBA or an MPA can be a good match.

People with these backgrounds will usually have the same challenge that MPH graduates face in breaking into the field—employers want experience in global health before they will give you that first job. Again, networking, volunteering, and pursuing education specific to global health can all help you get started.

An Online Introduction to Global Health Education

The Global Health eLearning Center (www.globalhealthlearning.org) is sponsored by USAID, but access is free to anyone who registers. There are online courses on a wide range of global health issues, from disease control to supply chain management.

Peace Corps and Related Programs

Joining the Peace Corps has long been a popular choice for young people interested in international health work. However, while a Peace Corps experience does give excellent experience living and working abroad, it does not necessarily offer thorough preparation for a career in public health.

One option is to enter the Peace Corps Master's International program. In this program, you apply to the Peace Corps and to graduate school at the same time. The Peace Corps partners with schools that offer degrees in subjects where skilled volunteers are specifically needed. There are many MPH programs that participate.

Graduate students in the program receive Peace Corps training while completing their coursework and then embark on their Peace Corps assignments. If the degree requires a research project or other major project or paper, the Peace Corps work becomes the basis for this assignment. The program is intended to meet the needs of Peace Corps host countries by giving them educated, skilled volunteers, and to serve participants by helping them earn their degrees. It also gives participants the opportunity to build their resumes by putting their education into real-world practice.

The Peace Corps also offers a graduate fellowship program for Peace Corps volunteers after they return, including financial assistance to help with tuition.

Doctors and nurses may want to consider the Global Health Service Partnership. This program, a collaboration between the Peace Corps, Seed Global Health, and the U.S. President's Emergency Plan for AIDS Relief (PEPFAR), was established to meet needs for clinical teaching and capacity-building in selected countries. In 2013, the program placed clinicians in Malawi, Tanzania, and Uganda.

United Nations Volunteers

The United Nations (UN) Volunteers Program is another established way to get experience overseas. Volunteers must have a university degree, at least 2 years' relevant work experience, and knowledge of English, French, or Spanish; and assignments are greatly dependent on specific needs. More information about how to get involved is at www.unv.org.

FINDING YOUR FIRST JOB

With more and more public health schools and programs opening up and global health becoming a popular topic of study, job applicants will need to plan carefully to stand out from the competition.

One option is to focus in on a particular skill set. Employers look for people with concrete skills. An organization looking for help with malaria prevention, for example, might prefer an applicant with a lot of knowledge about practical aspects of disease control. Monitoring and evaluation is a common job category but not a standard MPH concentration, so putting extra effort into this area could help. While focusing your studies may limit the jobs you feel qualified for, it may also give you an edge with an employer that is looking for that specific skill. Check with your school's career office and talk with your professors and other mentors about what is likely to be in demand around the time you graduate.

Make the Most of Studying Abroad

There are many chances to work or study abroad, but not all of these will stand out on a resume. People experienced in global health tend to have much more respect for a solid research project or hands-on experience with program development than for a few weeks spent on a "volunteer vacation," no matter how worthy the cause. Similarly, there is a big difference between a practicum experience that is largely "shadowing" project staff and one in which you are an active member of a team.

Some students have the good fortune to be hired on at the organization where they do their MPH practicum experience. However, even when a student shines during a practicum, the organization may not have a job to offer, or they may be looking for someone with more experience or different skills.

Use Your Resources

Do not be afraid to network. Use your school's career guidance office to get in touch with alumni who are doing the kind of work you are interested in. Ask them for an "informational interview," which is just a conversation about their career and a chance to ask for advice on getting into the field. You can also use the website LinkedIn.com to find people who went to your school or work in the area you are targeting.

Join APHA and get involved. Take advantage of their affordable membership rates for students and others who are not yet public health professionals. Look for other professional organizations that focus on your interests. (Check the "For Further Information" sections at the end of each career description in this book.) If you can afford it, attend conferences, go to the panels on global health, and chat with the people around you.

Keep in touch with your professors and mentors, and let them know you are looking for work. And, again if your budget permits, look for opportunities to volunteer with an organization that is doing work you admire.

Consider Taking a Chance

Workers with an MPH or clinical skills are often in demand in less developed countries. Some people working in global health got started by simply going to the country they were interested in, getting to know the organizations and people there, and either volunteering or applying for jobs at local agencies. If you decide to try this, you will need your best networking skills and it helps to know the local language. You should make sure you are legally eligible to work. And it is best to have a backup plan, in case things do not work out.

Entry-Level Employment Programs

Large agencies and organizations will sometimes offer recruitment programs to try to fill specific needs. It is worth checking their websites to see whether there is any current outreach for new graduates or early career professionals. For example, the United Nations Refugee Agency (UNHCR) has an Entry-Level Humanitarian Professional Programme specifically to identify and recruit young professionals to meet current and future needs (www.unhcr.org).

Fellowships and Internships

Fellowships in global health are opportunities for advanced students or recent graduates to continue learning and getting that essential experience, often while earning a modest income. Internships are generally shorter programs offered to students, to give them an early introduction to global health work. Some universities offer their own internships and fellowships to their students and recent graduates. There are also some programs from government agencies and NGOs.

Some of these opportunities are open to people from backgrounds including education, management, finance—not just people who have studied public health.

The websites for universities with global health programs often list volunteer, internship, and fellowship opportunities. Here are just a few examples:

- Global Health Corps accepts fellows from diverse backgrounds and varied levels of education and experience. In 2014, they had 128 fellows from 22 different countries. *ghcorps.org*
- The Association of Schools and Programs of Public Health (ASPPH) offers global health fellowships for recent graduates of Council on Education for Public Health (CEPH)-accredited, ASPPH member schools. *fellowships.aspph.org*

- USAID has a fellowship program geared toward more advanced professionals, but also an internship program for undergraduates to give students a first experience working in global health. *www.ghfp.net*
- GlobeMed is a national organization with student-run chapters at more than 50 universities. Student groups are paired with grassroots health organizations throughout the world, and students have opportunities to work directly with these organizations. *globemed.org*
- The Fogarty International Center at the National Institutes of Health (NIH) has a Global Health Program for Fellows and Scholars designed for doctoral degree students and recent graduates, and offered in collaboration with several universities and international sites. *www.fic.nih.gov*

Opportunities for Federal Employees

If you are already working in public health for a federal government agency, you may be eligible for the International Experience and Technical Assistance (IETA) program. This program was created to help build a stronger federal workforce for global public health work. The year-long program includes in-person workshops at the CDC in Atlanta and a minimum of 12 weeks in an overseas assignment. More information is at www.cdc.gov/globalhealth/IETA.

JOB LISTINGS ONLINE

There are too many organizations and websites with global health job opportunities to list here. NGOs, government agencies, and companies that do global health work often list available job openings on their websites.

Here are some places to start:

- *devex* is a website focusing on global development, where you will find news, career advice, and job listings. The site focuses on global development, so it includes jobs in economic development, renewable energy, environmental protection, agricultural systems, and more. There is usually a long list of job openings in public health, in many places around the world. You can narrow your search to just entry-level jobs, although—as with many global health jobs—even "entry level" often means a year or two of relevant experience is expected. There are also volunteer and internship listings. *www.devex.com*

■ *Idealist* is not specific to global health, but it is specifically for organizations that are aiming to make a difference in the world. Some of the jobs are with global health organizations, including some at entry level. Idealist also lists internships and volunteer opportunities. *www.idealist.org*

■ *ReliefWeb* is sponsored by the United Nations Office for the Coordination of Humanitarian Affairs. The site includes news, job listings, and training opportunities. It focuses on disaster and crisis relief, but its job listings include a range of global health opportunities, including some internships and entry-level jobs. *reliefweb.int*

PHYSICIAN/GLOBAL HEALTH

Job Description

Doctors have many opportunities to shape public health programs in the developing world, serving as advisors or working directly in research, systems and program design, and evaluation. For example, there are doctors involved in building capacity for HIV prevention and treatment in countries in Africa. They help to decide what training local health care providers need and contribute to the design and implementation of that training. They travel to clinics to make sure they are properly staffed and that they have the necessary space and equipment. Physicians are also involved in decreasing the impact of other chronic or infectious diseases, designing mental health services, and many other aspects of public health in the developing world. They may be based in the United States and travel to other countries periodically, or be based overseas.

Education and Certification

A medical degree is essential. Each job has its own requirements, depending on the work to be done. Some physicians who do international public health work specialize in tropical medicine. Some are preventive medicine specialists. Some have other specialties plus training in public health. Employers look for doctors with skills and training that match a particular program or population's needs. They also look for people with experience living and working abroad, ideally in the region where the work will be focused. A physician who wants to improve his or her knowledge and skills could consider a global health master's degree, particularly in a program designed for clinical professionals, or an MPH with a focus on global health. These programs can also provide useful connections for fellowships and initial jobs.

Core Competencies and Skills

- Adaptability
- Interest in other cultures and awareness of local climate, customs, and politics
- Fluency in a relevant language or the ability to learn (helpful and sometimes essential)
- Strong knowledge of epidemiology
- Expertise in the field of work to be done
- Understanding of the local health care capabilities and how they differ from what is available in the United States

Compensation

Salaries differ according to agency, duty location, and specific job. Here are some recent examples. Current listings for WHO medical officers assigned to help with infectious disease control, with at least several years' experience in this type of work, offer about $130,000 per year. In 2015, a typical listing for a CDC medical officer serving overseas offered a salary range from $73,000 to $130,000; some jobs include pay allowances for location, housing, and moving expenses.

Workplaces

The WHO, the USAID, and the CDC all employ medical officers to do global health work. Physicians can work for consulting firms that contract with international health agencies. There are many nonprofit organizations that employ physicians to help with global health efforts, and there are opportunities for international public health work in the military. The U.S. Public Health Service Commissioned Corps is another option.

Employment Outlook

Jobs for physicians, often listed under "medical officer," are frequently available at federal agencies, multinational organizations, and nonprofits. Other job titles to look for are "technical officer" and "health scientist," which often require an MD or PhD. Getting started can be a challenge, however, because many jobs are for people with experience in global health. As with other jobs in this field, look for fellowships and volunteer opportunities to start building your credentials. Once established, physicians who are international public health experts often enjoy long and interesting careers.

For Further Information

There are too many organizations concerned with global health and prevention to list them all here. Many of them post available jobs at the sites listed earlier in this chapter. There is a useful introduction to CDC career opportunities at:

- Centers for Disease Control and Prevention (CDC) Global Health—Jobs Overseas
  www.cdc.gov/globalhealth/employment

PROGRAM MANAGER

Job Description

The title "program manager" can have different meanings, but a typical role for a program manager at an international public health organization involves oversight of multiple projects in the developing world. Often, the projects are all working toward the same goal, such as the prevention and control of HIV/AIDS in a particular region. In some cases, an organization collaborates with local, in-country NGOs that provide the staff to carry out the projects; in others, the program manager is managing work within his or her own organization. When a new program is being launched, the program manager guides the planning, making sure that projects and activities are based on sound science, are feasible and sustainable, and match the organization's and outside donors' goals. The program manager assists with development of the budget and may help to write applications for funding. As the program gets underway, the program manager provides support to the staff, ensuring they have necessary supplies, training, transportation, and other needs. He or she tracks the progress of each project and makes sure that all work is in keeping with funders' rules and requirements. The program manager keeps funders, organization administrators, and others with a stake in the program informed about how the work is proceeding. Responsibilities also include communicating with other NGOs and with the country's Ministry of Health as needed to coordinate efforts, streamline the work, and ensure that local laws and regulations are followed. This job can involve significant travel to project sites, often in areas with little development and few amenities.

Education and Certification

A typical requirement for a public health program manager is an MPH with a concentration in global health or a degree in international health or another related field. A bachelor's degree in a field such as public health is sometimes acceptable, with appropriate experience. Program managers usually have at least a few years of experience in roles related to program administration; this can be a next step from the role of "project manager," overseeing just one part of a larger program.

Core Competencies and Skills

- Love of travel and the ability to handle adverse conditions
- Familiarity with key public health issues and the ability to learn new information quickly
- Understanding of public health programs in both theory and practice
- Familiarity with local politics and culture
- Knowledge of rules and regulations that apply to funding from foundations and from the U.S. government
- Strong management skills, including organization, budgeting, and personnel management
- Ability to handle pressure and meet deadlines
- Excellent spoken and written communication skills

Compensation

Salaries increase with experience and responsibility; there is too much variation among jobs to give a single salary estimate. As a rough example, the average salary for a lower-level program manager at a nonprofit organization is about $55,000, but at a large agency, the salary for an experienced manager of a major program can be over $100,000.

Workplaces

Program managers doing international public health work are often found at nonprofit organizations and at consulting firms that contract with government and intergovernmental agencies. Some program managers are based in the United States, with travel to project locations, and some work in the country where the work is being carried out.

Employment Outlook

Finding this type of work can take some determination. As with other global health jobs, good ways to get started including volunteering overseas, making connections, and being willing to accept a lower-level job and work your way up. Program manager can be a step along the way to a job with more responsibility and higher pay.

For Further Information

- There are many examples of program manager jobs on the job search websites in the introduction to this chapter. Also, check the websites of organizations that do work you are interested in.

PUBLIC HEALTH PROFILE: International Programs Manager
April Davies, MPH
International Programs Manager, Water.org, Kansas City, MO

Describe the sort of work you do.

Water.org is a U.S.-based NGO that works with partner organizations in other countries to support water, sanitation, and hygiene projects. Water.org aims for a few specific elements in our projects. We like to see that women are involved, we like projects to be community driven, and we prefer to know that after the project is completed, the community will be able to sustain it. I'm the person who manages the projects, either working directly with our partner organizations or working with our country offices in Kenya and India. It's rare that I go long-term to our overseas offices, but I'll travel to our project countries for a week or two at a time.

(continued)

(continued)

What is a typical day like at your job?

My day at headquarters starts with conference calls in the early morning, because we have a 9-hour time difference with our partners in East Africa. Then I might work on reviewing project proposals or writing grant proposals. Sometimes I prepare information for our communications department to share with reporters, donors, or other nonprofits.

I often communicate with our partner organizations by e-mail, too, answering questions and handling administrative issues. If the price of cement goes up, for example, they might want to know if they should ask for more funding or scale back their activities. I also hear from other organizations in the regions we serve. A smaller NGO might be looking for a drilling rig, and they'll ask if one of our partners has one.

When I'm overseas, I meet with partner organizations and visit project sites. Some are in urban areas and some in remote locations. One project I've gone to see is in a very rural area of Ethiopia—you can't even travel to the communities during the rainy season. The communities have hand-dug shallow wells, and our partner organization goes out to cap each well and put a pump on it. For a sanitation project that involves building model latrines and then providing education so people can build their own, I'll talk with the educators and go out to see the latrines.

What education or training do you have? Is it typical for your job?

I have bachelor's degrees with majors in Spanish and journalism, and I have an MPH with a global health concentration and a community health and development focus. Water.org also employs engineers to tell us if projects are sound, and we have people who are experts in development and in microfinance.

What path did you take to get to the job you are in today?

My first major international experience was the Peace Corps, right after college. I was assigned to a rural area in El Salvador. When I got there, the community had wells and a river but no water from a tap or

(continued)

(continued)

a faucet. They wanted a water system that would be reliable and safe year round. I helped them get funding, purchase materials, and manage the finances. After the Peace Corps, I managed an AmeriCorps program that placed workers in safety-net clinics in underserved areas in Kansas. When I decided I wanted to go back to international health, I chose to earn an MPH at a school with good opportunities for field experiences. I got a work–study job with the school's water and sanitation group and stayed with them for a while after graduation, including spending 6 months in Kenya. I found my current job through an ad, but I'd been collaborating with Water.org on some projects already, so I was aware of them, and they were aware of me.

Where might you go from here, if you wanted to advance your career?

I've only been here for a short time, so I can see myself staying for a while. A more senior, supervisory position would be the next step, if I wanted to move straight up. Another option would be to move to an organization that hires people to manage work abroad, and to work in an office overseas.

What is the worst or most challenging part of your job?

I love having the opportunity to travel, but my colleagues and I don't like flying on small planes in other countries. It can be scary! In terms of the work itself, it's difficult when we have to disappoint our partner organizations, when we don't have the funding that they need to run at their ultimate capacity. Sometimes I see programs from other organizations that have good funding but aren't very effective or sustainable, and that can be frustrating.

What is the best part?

I'm working with organizations all over the world to solve water, sanitation, and hygiene challenges. I especially like the solutions our partners come up with, and I like sharing ideas with them. It's exciting to see that things work. It's also exciting to discover what doesn't work out that well and to take those lessons to create more solutions.

(continued)

(continued)

What advice do you have for someone who is interested in your career?

Gain international experience. Live and work in another country. And do it early on, because it's difficult to find organizations that will hire people to do international work if they haven't had international experience. Volunteering is one option, and studying abroad doesn't hurt. Learning another language is also a good idea. Be flexible about the part of the world you go to. If it's in a country you weren't interested in, but it's a job you would like, go!

MONITORING AND EVALUATION SPECIALIST

Job Description

Monitoring and evaluation (often abbreviated "M&E") is increasingly a part of public health in the United States, but it is already a well-established role in global health efforts. The M&E specialist is responsible for measuring the success (or failure) of global health programs and activities. Evaluation is essential to know if a program is being carried out as intended, if it had the intended effect, if it caused any unintended problems, and ultimately if it should be continued, replicated, or shut down.

Ideally, M&E work begins as the program itself is being designed. The planning process determines what data will be collected, how monitoring will be carried out, and what result will be necessary to consider the effort a success. The M&E specialist looks for risks to the project and any assumptions that could influence how results are interpreted. They make sure that the baseline information and outcomes to be measured are actually relevant, and not just incidental to the program's goals. Then they work with the rest of the planning team to decide how data will be gathered and when. The role can include varied activities such as actually watching workers at their jobs, going out into communities to observe for changes, collecting data from health records, reading reports, and analyzing data. Traditional methods such as surveys and focus groups are still widely used. Often, M&E experts also use specialized techniques such as geographic information systems (GIS), which literally map out information such as health statistics, economic information, and environmental pollutants to uncover correlations in specific locations. The M&E specialist may train staff to help with information-gathering and other aspects of the process. They may also work with local community members to hear their priorities and involve them in the process.

Monitoring is done periodically throughout the project and tends to focus on making sure the work is done as planned, that efficient processes are being followed, and that rules for ethics, safety, and quality are followed. There may also be periodic checks to see if progress is being made. The M&E specialist reports back to the project team during this process, so they can make changes if necessary to keep the work on track. A more complete evaluation is often carried out at the midpoint and again at the end of the project. Evaluation focuses in on the actual effectiveness of the effort, the size of its impact, and whether or not it was cost-effective. The M&E specialist's final evaluation report may be shared with upper-level administration, funders, local government agencies, community leaders, and other stakeholders.

Education and Certification

Employers generally look for someone with relevant training and experience, typically with at least a master's degree. Some MPH programs have tracks or certificates specifically focused on M&E; more commonly, a student interested in this work might choose to emphasize courses in M&E, statistics, and data management while pursuing a different specific concentration. Other degrees that could provide an appropriate background include mathematics, business, statistics, international relations, and the social sciences. Demonstrating knowledge of M&E methods tends to be most important, rather than any specific degree subject; this may be learned through certificate programs, courses, or on the job.

Core Competencies and Skills

- Strong math and statistics skills
- Ability to translate complex statistical information into ordinary language
- Familiarity with guidelines and regulations related to the project or program
- Good computer skills, including use of databases
- Strong written and oral communication skills; fluency in local language is very helpful
- Good observational ability
- Familiarity with public health methods, processes, and pitfalls

■ Understanding of (or willingness to learn about) local culture and how it may influence behavior

Compensation

This is another role with a wide range of salaries, and no aggregate data to confirm what is typical at different levels. In the United States, $60,000 to $70,000 is not uncommon for someone with a master's degree, and some current global health openings are in a similar range; however, actual salaries will depend on the employer, level of responsibility, amount of experience, and country where the work is located.

Workplaces

These jobs are often based in the countries where the work to be evaluated is carried out. Consulting firms, nonprofits, and NGOs are common employers.

Employment Outlook

M&E is a well-established role in global health work. With increasing awareness of the need to spend funds wisely and protect against unintended consequences, these jobs should continue to be available. As with most global health jobs, the strongest candidates will be those with not only appropriate training, but also experience in the field.

For Further Information

■ There is no single organization or association for M&E specialists in global health. To get a better idea of this role, one place to start is the free, online M&E courses at the Global Health eLearning Center, www.globalhealthlearning.org.

LOGISTICIAN

Job Description

Most international public health programs require supplies. It could be posters and handouts for a social marketing campaign, or it could be clean syringes for a vaccination program. It could be vaccines, medications, protective gloves, equipment for water purification, or countless other items. A logistics expert helps an organization or local government forecast their supply needs and prepare to meet them. For example, tracking the past year's use of vaccines, looking at plans to expand an immunization program, and figuring out how many vials, syringes, and alcohol wipes will be needed is a logistics job. The vaccines must be stored, shipped, and distributed in the right amounts to the right places; that is a logistics issue, too. Does the country have the capacity—transportation, storage space, electricity and refrigeration, communication networks, tracking programs, and workers—to handle a huge supply of vaccines all at once? If not, how can the system be improved, streamlined, or expanded? Will current funds be enough to purchase and deliver supplies, and if not, how can the program trim spending or obtain more funding? Logisticians also manage the flow of information and products so that supplies do not expire before they are used, do not run out, and do not wind up sitting in a warehouse in one city while a clinic in another region has none to distribute.

Some logistics experts work directly for organizations carrying out public health programs. Others serve as technical advisors, advising local organizations or governments so that they can eventually take over this work themselves.

Education and Certification

The most common educational background for a logistician is a bachelor's degree in business, supply chain management, or a related field, but this includes logisticians who work in business and industry, handling manufacturing supplies. Logistics experts in global health need more specialized knowledge and are often expected to have a master's degree, such as an MPH. A pharmacy degree, an MD, or a master's in business or logistics is also appropriate for some jobs. An online course and certification program in humanitarian logistics, designed for entry-level or mid-career workers at aid organizations, is available at www.hlcertification.org.

Core Competencies and Skills

- Excellent organizational skills
- Strong time management skills
- A knack for financial management
- Ability to handle complicated problems with many elements

- Language skills or the ability—and patience—to work with translators
- Strong analytical and problem-solving skills
- Adaptability and a high level of comfort with unpredictable or changing situations
  - Understanding of politics and the diplomatic ability to facilitate a discussion, negotiate delicate issues, and bring people to consensus
  - Tendency to be detail oriented, combined with the ability to see the "big picture"
  - Understanding of public health issues, with the ability to learn quickly about new topics and recognize the major issues

Compensation

In 2014, the median salary for a logistician was about $74,000 with most earning between $46,000 and $114,000.

Workplaces

Logistics experts, including technical advisors, work at international health and aid organizations, including government and intergovernmental agencies and nonprofits, as well as at consulting firms that contract with these types of organizations. Organizations concerned with relief efforts following disasters also employ logistics experts.

Employment Outlook

According to the Bureau of Labor Statistics (BLS), logistics is a rapidly growing field—but they are primarily talking about the business world. This is a relatively small, specialized area in public health. There have been efforts over recent years to strengthen supply chains in developing countries, including funding for research and for technical advisors; the levels of continued interest, funding, and need will determine the number of future jobs for logistics experts.

For Further Information

- U.S. Agency for International Development (USAID) Deliver Project *deliver.jsi.com*

- International Association of Public Health Logisticians (IAPHL)
  www.iaphl.org
- Chartered Institute of Logistics and Transport
  www.ciltinternational.org
- Fritz Institute
  www.fritzinstitute.org

PROCUREMENT MANAGER

Job Description

In large global health organizations and programs, there is often a separate job or department for purchasing supplies. However, it is not as simple as just placing an order! Procuring enough supplies for a regional or nationwide program takes time, and it takes planning. Whether it is vaccines, medicines, water purifiers, condoms, posters, or any other health-related item, the manufacturer may not even have a large enough supply on hand. The procurement manager helps program directors plan far in advance, to allow for manufacturing, shipping, clearance through customs, and distribution. He or she works with them to decide how to get the most for their money without compromising on quality or time, and ensures that the product will meet the program's needs. Then he or she gives manufacturers the requirements and timeline, obtains price quotes, and advises on any changes to the budget. After placing the order, the procurement manager keeps track of progress, arranges for quality testing, and reviews the results. The procurement manager plans in advance for shipping, considering everything from the method of transportation to problems that might arise at customs, and then monitors the shipment to make sure it arrives safely at its destination.

Education and Certification

A bachelor's degree in business, public administration, marketing, or a related field is a good place to start. An MPH can be helpful, too. Special training in procurement and contracts management is available through certificate programs at some universities. For those with experience who want professional certification, there is a Certified Professional in Supply Management credential available from the Institute for Supply Management (ISM).

Core Competencies and Skills

- Excellent organizational and planning skills especially for working within bureaucratic organizations
- High degree of common sense
- Good negotiating skills
- Good math skills and financial sense
- Ability to gather information effectively and determine what is important
- Understanding of how to differentiate between theory and practice
- Knack for explaining needs clearly, so that manufacturers know what is expected
- Ability to read and understand contracts
- Willingness to learn and gain experience over time

Compensation

The ISM's 2014 salary survey found an average of $66,000 for an entry-level supply management professional, to $108,000 for a mid-level manager, and $158,000 for a director. The average salary for those with 9 to 20 years of experience was $100,000.

Workplaces

There are opportunities available at consulting firms that contract with international agencies, nonprofits, and foreign governments, as well as at agencies and organizations that manage large public health programs.

Employment Outlook

There are not a lot of people with the specific skills and knowledge to do this type of work. After the entry level, opportunities should be good for someone who is willing to take the time and make the effort to gain experience.

For Further Information

- Institute for Supply Management (ISM)
  www.instituteforsupplymanagement.org

- International Federation of Purchasing and Supply
  Management (IFPSM)
  www.ifpsm.org
- Council of Supply Chain Management Professionals (CSCMP)
  cscmp.org

PUBLIC HEALTH PROFILE: Procurement Manager
Paul Stannard
Deputy Procurement Manager
Crown Agents, Based at John Snow Inc., Arlington, VA

Describe the sort of work you do.

I'm currently assigned to work with John Snow, Inc., where I supervise a procurement team and also do a lot of the hands-on work
myself. We procure products for international public health programs supported by USAID. That includes pharmaceuticals, medical
devices, contraceptives, diagnostic tests, mosquito nets, and more.
Purchases are informed by the receiving country's needs, what other
donors are funding, and that country's own budget. My team and I
work with the stakeholder in-country to figure out what to buy, how
much to buy, and when. Then we handle purchasing, quality assurance, and shipping. If the country doesn't have the capacity to handle in country-transport, we'll arrange that too, all the way to local
clinics or even individual households.

What is a typical day like at your job?

I'm in frequent contact with our field offices and U.S. embassies
overseas, talking about requirements. For example, I'll talk with
someone in Senegal about what supplies they need for their malaria
control program. I speak regularly with manufacturers to negotiate
terms, follow up on orders, and see whether they are on schedule.
Sometimes I'll be calling a manufacturer with an emergency order.

I also speak daily with my counterparts at USAID in Washington.
Sometimes we need to discuss budget problems. Often, someone from
USAID will call and ask my advice. I also keep in touch with our quality
assurance experts about policies and practices, such as whether we
need to sample more of a given product or can sample less.

(continued)

(continued)

About twice a year, I travel overseas. I go for a week or 10 days at a time. I do briefings for our field offices, explaining what we are doing, how we do it, and what they need to know. I also visit manufacturers' production facilities to discuss what we expect and what quality standards they need to meet.

What education or training do you have? Is it typical for your job?

I went to high school in the United Kingdom, and my higher exams were in the sciences. A lot of my colleagues have bachelor's degrees, which is expected for new people coming in. Many either have an MPH or are in the process of earning one. Very few have specific degrees related to procurement.

What path did you take to get to the job you are in today?

My original plan was to be a dentist. I took a year off after high school, and I wanted to travel. My careers advisor recommended that I get some work experience, and I was fortunate enough to join Crown Agents. I started in their shipping department. I got to go to Lagos when I was just 21. I spent a total of about a year and a half there, came home to England for a couple years, and then was sent to be a company representative in Singapore. My public health involvement started after that, when I helped set up a program to manage essential drug procurement and distribution in Kenya. I spent a number of years running procurement projects and working in different African countries, and finally, as my last assignment came to an end, my wife and I decided to settle back in the United Kingdom. But then I was offered this posting in the United States, and here we are!

Where might you go from here, if you wanted to advance your career?

My plan for the future is to continue with supply chain work, whether directing a team, educating others, or consulting. It's difficult to

(continued)

(continued)

describe a typical career progression, because structures differ from place to place. You start in a role with a lower amount of responsibility and as you learn, you gain more responsibility—but each job is different, so you never stop learning.

What is the worst or most challenging part of your job?

Sometimes our own donor bureaucracy or the bureaucracy in-country delays things, or the people in charge will make decisions that don't seem to make sense. It's also hard when people don't understand the need for planning. If countries don't plan properly, or donors don't understand how little infrastructure there is before they give the money, we'll always be running to catch up.

What is the best part?

It's fun when we get a new request. It's exciting to work with the country to define what they need and how we can handle it. I'm less interested in the process once something's up and running smoothly—I always want to move on to the next new thing! And although one can get a bit blasé about the size of the shipments, when we're sending out two jumbo jets full of medicine to help moms and kids—it's still a bit of a buzz.

What advice do you have for someone who is interested in your career?

Procurement is a huge part of the budget for any private company or government agency. That includes not just procuring goods but finding consultants, office spaces, and things the organization needs. Have a look at the supply chains for hospitals, look at the supply chain side of public health programs, and look at donor programs and at the services that help them. If you're interested in international work it helps to have overseas experience, even if it's short-term. Look for volunteer opportunities, and go even if it's just for a week or a month. The first overseas assignment is the toughest one to get, so don't wait around for a 3-year posting.

WATER, SANITATION, AND HYGIENE (WASH) MANAGER

Job Description

In the United States, we have well-established water and sewer systems, with tap water that is safe to drink, efficient systems to carry waste away from living areas, and strong regulations around wastewater treatment and management. In many parts of the world, however, water and sanitation remain important challenges to public health. They are also major concerns after natural disasters, in refugee camps, and in other situations where day-to-day life is disrupted or people are forced to move en masse. WASH experts are involved in the development, planning, management and monitoring of water and sanitation systems in these types of settings.

The exact duties of a WASH manager will vary from place to place, according to need. The WASH manager may conduct onsite surveys to see what the sanitation infrastructure looks like, such as how water gets to a site and whether it is drinkable, what type of toilets or latrines are available and where they are located, and how wastewater is handled. Especially in emergency situations, they also consider laundry, bathing, and food preparation facilities. They may help to select contractors to carry out work needed to create or improve these systems, and then review contracts, supervise work, and analyze data to be sure the work was done appropriately and is effective. When working in a disaster area or a refugee setting, the WASH specialist may be helping to coordinate temporary solutions; in more permanent settings, they must make sure that the system will be sustainable based on local resources and level of use. A WASH manager also keeps an eye on the budget and reports regularly on progress. Some WASH jobs are very technical, and include creating technical drawings and specifications for water and sanitation infrastructure, and helping to find solutions to problems that arise during construction. Others lean more toward project management or even social science, focusing on how to encourage people to adopt sanitation hygiene practices that will reduce transmission of disease. In some cases, this is a technical advisor job, helping to train staff and support the work of local agencies and organizations.

Education and Certification

These jobs require at least a bachelor's degree and often more advanced training specifically related to water and sanitation. In many cases, employers will accept a degree in one of several disciplines, such as public health, civil engineering, or environmental health, so long as the candidate has training specifically in water and sanitation work. Some jobs require specific computer skills, such as computer modeling or understanding of GIS; some look for specific technical expertise, such as experience with borehole drilling and pump installations.

Core Competencies and Skills

- Understanding of civil engineering principles and water and sanitation needs
- Ability to assess how local culture influences use of water and sanitation systems
- Good project management skills, including organization and budgeting
- Ability to manage contractors and other staff
- Willingness to travel and to spend time at sites with limited sanitation infrastructure
- Flexible and innovative thinking
- For emergency and humanitarian aid work, ability to work under pressure and in unstable security environments
- Good computer skills, including word processing and spreadsheets but also technical software

Compensation

As with other global health jobs, salaries will differ according to location and specific responsibilities. In the United States in 2015, the median salary for civil engineers (a category that includes water and sanitation) was $82,000, with most earning between $52,000 and $128,000.

Workplaces

Major employers of WASH experts in global health include international aid organizations, nonprofits and NGOs, and consulting firms.

Employment Outlook

The closest job category with national statistics is civil engineer, and this job category is expected to grow rapidly over the next several years. In global health, there is an ongoing need for improvement in water and sanitation infrastructure in order to combat disease and promote overall health. There is also an ongoing need for WASH experts in disaster management and in protecting the health of refugees and other displaced persons.

For More Information

- CDC Global Sanitation, Water, and Hygiene website
  www.cdc.gov/healthywater/global
- USAID Water and Sanitation
  www.usaid.gov/what-we-do/water-and-sanitation
- WHO Water Sanitation Health
  www.who.int/water_sanitation_health/en
- UNHCR (the UN refugee agency, has information on WASH in refugee camps)
  www.unhcr.org

NGO FOUNDER/DIRECTOR

Job Description

NGO is a term used to describe a broad range of organizations that provide services or work toward influencing public policy. NGOs are usually not-for-profit organizations, although some are for-profit companies with strong public service orientations. Public health-oriented NGOs include large international foundations, tiny grassroots groups in developing countries, and everything in between. The director or president of a large NGO has responsibilities similar to those of the leader of any large organization. However, running a small NGO in a developing country can be a different job entirely. These leaders are intimately involved in the day-to-day functions of the organization. Together with a small staff, they come up with ideas and do what is needed to get projects done. They track down potential funders, write grant proposals, plan events, meet with government officials, train staff members, and even take part in providing services.

When an American sets out to start or lead an NGO in a developing country, he or she is often coming in as an outsider, so one of the most important tasks is to gain the trust and cooperation of the local community. There is no point handing out mosquito nets if people have no intention of using them—or if they already have plenty. Long-term planning is another vital responsibility. If the NGO is digging wells to provide water, it is important not only to install pumps, but also to provide for safety monitoring and maintenance. Many NGOs in developing countries hire primarily local citizens, who often have little experience creating or running social programs. Another of the NGO leader's tasks may be to train these local workers, with the goal of eventually giving them ownership of the organization.

Education and Certification

Educational requirements depend on the specific needs and purpose of the organization. Only people with demonstrated leadership skills and experience with the specific locations and programs will be hired to run established NGOs. Anyone can start an NGO, but only those with strong organizational and leadership skills will succeed. The skills and knowledge gained while earning an MPH can be very helpful, as can the experience of running a business or another nonprofit. Overseas experience is almost essential, because trying to get things done in a developing country can present challenges wildly different from anything Americans have experienced at home. A good way to get this experience is to begin with an entry-level job or even a volunteer position in an NGO whose goals match your passions.

Core Competencies and Skills

- Flexible thinking
- Adventurous spirit
- Optimism
- Persistence
- Exceptional managerial and financial skills
- Fluency in the local language (not always essential but very helpful)
- Thorough understanding of local culture and needs
- Excellent networking skills, with the ability to convince others to contribute funding, expertise, or time

Compensation

It is impossible to give a "typical" salary for the leader of an NGO focusing on public health issues overseas. Large organizations pay their executive directors handsomely, and they have staff members who work full time to bring in grants and donations. The leaders of small NGOs often must raise the funds to pay their own and their employees' salaries.

Compensation may reach the level of a modest salary by U.S. standards. If funding is tight, the leader of a new organization may even forgo payment while working to get the NGO off the ground.

Workplaces

NGOs exist in countries throughout the world. Depending on the size and structure of the organization, the job can mean living in a developing country or being based in the United States or another developed country and traveling to local sites as needed.

Employment Outlook

It is likely that there will always be a need for public health-oriented NGOs, because there will always be a need for improvement in public health infrastructure, services, and policy. There are organizations already in existence to meet many needs, and there are numerous opportunities to work at established NGOs and eventually achieve a leadership role. Those interested in starting new organizations should assess the need carefully, to avoid duplicating efforts already in progress.

For Further Information

- Global Health Council
  www.globalhealth.org
- InterAction
  interaction.org

PUBLIC HEALTH PROFILE: NGO Founder/Director
Asheesh Bhalla, MPH
President/Executive Director
The Friends of Humanity Organization of Afghanistan (FHO), Kabul, Afghanistan/Washington, DC

Describe the sort of work you do.

I direct a small NGO based in Afghanistan. Our goal is to strengthen the public health infrastructure of Afghanistan through the delivery

(continued)

(continued)

of clinical treatment, public health education, and social development programs, with a focus on women. Women are key to Afghan
society, but after 30 years of war, many have been left without
resources. Their husbands may have died or been seriously injured,
their extended families may have died, and many are caring for seven
or eight children. And when the Taliban were in control, there wasn't
much access to women's health care, so there isn't much infrastructure. The capacity just isn't there.

We run a 20-bed clinic in Kabul and a 30-bed clinic in Jalalabad.
We do everything from checkups to treating pneumonia to emergency
deliveries. We have classrooms to train nurses and community health
workers. We do seminars where our maternal health director teaches
clients about nutrition, hygiene, what to expect during pregnancy.
We're also doing a community dialogue program with women. We give
them a safe space to talk about issues that concern them, such as
religion or economics.

What is a typical day like at your job?

Developing a small organization in Afghanistan requires a lot of work
in different areas. Right now, I'm based back in the United States, but
until recently I was living full time in Afghanistan. On a typical day, you
might have found me collecting statistics, writing proposals, discussing partnerships, or looking at plans at a construction site. I'd start
by checking my e-mail. Then I'd talk with my colleagues about what
we were working on, and I'd meet with the doctor at the clinic about
what we needed. Sometimes I'd have a meeting with a government
official or someone from another organization. When we were building
the clinic, I'd visit the construction site. Some days I'd spend thinking about how to get past roadblocks, what to do if a funder changed
their mind, or where to look for what we needed. We also have a program that provides Vitamin A and antiparasite medication to children
at orphanages, and some days I would go to help give these medicines.

What education or training do you have?
Is it typical for your job?

I have a BA from an individualized study program. My concentration was political and economic trade policy and its effects on social

(continued)

(continued)

development. I also hold an MPH with a concentration in health policy and management. There is no minimum education for a job like this, but I think that a strong education in public health is one of the best backgrounds you could have.

What path did you take to get to the job you are in today?

During college and graduate school, I worked on political campaigns, did an internship at the United Nations, and was a research assistant for Doctors without Borders. For my summer practicum for the MPH, I worked with an NGO affiliated with the best hospital in Afghanistan. I wrote hospital policy and did management training. I had all these great ideas from my public health training, but I found out that working in the real world is very different. Many of the things I tried to do failed! But what I learned, I was able to apply to starting a new NGO.

I came back to the United States and finished my MPH, but I wasn't interested in any jobs here. I tried to get a job with the U.S. government in Afghanistan, but I didn't have the right experience. I was asked to start the NGO by my two Afghan partners, whom I met while working in Afghanistan that first time.

Where might you go from here, if you wanted to advance your career?

Right now, I'm attending law school while continuing to serve as executive director of FHO. I'm not sure what I'll do next. Starting a business in the health care sector is a possibility. I think with a couple more years' experience, I could be hired to run another NGO, but I'm not sure I want to do that. I feel an attachment to the one I helped start.

What is the worst or most challenging part of your job?

Sometimes things take longer than you'd like. When we were building a clinic, I thought it would be finished by the end of June, but construction didn't finish until October!

(continued)

(continued)

What is the best part?

I get to brainstorm and plan projects and come up with programming ideas. So much is needed, and there are a lot of different things you can do. And our work environment in Afghanistan was so collegial. I was surrounded by people starting other NGOs, so we were bouncing ideas off each other and getting each others' perspective.

What advice do you have for someone who is interested in your career?

Stay hungry and stay foolish. I was told by plenty of people that I was crazy for going to Afghanistan and trying to work there, much less start an NGO. But when I first came to Afghanistan I was lucky to have a position that gave me so much responsibility and experience, and I used it to my advantage.

Profile Update

Mr. Bhalla still serves as an advisor with the NGO he founded, which has continued to work on identifying and meeting needs and is now called the Family Health Organization of Afghanistan. Since his original interview, he has completed law school and spent about 2 years working as assistant general counsel with the Mayor's Office of Housing Recovery Operations in New York City. He has also been a consultant for the World Bank and done legal policy fellowships with the National Archives and Records Administration and the U.S. Department of the Treasury. He recently started working with Scrimbox, a startup that connects gamers for online events—a very different angle from public health but an interesting challenge!

GLOBAL HEALTH LAWYER

Job Description

Those in the relatively new field of global health law focus on how international law and the laws of individual nations affect health care (Gostin, 2014). Every nation sets a health policy via its laws pertaining to health, and by how its institutions, such as legislatures and courts, create and interpret those laws. Beyond individual states, there is a network of regional and international agreements pertaining to health, such as the WHO's regulations as to how epidemics are to be handled. Finally, there are activities now common in a global, integrated world—agricultural trade, arms control treaties, and economic development projects, to name a few—that can affect the health of populations for better or worse, sometimes intentionally and sometimes as an unintended consequence.

Global health law practitioners evaluate the legal and governmental practices within a nation. They also look at the legal frameworks that support regional agreements and for-profit economic projects. They advise, through analysis, policy suggestions, and discussion, on how those practices and legal frameworks can be used to advance the health of people in the region. Some in global health law work at the level of international treaties, such as helping to develop a treaty to curb tobacco use, which has spread across the globe. Others work to bring a smaller number of nations together in cross-border agreements that will improve health, such as an agreement to clean up the regional environment. Still others work with the government and people of a nation to change laws, governmental processes, or informal practices in order to create access to high quality health services. With different levels of government, different legal instruments, and different subjects, global health law work is complex. Sometimes a conflict arises, as when a health organization is accused of violating a medical device patent; then, experts in global health law might be called in to argue for each side or to mediate the dispute.

Education and Certification

Practicing global health law requires a law degree and a license to practice. To learn about legal issues in global health, specifically, a lawyer can pursue an LLM (Master of Laws), an advanced specialty degree. Several schools offer an LLM in global health law.

Core Competencies and Skills

- Ability to understand complex laws, rules, and policies
- Appreciation for the differences among cultures and societies
- Good negotiating skills, including both persuasion and compromise
- Strong sense of responsibility and ethics
- Excellent reading and writing skills

Compensation

The details of these jobs vary widely, and there are opportunities around the world. There is too much variation to give a good salary range.

Workplaces

Global health lawyers work for international organizations (like the World Bank and WHO), government agencies (including the U.S. Department of Health and Human Services and foreign governments), NGOs concerned with health and development, and sometimes at private law firms.

Employment Outlook

This is a growing field, as globalization in both health and commerce continues to increase. Some of the areas with the strongest interest or clearest need are ministries of health, academia, civil law and law firms, and pharmaceutical companies.

For Further Information

- O'Neill Institute for National and Global Health Law, Georgetown University
  www.law.georgetown.edu/oneillinstitute/index.cfm

BIOMEDICAL ENGINEER

Job Description

Biomedical engineers use engineering principles to solve real-world problems in the fields of medicine and biology. One way this work is applied is to create medical devices that assist physicians and nurses with evaluation, diagnosis, and treatment. While many biomedical engineers work on innovations for the U.S. market, experts with these skills can have an important impact in global health. Imagine needing to rely on an EKG machine in a remote setting where electricity is intermittent and, if it breaks, there is no repairman to fix it. Imagine you have medical devices that are supposed to be tested regularly for accuracy, but there is no testing equipment available. It may be too expensive to maintain delicate equipment or even to buy it in the first place. A piece of donated medical equipment might work fine, but require a disposable testing cartridge for each patient—and what if there is no budget to purchase them? There are other problems that need engineering solutions, too. For example, there are vaccines and medications that need to be refrigerated, but how do you keep them protected when there is no fuel for the back-up generator?

Biomedical engineers can make important contributions in global health by making devices sturdier, less expensive, or easier to repair. They also look for ways to make equipment easier to use, which can be particularly important when the availability of training is limited. Some other examples of bioengineering projects are simplified machines to test for lung disease; incubators for premature babies that use inexpensive, easily obtainable parts; and a way to send EKG results by cell phone, so a rural health worker can get input from an expert doctor at a hospital many miles away.

Another role for bioengineers in global health is helping to build capacity in less developed regions: collaborating with local engineers and health care providers and helping to train local technicians to do maintenance and repair.

Education and Certification

There are bioengineering degree programs at the bachelor's, master's, and doctoral levels; they combine biological studies with engineering coursework. People who create, refine, or redesign medical devices typically have advanced degrees. Some have an undergraduate degree in another engineering field and a graduate degree in biomedical engineering. Because this is a relatively new field, it is also possible to enter this type of work without a specific biomedical engineering degree, if you have the right combination of other training. There are some fellowships available to support bioengineering students and recent graduates interested in international research and collaborations. The Whitaker International Program, for example, sends students and recent graduates to work on self-designed projects overseas. This program is currently scheduled to end in 2018; other places to look are academic departments' websites and the website for the National Institute of Biomedical Imaging and Bioengineering (NIBIB) at the NIH.

Core Competencies and Skills

- Knowledge of medical and physical sciences (such as physiology, biochemistry, material sciences, electronics)
- Strong research skills
- Creativity, a desire to innovate, and perseverance

- Open-mindedness
- Ability to work with a team
- Interest in traveling to less developed countries and low-resource areas
- Good communication skills

Compensation

Pay for bioengineers varies with the level of training, the size of the organization, the degree of responsibility on the job, and how successful they are at solving the problems that are brought to them. The BLS places the median salary for bioengineers at $87,000 in 2014; most earn between $53,000 and $139,000.

Workplaces

Biomedical engineers may work for private industry, at hospitals, or at universities, where there tends to be more freedom to work on humanitarian projects that may not have large financial returns. There are also bioengineers at government agencies, such as the NIBIB, the Food and Drug Administration's product approval arm, and the U.S. Patent Office.

Employment Outlook

According to the BLS, the outlook for employment for bioengineers in general is very good. However, the field is small and it has been promoted as a good career opportunity—so it is possible there will be increasing competition for jobs even if the market expands. There can already be strong competition for research jobs, such as academic appointments at universities.

For Further Information

- Biomedical Engineering Society (BMES)
  www.bmes.org
- National Institute of Biomedical Imaging and Bioengineering (NIBIB)
  www.nibib.nih.gov
- American College of Clinical Engineering (ACCE)
  accenet.org
- IEEE Engineering in Medicine & Biology Society (EMBS)
  www.embs.org

ENTOMOLOGIST

Job Description

Entomologists study bugs. That includes the insects that eat our crops and the honeybees that pollinate flowers. So what does this have to do with global health? Public health entomologists work with the insects that carry disease. Here in the United States, mosquitoes are mostly just a nuisance. But in many places in the world, mosquitoes carry malaria—one of the world's biggest killers. Dengue fever, another mosquito-borne infection, is a leading cause of childhood illness and death in some parts of Asia. Certain types of flies, ticks, fleas, and other insects can carry serious diseases, as well. There are public health entomologists studying these insects in laboratories, looking for ways to control their populations or reduce the risk of disease transmission. There are public health entomologists working in the field, doing surveillance of insect populations, studying local conditions, and helping to plan programs for insect control. This job can involve hands-on work examining sites and collecting samples; time in a lab or in front of a computer, pulling together data from multiple sources; and meetings, trainings, and presentations to share information with other public health professionals.

In addition to international jobs, there are entomologists working on insect control here in the United States, to protect us from infections like tick-borne Lyme disease and mosquito-borne West Nile virus. Public health entomologists also had a role in pest control after Hurricane Katrina.

Education and Certification

Many jobs require a master's degree, and an entomologist usually needs a PhD to conduct independent research. A small number of universities offer bachelor's degrees in entomology; master's and PhD programs are more common. Entomologists can earn board certification from the Entomological Society of America.

Core Competencies and Skills

- Interest in problem solving
- Passion for science
- Understanding of epidemiology
- Appreciation for local culture and an understanding of local practices
- Knowledge of the principles of vector control

- Ability to work with administrators and other nonscientists
- Relevant technical knowledge, such as how to use GIS (mapping systems to track disease)

Compensation

Salary will depend on the specific job and location. Income can range from the $30,000s for someone just starting out with a bachelor's degree to over $100,000 for a PhD in a leadership role.

Workplaces

Public health entomologists are doing work related to global health at universities, nonprofit organizations, government agencies, and consulting firms. Some entomologists work for the military, finding ways to protect soldiers from vector-borne diseases in locations throughout the world. There are even entomologists at for-profit companies developing products for insect control.

Employment Outlook

There are many job opportunities for entomologists, but the number of jobs in global health is fairly small. Jobs in academia, where much of the international health research is carried out, can be very competitive.

For Further Information

- Entomological Society of America (ESA)
  www.entsoc.org
- CDC Division of Vector-Borne Diseases (DVBD)
  www.cdc.gov/ncezid/dvbd
- See also the organizations listed with disease ecologist.

REFERENCES

Fried, L. P., Bentley, M. E., Burke, D. S., Frenk, J. J., Klag, M. J., & Spencer, H. C. (2010). Global health is public health. *The Lancet, 375*, 535–537.

Gostin, L. O. (2014). *Global health law*. Cambridge, MA: Harvard University Press.

Koplan, J. P., Bond, C., Merson, M. H., Reddy, K. S., Rodriguez, M. R., Sewankambo, N. K., & Wasserheit J. N.; Consortium of Universities for Global Health Executive Board. (2009). Towards a common definition of global health. *The Lancet, 373*, 1993–1995.

CHAPTER 23
Military

People outside the military often do not realize it, but public health is a major priority in the Armed Forces. The Army has a strong focus on preventive medicine as well as its own U.S. Army Public Health Command (USAPHC), the Air Force has its medical division and public health officers, and the Navy and Marines together have the Navy Marine Corps Public Health Services. The Defense Health Agency (DHA), established in 2013, is an effort to enhance collaboration and efficiency among the Army, Navy, and Air Force medical services. As part of their goal of a "medically ready force" and a "ready medical force" for both peacetime and wartime, the DHA established a public health division in 2014.

The military uses the principles of public health to maintain the health and combat readiness of the troops and to help protect them from illness and injury on deployments. In peacetime, many of the issues are the same as in any public health department: monitoring of disease outbreaks, maintaining food safety, and ensuring clean water and sanitation. The military has a high emphasis on occupational medicine and industrial hygiene, and it has the authority to track injuries and preventive measures closely. Public health experts in the military must also take some special situations into account: Members of their population often live in close quarters, so communicable disease can spread quickly. There are many young people far from home for the first time and under significant emotional stress. Worldwide travel can put members of the military force at risk of diseases not usually seen in the United States.

In wartime, new issues arise, and public health experts are closely involved in preparing for them. For example, one concern is recognizing and protecting against biological or chemical warfare. Another is planning sanitation for temporary camps and longer term installations. There are even public health experts involved in improving body armor to better protect soldiers in combat. In times of war or increased political tension, public health teams deploy to help protect the health of the troops and keep them ready for whatever action is needed. They also can be sent to disaster areas to help provide humanitarian aid.

An important goal of military public health in recent years has been suicide prevention. The Armed Forces have been working hard to destigmatize the idea of asking for help and to teach all members of the military how to help a comrade in need.

These are just a few examples. A visit to the website for the USAPHC is a good way to get a sense of the true extent of public health in our Armed Forces. Here are some of the other things happening within the USAPHC:

- Animal medicine, including care of working dogs and horses and defense against zoonotic (animal-borne) diseases
- Injury prevention, from how to select running shoes to how to reduce risk of parachute accidents
- Hearing protection, in peacetime work and in combat situations
- Entomology and pest management, including minimizing transmission of disease from insects and guarding against toxic effects of pesticides
- Air quality management, with sampling, monitoring, and computer modeling to predict future hazards
- Waste management, including hazardous waste
- Health promotion and wellness, from everyday fitness to stress management in combat

The bulk of the military's public health staff is made up of enlisted personnel and officers, many of whom are trained by the military for the jobs that are needed. There are also roles for civilians, who make up for manpower not available in the ranks or fill positions that require specialized training that the military is unable to sponsor. There are Oak Ridge Institute for Science and Education (ORISE) fellowships (orise.orau.gov) based in the Department of Defense, in roles with military branches.

Those with an MPH often have leadership roles, such as department heads. The military will sometimes sponsor a serviceman or servicewoman in an MPH program, and there are also opportunities to have tuition covered in return for joining the service after graduation. The military does also employ civilian MPH graduates, depending on the needs of a program. In some cases, a civilian is asked to attend Officer Development School in order to learn how the military operates; they may need to get a security clearance and make a commitment to stay on the job for several years.

The basic job descriptions for military public health jobs are similar to those in the civilian world, so this chapter includes just a few more specific examples, two for officers and one for civilians. There are many other opportunities for people at various educational levels, from high school or general equivalency diploma (GED) up to MD or PhD. To better show how public health roles fit into the structure of the Armed Forces, the chapter also includes an example of a public health unit and a health and readiness campaign.

There is more information online at the websites for each branch of the uniformed services. Each branch also has a recruiting website with contact information for local recruiters, who can give the latest information about what roles they are seeking to fill and how to qualify.

AIR FORCE PUBLIC HEALTH OFFICER

Job Description

Public health officers in the Air Force can have many different roles. They manage programs addressing a wide range of public health issues, including disease surveillance and prevention, food and water safety, clinical preventive care, and occupational and environmental health. In the area of communicable disease surveillance, public health officers need to know what diseases occur in different parts of the world and how to protect against them. They become experts on where malaria occurs, how Lyme disease is transmitted, and the biggest disease risks in Southeast Asia, the Middle East, and everywhere else airmen might be carrying out their work. There are public health officers managing surveillance and prevention for sexually transmitted diseases, screening for tuberculosis (TB), and monitoring programs to watch for outbreaks in the Air Force community. In the area of occupational health, public health officers oversee programs for hearing conservation, monitoring the use of hazardous chemicals, and watching for patterns in occupational injury to try to catch problems early. Another role is making sure food service facilities are properly run and inspected to prevent foodborne illness.

Education and Certification

Public health officers in the Air Force must have advanced degrees specifically related to the work, such as an MPH, a master's in epidemiology, or a veterinary degree. For degrees that require a license to practice, an active license is required. New officers must participate in a 5-week training course to orient them to the military and military health care, including physical conditioning and leadership training. The Air Force also sets an age limit for joining in this role, which most recently was in the low 40s.

The Air Force also has a public health role for airmen with more limited training. Public health specialists are enlisted airmen with a minimum of a high school education or GED, who receive special technical training. These technicians help to carry out the day-to-day work of prevention programs, such as inspecting food service facilities or educating other airmen on proper sanitary procedures to minimize transmission of disease.

Core Competencies and Skills

- Good understanding of public health principles
- Ability to work as part of a team
- Flexibility to take on new roles as needed
- Willingness to move or travel as needed for assignments and deployments
- Ability to follow orders and procedures
- Appreciation for the goals and values of the U.S. Armed Forces

Compensation

New public health officers typically start at a low-level officer rank, such as first lieutenant, but have opportunities to rise to higher levels with experience and time. Base pay for a first lieutenant starts at about $40,000 but pay rises substantially as an officer advances. There also may be adjustments to pay according to location and additional benefits.

Workplaces

Public health officers serve on permanent bases in the United States and abroad, and as needed on deployments around the world. Candidates must be willing to relocate and travel as needed.

Employment Outlook

Opportunities to join depend on the needs of the Air Force at that time. Officer positions can be competitive, much like any other job application. The recruiting service looks at experience, evidence of leadership ability, and potential for growth and advancement, as well as education and grade point average. Public health officers must also meet physical requirements.

There are similar roles and opportunities in the other branches of the military.

For Further Information

- Air Force Recruitment
  www.airforce.com/careers
- Navy and Marine Corps Public Health Center
  www.med.navy.mil/sites/nmcphc/Pages/Home.aspx
- Army Recruitment
  www.goarmy.com

ARMY PREVENTIVE MEDICINE OFFICER

Job Description

In the Army, preventive medicine officers are doctors who combine clinical practice with public health. The work can include occupational medicine, such as treating on-the-job injuries, making sure vaccinations are up to date, and doing regular monitoring for safety. It can also include treating infectious diseases, as well as looking at patterns of infections and at ways to prevent them. A preventive medicine officer might have a regular TB clinic, an STD clinic, and a clinic that provides primary care for people with HIV. The work can involve some treatment and prevention of chronic diseases, such as running a smoking cessation program. Often, there is an emphasis on tropical medicine, because of the types of places that the Army is deployed. There is also a research component, as the Army is always looking for ways to provide better care for the troops and minimize outbreaks, injuries, and chronic diseases. Preventive medicine officers can serve as teachers in the Army's preventive medicine residency program.

The job can include significant amounts of travel. A preventive medicine officer might be deployed to work with troops overseas or to help with an outbreak in another country.

Education and Certification

A preventive medicine officer in the Army needs an MD or DO degree and a license to practice, and needs to complete a residency in preventive medicine, which includes earning an MPH.

Core Competencies and Skills

- Interest and skill in both clinical care and public health
- Willingness to travel
- Ability to work with people of many different ranks and educational backgrounds
- Ability to work within a military system
- Strong problem-solving skills and the ability to make good decisions quickly
- Ability to cope with stress and high levels of responsibility

Compensation

Active duty preventive medicine officers in the Army receive compensation that is considered competitive with civilian salaries. They receive pay at the level of commissioned officers as well as special pay incentives. There is funding for educational loan repayment and for continuing education. There is also retirement pay for those who serve at least 20 years.

Workplaces

Preventive medicine officers are assigned where they are needed. For the first few years, the work may be heavy on direct clinical care; they may serve at a base medical center or clinic as their main assignment. Later, there are opportunities to focus more on leadership and research. Preventive medicine officers can be deployed for months at a time to work with troops or on special projects, or to help with humanitarian missions.

Employment Outlook

Openings depend on the current needs of the Army. Talking to a recruiter is the best way to find out about opportunities. There are also preventive medicine officers in the Air Force and the Navy. Coast Guard physicians are assigned via the U.S. Public Health Service Commissioned Corps.

For Further Information

- Medicine + The Military
  medicineandthemilitary.com

PUBLIC HEALTH PROFILE: Preventive Medicine Officer
James Mancuso, MD, MPH, DrPH
Program Director
Preventive Medicine Residency, Walter Reed Army Institute of Research, Silver Spring, MD

Describe the sort of work you do.

As the director for the preventive medicine residency program at Walter Reed Army Institute of Research (WRAIR), I teach residents, medical students, and MPH students both at WRAIR and at the Uniformed Services University of the Health Sciences (USUHS). TB research is a particular area of interest for me, and I get called a couple times a week to consult on military TB issues. I have clinical activities at nearby civilian and military facilities, typically in those clinics, which involve communicable disease control, such as TB, sexually transmitted infections, and travel clinics.

I also go out on field operations. I just went to Japan for 3 months to augment and assist the military response after the 2011 nuclear meltdown at Fukushima. I was doing work on health effects, risk assessments, and risk communication for U.S. forces over there. We also participate in outbreak investigations. For

(continued)

(continued)

example, in 2010, I went to Detroit to help investigate an outbreak of severe cases of *Legionella* at a military facility. I travel to places like Honduras, Guyana, Tanzania, and India to support training missions to teach military physicians about tropical medicine.

What is a typical day like at your job?

It's a nice mix. I really enjoy getting to do different things—I think that the wide variety of activities I get to experience is what attracted me the most to preventive medicine. I do clinic about 20% of my time, then probably another 20% is spent on research, 20% on administrative activities, and the remaining 40% on educational activities. Today I went to the TB clinic in the morning, and then in the afternoon came back to the office to complete a research proposal and work on a manuscript. Tomorrow I will do administrative work to set up some 4-week rotations in tropical medicine for our students (including some preventive medicine residents) to countries like Kenya, Peru, and Thailand. Later in the week, I will be teaching medical students and MPH students, including lectures on epidemiology and disease prevention, and a lab exercise on outbreak investigation. I also have a meeting in downtown Washington, DC, to talk about preventive medicine and the uniformed services' role in the American College of Preventive Medicine, and another later this month at the Centers for Disease Control and Prevention where I will provide military perspective to the National Advisory Committee on the elimination of TB.

Days are different on field exercises. When I was in Japan, I spent about half the time involved with tracking radiation in the environment and radiation exposures. The other half was answering questions and communicating about the radiation risks, which weren't very significant for U.S. personnel. I would explain to commanders what the effects were, write articles for scientific and lay publications, and talk to the media. I did a lot of the writing. I went with the Army medical laboratory and then stayed on longer with an environmental health scientist, an entomologist, and a health physicist.

(continued)

(continued)

What education or training do you have? Is it typical for your job?

You need a medical degree and you need to go through a residency in preventive medicine, which takes 3 years. During the residency, you must complete an internship, an MPH, and other clinical and nonclinical rotations. After that, you typically do 5 or 10 years out in the field and then might move on to a more teaching or research-oriented role.

I received an MD and an MPH during my medical training. However, I was still hungry for more education after that, so I also earned a DrPH, which took another 3 years. Preventive medicine physicians can also have degrees other than an MPH, such as a Master of Tropical Medicine and Hygiene or other public health degree.

What path did you take to get to the job you are in today?

I enlisted in the Army right after high school and spent 2 years in the infantry, and then I left the military and went to college. After undergraduate school, I came back into the military to attend the USUHS, the military medical school. I got interested in medicine when I was in the infantry. We had a Combat Lifesaver course, which was a little beyond basic first aid, and I was sort of the medic for the platoon. When I went to college, I was a chemistry major and I knew a lot of people who were pre-med.

At USUHS, you have a first-year class in epidemiology, which I really enjoyed. I got to know the course director pretty well, and he helped me set up a summer rotation in Panama with preventive medicine staff there. There was a dengue outbreak at the time, so I was able to see how that worked. And then I went to the Jungle Operations Training Center, which was still in Panama at the time, where I was able to see a lot of heat-related illness and other injuries. The whole experience really deepened my interest in the work that the preventive medicine physicians were doing.

I was always interested in teaching residents. During my residency training, I told my residency director I was interested in taking her job one day, and once I'd completed the DrPH it was sort of a natural fit.

(continued)

(continued)

Where might you go from here, if you wanted to advance your career?

In terms of military advancement, I would like to get promoted to colonel. Since I am on an academic track, it is unlikely for me to get promoted beyond that—that is to become a general. My goals are more research and service-oriented. I would like to continue to work in tropical medicine, and I hope that a substantial portion of that work will be outside the United States. After the military, I might consider a position at a major agency or program focusing on tropical medicine or global health.

What is the best part of your job?

The best part is teaching the residents and other students. We're molding the future of the specialty and helping grow future public health leaders! We're giving them some great experiences in both didactic and experiential medicine. The next best is probably doing research. For example, I've been looking at discordance between the traditional TB skin test and a newer blood test in identifying those with latent TB infection (LTBI). Both of these are good tests, but they don't always agree, and this discordance is often difficult to interpret because there is no "gold" standard for diagnosing LTBI.

What is the worst or most challenging part?

My least favorite part is the administrative work. In the Army, we have a lot of mandatory trainings and paperwork. Also, dealing with personnel who aren't doing well or are having problems is challenging. It's not bad, because I want to help them, but it takes up a lot of time.

What advice would you give to someone who is interested in your career?

If you like variety, to me that's what the preventive medicine specialty is all about. You can do so many different things, including international health, policy, epidemiology—there are so many opportunities.

(continued)

(continued)

The more of those different categories that you like, the more you will enjoy this work.

Profile Update

Since his initial interview, LTC Mancuso has moved on to become Director of Tropical Public Health at USUHS. As an associate professor in the Department of Preventive Medicine and Biostatistics, he still enjoys teaching medical students, residents, and MPH students. He continues to serve as an active duty Army physician.

ARMY HEALTH PROMOTION OFFICER

Job Description

Army health promotion uses a range of modalities to support and improve the health and well-being of service members and their families. The Army considers health promotion to include not just health education, but organizational, economic, environmental, and policy interventions that facilitate good health. The goal is for health and well-being to be integral to the Army community. Some current priorities are preventing drug and alcohol abuse, promoting tobacco-free living, enhancing mental and emotional health, reducing STDs, and supporting healthy eating and active living.

On an Army installation, the health promotion officer (HPO) develops a strategic plan for health promotion and then creates and markets health promotion and wellness programs to carry out that plan. An important part of this role is facilitating the installation's Community Health Promotion Council (CHPC). The CHPC is headed by the senior commander and includes officers and other leaders who are closely connected with the health of services members and the functioning of the Army base. As a team, the CHPC identifies health promotion needs, evaluates resources, decides how to prioritize and address needs, and reviews the results. They also make sure that programs do not duplicate each other or work at cross-purposes. The HPO integrates input from the various CHPC members and consultants, advises the senior commander on both health promotion and on the CHPC process, and brings in other subject matter experts as needed.

Education and Certification

The Army looks for people with at least a few years' experience and also provides specific training to HPOs on community health assessment, how to identify gaps in programs and services, and how to identify strengths and weaknesses of programs. An HPO must have at least a bachelor's, although a master's degree is preferred, in a subject such as business or organizational management, or in a subject related to health, such as health education, nursing, or health promotion.

There are also roles for health promotion program assistants (HPPAs), who provide day-to-day administrative support for the health promotion process, including maintaining records and creating reports on data and trends. HPPAs must have a bachelor's degree and relevant experience. Health promotion technicians help with organizing events and maintaining supplies and equipment. This role requires a bachelor's or master's degree in public health or a related subject.

Core Competencies and Skills

- Strategic planning skills
- Ability to facilitate a multidisciplinary committee
- Knowledge of the theories behind successful health promotion efforts, and of how to apply this information to program development
- Ability to monitor and evaluate programs and to convey the results to stakeholders
- Ability to manage multiple tasks and to prioritize

Workplaces

HPOs are currently civilian employees of the USAPHC. They are placed on Army bases both in the United States and internationally.

Compensation

Recent HPO stipends have been set according to the government's "general schedule" pay scale, at GS-12. Depending on the region, this starts around $70,000 to $80,000.

Career Outlook

As part of the Health Promotion Operations Program, the USAPHC aims to have HPOs at all Army installations. In 2015, HPOs were being hired as part of the ORISE fellowship programs, for appointments of up to 5 years. Working as an HPO should give solid experience in program planning and project management, as well as inside knowledge of how military public health works.

For Further Information

- United States Army Public Health Command (USAPHC) *phc.amedd.army.mil/Pages/default.aspx*

ADDITIONAL EXAMPLES OF PUBLIC HEALTH AT WORK IN THE MILITARY

The following are just a couple of examples of how the military makes use of public health principles. These special programs are set against a backdrop of ongoing work in epidemiology, health promotion, injury prevention, occupational medicine, research, sanitation work, and other regular public health efforts.

Navy Environmental and Preventive Medicine Units

Navy Environmental and Preventive Medicine Units (NEPMUs) represent one way that the Navy makes use of its public health personnel. There are several NEPMUs located around the United States. Each serves a different region of the globe. A NEPMU is composed of people skilled in environmental health, entomology, preventive medicine, microbiology, and other public health specialties, as well as medical doctors, biochemists, and audiologists. During peacetime, these professionals work with Navy and Marine Corps personnel and their families in the United States and carry on ordinary medical and public health processes. Should tensions rise overseas or war break out, members of a NEPMU deploy in order to protect the health of the troops. They also go to the scenes of natural disasters in order to provide humanitarian assistance, such as preventing the spread of disease and protecting the food supply from destructive pests.

For Further Information

- Navy and Marine Corps Public Health Center Field Activities
  *www.med.navy.mil/sites/nmcphc/field-activities/Pages/default
  .aspx*

Army Ready and Resilient Campaign

The Army recognizes that caring about the physical health of its soldiers is not enough; it needs to pay attention to the emotional and interpersonal skills of its soldiers if they are to be ready and effective. The "Ready and Resilient Campaign," or "R2C," is intended to enhance troops' ability to face adversity, adapt to change, and overcome problems through individual and team efforts. Individuals who are resilient are better able to bounce back from physically and emotionally trying circumstances. Among R2C's goals are encouraging self-awareness and good decision making, identifying soldiers who need help coping in order to forestall substance abuse and suicide, and motivating soldiers to perform at an optimal level in all circumstances. It also includes helping soldiers cope with injury and grief, and it aids them in the transition back to civilian life. The program reaches out to soldiers, their families, and civilians working for the military.

R2C employs public health specialists from a variety of disciplines, including mental health professionals, medical experts in traumatic brain injury and other battle-caused conditions, and trainers in leadership and teamwork for overcoming adversity on the battlefield. Another part of the R2C program is to embed behavioral health specialists with the Army units on deployment to make support available on scene.

For Further Information

- Ready and Resilient (R2C)
  www.army.mil/readyandresilient

CHAPTER 24

On the Cutting Edge

Public health has been around, in one way or another, for hundreds of years—but it is still very much an evolving discipline. Schools of public health are introducing new programs, health departments are looking for innovations, and new diseases and challenges continue to appear. The careers in this chapter address some of the newest and fastest evolving areas of public health, from new technology to new ways of looking at familiar work. They are heavy on research, because even the top experts are still figuring out the best approaches and the smartest policies.

These careers are just a sample of what is currently happening in the evolution of public health. Over the next several years, it will be interesting to see where these fields are headed, and what other new developments occur.

For more ideas about emerging careers in public health, check out the course catalogs from some schools of public health—there are often classes that cover new developments and trends. And there are always interesting people to meet and careers to discover at the American Public Health Association's annual meeting, where innovations from all areas of public health are presented and discussed.

PUBLIC HEALTH GENETICS

Job Description

Knowledge about genetics has always been important in health care, but it has become a more prominent topic in recent years. Genetic studies have shown why certain medications do not work the same way for everyone. More and more genetic tests are becoming available, promising to predict the future in terms of health and disease. At the same time, our understanding of genetics remains limited. We do not always know how to interpret test results, because even if we know a certain gene is associated with a disease, we may not completely understand all the other influences. We only know how to tailor a very few treatments to genetic makeup. And we are only just starting to explore the connection between genetic expression and the environment.

Public health geneticists straddle the line between genetics research and the development of public health programs and policy. Historically, public health has incorporated genetics mainly in the form of newborn screening programs, which look for genetic diseases. However, this has been expanding as we learn more about the human genome and how genes work. The human genetics department at the University of Pittsburgh, which was the first genetics department at a School of Public Health in the United States, identifies three roles: looking at causes and treatments for both acquired and inherited diseases, understanding genetic differences among human populations, and looking at how genetics impacts public health and the prevention of disease. A public health geneticist might focus on how genetic makeup influences the development of common diseases, so that prevention efforts can take this into account. They might look at all those new genetic tests and how much the results *really* tell us, so they can be used wisely and not cause harm. They might study how environmental factors, from pollution to emotional stress, can influence genetic expression, or how different genetic variations allow some people to avoid a disease while others are affected. Some public health geneticists focus on the ethics of genetics in medicine and public health. Some translate research results into education for legislators, doctors, and the general public, and advise on policies that will benefit the public's health.

Public health genetics is often an office job that includes analyzing data, writing reports, collaborating with other scientists, and educating various stakeholders.

Education and Certification

The best degree for a public health geneticist depends on career goals. For a research-focused career, a PhD in human genetics would be a good choice. If your interest is more in applied research (figuring out how current genetics knowledge can be used to improve health on a population level), it is possible to earn an MPH or a PhD with a focus on public health genetics. However, only a small number of schools of public health offer a specific genetics track. Some incorporate the study of public health genetics into a more general epidemiology track. Because this is still an evolving field, many of the current experts come from other backgrounds, having incorporated genetics and public health into their work.

Core Competencies and Skills

- Understanding of scientific and clinical research methods
- Strong knowledge of applied statistics
- Good background in molecular biology and genetics
- Knowledge of core public health principles, particularly epidemiology
- Scientific curiosity
- Ability to understand how information from basic research and human behavior interacts
- Ability to translate difficult concepts into straightforward language

Compensation

The National Human Genome Research Institute gives a salary range for public health geneticists starting at about $36,000 and rising to $101,000, with a median of $65,000. Upper-level professors, researchers, and public health leaders can earn more.

Workplaces

There are public health genetics experts working in research and academic settings, in laboratories, and at health departments and the Centers for Disease Control and Prevention (CDC).

Employment Outlook

Public health genetics is a growing field, and there seems to be room for both MPH and PhD graduates. The CDC has a special division for public health genomics. (Genomics is a subset of genetics that looks at a person's whole genetic makeup, and how genes interact with each other and the environment.) Some state health departments have special sections dedicated to the connection between genetics or genomics and public health. There has been increasing interest in tailoring prevention and treatment to individuals' specific genetic variations, which may lead to more jobs in industry; although not strictly "public health," these roles use many of the same skills. It seems likely that this field will continue to expand as more is learned about the connections between genetics and health.

For Further Information

- Human Genetics department at Pitt Public Health, University of Pittsburgh
  www.publichealth.pitt.edu/human-genetics
- Institute for Public Health Genetics, University of Washington School of Public Health
  depts.washington.edu/phgen
- World Health Organization (WHO) Human Genetics Programme
  www.who.int/genomics/en
- American Society of Human Genetics (ASHG)
  www.ashg.org
- Centers for Disease Control and Prevention (CDC) Office of Public Health Genomics
  www.cdc.gov/genomics

PUBLIC HEALTH PROFILE: Public Health Genetics
W. David Dotson, PhD
Senior Coordinating Scientist
Office of Public Health Genomics, Centers for Disease Control and Prevention, Atlanta, GA

Describe the sort of work you do.

My job title is health scientist, and although I sit at a desk most of the day, I am often doing research at the same time. My area of expertise is in the development of evidence-based information on the use of genomic applications in clinical and public health practice. For example, with the increasing availability of tests that

(continued)

(continued)

pertain to common, complex conditions that have been made possible following completion of the Human Genome Project in the early 2000s, we need to look at which tests are ready for safe and responsible use at the population level. The research that I do is typically based on analysis of existing scientific literature, so I don't need to be in a laboratory. I also help design and implement databases and online tools intended to inform stakeholders (including health practitioners, researchers, health care payers, and the general public) and help integrate evidence-based genomic applications into practice.

What is a typical day like at your job?

Usually the first thing I do every morning is to check my e-mail. I get anywhere from 1 to 20 e-mails per day that need a response. I answer a lot of questions from people, both at the CDC and elsewhere, who need to know about genomic research and information for their own work.

I attend at least one meeting per day, and occasionally even three or four. Some are weekly team gatherings to plan and implement new databases, or to prepare our weekly e-newsletter update. Other meetings are phone calls with representatives from state public health genetics programs that work with the CDC through cooperative agreements. I also plan meetings for an independent panel that our office supports, which is devoted to the evidence-based evaluation of genomic tests.

I would say that approximately half of my day is spent working collaboratively on projects that require face-to-face or virtual team activities. Even when I am working alone in my office, however, the projects I am doing are part of larger products that are owned by various teams. So I could be writing commentaries on current policy issues in genomics for publication in a journal, or writing a blog to inform people what the evaluation panel has determined, or writing an e-mail to invite someone from another office within the CDC to consider collaborating with us on a project. In every case, I am working to help develop, support, and maintain activities and programs that support both the mission of my office and of my agency.

(continued)

(continued)

What education or training do you have? Is it typical for your job?

I earned a BS in biochemistry and PhD in microbiology. After deciding that I wanted to pursue a career in public health, I completed an online graduate certificate in the core concepts of the field from the University of North Carolina at Chapel Hill. I also earned an online graduate certificate in applied statistics from Penn State University, as a means to expand my analytical skills. I think it would be more typical to go straight for an MPH or even DrPH.

What path did you take to get to the job you are in today?

During graduate school, I did laboratory research in fungal genetics and molecular biology. I also worked as a teaching assistant for an undergraduate microbiology laboratory class. After I earned my PhD, I went to work as a postdoctoral fellow in the biotechnology industry, doing research on similar topics. My first job after completing that training was in the pharmaceutical industry. My title was senior medical writer, and the work included medical writing, project management, and reviewing promotional materials for accuracy and regulatory compliance. But I wanted to feel more like my work was making a difference in the world, and I found an opportunity to work as a contractor at the CDC through a public health jobs website. Later, when a full-time federal position opened up that I was qualified for, I applied and got that job, where I remain today.

Where might you go from here, if you wanted to advance your career?

I really enjoy working for the CDC, and they are involved in a wide range of really important health areas, so I would look for opportunities to advance here.

What is the worst or most challenging part of your job?

Working collaboratively on writing projects is both the most rewarding and the most challenging part of my job. It is rewarding because I get

(continued)

(continued)

to meet and work with a lot of really wonderful people, and the final products turn out better than if only one of the authors had done all the work. It is challenging because often you need to build consensus around ideas that people may feel strongly about. It can be difficult, and sometimes frustrating, but when you achieve that, and finish the project, there is a great feeling of accomplishment.

What is the best part?

The best part of my job is that I feel like I am contributing to something that has value and will be helpful to society. On top of that, I get to meet a lot of really talented, kind, and hardworking people who devote their lives to trying to improve health. It is really inspiring!

What advice do you have for someone who is interested in your career?

I recommend developing a solid background in the aspects of genomics that interest them—that is, they may have an interest in pathogen genomics, or human genetics, or laboratory aspects of genomics, or bioinformatics. But don't neglect social science courses! So much of public health, genomics or otherwise, requires an understanding of behavioral, economic, ethical, and societal issues. Likewise, statistical analysis is a valuable skill across disciplines in public health. Whether someone actually does numerical analyses or not, it is absolutely critical to be able to understand what the results mean.

IMPLEMENTATION SCIENCE

Job Description

Implementation science can be considered an offshoot of translational research, which looks at how the results of basic scientific studies, such as in the laboratory, can be "translated" into treatments or practices that directly benefit health. In public health, implementation science aims to find better ways to disseminate effective innovations, replicate successful programs in different communities, and prevent useful knowledge from being overlooked or lost. Even in the Internet age, there is no single repository for evidence-based public health knowledge, and no efficient way for public health practitioners at local health departments to keep up with each others' work. Furthermore, it is not always clear how best to translate a successful program from one location to another: What works in one setting often fails in a different one. Sometimes a program will work for a while but then start to fail, without an obvious reason. Often there is more than one way to approach a problem—and it is not clear which one to choose, or if it would be better to combine them. Implementation science looks at social, behavioral, economic, and administrative influences to see what might be acting as a roadblock and what might be helping a program or policy succeed. This research can involve community-level programs, laws, and policies, or direct-care health services that need improvement on a wide scale.

Methods developed by implementation science can be put into practice at all levels of public health, but careers specifically in this area tend to be research oriented. Implementation science researchers combine knowledge on topics such as systems analysis, monitoring and evaluation, comparative effectiveness, behavioral sciences, economics, and more to investigate best approaches in public health. Examples in health care delivery include looking at what helps HIV patients in different settings to follow up with treatment, or figuring out how to encourage doctors to follow guidelines for managing heart disease so that evidence-based practices will be more widely used. In community-level work, a researcher might look at the effects of different programs to encourage exercise and why some are more successful than others, or at how a successful program to promote safer driving can best be disseminated to other communities. The job may involve travel to sites where programs or policies are being implemented, to observe and gather data. Researchers who are also professors will generally teach classes in addition to their research work. Depending on the researcher's interests, the work can range from local to global.

Education and Certification

As of 2015, the Association of Schools and Programs of Public Health did not include implementation science in its list of public health focus areas, and it was not common to find degree programs specifically in implementation science focusing on public health. More often, implementation science is taught as part of other disciplines such as health services research and quality improvement, health policy and management, or social and behavioral health sciences. Because this is still a new field, it is likely that more educational opportunities will be developed in future years. Meanwhile, there are some brief training courses and certificate programs that can provide an introduction to the field, and a limited number of fellowships for PhD or MD graduates.

Core Competencies and Skills

- Understanding of how to carry out and interpret research and conduct statistical analyses
- Ability to collaborate with public health professionals who are implementing programs and policies
- Understanding of how clinical practice works and how clinicians think
- Ability to think creatively about problems and obstacles
- Understanding of cultural differences and how they can impact approaches to health

Compensation

Job descriptions that incorporate implementation science vary, and there are no national salary statistics. Salaries for university-based researchers would be expected to be typical for professors.

Workplaces

Implementation science researchers and specialists work at universities, government agencies and health departments, intergovernmental agencies like WHO, and major nonprofit organizations and consulting firms.

Employment Outlook

There is a lot of interest in what implementation science can offer. As both public health and health care focus more and more on measuring outcomes and impact, the demand for implementation science experts is likely to grow. Applying the tools of implementation science in real-world scenarios holds great promise for the future of public and global health.

For Further Information

- Several of the agencies within the U.S. Department of Health and Human Services (HHS) are doing work in implementation science; in 2015, some of the agencies with information on their websites were the National Institutes of Health (NIH),

the CDC, the Substance Abuse and Mental Health Services Administration (SAMHSA), and the National Cancer Institute.
■ University websites are another good way to start learning about implementation science. Look for programs based at global health programs or schools of public health.

NANOTECHNOLOGY

Job Description

It is only in the past few decades that we have started to understand the properties of matter on the nanoscale level. Nanoscale is really, really small: According to the National Nanotechnology Initiative, a single sheet of newspaper is about 100,000 nm thick. The basic properties of materials—such as melting point, chemical reactivity, and even color—change as they get down to this size. Most biological processes occur at the nanoscale level, which makes knowledge about what happens very useful for developing new medical technologies. But it also raises questions about the safety of nanoparticles for human health.

Nanotechnology has become a very important part of industry. It has been estimated that by 2014, 15% of all products would use nanotechnology in some way, totaling nearly $2.6 trillion in manufactured goods. Cosmetics companies are advertising wrinkle treatments and cleansers made with nanoparticles. Nanoscale materials are being used on clothing to help resist staining and wrinkling. They are in our eyeglasses and computer displays, because they can make surfaces nonreflective and scratch resistant. They are in food packaging, helping to keep sodas bubbly and food fresh. Nanotechnology is used in electronics, in fuel production, in medical devices. And yet we do not know the full impact of absorbing or ingesting nanoparticles, the true spectrum of risks in manufacturing, or what happens when recycling releases nanoscale particles into the environment. Workers in industries using nanotechnology may need special protections. There may be new concerns about air or water pollution.

Nanotechnology experts in public health can do a variety of different jobs. One role is in academia, as a faculty member doing research on the safety, ethics, and public health risks of nanotechnology. Others work for federal or state governmental agencies, on research, regulation, or policy development. Some experts with public health training have jobs in the private sector, such as working with an industry to ensure the health and safety of workers using nanotechnology in science or manufacturing. There are also opportunities to work on developing nanotechnology applications for health or environmental purposes. Public health and environmental health professionals in nanotechnology often interact and collaborate with a wide variety of other highly trained professionals, such as engineers, biologists, chemists, physicists, and business experts.

Education and Certification

Depending on the type of job and the employer, there are many different paths to a career in nanotechnology and public health. Physicians may work in occupational health and safety, for example, in a clinical capacity, research, or both. A public health degree, such as an MPH, DrPH, or PhD, can lead to research-based, policy-based, or other types of positions within academia, government, or industry. Many of the people who have found their way to public health nanotechnology research come from other backgrounds. For example, faculty working on nanotechnology at schools of public health include physicists, bioengineers, environmental science experts, pathologists, and other types of specialists.

Core Competencies and Skills

- Interest in scientific and medical information
- Knowledge of public health, occupational medicine, and environmental health and safety
- Strong understanding of scientific research and (for researchers) knowledge of how to design a scientific study
- Good understanding of risk assessment
- Ability to work with people from varied other disciplines—such as engineering, business, physics, and chemistry
- Ability to explain complex ideas to people from different fields

Compensation

The opportunities in this emerging field are too varied to give a single estimate for salary. For a general idea, look at the salary ranges for more specific roles—such as public health advisor, public health physician, bioengineer, professor, and so on.

Workplaces

Work concerning nanotechnology's impact on public health is going on at colleges and universities, at nonprofit organizations, and at state and federal agencies. There are also opportunities at private companies for people with public health training, such as overseeing worker and consumer safety.

Employment Outlook

Nanotechnology is a rapidly growing field with a quickly expanding workforce. Although right now nanotechnology is still an emerging specialty in public health, it is likely that there will be increasing needs and opportunities in the future, particularly relating to occupational medicine, health care, and environmental health.

For Further Information

- National Nanotechnology Initiative
  nano.gov

PUBLIC HEALTH PROFILE: Nanotechnology
Sara Brenner, MD, MPH
Assistant Vice President for NanoHealth Initiatives, Assistant Professor of Nanobioscience
Colleges of Nanoscale Science and Engineering (SUNY Poly CNSE), SUNY Polytechnic Institute, Albany, NY

Describe the sort of work you do.

As a faculty member at SUNY Poly, I have three main jobs: research, teaching, and service to the university. The primary focus of my research is occupational exposure assessment for the nanotechnology workforce, which includes developing methods to measure inhalation and cutaneous (skin) exposure for workers in the semiconductor industry. I collaborate with colleagues who have very different areas of expertise from me. Only through interdisciplinary teams are we able to advance the state of the science with regard to measurement (quantification) of nanomaterials and how exposure relates to health outcomes. My research group also links occupational health to nanotoxicology research where we investigate biological responses to specific nanomaterials. Another related aspect of interest is

(continued)

(continued)

environmental health. For example, my team investigates how engineered nanomaterials move through the industrial waste stream and the potential effects they may have on the environment.

For my role as a teacher, I designed a nanomedicine course focusing on applications for prevention, diagnosis, and treatment of disease. I also teach an ethics course on the societal implications of new and emerging technologies. Additionally, teaching includes day-to-day mentorship and guidance of graduate students (PhD and MS) in their research, as well as coordination of teams of students including undergraduates and high school students who work under my guidance on health-related projects.

My service activities are quite varied and include activities such as serving on our admissions committee and institutional review board (which helps ensure that research is ethical), as well as designing and delivering education and outreach activities related to my work that engage the greater community. I am also responsible for helping to build new programs (such as the MD/PhD program in nanomedicine), centers (such as the NanoHealth & Safety Center), and initiatives (such as partnerships with federal agencies, companies, and other groups), and scope out new directions for SUNY Poly CNSE in health and medicine.

What is a typical day like at your job?

Every day is different—which is part of what I love about my job—but each week typically contains a few main themes. One is conducting research and orchestrating my research team, which includes staff, undergraduates, and graduate students. I spend a lot of time training, mentoring, and working with them. I do a great deal of writing—such as scientific research papers, book chapters, proposals, and grant applications. I also review and prepare feedback on writing prepared by others, such as scientific papers being considered for publication and grant applications being considered for funding. For my classes, I prepare lectures and grade papers, and, of course, there is time spent teaching and meeting with individual students who are taking part in SUNY Poly CNSE's immersive educational experience, enabling them to pursue a growing number of high-tech careers across New York State and beyond.

(continued)

(continued)

Another part of each week involves strategizing and preparing information and presentations for colleagues, collaborators, administrators, and the public. This is where I link the nitty-gritty details of my research and other activities of the college to the "bigger picture" of what is going on with the nanotechnology community as a whole, locally, nationally, and internationally. I do a lot of thinking about national priorities and strategies for the future of nanotechnology and health. That includes doing talks for federal agencies, scientific conferences, local or community organizations such as professional groups or schools, as well as presentations for the general public such as those hosted by museums. Another big slice of time is spent on building partnerships and strategic or research-focused relationships with the clinical community, the public health community, federal agencies, and industry. That can include phone calls, meetings, and e-mails, or travel to in-person meetings. In addition, I spend time each week learning, either through these activities or through time dedicated solely to expanding my own knowledge base. I devote time each week to reading papers and learning from many different disciplines that are important to understanding nanotechnology and its implications. The science is moving so quickly that if you take your foot off the gas for even a short time, you're way behind!

What education or training do you have? Is it typical for your job?

My path is rather serendipitous and definitely not typical. However, in the future, I don't think there will be a "typical" route into nanotechnology. I did my BS with a focus on genetics and philosophy before going to medical school. I realized early in medical training that I was different than other physicians-in-training. I was always interested in disease prevention (even more so than treatment, from a philosophical standpoint) and became increasingly interested in health care systems, the delivery of medical services, and health policy. I completed my MD and went on to residency training in internal medicine and then specialized in preventive medicine and public health (including an MPH). I'm the only faculty member at my institution with an MD; other faculty members have PhD terminal degrees. Medical doctors

(continued)

(continued)

who do research are more often located at academic medical centers; however, the MD degree is becoming one of the most versatile degrees out there, and many physicians are forging careers outside of clinical practice. I believe this is a good thing, as the role of physicians in the health care system and in society is changing and will evolve in coming generations due to a variety of factors, including the integration of advanced nanotechnologies into medicine.

What path did you take to get to the job you are in today?

I started this job right after residency. My main focus during medical school and residency was federal health policy, and I was solely interested in moving to Washington, DC, to pursue a career in the federal government. At the tail end of residency (literally in the final weeks), I happened to attend a lecture on nanotechnology and medicine, and it really piqued my interest—so just out of curiosity, I asked if I could do a short rotation with the head of the nanobioscience department here; he said, "Sure!" and I quickly discovered how fascinating and transformative nanotechnology will be in all industries, including medicine. I became so fascinated that I still haven't left.

Where might you go from here if you wanted to advance your career?

There is a lot that I want to do right here! SUNY Poly is growing at lightning speed, with more than $20 billion in investments at its world class Albany NanoTech Complex alone, and nanotechnology is the future in so many industries. I want to help advance this technology and also safeguard the advancement from a health and safety perspective. SUNY Poly CNSE is a unique institution, where we are connected to all sectors—academia, industry, and government. There's no better platform for the type of work I want to do.

What is the worst or most challenging part of your job?

The most difficult part of being on faculty is wanting to do more than I can fit into each day! I know many colleagues feel this way

(continued)

(continued)

as well. Time management can be challenging, because there are so many different activities going on and all of them are interesting and important.

What is the best part?

The most rewarding part is helping shape the future, in the sense that we are advancing science that will propel humanity forward. Nanotechnology has been heralded as the next industrial revolution, it's the nexus of thinkers, scientists, entrepreneurs, humanitarians, and futurists. The other way in which I can shape the future is through teaching and mentoring students who will carry on this work. They will carry the torch, they will create what comes next. And I love the diversity in my work—from the activities every day to the progression of science to the different people I work with.

What advice do you have for someone who is interested in your career?

Follow your passion. Embrace risk. Create opportunity. Engage tenacity. Don't be afraid to pursue a direction that others don't understand. The future is defined by those who see things differently and who do things differently. If you can envision a path that doesn't yet exist, don't let the unknown dissuade you. And preserve your sense of curiosity and wonder along the way.

CHAPTER 25

Off the Beaten Path

In the preceding chapters, you have learned about many traditional (and some nontraditional) careers in public health. This chapter is a mix of "everything else." Some of these jobs are already being accepted as part of the future of public health, even though they are really based in other disciplines. Some are here because they are particularly exciting or fun. As you review these careers, keep in mind that public health is constantly changing and evolving. There is always room for new connections in unusual or unexpected ways.

DANCE INSTRUCTOR

Job Description

Maybe it is not fair to include dance instructor in a book about public health careers, because it is not something you would find as a full-time job at the health department. But dance does have a role in public health. We have learned that it is not enough just to tell people to go out and exercise, that it will improve health and fight diseases related to obesity—exercise has to be something they *want* to do. And we are all more likely to do things if they are fun. That is what is great about dance. A few years ago, more than 30 cities around the United States shared in a "Day of Dance" as part of a heart health campaign to help people see that getting fit can actually be fun. Many local health departments link citizens to dance classes at city recreation centers. Dance also turns up in campaigns focused on other issues—hip-hop dance and music being used as a medium to teach kids about health, for example.

Education and Certification

There is no single path to becoming a dance instructor. Some instructors learn at for-profit dancing schools. A degree (bachelor's, master's, or even a PhD) in dance or dance education is one option. For those who are sure they want to go into public health, there are some programs offering an undergraduate degree or MPH that combines exercise science, health education, and public health. Public school dance teachers must have state certification to teach.

Core Competencies and Skills

- Excellent teaching skills
- Ability to inspire enthusiasm
- Patience with people who are not natural dancers
- Ability to design classes for specific needs
- Initiative to create new programs and seek funding to support them
- Knowledge of the evidence for a connection between dance and fitness—and the ability to explain it

Compensation

There are not enough dance instructors working solely in public health to give an accurate salary range. Dance performers typically earn about $9 to $34 per hour. Fitness trainers can earn a wide range of salaries, from about $18,000 at the lower end to $67,500 or more; the range is similar for instructors who teach "self enrichment" classes (classes that are essentially for fun, as opposed to professional training).

Workplaces

Dance instructors work at community centers, dance studios, schools, senior centers, day-care centers—anywhere there is room to dance and where people are interested in learning.

Employment Outlook

The future of dance in public health is not clear. Combating obesity and sedentary lifestyles has been an increasingly strong focus of public health in recent years, and there is a need for new and creative programs with a basis in sound science. There are no guarantees, but learning what is known about the health benefits of dance and then networking with people from the local schools and health department could lead to interesting opportunities.

For Further Information

- SHAPE America
  www.shapeamerica.org
- Let's Move
  www.letsmove.gov

URBAN PLANNER

Job Description

Urban planner may not be "off the beaten path" of public health for much longer, as awareness continues to increase about how much our built environment contributes to our health. Urban planners use computer programs and databases to collect and analyze information about population, transportation, and housing. They map out land areas and look at population density, demographics, roads, and public transportation. They make recommendations for zoning, for the location of roads and schools, and for other aspects of city infrastructure, keeping local laws and regulations in mind. The job combines visits to development sites and time in the office, plus meetings with government officials and community groups.

Historically, urban planning and public health were closely connected. As sanitation improved, the two disciplines became disengaged. But with more and more attention to the impact that the environment has on people's health, there is a movement to bring urban planning and public health together. Public health professionals are asking whether neighborhoods can be built in a way that promotes diversity and reduces health disparities. They are looking at building safety into street designs, thinking about pedestrians and bicycles, not just cars. Some urban planners are already working on these types of issues, and the future may see the two disciplines becoming closely integrated once again.

Education and Certification

A good option for those interested in urban planning and public health is a dual degree—an MPH combined with a master's in urban planning. Certifications that can help with advancement are available through professional organizations such as the American Institute of Certified Planners. A few states require licensing or registration for urban planners.

Core Competencies and Skills

- Creativity
- Understanding of the intersection between the built environment and public health
- Ability to see how two-dimensional plans will translate into three-dimensional space
- Ability to both give and accept constructive criticism regarding plans
- Strong computer skills, including the ability to use geographic information systems

Compensation

In 2014, the median salary for urban and regional planners was about $67,000. Most earned between $42,000 and $99,500.

Workplaces

Most urban planners work for local governments. A few are at the Centers for Disease Control and Prevention. Planners also work for private companies at architecture and engineering firms. Planners with a specific interest in public health can often be found at universities, doing research and teaching the next generation.

Employment Outlook

Employment growth is expected to be about average for this career, between 2012 and 2022. Opportunities will depend on city budgets and the state of the economy. In times of economic slowdown or recession, there is less money for development projects, but then jobs tend to open up as the economy recovers. The increasing focus on sustainable, environmentally conscious planning is also expected to drive job growth.

For Further Information

- American Planning Association (APA)
  www.planning.org

HOSPITAL ADMINISTRATOR

Job Description

Being the top administrator at a hospital is not always a "public health" sort of job. The head of the hospital has to ensure that the place is profitable (or, for a nonprofit hospital, that income is meeting financial needs), in addition to keeping an eye on the services delivered and ensuring that the board of directors, medical staff, and department heads are all working toward the same goals. But some administrators make it their business to take a public health stance. Hospital administrators can spearhead quality improvement efforts. They can launch community health programs and support research into the community's needs. They can partner with local organizations and health departments to help meet current needs and prepare for future ones. And they can ensure that the hospital is prepared for epidemics and other potential crises. In addition to the top job, larger hospitals also have mid-level administrators who oversee various aspects of the hospital's services and behind-the-scenes management, and who report back to the top administrator. This is an office job with many meetings and obligations. Administrators also visit the various hospital departments so that they can see what is really happening in management and patient care.

Education and Certification

A typical way to prepare for a career as a hospital administrator is to earn a master's degree in health services administration, public administration, or business administration, and to start with a low-level administrative job at a hospital or health care center. More experience allows access to higher-level jobs with more responsibility. Some hospital administrators start out as physicians and gradually move from a clinical to an administrative role. Administrators who are members of the American College of Healthcare Executives (ACHE) can earn board certification and the title of ACHE Fellow by meeting certain professional requirements and passing an examination.

Core Competencies and Skills

- Strong leadership skills and the ability to inspire others
- Ability to handle multiple complex tasks
- Confidence in decision making
- Good political and networking skills
- Significant administrative experience, including strategic planning and finance
- Understanding of the many needs within a hospital, from the cafeteria to the intensive care unit
- Understanding of the laws, regulations, and policies that apply to hospitals, from workforce issues to infection control

Compensation

At a large hospital network in a major city, the chief executive officer (CEO) can take home a base salary of well over half a million dollars each year, not counting bonuses and other benefits. According to a 2014 survey by *Modern Healthcare*, average compensation for hospital executives was $319,400. A report from the consulting firm Yaffe and Company breaks down salaries further; at a small hospital in a rural area, pay tends to be more in the range of $100,000 to $200,000.

Workplaces

Hospital administrators work for both for-profit and nonprofit hospitals. Some oversee networks including multiple hospitals and outpatient offices, while others are responsible for just one hospital.

Employment Outlook

There are plenty of lower-level administrative jobs, and the Bureau of Labor Statistics estimates that the job outlook for medical and health services managers will be good in the next few years as the population ages and health care continues to expand. However, the top job of hospital president or CEO is extremely competitive, and only the best qualified people will have a shot at these jobs.

For Further Information

- American College of Healthcare Executives (ACHE)
  www.ache.org

CHEF

Job Description

Several years ago, celebrity chef Jamie Oliver demonstrated how far our culture has gotten away from fresh, healthful food. He showed a group of American schoolchildren a tomato and asked them what it was. They did not know. They could not name a cauliflower or an eggplant, either. There has been a lot of talk in public health about combating obesity by encouraging healthier eating, but if you just put an apple on a child's lunch tray, there is a good chance it is going to end up in the trash. You can offer adults all the fresh produce in the world—but if they do not know how to prepare it, they are not likely to choose fresh broccoli. A lot of people do not even know how to cook. And these days, many of us in front of the television or computer screen, which can mean gulping down calories without noticing what we have eaten.

There is a small but dedicated movement among talented cooks to change all this. These chefs are showing communities how to *enjoy* fruits and veggies—how to make them a practical part of everyday meals that are not just good for you, but absolutely delicious. Some chefs teach for love of food and the social sharing around the table, some are thinking of the environment, and some have health specifically in mind—but in each case, home cooking leads to healthier food choices. Chefs are helping revamp school meals, pushing to make cooking classes part of the school day, teaching parents and children to cook together, and running garden-to-table programs where kids grow their own produce and then learn to prepare it. Just like the dentists who come to our schools and teach our kids about oral hygiene, these chefs are giving kids the skills they need to make healthy habits part of their everyday lives.

Education and Certification

Chefs often have associate's or bachelor's degrees in culinary arts. There are also many chefs who learned their skills on the job.

Core Competencies and Skills

- Love of food
- Ability to create enthusiasm in others

- High level of comfort with public speaking
- At least a basic understanding of nutrition
- Strong teaching skills and the patience to teach people who know nothing about cooking
- Understanding of differences in people's food preferences, including cultural differences

Compensation

The median salary for a chef or head cook is about $42,000, with most earning $23,000 to $74,000. These numbers are for traditional chefs, though, who direct the cooking at restaurants and other food establishments. The rate of pay at a school cooking program will depend very much on the funding available.

Workplaces

Chefs who are involved in public health work often work for nonprofit organizations. Some chefs partner directly with schools, health departments, or universities.

Employment Outlook

The percentage of schools with cooking classes and gardens is still small, but it is growing. Cooks who are interested can look for local programs or talk with school authorities, local foundations, or the health department about getting something started.

For Further Information

- The Edible Schoolyard Project
  edibleschoolyard.org
- Slow Food USA National School Garden Program
  www.slowfoodusa.org
- Food Corps
  foodcorps.org
- Chefs Move to Schools
  www.chefsmovetoschools.org

PUBLIC HEALTH PROFILE: Chef
Esther Cook
Chef Teacher
The Edible Schoolyard Berkeley, Berkeley, CA

Describe the sort of work you do.

The Edible Schoolyard Berkeley provides gardening and cooking classes at a public school in Berkeley, California. The kids have garden classes through the science department and come to the kitchen through their history and humanities classes. We grow a wide variety of foods in the garden, so that the students can see what different crops look like. Hopefully, we're taking away the idea that good, fresh food is an elitist thing, and we're showing that everyone can have good food. The founder of the Edible Schoolyard, the chef Alice Waters, is committed to child nutrition as a basic right as well as an essential component of the learning process. She believes that mealtime, shared with family and friends, is an important ritual that teaches values and builds community. This tradition is getting lost as fewer families eat together.

Part of my job is to illuminate for the kids that healthy is not synonymous with unpleasant. We don't focus on calories or a lot of nutritional information, because they're not there yet. Instead we seduce them with delicious food. For example we'll do an apple tasting. We'll try nine different apples, and they can see which ones they like.

What is a typical day like at your job?

My assistant and I teach two classes a day, sometimes three. We'll have all the food and vegetables laid out on the table and encourage students to use all of their senses as they cook their way through a lesson. We'll show them kale, and we'll talk about what it looks like and feels like. We'll show them neat things like how water beads up on the leaves when you rinse it, which elevates the experience from simply washing food to observing how beautiful an ordinary task can be.

After the kids do all the prep and the cooking, then we'll clear the table and set it with a tablecloth. We sit down together, and we eat together. For some kids, that's their only experience of eating

(continued)

(continued)

together—their families don't do this. They learn how to have a conversation at the table and how to pass food, and in the process they gain a sense of accomplishment and pride. The kids do the cleanup, too.

In addition to the class time, I also go shopping at farmers' markets, because not everything we use comes from our garden. There's lesson planning and research. We've written manuals, and we do what we call academies for educators who want to start programs like ours. We also have staff meetings, we have visitors, and there is a fair amount of media attention.

What education or training do you have? Is it typical for your job?

I don't know what's typical, because not a lot of people have my job. Hopefully it's becoming more common, though. There are a lot of cooking programs you can go to if you want to learn to be a chef, but I just worked in restaurants and learned that way. Because the Edible Schoolyard is a nonprofit program, I don't have to be a certified teacher. A certified teacher does have to be present, though.

What path did you take to get to the job you are in today?

I went to college for fine arts and I've taken classes in child development. I ended up as a cook because for me it was a way to continue to do art, but still earn money. I started volunteering for the Center for Urban Education about Sustainable Agriculture. We would go into schools and do little cooking projects, with desks pushed together and no running water. And the kids would get so fired up—it was great to see that!

A friend told me about the chef teacher job. I'd been running a similar program in a community center, but it was only for 6 weeks at a time. I hadn't known about the Edible Schoolyard program, but I knew who Alice Waters was. And my parents were teachers, so even though I'd never been a teacher, I understood about teaching and really appreciated it. I got the job, and I became a founding teacher here. It's been 13 years, and I've never looked back!

(continued)

(continued)

Where might you go from here, if you wanted to advance your career?

I joke that they're going to have to blast me out of here eventually, because I'm not leaving. I've always been fascinated by the therapeutic aspects of cooking, though, and I'd like to look into cooking in the same way that art therapy came about. There are some troubled kids at the school, and I've been really moved by the transformations that you see in them when they're in the kitchen.

What is the worst or most challenging part of your job?

Sometimes it's just hard to see other people's realities. To realize that not every child is getting this experience. As wonderful as it is to have the Edible Schoolyard, it should be a part of every school.

What is the best part?

Absolutely, without a doubt, the kids are the best part. Getting to be a part of their lives on a daily basis gives me so much optimism for the future. They are so bright and so funny and so insightful.

What advice do you have for someone who is interested in your career?

Volunteer! We've had so many volunteers move on to paid positions. Look at places you admire and offer to help them for a few months, and see if you like it. And if the program you are interested in does not have an opening, look for other programs that might.

Profile Update

It's been a few years since her interview, and Esther continues to love her job with the Edible Schoolyard. She's proud to say that the program serves over 1,000 children at Martin Luther King, Jr. Middle School in Berkeley. They've also expanded to teaching adults, training other educators to create edible education programs in their own communities.

WORKSITE WELLNESS MANAGER

Job Description

Health and wellness programs have become common in corporate settings across the United States. Employers like them because they have the potential to reduce health insurance costs and boost productivity. The motive is often profit—but one result, if it is done right, is better health for employees. The person responsible for corporate wellness designs programs and policies (or purchases services from outside vendors) to encourage employees to quit smoking, exercise more, eat better, cope with stress more effectively, and generally make better choices for their health. Ideally, these are evidence-based efforts with a focus on concrete results. The wellness manager collects information about health challenges common among employees and about employees' interests. The manager devises interventions based on that information, then collects more data once the interventions are underway to be sure they are working. An important goal is to make the work environment conducive to health. Examples of interventions include posting calorie information in the cafeteria, creating special discounts on healthier lunches, and working with vending machine suppliers to include more healthful snacks. A wellness program could offer flexible work hours to decrease employee stress levels. Some include financial incentives for employees who participate in weight management programs, keep their cholesterol under control, or try to quit smoking. If employees are interested, the wellness manager might even distribute pedometers to all employees and hold a walking contest, with prizes for the team that walks the most each week.

Education and Certification

Employers often look for a bachelor's or master's degree in a field related to health promotion or exercise science; some ask for an MPH. Managing a program usually requires some experience in this field. Wellness practitioners can complete training programs and certifications through the Wellness Council of America (WELCOA).

Core Competencies and Skills

- Creativity to keep wellness programs fresh, even if the issues do not change

- Patience for employees who may start wellness activities, but not finish them
- Good skills in persuasion and negotiation, for working with administrative staff to implement changes
- Knowledge of basic survey techniques and statistical methods
- Knowledge of how to translate research into practice and design evidence-based programs
- Understanding of outcomes assessment and quality improvement methods
- Understanding of social marketing

Compensation

A 2012 survey by WELCOA found a median salary of $70,000 for wellness program directors, $65,000 for wellness program specialists/coordinators, $61,000 for wellness program consultants, and $41,000 for health/wellness coaches.

Workplaces

There are worksite wellness programs at all types of organizations, including for-profit companies, nonprofits, and government agencies. Wellness managers also work for outside agencies and consulting firms that provide wellness services, and for insurance agencies.

Employment Outlook

Worksite wellness is a rapidly growing industry. According to a 2013 report from the RAND Corporation, worksite wellness programs were already being offered at about half of all companies with 50 employees or more. Future demand for wellness managers will be influenced by developments in health care reform and by the results of research on the effectiveness of wellness programs as money-saving efforts.

For Further Information

- Wellness Council of America (WELCOA)
  www.welcoa.org

MEDICAL EXPERT/MEDIA

Job Description

When President Obama floated the idea of television celebrity doctor Sanjay Gupta as Surgeon General back in 2009, a lot of public health doctors were outraged. Dr. Gupta is a neurosurgeon and a journalist—but not a public health expert. But the president did have a point. A doctor with a strong presence in the media can have a huge impact on how we think about health and on the choices we make. An awful lot of people got answers to questions about a flu pandemic from Dr. Gupta's broadcasts. Daytime talk shows starring or featuring segments with personable doctors have huge audiences. People listen to the local doctor who does the "medical minute" on the evening news, too. There are also doctors working behind the scenes advising movie and television scriptwriters, trying to keep drama from trumping accuracy, and sometimes even sneaking public health messages into the story. There are doctors helping with nonfiction television shows, ensuring that weight loss advice or a story about the latest way to prevent a heart attack is actually correct. Some doctors advise on social marketing efforts or write magazine and web articles about health and prevention. And we know that media can have an impact. Studies have shown that teens picked up messages about condoms from a television sitcom and that viewers remembered advice about cancer prevention from storylines on favorite dramas. And of course, the media is a major source of information whenever there is an immediate public health concern.

Education and Certification

A clinical degree is essential for credibility. Media advisors on medical issues are typically doctors, but nurses and nutritionists can have a role here too. For doctors, having completed a clinical residency and being licensed is usually expected if not absolutely required.

Core Competencies and Skills

- Creativity
- Excellent networking skills

- Knack for translating medical information into plain language
- Good sense of what will hold the public's interest
- Awareness of how the general public uses and reacts to health information
- Media skills—not just public speaking skills, but an understanding of what works on camera
- Understanding of how media works, including video production, web design, and publishing

Compensation

A top "media doctor" with national exposure can earn far more than he would in private practice. Dr. Gupta would have taken a substantial pay cut if he had accepted the job as Surgeon General! Working in the media does not guarantee a fabulous salary, though. It very much depends on the job, the hours, and the audience reach. A reporter or freelance writer would not necessarily be paid extra just because he or she is an MD.

Workplaces

A doctor working in media could be a freelance writer or consultant, or an employee at a production company or television network. Some doctors collaborate with scriptwriters and producers part time, while maintaining a clinical practice or working as a professor at a medical school.

Employment Outlook

A lot of doctors want to do this kind of work, and there are only a handful of jobs—most of which are never advertised. That does not mean it cannot happen. But it can take a lot creativity and perseverance, not to mention being in the right place at the right time.

For Further Information

- National Association of Medical Communicators (NAMC) *www.namc.info*

PUBLIC HEALTH PROFILE: Medical Expert
John Whyte, MD, MPH
Chief Medical Expert, Vice President of CME
Discovery Channel, Silver Spring, MD

Describe the sort of work you do.

My job at Discovery Channel is to create medical education and patient education programming. My department makes television shows that appeal to a physician audience as well as a lay audience, and we create media for Discovery's digital properties, too—websites, online games, podcasts, and streaming video. Discovery's strength is the power of storytelling, and everything we do is consistent with the theme of "Entertain your Brain." So a big part of my job is trying to reach a balance between giving quality, credible information, and providing entertainment. You can have the best health message out there, but if no one's listening it doesn't matter.

What is a typical day like at your job?

My day is split among working on new proposals for shows, helping to oversee production and editorial content, and managing the health aspects of our digital properties. I also have to stay current with the medical literature, so I read medical journals and articles from clipping services.

When we're planning our medical education shows, the first thing we do is figure out where physicians are not doing a good enough job in caring for their patients. What do they need to know? We also ask where patients need help in improving their own care. Then we look at potential funders, like pharmaceutical companies and large foundations, to see what they might be willing to sponsor. I work with members of my team as well as outside contractors to create grant proposals, and I look over the proposals before they go out to make sure they are medically accurate.

Our production team doesn't have medical knowledge, so I educate them about each show's topic. I contact outside experts to invite them to participate in the programs, and I approve the subjects for documentary-style segments. As the show is being produced, I review the video and give comments.

(continued)

(continued)

I'm the only physician at Discovery, so producers from other departments come to me for medical information, too. For Discovery's National Body Challenge, I make sure the experts they plan to use are qualified, and I give input on the fitness and weight loss recommendations. I also do a lot of digital video shorts, where I'm actually the one on camera. For a recent one, I went out onto the street and talked with people about aging and health.

What education or training do you have? Is it typical for your job?

I have an MD and an MPH, and I'm board certified in internal medicine. I think in media, especially if you want to be on television, it helps to be board certified in a specialty. People really equate that with quality. I also think having done a full clinical residency helps my work here. If you want to impact patients' behavior or physicians' practices, you have to understand how patients think, and you have to understand the process of medicine. I still do some direct patient care, and that adds tremendous value.

What path did you take to get to the job you are in today?

I never expected to be working in media. I thought I would be a faculty member at a medical school, and eventually a department chair. But even in college, I was interested in health policy. During medical school, I took time out after my second year to earn an MPH. After my internal medicine residency, I did a health services research fellowship, and I enjoyed that a lot. And then I had to figure out how to combine policy and clinical practice. I had some contacts in government who knew about my interests, so I reached out to them. It turned out they wanted to bring more physicians into Medicare policy work, and they created a spot for me. I really had to go out and make that opportunity, though. After that, I worked on childhood obesity issues at the Agency for Healthcare Research and Quality. That job included working with the media, which is how I met the people at Discovery. At first, I wasn't interested in taking this job. But then I started thinking about how I could use the position to translate medical research into

(continued)

(continued)

actual practice. Discovery is truly a global multimedia company, with many opportunities to have an impact.

Where might you go from here, if you wanted to advance your career?

I want to find even more effective ways to change behavior and to communicate health messages. This is complex information, and people often don't want to hear it. They don't want to be preached to. I don't necessarily have another job in mind, but I'm always interested in opportunities to learn to communicate health message better.

What is the worst or most challenging part of your job?

I may have a great idea for a show, but I need to find the funding. That can be very challenging, especially in a tough economic climate. And we have to keep seeking funding constantly for all our shows—it can be exhausting!

Traveling does get tiresome after a while, too. I spend a lot of time in airports and trains, when I could be attending to other priorities. But what's cool is that our shows have taken me to every continent except Antarctica.

What is the best part?

The best part of the job is having the ability to create a show on a health topic where I know there needs to be improvement. I can wake up one day and say, "I really want to educate people about taking better care of type 2 diabetes." And I can go out and obtain funding and make a program that will be seen by millions of people.

It's also exciting, here at Discovery Channel, to be surrounded by some of the most creative people around. You don't usually get that when you're practicing medicine.

What advice do you have for someone who is interested in your career?

I would say to get a good education, to have good clinical knowledge so that you can be a medical advisor. You also need to be willing to

(continued)

(continued)

network and to develop a group of people who know and respect you. Often you can reach out to people who have careers similar to what you would like to do and ask them about their career path and how they got involved. Some of the best career opportunities are not listed in any job description. You have to create them.

Profile Update

Since his original interview, Dr. Whyte has transitioned to the Food and Drug Administration, where he serves as Director of Professional Affairs and Stakeholder Engagement (PASE) at the Center for Drug Evaluation and Research (CDER). His role is to serve as the eyes, ears, and voice of CDER when it comes to understanding and communicating with stakeholders. This includes physicians and their professional societies, patients, and their advocacy groups, CDER officials, and all others with a shared interest in drug development, review, and safety. PASE encourages and facilitates two-way communications between CDER and these stakeholders, in order to foster true and lasting collaboration.

Dr. Whyte is also responsible for building relationships with representatives from other offices within CDER, learning which topics are of particular importance, and devising ways to disseminate information. Examples include creating infographics for both patients and physicians, speaking to outside groups on topics such as drug development or the expedited approval process, and writing scientific articles.

PART III

The Future of Public Health

CHAPTER 26

The Future of Public Health

COLLABORATION WITH THE COMMUNITY

Community-level public health efforts are strongest when the unique needs of a location, population, and culture are taken into account. But in many situations, public health professionals come from very different backgrounds than the people they are trying to help or protect. Picture an MPH grad from the suburbs trying to do injury prevention work among low-income migrant workers, many of whom have not finished high school. Imagine an American-born PhD trying to plan reproductive health programs among the favelas (urban shantytowns) in Brazil. Who are the true "experts" on what is needed and what will work in these places? Is it the public health graduates—or the people who live their lives in these communities?

More and more, public health is emphasizing the importance of involving community members in the creation of programs and policies that will affect them. This is not just doing a few focus groups or taking a survey: It is bringing community members directly into the planning and decision-making process. The interest in this type of approach stems, in part, from recognizing that the underlying causes of health disparities are complex, and that inequities are unlikely to be overcome from the outside alone. The thinking is that when a public health effort comes up from the community, rather then down from an outside authority, research results will be more accurate and policies and programs will be more efficient and effective.

Community-based participatory research (CBPR) is one way that public health experts are recognizing that communities ultimately have power over their own health, and that programs may be more effective when that is recognized from the start. Traditionally, a public health professional or academic researcher would consider a community, decide on a research question, choose how to explore that question, and decide what results were important. Sometimes this yielded information useful to the research subjects. But sometimes the results were not of interest to community members at all. And all too often, people living in the community were not even informed of the research results.

The traditional approach to research can leave community members feeling taken advantage of. When they cannot see the purpose of the study, there is little reason to participate. If they do not find out the results or do not understand them, there is no apparent benefit. Further, populations that experience lower levels of health are often marginalized in other ways. Even if policies and programs are created based on good data, they may not resonate with a community that feels that an outside entity is telling them what to do about yet another issue.

CBPR turns the research system around. Although the researcher may bring the general topic, such as infant mortality or rates of heart disease or depression, it must be something of interest to the community. Instead of being "research subjects," community members become active participants. Development of specific research questions and decisions about how data will be gathered and what will be done with it are collaborations among researchers, community members, representatives of community organizations, and others with a stake in improving the local population's health.

CBPR emphasizes that although public health professionals may have a high level of knowledge about, say, biostatistics and program planning, it is the community members who know whether it is common for men to use condoms, which blocks the drug dealers frequent, and whether fresh vegetables are available and affordable. Community members have knowledge of local culture, common beliefs related to health and lifestyle choices, and common challenges.

Carrying out true CBPR is challenging. It requires working with people with varied education levels, many of whom have no formal training in how to design or carry out a study. The researcher needs to be able to support collaborators in learning how to do research, how to frame a question, and how to interpret the results. At the same time, they must maintain a high degree of humility, with the understanding that the exchange of knowledge goes both ways—and that they have much to learn, themselves.

As the work progresses, the researcher must be able to encourage and support continued collaboration, even as different priorities tug at participants' interest and time. At the end of the project, they must make sure that the results are shared throughout the community, and that the information is presented in a way that is understandable, useful, and relevant to people's lives. And finally, ideally, the research should lead to some sort of beneficial change.

The overall effectiveness of public health efforts based on CBPR, compared to more traditional approaches, is difficult to measure. Different studies use the principles of CBPR to different degrees, so there is no good way to combine or compare them. Further, public health researchers and practitioners are still learning how best to carry out this type of work. However, a look at academic departments, government grants, and federal, state, and local health agencies shows that community engagement is a goal in many areas.

CBPR is part of a broader concept of "community engaged research," essentially a paradigm encompassing the idea that research should be done with communities, not to them. "Community-based public health" is another broad term referring to a partnership among public health professionals, academic faculty, and communities to recognize problems, identify and make use of resources, and create and implement public health policies, programs, and other efforts that will meet the community's needs.

Given the increasing recognition of how hard it can be to change health behaviors, of the impacts of personal, cultural, and geographic influences, and of the possibility that communities may best understand their own needs, it seems likely that community engagement, at least in some form, will be an important part of the future of public health.

CLIMATE CHANGE AND PUBLIC HEALTH

What does climate change have to do with public health? Quite a lot! If projections are correct, we may see significant changes not only in weather, but in patterns of disease—and we may need more public health professionals to combat these effects.

Many infectious diseases are strongly influenced by climate. Climate change can alter both the geographic range and the transmission seasons of insect-borne diseases like malaria. Millions or even billions more people around the world could be affected. No one knows for sure whether we will start to see tropical diseases like dengue fever moving into the United States, but it is possible. We could also see more cases of diseases that already occur here. Lyme disease is one example. The ticks that carry the disease are expected to thrive in warmer weather, and humans could be at increased risk from higher tick densities and from simply spending more time outside (World Health Organization, 2014a).

Climate could also impact our water supply, with complex effects on health. Changes in rainfall can influence the supply of drinking water, through droughts or floods. Floods can overtax drainage systems, leading to contamination of drinking water. This is likely to be particularly serious in the developing world, where diarrheal disease is already a major cause of childhood mortality and sanitation systems are limited. Climate change can also disrupt agricultural rhythms, if drought or excess rainfall interferes with a season's crops. The collapse of agriculture in a region can lead to widespread malnutrition and a range of associated health problems. It can also contribute to problems with sanitation and disease transmission, particularly if people must leave villages for crowded camps or big-city slums (World Health Organization, 2014a).

Climate change can affect air pollution, with higher temperatures raising the levels of pollutants. Air pollution worsens asthma and can cause or worsen other forms of lung disease. Studies have shown that deaths from heart disease go up in parallel with certain types of air pollution, as well.

Other health risks related to climate change include increased injuries, fatalities, and mental health stressors from weather-related disasters, heat-related illness and death, and even civil strife if degradation of the environment destabilizes cultures or economies (World Health Organization, 2014a).

In 2014, the World Health Organization (WHO) released a report looking at some specific categories of health impacts, part of an ongoing effort to quantify the number of deaths expected due to climate change (World Health Organization, 2014b). Each year between 2030 and 2050, and assuming current medical and economic progress continues, the researchers expect we will see an additional 38,000 heat exposure deaths among elderly people, 48,000 deaths due to diarrhea, an extra 60,000 deaths from malaria, and 95,000 deaths attributable to malnutrition in childhood.

Public health organizations are beginning to focus in on both prevention of and response to climate change. In 2015, the Centers for Disease Control and Prevention's (CDC) Climate and Health Program was funding 16 states and 2 cities to work on planning and testing methods to respond to the health effects of climate change (Centers for Disease Control and Prevention, 2014). One aim of the Arizona health department was to prepare for the health effects of extreme heat. New York State was working on issues including the impacts of extreme weather, food- and waterborne illness, and vector disease. Oregon's interests included food- and waterborne disease, extreme weather, and effects on ecosystems.

Other U.S. agencies working on climate change include the National Institute of Environmental Health Sciences at the National Institutes of Health, the U.S. Department of Agriculture (USDA), and the Environmental Protection Agency. Major nonprofits and other nongovernmental organizations support initiatives to mitigate climate change impacts. As an example, the Public Health Institute's Center for Climate Change & Health pulls together public health professionals, policy makers, scientists, and others to figure out how to reduce climate change and, at the same time, help communities be resilient and become or remain healthy as climate change occurs. On a global scale, the WHO recognizes climate change as a major public health risk. Among other initiatives, the World Meteorological Association and the WHO have teamed up to improve collaboration between those who predict weather changes and events, and those who plan for and respond to the impact of these changes (World Health Organization, 2014c). As the United Nations and world governments work to reduce the causes of climate change, its current and potential effects will likely resonate throughout the world of public health.

PUBLIC HEALTH AND CHANGING POPULATIONS

Changes in populations, including population density, age distribution, and wealth all have significant impacts on people's health. In the developing world, migrations from rural to urban areas lead to changes in disease distribution, new sanitation issues, and new challenges to mental health. Even improvements in health care can create new challenges, such as a decrease in infant mortality leading to larger families with more mouths to feed.

Here in the United States, immigration patterns are also changing public health needs. An influx of new immigrants to a city can mean an increase in the ratio of children to adults, requiring the health department to shift funds and focus to meet different needs. People from different places may have different disease risks; hepatitis B, for example, is much more prevalent among immigrants from certain places than among the U.S. population as a whole, due to differing patterns of transmission. In places where the population is aging, a greater focus on elder health issues will be needed. (See the chapter on aging [Chapter 8] to see how public health is adapting to the increasing numbers of older adults in the United States.)

Funding for public health does not always parallel population needs, and it can be slow to catch up. But keeping an eye on shifts in local demographics, both here in the United States and in populations in other regions or nations around the world, can be helpful in predicting where new public health efforts will be needed.

NEW MEDIA AND PUBLIC HEALTH

Public health organizations and agencies are on Facebook. You can follow the WHO on Twitter. The CDC has an Instagram account. They have dabbled with videos on Vine. They are even on Pinterest. (And by the time you are reading this, there will probably be new services where you can follow them, too!)

Public health is probably never going to be a major source of viral videos or share-worthy memes. It is just not that kind of cool. But there is promising work in disease prevention and health promotion based on social media. During flu season, the CDC uses Twitter updates, Facebook posts, videos, an RSS feed, and e-mails to promote flu prevention and keep people informed about symptoms and treatment. They also offer a series of widgets, computer programs that can be embedded in web pages and updated automatically as new information emerges.

When the Ebola outbreak ravaged parts of West Africa in 2014, the United States devoted a great deal of effort to help stop the epidemic. At the same time, there was great concern about the possibility that Ebola could spread here at home. Even with our high-technology medical care, there was no reliable treatment and no cure. And there was a lot of confusion and misinformation about how the disease spreads and who might be at risk. The CDC created infographics to make the facts and recommendations clear to doctors and the public across the United States. A series of webinars kept clinicians and health care administrators up to date on pre-paredness planning and needs. The public was invited to use Twitter to ask questions and get answers from experts. A social media team monitored online conversations to watch for trends and catch misunderstandings.

The CDC was far from the only organization using new media to address the situation. When the CDC seemed slow to update informa-tion on protective gear for doctors and nurses, many health care provid-ers turned to Nebraska Medical Center's Biocontainment Unit, which used their own website to disseminate information on how to stay safe while caring for patients with Ebola. By mid-2015, they offered a wealth of links including downloadable graphics, webinars, algorithms, and a screening checklist.

There are many other uses for new media in public health. New York City offers smartphone apps that address some of the basics of public health: There is one to look up restaurant ratings, one to calculate calories and suggest healthier recipes, one for teens to access reproductive health services and treatment of sexually transmitted diseases, even one that lets you enter your address and find the nearest place to get free condoms. Some health departments and hospitals have apps to report local public health risks and disease outbreaks. The American Cancer Society and the National Cancer Institute offer apps to help people quit smoking. The California Poison Control System even created an app in the form of a game that teaches how little kids could get pills confused with candy.

Websites have become a major resource for people looking for health and safety information. There is a lot of poorly sourced and incorrect information out there on the web, which can lead to health scares and fads for remedies that do not actually work. But the Internet has also made it easier for public health organizations to offer safe and reliable information and resources. A website called recalls.gov links users to the Food and Drug Administration, the USDA, the Consumer Product Safety Commission, and the CDC for safety warnings and recalled products, and offers the opportunity to sign up for e-mail alerts. The National Library of Medicine offers MedlinePlus, which lets members of the public search for verified information about health, disease, tests, and treatments. There are also educational videos, quizzes, risk calcula-tors, and even links to games created by a range of other agencies and organizations.

Texting is becoming more and more mainstream in public health efforts. In many areas, people can sign up for a city- or county-wide tex-ting service that lets citizens know about weather emergencies, temporary boil alerts (when water may be contaminated and must be boiled before drinking), disease outbreaks, and other important happenings. Texts are being incorporated into emergency preparedness plans. Programs to promote prenatal care are using text messaging to send women information about pregnancy. Crisis hotlines are starting to invite texts as well as phone calls, and public health programs are trying texting as a new way to address mental illness and promote mental health. In 2015, for example, New York City piloted a program that invites teens to text with counselors about their mental health questions and concerns, because people in this age group are often more comfortable texting than talking.

Some of these efforts have been very successful. Some have been less so—in part because public health professionals are not always in tune with what laypeople will find interesting or entertaining. (How exciting can a handwashing video game possibly be?) Public health organizations are still figuring out where new media will best fit into their efforts, so it is not clear yet how this job market will evolve. But it is clear there is a need for people who understand the Internet, social networking, and other forms of new media, and who can make them work for the cause of population-level health.

REFERENCES

Centers for Disease Control and Prevention. (2014, December 22). *Climate-ready states & cities initiative grantees.* Retrieved June 6, 2015, from http://www.cdc.gov/climateandhealth/crsci_grantees.htm

World Health Organization. (2014a, August). *Climate change and health fact sheet.* Retrieved June 6, 2015, from http://www.who.int/mediacentre/factsheets/fs266/en/

World Health Organization. (2014b). *Overview: Quantitative risk assessment of the effects of climate change on selected causes of death, 2030s and 2050.* Retrieved June 6, 2015, from http://www.who.int/globalchange/publications/quantitative-risk-assessment/en/

World Health Organization. (2014c, August 27). *Call for stronger action on health and climate* [Press release]. Retrieved from http://www.wmo.int/media/content/call-stronger-action-health-and-climate

PART IV

Public Health or Medical School?

CHAPTER 27

Public Health
or Medical School?

It is a common question. After the first edition of this book was published, many readers reached out to ask about going to medical school versus earning an MPH. Can you have a rewarding career in public health without a medical degree? Will clinical training add enough to a public health degree to be worth all those years of study? Most of the people who have asked about this have been weighing an MPH versus medical school (as opposed to nursing or other clinical degrees); so this chapter focuses mainly on that decision.

As a public health doctor, I can tell you that I use both my public health knowledge and my medical education every single day in my work. But I can also tell you that there are plenty of jobs in public health that do not require an MD. And medical school is an awful lot to go through if you do not really need to!

I have found that many people just starting out do not really understand the differences between clinical medicine and public health, so I will start by explaining. If you are already familiar with this information, later in the chapter you will find more on the intersections between clinical medicine and public health, and some options for those who want to do both.

A couple of quick notes: First, it is worth remembering that there are other health care professionals who can combine their work with public health—nurses especially, but also physician assistants, nutritionists, and so on. These educational programs can be completed in much less time and at a lower cost than becoming a doctor. They are worth checking out, if you think you might be interested. And second, you will see two medical degrees mentioned here: The MD or "medical doctor" is the more common. A DO is a "doctor of osteopathy." The training takes similar amounts of time and they receive the same license to practice, although historically their approaches are somewhat different.

CLINICAL MEDICINE VERSUS PUBLIC HEALTH PRACTICE

As mentioned at the beginning of this book, public health is something that people do not tend to think about until there is a problem. That may be the reason why so many people get confused about what public health actually is and how it is different from clinical medicine.

Here are a couple of ways to think about the differences:

- Clinical medicine focuses on individual patients. Public health focuses on systems, groups, and communities.
- Both disciplines aim to improve health, fight disease, and keep people well. But clinical medicine is more about identifying and treating illnesses and injuries. Public health has a stronger focus on patterns and prevention.

To practice clinical medicine, you need a very broad range of knowledge about:

- How the body works
- How to recognize a large number of diseases and illnesses
- How to treat these diseases and what to expect as the result of treatment
- How to use many, many different medications, how they work, and how they interact with each other
- When to order and how to interpret x-rays, laboratory results, and other tests
- What will happen if a disease is left untreated or not treated correctly

To practice public health, you need a separate set of skills. Different public health jobs will emphasize different skills, but most public health professionals have at least this basic knowledge:

- How to recognize patterns of disease in a population or patterns of risk in an environment

- How to identify the causes of these patterns
- How to determine what can be done to change them
- How to promote, encourage, or carry out this change
- How to tell if the effort made a difference.

You would not want to rely on someone with an MPH, but no clinical training, to do your surgery or treat your pneumonia. And, although some doctors do think in "public health" terms and lead successful public health efforts, for the most part a doctor who has never studied public health is not the best choice to lead the way in a public health emergency.

TREATING PATIENTS VERSUS TREATING COMMUNITIES

When someone tells me they are trying to decide between medical school or an MPH, I usually ask: Do you see yourself treating patients?

If the answer is yes, then medical school is a serious consideration. If you are picturing yourself in the role of a doctor who does public health work in addition to, say, treating heart disease, working in an inner city clinic, or saving lives after a natural disaster, an MPH just is not going to be enough. One option is to start with the year or two it takes to earn the MPH, and then go to medical school if it is still a burning desire—but keep in mind that it may be easier to get through medical school when you are young and can more easily handle the heavy workload, late nights, and early mornings.

I also ask, are you interested in clinical medicine? There is a whole medical specialty that focuses on public health, and many of us do not do direct patient care. We fill an important niche, because we know what it is like to treat patients on an individual level, but we also have skills to treat and prevent disease on a population level. We have an insider's view of the health care system that many public health professionals lack. And, although there are public health professionals with deep knowledge of specific diseases (such as tuberculosis or HIV), we have broad knowledge about many different things that can go wrong with the body and how they can be interconnected.

However, most of us went to medical school thinking that we would be traditional doctors. We found our way into public health because we saw problems we wanted to help solve. If you have no intention of ever doing one-on-one patient care, and you do not have a deep desire to learn about clinical medicine, then medical school seems like an awfully big commitment of both time and money. It is an incredible privilege to get to study and practice medicine, and it certainly gives you a depth of knowledge about health and disease and a perspective on human nature that no public health training can duplicate. It will inform every decision you make in public health practice. But it is an enormous commitment, and it is important to know what you are getting into before you start. I have known medical students and residents who regretted the decision to go to medical school, but felt they were too far in debt to change direction.

There are some public health jobs that absolutely require a medical degree. In some places, you cannot head up the health department unless you are a doctor. And without a medical degree you will never get to be Surgeon General. But an MD or DO definitely is not necessary for a successful, influential, and meaningful public health career.

In fact, for many jobs, you will do better with a background in the social sciences...or engineering...or biology...or social work.... Look back through this book and see how many jobs require something other than an MD!

MEDICAL SCHOOL VERSUS PUBLIC HEALTH SCHOOL

Both medical school and MPH programs are considered professional training, intended to create graduates who can go out and do practical work in their fields. But there are very important differences.

Studying Medicine

Medical school is designed to prepare students to practice clinical medicine. To be able to apply, you will need to study "pre-med" courses at college, including biology, chemistry, and physics.

Typically, the first two years of medical school are devoted to classroom learning. You will study the respiratory system, the circulatory system, how the kidneys and liver work. You will learn what is normal and the different ways things can go wrong. You will study bacteria, viruses, genetic diseases, and the effects of unhealthy lifestyles. In anatomy lab, you will dissect a human cadaver to get firsthand knowledge of how the body is structured. You will look at cells under the microscope and learn how to interpret what you see. You might also spend some time in a clinic or hospital, starting to learn what it is like to see patients. You will learn a little bit about public health—but it is just a small part of 2 solid years of studying a huge amount of information.

Years 3 and 4 are usually dedicated to more hands-on training. Students are placed on "rotations" of a few weeks at a time, moving from one department or specialty to another. You will experience the intensive care unit, the maternity ward, the pediatric floors, the general medicine service, surgery, and specialties like cardiology and oncology. On each rotation, you are assigned to a team led by an experienced "attending" doctor and consisting of students and residents at different levels of training. It is common to spend some time in outpatient clinics, seeing patients with less serious problems. You will also learn about "taking call," which means spending the night in the hospital, responding to emergencies, and helping to check in patients who arrive after hours. Years 3 and 4 are notorious for being grueling, as you spend long days in the hospital and then go home to study at night. Medical students tell a lot of rueful jokes about these years: Our boyfriends and girlfriends never see us, our pets forget who we are, we survive on coffee and those peanut butter crackers from the vending machine.

And then after medical school, you are not done: The next step is residency, which is 3 years at minimum. For some specialties, it is 4, 5, or even 6 years. Residency is like a more advanced version of third and fourth year in medical school. You are still part of a team, but now you have more responsibility, manage more patients, and do more and more on your own. You also help teach the students and the residents who start after you. Although some specialties have easier hours, for most, residency is another period of long days, hard work, and limited sleep. In recent years, laws have been passed to limit how many hours a resident can work. In 2015, the limit was 80 hours each week, averaged over a 4-week period, with at least 1 day off per week. First-year residents are allowed to work for no more than 16 hours in a row. In the years after that, it is 24 hours of patient care plus up to 4 hours to finish paperwork and make sure the next resident coming on shift knows what is happening with the patients. The Accreditation Council for Graduate Medical Education actually encourages "strategic napping" after the first 16 hours!

By the time you finish residency, you are ready to start your first job as a full-fledged doctor. That is, unless you want to focus in on a particular specialty even further, in which case you will add on a fellowship that could last another year or more. For example, you might do a residency in general internal medicine (3 years) and then focus in on cancer treatment (2 more years). Or you could do your residency in family medicine (3 years) and then a fellowship in geriatrics (another year).

Studying Public Health

Studying for a public health degree is no cakewalk, but it is a very different experience. For the undergraduate major, public health classes will be part of your broader 4-year education. The Association of Schools and Programs of Public Health (ASPPH) recommends that undergraduate programs include experience at local public health agencies or working with public health professionals, plus a capstone project that involves either research or applied experience. An undergraduate major is a good introduction to public health. It can be sufficient for some entry-level jobs. It is not required for entry into a public health master's degree program. Many MPH students come from other backgrounds. For example, ASPPH suggests a math or science major if you are interested in epidemiology or biostatistics. Sociology, anthropology, or psychology can be good matches if you would like to go into health education. And there is room in public health for many other interests.

MPH programs typically take about 2 years to complete, but there are programs designed to be finished in a year and some that take longer. It depends on how classes and semesters are arranged and also on whether you do the program on a part-time or full-time basis. Some schools offer online programs. Prerequisites vary from school to school; some require a few undergraduate math or science classes, some prefer candidates with work experience.

In an MPH program, you will take a series of core courses in topics like environmental health, public health policy, epidemiology, and biostatistics. You will also take classes in your area of concentration, which might be global health, community health, epidemiology, or one of many other options. (Different schools offer different selections of concentrations.) And you will usually have room for a few classes to explore other interests. It is common to spend a few hours in class each day, most or all days of the week. You will spend many hours outside of class reading textbooks and journal articles, writing papers, and doing other homework. You may have group assignments, where you work with other students to complete a project.

Generally, once you have completed some initial coursework, you will begin planning for a practicum experience. Precise requirements differ from school to school, but it is meant to be a substantial experience over weeks to months, in which you make a real contribution to an organization or research project. You will also be expected to do a "culminating experience" that brings together what you have learned and shows you are able to apply it to real-world practice. In some schools, this is a paper based on your practicum experience. Other models include a comprehensive exam, a thesis paper, an applied research project, or a "capstone" seminar.

An MPH program is a fairly typical grad school experience. You will have some late nights and stressful times, but most full-time students find they are able to maintain a social life or hold a part-time job. Part-time programs allow students with full-time jobs or family obligations to take fewer classes and stretch out the process over more time.

A WORD ABOUT DEBT

It is distressing to have to consider money when you just want to go out and do some good in the world. But it is a very real issue in the American higher education system, and if you are not independently wealthy, you will want to do a little math before you make your decision.

There is always a small percentage of students whose families can afford to pay for tuition outright. Some students are able to pay for medical school by joining an Armed Forces program, which requires a 4-year commitment after completing residency, or by committing to a number of years working in underserved communities. But according to the Association of American Medical Colleges (AAMC) in 2014, 84% of graduates finished school in debt. On average, they owed $180,000. Forty-three percent owed $200,000 or more. Ten percent owed $300,000 or more. And this is not because students are not careful with their spending. Median tuition for medical school that year was $34,540 at public schools and $53,714 at private ones. Including books, living expenses, and other costs, the total to attend 4 years of medical school was $226,447 at public schools and $298,538 at private schools. The interest on loans can add up fast—typical repayment plans take 10 or more years and interest can be well over $100,000.

Can you pay back these loans once you are in practice? Absolutely, if you are working full time on a typical doctor's salary. However, it can take many years, especially if you are a primary care doctor at the lower end of the pay scale and have other financial obligations. If you are running your own practice, just the cost of malpractice insurance can be staggering. But yes, it can be done.

However, it is common for doctors to feel constrained by debt, especially if they would like to try another field or take a lower paying job doing interesting and worthwhile work. It does not feel like you have many choices when interest is piling up and monthly payments are due.

What about debt from an MPH? This can be an expensive degree, too, depending on where you decide to go. Tuition varies from less than

$10,000 to well over $30,000 per year. And then there are campus fees, textbooks, and living expenses. It is smart to look at salaries for the type of job you want and plan your expenses accordingly—you may not want to go $100,000 into debt if the career you want only pays $50,000 per year. Some students will find financial assistance from scholarships or programs such as the U.S. Department of Education's Public Service Loan Forgiveness Program, which applies to certain government loans.

REFUSING TO CHOOSE

Not intimidated by medical school? Still want to get that MD or DO degree and combine it with public health work? You would not be alone. There are many of us who took that plunge and are glad we did! I have worked as a doctor at a rural clinic, seeing patients and also serving as the town's public health doctor, managing outbreaks and shoring up plans against future ones. I have worked on improving a health care system by integrating different clinical services and creating related community programs. I have even consulted and written for educational shows on television.

If you are serious about combining medical practice and public health, you have a few different options. It is possible to become a public health doctor without formal public health training, but as the MPH becomes a more common degree, you may find you are not very competitive on the job market without it.

Many medical schools have partnerships with schools of public health, so that you can earn an MPH before you graduate from medical school. This usually adds a year to the time it takes to get a medical degree. AAMC maintains a list of programs including information about costs and duration of training at their website, www.aamc.org.

You can also earn an MPH as a separate process, either before or after your medical training.

Some residency programs have public health tracks that allow time and provide funding to earn the MPH. Some combine public health training with a clinical specialty. There is also an option to make public health the main focus of your residency training.

THE PUBLIC HEALTH MEDICAL SPECIALTY

To this day, I tell other doctors that my specialty is preventive medicine, and they say, "Huh? I didn't know you could specialize in that!" The full title of my specialty is Public Health and General Preventive Medicine. A preventive medicine residency is substantially different from other residency programs. We spend 1 year training in the hospital, just like doctors going into any other specialty. But then we spend the second and third years earning an MPH and working in public health settings. We do our rotations at health departments, quality improvement organizations, nonprofit organizations focused on public health issues, and so on. It is a fascinating opportunity, if you are interested in combining medicine and public health. And it has the added bonus that health departments follow a normal workday; so for most of those 2 years, we get to go home in the evenings, eat a proper supper, and get a decent night's sleep!

You will find preventive medicine doctors at the Centers for Disease Control and Prevention and other federal agencies, in the military, heading up health departments, running programs to promote wellness or improve medical care, and in many other interesting roles.

Preventive medicine doctors are licensed to practice medicine just like any other physician. One warning, however, if you only do a preventive medicine residency, you may find that employers will not hire you for clinical jobs. There are definitely preventive medicine doctors who practice clinical medicine—I am one of them!—but it is not the standard path and many employers will want you to have completed a more traditional residency. If clinical medical practice is an important goal, you should strongly consider pursuing preventive medicine in addition to another specialty. The American Board of Preventive Medicine lists a few combined programs at www.theabpm.org, or you can take an additional 2 years to pursue preventive medicine after completing your other training.

GETTING A JOB AS A PUBLIC HEALTH DOCTOR

A challenge that many "prev med" doctors share is that we are considered overqualified for a lot of public health jobs. Why should an employer pay a doctor's salary when someone with an MPH can do the job? On the other hand, for certain complex jobs and leadership roles, nothing but a medical degree will do.

Before you make your final decision, take some time to search job listings for the kind of work you are interested in. Look specifically for jobs that require a medical degree and compare them to the ones that ask for an MPH alone. You can also look back through this book to review some of the public health jobs that are reserved for doctors. Would you be happy doing the MPH-level work? If so, a medical degree could price you right out of the running. But if the doctor jobs are the ones you really are aiming for, you have your answer.

Many public health doctors work at federal agencies and at state and local health departments. To see what types of jobs are available at the federal level, you can search for "medical officer" at usajobs.gov. (Try limiting your search to the agencies most concerned with public health. Listings with the Indian Health Service and Department of Veterans Affairs tend to be for jobs that are primarily clinical practice.)

The website for the U.S. Public Health Service Commissioned Corps (www.usphs.gov) is another place to learn about public health roles specific to physicians.

Also take a look at career opportunities in the military. The U.S. Armed Forces seem to be particularly aware of the value of public health physicians, and the Army and Air Force even have their own preventive medicine residency programs.

WHERE TO LEARN MORE

In addition to the resources mentioned earlier, I always recommend that students interested in combining medical training with a public health career check out the American College of Preventive Medicine, which is the professional association for the preventive medicine specialty. Their website is acpm.org.

You may also want to get in touch with the American Association of Public Health Physicians at www.aaphp.org. This is a small organization, but its members tend to be knowledgeable and enthusiastic about the field.

PART V

Advice From Career Counselors

CHAPTER 28

Advice From Career Counselors

If you are working on a public health degree, your school's career counselor can be very helpful. But what if you are still deciding whether to go for that degree, or you are looking into changing jobs and do not plan on going back to school? Wouldn't it be great if you could get some advice early in the process of making your decision?

This chapter will share some wisdom on trends in the public health job market and ideas on how to land the job you want, including thoughts on networking, using social media, preparing a resume, and putting your best foot forward in an interview. There is also some advice on common mistakes to avoid. In compiling this chapter, I included ideas from the career counselors at two highly respected schools of public health: Betty Addison, MS, at Johns Hopkins Bloomberg School of Public Health and Heather Krasna, MS, from Columbia University's Mailman School of Public Health.

THE JOB MARKET: SOME CURRENT TRENDS

Career counselors at schools and programs of public health usually have a good idea of trends in hiring. They get to see which graduates are snapped up and which ones struggle to find a job. Be aware that the "hot" jobs do change over time, according to funding, public and government interest, and world events. It is worth taking a look at current job listings at sites like publichealthjobs.net to see what new trends are developing.

In talking about which skills are most in demand, Addison noted that MPH graduates are fortunate—the "core competencies" that all MPH graduates share can translate to many different roles. MPH graduates have training in statistics, budgets, communications, cultural competency, systems-level thinking, and many other areas that would serve well in any number of jobs.

One set of skills that has been particularly in demand recently relates to "eHealth." This is an evolving term but, essentially, it encompasses all the ways that information technology is being used in health care. Examples of eHealth include electronic health records, telemedicine, online health information for consumers, information to support clinical decision making for doctors, and smartphones to gather and disseminate health information. Addison has noticed that many Hopkins graduates are able to combine computer technology skills with their public health training to do jobs such as evaluating global health programs using data from afar, or teaching workshops to organizations around the world via teleconferencing or webinars. These jobs might be found under titles such as "global health," "eHealth," "mHealth" (which involves mobile devices), and "tele-advising."

According to Krasna, one of the hottest fields for Columbia's public health graduates is now statistics and biostatistics. There has been increased interest in using data to reduce health care costs, improve quality, and fight illness and injury. With electronic medical records, Geographic Information Systems, Internet search data, and more, we have a whole range of new options for looking at public health trends. We can track disease, treatment, and outcome information from thousands or even millions of medical records. We can collect hundreds of thousands of data points about changes in bacteria. We can plot out grocery store locations, sidewalks, and bus routes across huge areas. The need to analyze, interpret, and make use of what has come to be called "big data" is driving jobs for graduates who truly understand statistical analysis and can use the major statistics programs and languages (such as SAS, STATA, and R).

Health policy and management, including hospital administration, health care administration, and health care consulting, is another area where graduates can do well. Hospital and health care regulation and administration are areas of high interest for employers as providers face increased regulations and constraints on payment.

Program managers and project managers with public health skills have continued to be in demand. The Washington, DC, area has an ongoing demand for public health graduates to assist with research and other projects at major nongovernmental organizations, nonprofits, and consulting firms.

Health promotion and wellness programs now seem to be looking for public health graduates, notes Krasna. These programs have become more and more common in recent years, and they often specify a public health degree in their job listings.

An interesting change in the market for public health graduates, which both Krasna and Addison have observed, is an expansion of jobs in for-profit markets. It is not clear why the change has taken place. Part of it could be budget cuts at local-level health departments, so that students have had to look elsewhere for work. It also appears that the for-profit world—including pharmaceutical companies, insurance companies, health marketing and technology companies, and certain health care systems—has discovered that public health training translates well to their own companies' needs. Addison notes that some graduates go to work in industry for a few years to pay off their loans and then switch over to work that is more in line with their public health interests. It is up to each individual whether work in the for-profit realm is of interest, or whether he or she prefers the more traditional domains of public health work. Another option to investigate is the Public Service Loan Forgiveness Program, through which certain student loans can be forgiven if you choose a nonprofit or government career path.

What are the difficult markets right now? Global health remains a challenge, although Addison has seen graduates with strong computer and eHealth skills do well in this area. Many graduates share an interest in global health, and there are only so many entry-level jobs to go around. (See the Global Health chapter [Chapter 22] for some ideas on how to break into this area of public health.)

Environmental health is another area where it can take some extra effort to find that first job. Many "environmental health" jobs actually require engineering skills, which is a different type of education from the MPH. Krasna observes that for-profit companies sometimes seek MPH graduates for environmental monitoring, but it is often in the interest of building new developments or getting permission to do things that put the environment at risk. Jobs focusing on protecting human health through saving the environment are out there, but they are sometimes harder to find.

Epidemiologists are always needed in public health, and Addison notes that this is a consistently popular job goal for graduates. However, she cautions that many job openings are for epidemiologists with additional training or at least a few years' experience. Graduates may find they need to pursue a fellowship or other additional education to be employed as epidemiologists.

Addison recalls many conversations with students who hope to work for the World Health Organization (WHO) immediately after graduation. But the WHO is not an easy place to find an entry-level job. They typically look for people with at least several years' work experience and often prefer MDs or PhDs.

COMMON MISTAKES

I talked to Heather Krasna about common mistakes she sees students and recent graduates make, and also reviewed career advice from other public health experts and employers. Here are some mistakes to avoid.

Setting narrow goals. If you insist on one particular job description or one specific organization, you may find the job search very frustrating. Krasna observes that students studying sexual and reproductive health often have their sights set on a certain foundation based in New York City. It has a great reputation and does good work, but it only has about 70 people on staff—which is why there are not many job openings. Plus, most jobs there are either too basic (no master's degree necessary) or too advanced for a recent graduate.

Instead: Broaden your job search. Think about why you were attracted to your area of focus and look for other organizations with similar values, or other opportunities that use similar skills. You can still keep that one employer or one job title as your long-term goal. If you are smart about building your skills and your network, you will eventually have a chance to get there.

Failing to focus. Your job search may need to be broad, but your skills should be identifiable. You may have taken a wide range of classes on different topics in public health and have all kinds of ideas. But sometimes students forget that employers will be looking for practical skills with some experience to back them up.

Instead: When you find something that interests you, get good at it. Look at job listings for the work you want to do and see what skills they are looking for. Take multiple classes on related topics, so you will really understand the issues and be able to practice the skills. Consider focusing in on a specific population or demographic group, such as aging adults or inner-city residents, or learning a second language. When it is time to do your practicum, seek out opportunities to use your knowledge in the real world so you will not just be telling employers, "I learned about this." You'll be saying, "I've done this."

Not using your network. It can be tempting to just fill out applications on job search websites. You can do that from home, in the middle of the night, in your pajamas. You do not even have to talk to anyone! The truth is, although some people do get jobs this way, you may be setting yourself up to wait for months without a single reply. If all you do is fill out online forms, you are just another faceless graduate with the same degree as a lot of other people.

Instead: Talk to people. If you do an internship, let them know you are going to be looking for a job. If you meet someone in the field you are interested in, ask for their advice on the job search. Use the alumni network from every school you have been to. When you apply for a job online, and there is someone at the company or agency who already knows and likes you, ask if they can put in a word on your behalf. There is more information about networking later in this section.

Applying for jobs you are not qualified for. It is common for employers to receive applications from people who do not seem to have read the job description. They are underqualified, or have no experience, or go on about their interest in something that is barely related to the job. Maybe they are just applying to everything that mentions public health. Maybe, they think that someone in Human Resources will admire them for taking a chance. It is fine to take that chance, but the most likely result? Your application ends up in the recycle bin.

Instead: Read every single word of the job description. Read what the job is, what the responsibilities are, and what skills and qualifications are expected. Then tailor your resume and your application to show that you know what you are applying for and that you are qualified to do the job. When in doubt, you are probably better off applying for a job rather than missing a chance—as long as you have read the description and feel you meet enough of the requirements that you can make a strong case for yourself.

Not filling out applications properly. A lot of companies use computer algorithms to sort through applications. If you leave out required information or are not clear about how you meet their criteria, your application may never even reach a human being. Even if you have someone who can get your application on the right desk, you can still lose out if you are careless with the forms or with your proofreading.

Instead: After you read every single word of the job description, read the application instructions and follow them. Answer all the questions, fill in all the blanks, and make sure to show how you meet the qualifications. Then, proofread to be sure you did not miss anything and did not make errors in spelling or grammar. If you can identify keywords in the job description ("biostatistics," "managerial experience," "global health") and they apply to your experience or training, use them. Remember, you may be trying to get past a computer—and computers do not overlook mistakes.

ONLINE NETWORKING

The Internet changes fast. What is hot this year could be the punchline of next year's jokes. The sites mentioned here have been around for at least a few years, so there is a chance they will last. But even if they do not, the general advice offered here should hold for the next new thing to come along.

LinkedIn. LinkedIn is a social networking site for the career minded. It takes advantage of the fact the people are more likely to help you out if they feel they know you or that you have something in common. Maybe you are from the same hometown, maybe you are a friend of their former colleague—anything that makes you a little more "real" to them can be a point in your favor.

Once you sign up, LinkedIn helps you find existing members that you already know. It also gives you the opportunity to invite friends and colleagues to join. (Be careful—sometimes people accidentally give the site permission to invite their entire address book. This can be awkward with ex-boyfriends, ex-girlfriends, and current employers!) The system then allows you to see and communicate with friends of friends, colleagues of colleagues, and others who are connected to people you know.

So how do you use the site? Do not just send out a blanket "help me find a job" message. Instead, target specific people who might be interested to hear from you.

- Alumni from your school who have jobs that match your interests
- Someone with a job at a place you would love to work
- Someone at the health department in a city or town where you would like to live

If it turns out that you know someone who knows them, you can ask for a personal introduction. If it is a more distant connection, or no connection at all, you can still reach out to them directly. Just be very respectful, and be clear about what you are asking. Each message should be tailored to the person you are writing to. You could ask for advice on your career path, because someday you would like to do the same kind of work. You could ask if there is an active, local public health association that you could join. (Just make sure to try Google first, so you are not asking something with an obvious answer!)

Be careful not to overwhelm an area or industry with dozens of messages. People do talk to each other, and you want to be that smart person who asks intelligent, targeted questions—not that annoying student who is taking up everyone's time.

LinkedIn can also be helpful in a more passive way. Your own profile is searchable by employers. Put your best foot forward. Be specific about your experiences, skills, and goals. It is possible you will be invited to apply for a job that matches your skills.

Facebook. Facebook is a more personal medium, which friends and acquaintances use to keep in touch by posting brief messages, pictures, and web links. You can make your page public or set it so that only people you have agreed to connect with can see your posts. You can certainly use it for networking, but more often it is purely social. On Facebook, reaching out to someone you have never met may feel a bit like approaching a stranger when they are out with friends, announcing that you know who they are, and asking them for a favor. However, your Facebook page can be a good place to broadcast that you are looking for a job and to ask if anyone has any leads. You may be lucky enough to have friends or acquaintances reply by linking you up with people they know. If your school has an alumni group on Facebook, that can be a good place for networking, as well.

You can also look on Facebook for pages from organizations you want to work for. Following their posts can give you a good idea of their values and priorities, which can be very helpful once you land an interview. You can also participate in discussions and post your own questions. Just make sure you are familiar with the culture of Facebook and of the company's page before you jump in.

One warning: More than one job applicant has been passed over because their own Facebook page was full of pictures of drunken parties or posts with extremist political views. If you are going to use Facebook to network, clean up your page, check your privacy settings, and be careful what you post!

Twitter. Twitter is a social network where celebrities, politicians, and ordinary people share messages that are limited to 140 characters per post. Many public health organizations use Twitter to broadcast news and information. As on Facebook, you can follow people or organizations you admire and you can post "tweets" for friends or the general public to see. Twitter has its own rules and etiquette, which can be confusing at first. Once you have spent some time and gotten to know the site, it can also be a way to find out about potential employers and communicate with people who could help in your job search.

IN-PERSON NETWORKING

Networking can feel awkward in person, especially in the Internet age. We are used to texting, e-mailing, and posting—but in-person events and meetings are still highly valuable in the job search. It is very common in public health to find a job not through an ad or through sending out resumes, but because you know someone.

Many people give up on this type of networking after a few tries because it "didn't work." But the secret to networking is to be open to whatever comes of it. You might connect with someone who has the perfect job for you or exactly the advice you need—or, you might hit it off with someone who turns out to be helpful years later, when they finally have a project that requires your skills.

Keep a few guidelines in mind:

- *Be curious.* Ask the other person about his or her work. People in public health tend to be enthusiastic about what they do. Listen. Compliment them if the work sounds interesting or important or innovative. If it sounds like a match for what you would like to do, say so.
- *Keep an open mind.* Even if the person's work is outside your area of interest, you will still learn something. Plus, the different fields in public health interact all the time. Later on you may find that you are glad to have the connection.
- *Do not be demanding.* It is off-putting to have someone in a networking setting ask outright for a job or a recommendation. Instead, ask for advice. Most people will be flattered.
- *Set aside your shyness.* It can be intimidating to approach a stranger, but it is expected in a networking setting. Although there will certainly be exceptions, public health professionals tend to be happy to welcome new people to the field.
- *Do not monopolize anyone's time.* It takes practice to end a conversation gracefully, but do not worry. It is normal to chat for a few minutes and then move on so you can each talk with more people. It is perfectly fine to wrap up a conversation with, "So nice to have met you."

- *Consider asking for an informational interview.* If you meet someone whose work seems close to what you want to do, you can ask if they would be willing to sit down with you another time and talk about their job. This type of meeting is called an "informational interview" and it can be a great way to get some career advice and tips on the local job market.
- *Bring business cards.* Even if you are still a student, you can make a card with your name, contact information, school, and the degree you are working toward.
- *Do not give up.* One of the secrets to networking is to keep going to events. You will start to see the same faces and get to know who is who in the local public health scene. Even more important, they will get to know you, your interests, and your skills—and when the right job does come around, you will have increased your chance of being invited to apply.

Networking can happen anywhere, not just at designated "networking events." Educational meetings, conferences, and planning meetings are all chances to get to know people, and there will usually be breaks or opportunities before or after the meeting to chat.

The American Public Health Association (APHA) website has a list of state public health associations around the country. It can be worth attending their meetings even if you have to drive a couple hours. If nothing else, people will be impressed at how far you traveled! If the nearest affiliate has an annual conference, consider going: You will meet people from around the state.

Also look for volunteer opportunities and charity functions that are within your area of interest. You will get to help out with a cause you believe in and meet people who are working toward the same goals. Volunteering lets you demonstrate your work ethic and show off some of your knowledge and skills.

MAKING THE MOST OF AN INFORMATIONAL INTERVIEW

An informational interview is a relatively informal meeting with someone in a job or at a company you are interested in. You get a chance to ask them all about the work, the organization, and how to maximize your chances of getting the kind of job you want.

If you have never done an informational interview before, though, it can be nerve-racking. What are you supposed to ask? How should you dress? Are you allowed to say you are looking for a job?

Here are some simple strategies to help you make the most of it:

- *Remind your contact of your background.* They might not remember where you are in your career or what you have done so far. Bring along a copy of your resume to offer, so they can see your history at a glance.
- *Be prepared with specific questions.* "Tell me about your job" makes it look like you have not done your homework. Instead, consider asking, "How did you get your first job here at the health department?" "What skills have served you best?" "What does the Robert Wood Johnson Foundation look for when they're hiring?"
- *Ask for other contacts.* Do not be afraid to ask if they know anyone else you should talk to. If you have your sights set on a particular organization or location, ask if they know anyone there who could give you additional advice. People in public health often work collaboratively, and that can include sharing contacts to help someone who is just starting out.
- *Resist asking outright for a job.* Do not expect them to "put in a word" for you or recommend you—especially if they just met you! It is ok to ask if they are aware of any job openings coming up, but do not put them on the spot to get you hired.
- *Send a thank you.* It used to be that you would write an actual thank-you letter on stationery and put it in an envelope with a stamp. These days, most professionals will think that an e-mail is fine. However you send it, a *thank you* makes a real impression, because it honors the fact that someone gave up an hour or two to help you—and not everyone will think to acknowledge that.

WRITING A RESUME THAT STANDS OUT

When a potential employer looks at your resume, it should be obvious what education you have, where you went to school, where you have worked in the past and when you held those jobs, and what experience you have. It is especially important to indicate what skills and talents you can bring to their company.

In the age of texting and e-mail, we tend to worry less about grammar, capitalization, and spelling in everyday life. But when you are applying for jobs, these things are important, and your resume is no exception.

The rules that apply to writing a resume for any job search also apply in public health:

- *Keep it short.* A resume should be just a page or two, unless you have had such a long and illustrious career that it cannot possibly fit. There are a few exceptions. If you are seeking a job in academia or research you will send a curriculum vitae (CV), which can be much longer. A longer format can be helpful in applying for federal government jobs, as well.
- *Keep it simple.* Resist the temptation to get fancy with different fonts, graphics, or complicated formatting. Also, do not make the print too small or too crowded. Your resume should be readable.
- *Tailor it to the job.* Do not use the same resume for a social marketing job as you would for a job in monitoring and evaluation. Highlight the skills that each employer is looking for.
- *Be specific about what you did, and use action words.* Do not say, "Was part of a project that created a social marketing campaign." Say, "Conducted focus groups of up to 20 participants. Designed effective outreach posters. Interviewed 30 stakeholders and prepared reports on priorities in the community, which were presented to senior public health experts." Including numbers and percentages will help employers get a better sense of your accomplishments.
- *Include full contact information.* That means name, address, telephone, and e-mail. If you have more than one page, put your name in the header or footer on the second and any subsequent pages in case they get separated.
- *Include any professional certifications or publications.* If you have earned the Certified in Public Health credential, for example, do not forget to include it. Also include any special continuing education or certificate programs that are relevant to the job.
- *Use keywords.* As with online applications, look for keywords in the job description. For example, for that monitoring and evaluation job, be sure to include the words "monitoring" and "evaluation" when you summarize your education or

your work experience. Do not get overlooked because you forgot to include words such as "global" or "international" when writing about your experience working in public health overseas.

ACE THAT INTERVIEW

There is nothing particularly unusual about interviewing for a public health job, versus other professions. But you can increase your chances of doing well with some advance preparation.

Be prepared. Pay a visit to the organization's website, whether it is a governmental unit, a nonprofit organization, or a for-profit company. You should learn basic information such as where headquarters is located, how big the organization is, and how long they have been around. You should have at least a basic knowledge of the company's history, the work they do, and current projects or programs, so you can be specific about why you want to work there. You do not necessarily need all the details, but you do not want to be asking about things you could have found out easily on your own.

Know your interviewer. You will not always be able to find out your interviewer's name in advance, but if you can, look them up online. Read their bio. Look on PubMed.gov (the journal catalog from the National Library of Medicine) to see if they have written any articles. Google or another search engine can show if they have been in the news recently, maintain a blog, or have any other claim to fame. You will feel like you are on more solid ground when you meet them in person. If their work comes up in the conversation, you will be able to say, "I understand you're an expert on …" or "I was really interested in what you wrote about." Again, you do not need every detail (and you do not want to look like you have been stalking them!), but people are usually impressed that you have bothered to find out who they are and what they have accomplished.

Dress the part. You do not always have to wear a suit to an interview in the public health world, but you should be neatly dressed. If you can find out how people typically dress at the organization (Suit and tie? Business casual?), you can tailor your look to match. One exception is the jeans-and-t-shirt job: Even if the office is extremely casual, employers tend to notice and appreciate that you dressed up a bit. Personal style is fine, but an outfit that is too quirky—or too high fashion—can distract an interviewer from your actual potential.

Focus on what you can offer. Employers are not usually in the business of "helping out" new graduates. They are looking for someone who will fill a specific need and make a real contribution to their workforce. Before your interview, review the job description and what it involves. Then think about how your training and experience so far can meet the identified needs. Be prepared with specific examples of how something you have done resembles what the employer needs. If you do not have strong experience, think about potential: How does your past experience prove that you can learn new skills on the job?

Stay on topic. It can be tempting to give the most thorough possible answer to every interview question. But remember, the interviewer is looking for someone who will be an efficient and effective member of a team. Someone who takes 10 minutes to answer a question probably is not going to fit in. If you struggle with nervousness and it makes you tend to ramble on, practice with a mentor or friend (or someone at your school's career services office) until you feel more confident.

Know the language. Public health has its own jargon, and so does each sector within the field. Do not just say you studied statistics. Be ready to say what types of statistical analysis you can do and how you would apply these to the employer's work. If you are applying for a water and sanitation job, be ready to talk intelligently about different types of latrines and the microbiological quality of drinking water. Also check for any current or recent major initiatives related to the work. You do not want to look like a deer in the headlights when the interviewer asks what you think about that new Gates Foundation project.

PLANNING FOR THE FUTURE

You probably should not pick a career or a job just because it is "hot" the year you are graduating or considering a career change. Public health is a great field and the work can be very rewarding, but it is also challenging and sometimes frustrating. It can even be heartbreaking. You may not want to commit to a career crunching numbers when what you really want is to be out working with people—and vice versa.

You will also find, as time goes on, that funding streams change and jobs in a given area become more or less available as needs evolve. There is almost always work to be had in the public health world—but in terms of specific positions, this year's hot job may be next year's budget cut. Many of the people who were interviewed for this book have made lateral moves or changed subject areas, either because they found a new interest or because needs around them changed. Look for opportunities that interest you and will allow you to build your skills, and you should do fine.

IN CONCLUSION

Public health jobs are extremely varied, and there is no one "best" way to get started in the field. Some of the people interviewed for this book have been in the same role their whole careers. Many have made multiple career moves, following their interests or responding to changes in the field. If you are connected with a school of public health, take advantage of the career services office and their resources. They will know who tends to hire graduates from your school, what skills are most in demand in your area, and how to get started on your job search.

If you are not a student or alum, the Internet has some good resources to guide you on the job hunt. Many schools of public health post advice from their career offices online, and anyone can access it. The APHA website has an online newsletter about careers in public health and contact information for leaders of the different member sections. You can also find insight on websites designed for students or job seekers. For example, studentdoctor.net has a forum on public health degrees, where people discuss getting into school and finding a job after they graduate.

Finally, follow your interests and do not give up. Learn to be a smart networker, resume writer, and interviewee. There is room in this field for so many backgrounds, so many interests—and there is so much good to be done.

Index

Made in the USA
Middletown, DE
25 January 2022

59646169R10289